Is It "Just a Phase"?

Is It "Just a," Phase?

How to Tell Common Childhood Phases from More Serious Disorders

Dr. Susan Anderson Swedo & Dr. Henrietta L. Leonard

Golden Books
NEW YORK

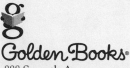

Golden Books®

888 Seventh Avenue
New York, NY 10106

Anafranil, Prozac, Luvox, Zoloft, Paxil, Tofranil, Norpramin, Elavil, Asendin, Pamelor, Sinequan, Ritalin, Cylert, Dexedrine, Wellbutrin, Catapres, Tenex, Haldol, Orap, Risperdal, Xanax, BuSpar, Klonopin, Ativan, Valium, Thorazine, Nardil, Inderal, Tenormin, Parnate, Desyrel, Serzone, Effexor, Eskalith, Lithobid, Stelazine, Mellaril, Clozaril, Zyprexa, and Tegretol are registered trademarks.

Golden Books® and colophon
are trademarks of Golden Books Publishing Co., Inc.

This book provides comprehensive information relating to children's health issues,
but should not be used as a substitute for medical advice. The readers should consult
a physician for individual medical problems.

Designed by Suzanne Noli

Manufactured in the United States of America

10 9 8 7 6 5 4 3 2 1

Library of Congress Cataloging-in-Publication Data

Swedo, Susan.
  Is it "just a phase"? : how to tell common childhood phases from
more serious disorders / Susan Anderson Swedo and Henrietta L. Leonard.
       p.   cm.
  Includes bibliographical references and index.
  ISBN 0-307-44050-8 (alk. paper)
  1. Child mental health.   2. Emotional problems of children.
3. Behavior disorders in children.   I. Leonard, Henrietta.   II. Title.
RJ499.34.S9   1998
618.92'89—dc21   98-17846
                                                         CIP

To our parents, husbands, and children—with all our love.

Contents

Part II - Problems That Are More Than "Just a Phase"

Introduction

"Amy, why don't you go outside and play with your cousins?" her mother, Celeste, asked.

"I don't want to. I'm busy," Amy responded, without looking up from her toys.

"Amy, I want to talk with your Grandma Rose alone for a little while, so you need to go outside and play."

"I don't want to go outside. I'm playing with my dolls," Amy whined. "If you want to have a private conversation," she continued, "why don't you go someplace else?"

"That's enough, Amy! You're going outside—right now!" Celeste got up and led her daughter to the back door. "Now, scoot!" she said and shut the door behind the reluctant eight-year-old.

"What's up, Celeste?" Rose asked her daughter-in-law as she returned to sit at the kitchen table.

"I'm worried about Amy," Celeste said. "She's been so difficult lately— always talking back to me and insisting on having her own way about everything. She's absolutely impossible!"

"She's not impossible, Celeste," Rose said soothingly. "She's just showing her spirit."

"Her spirit!" Celeste snorted. "I think it's more than that, Rose. Amy's being really obnoxious these days. It's not like her—she's always been so sweet and helpful. She'd have a smile on her face all the time, too. But, lately, all she does is sulk. And sass us. I can't count the number of times I've been tempted to wash that girl's mouth out with soap."

"Have you?" Rose gasped.

"No, of course not," Celeste answered. "But the fact that I've even considered it is a sign that there's something seriously wrong with Amy. I'm really worried about her."

"Don't worry, Celeste," Rose said. "It's just a phase—Amy will grow out of it soon. All kids go through difficult stages. They have to give you some grief and go through some tough times—it's a normal part of growing up. The key to being a good parent is to help them grow out of the problem phases as quickly as possible, and not to lose your cool until they do."

"Sounds like great advice," Celeste said. "But easier said than done—she really irritates me! And how do you know for sure that it's 'just a phase'?"

"That, my dear, is the million-dollar question," Rose answered.

While it may not be worth a million dollars, the question of whether a child's behavior problems are "just a phase" or something more serious is one that parents ask frequently during the grade school years. Problem phases occur so predictably that child development experts have even given them names, such as the Terrible Twos, the Ferocious Fours, and the Sensitive Sixes. Some children are a handful from the time they enter the Terrible Twos until they leave home sixteen years later. Others, like Amy, appear to sail through their early development without problems, and then challenge their parents by exhibiting the sassy independence common to eight-year-olds or the moody rebelliousness of adolescence. Parents who are prepared for these difficult stages can change their parenting style in preparation for the expected challenges. They will have an easier time handling the problem phases, and their child will pass through them more quickly and easily. This book provides parents with the information they need to anticipate the problem phases and to be prepared for the developmental challenges that face their child.

The book's title, Is It "Just a Phase"?, alludes to the old, outdated approach to pediatric behavior problems: "It's just a phase. Ignore it and wait for her to outgrow it." Bad advice! But often a worried parent can't just ignore her child's problem behaviors. Attempting to ignore the unignorable is not only frustrating to both the parent and child during the months (or years!) that the behavior lasts, but it also impacts on the child's development, which is shaped by the behavior she's practicing and by her parents' reactions to it.

For example, if a six-year-old child's bedtime fears are dismissed as "just a phase that she's going through—ignore it!" and her parents act as if nothing's the matter, they may insist on turning off her light, giving her countless hours of needless anxiety and creating further behavior problems. Because she's afraid to go to sleep and equally afraid to lie awake in the dark, she refuses to go to bed at night, or climbs into her parents' bed in the middle of the night despite warnings against doing so. She may also experience nightmares and insomnia, which further compound the problem. On the other hand, if her parents recognize that she is entering a phase in which nighttime fears are common, they can be prepared to provide her with extra measures of comfort and security so that she quickly accepts that "there's not really a monster under my bed" and "outgrows" her fears.

Clearly, the way that the child's parents handle her developmental challenges is an important factor in determining her future development. Although physicians have always known that this was true, we have only recently learned that this is because the child's brain is "plastic," or malleable, and is molded by many things, including her experiences. Scientific experiments have proven that the actual size and structure of the brain can be altered by factors in the environment; some experiences, such as practicing the piano or reciting poetry, result in improved brain function, while others, like drug and alcohol use, can dramatically decrease the child's potential capabilities.

The visual system is a good example of the brain's plasticity. When a child is born, her vision is limited to blurry images and indistinct colors, but it quickly comes into sharp focus as her brain is matured by the act of "seeing." The act of processing visual images causes some nerve connections to be strengthened and others to be eliminated. This shaping process is so important that it can make the difference between perfect vision and blindness. For example, if a child is born with cataracts, her brain doesn't receive any visual input and she's "blind." If the cataracts are removed soon after birth, she will have normal vision. But if the cataracts aren't removed until the shaping process is complete (sometime before the age of four), the child will always be blind—even though her eyes are now completely normal. She can't see because her brain hasn't learned how to process the images. The visual system is an unusually dramatic example of the plasticity of the brain, and there are no similar "all or none" periods during a child's emotional development. But since early experiences have such a tremendous impact on development, it is clear that a child's behavior problems are never something to be ignored.

The chapters in part I of Is It "Just a Phase"? provide parents with strategies for helping their children cope with a variety of common developmental problems, from hyperactivity, picky eating, naughtiness, and impulsivity, to shyness, excessive fears, sadness, and social isolation. A "real life" example, similar to Amy's story, introduces each chapter. These case histories are not based on any one child (in order to protect our patients' privacy), but are composites of our experience and training. The purpose of the stories is to give you a sense of the types of problems that fall under the category of "normal" childhood behavior. A case example of a "problem" behavior is also included so that you can decide which pattern is more similar to your child's behavior. If your child's behavior is in the normal range, suggestions are provided for helping her outgrow the problem, including ways in which you, your child's teacher, and her doctor can be of assistance. If your child's behavior appears more like one of the problem behaviors that are described, then you will be referred to the appropriate chapter in the second half of the book.

The second part of Is It "Just a Phase"? focuses on the symptoms of childhood psychiatric disorders—"problem behaviors," like attention deficit hyperactivity disorder (ADHD), depression, and obsessive-compulsive disorder (OCD). In addition to a case illustration, parents are provided with a diagnostic checklist so that they can accurately assess the nature and severity of their child's symptoms. Treatment strategies are presented and rated for safety and effectiveness. Suggestions are also provided for ways in which parents can help their child continue to grow and develop appropriately, even as she is recovering from the disorder.

It should be apparent by now that there is no shame or blame in this book. The problems described here can't be blamed on either the child or her parent, and neither of them should be ashamed when they occur. Difficult phases result when developmental challenges facing the child overcome her ability to cope, just as diabetes occurs when the blood sugar content exceeds the body's ability to make insulin. Psychiatric disorders occur when the brain malfunctions—they are medical illnesses, not a punishment for a child's weak character or a parent's mistakes.

Stomach ulcers provide the perfect analogy for our changing attitude toward mental illness. For generations, doctors thought that ulcers were brought on by stress and dietary indiscretions and patients were encouraged to "take it easy and avoid spicy foods." With that prescription, some of the patients got better, just as some patients with depression or anxiety disorders get better with rest and tender, loving care. Some ulcer patients' symptoms continued to worsen on the bland diet, however—not a surprise since the treatment failed to address the cause of the symptoms. A few years ago, an Australian doctor discovered that most ulcers are the result of a bacterial infection and, since then, antibiotics have become the treatment of choice—now 95 percent of the patients improve in the first six weeks. We haven't yet found the cause of most children's psychiatric disorders, so a true "cure" isn't immediately available, but important discoveries are being made every day. Recently, for example, researchers from the National Institute of Mental Health reported that some behavior problems may be caused by strep throat infections. If so, these disorders could be "cured" by immunologic treatments and possibly prevented by long-term penicillin treatment (see chapter 17 for a complete description).

It is our fervent hope that the cause and cure of children's psychiatric disorders are nearly at hand, and that our understanding of childhood development improves to the point at which we can prevent problem phases through early interventions by parents, physicians, and teachers. Until then, it is reassuring to know that these problems are real, they can be diagnosed accurately, and they will improve when given proper care and attention. The same holds true for undesirable developmental behaviors deemed normal, for no matter what the behavior problem, it's never "just a phase" that should be ignored.

Part I

Developmental Challenges and Challenging
Developments from Preschool Through Adolescence

1

"My Son Is Always 'On the Go'— He Exhausts Me!"

Excessive activity during childhood

"Zachary, get down off the back of that couch."

"Zack, I told you to get down off the couch. That means you shouldn't be jumping on the cushions, either. Come on, Zachary, it's not a jungle gym, it's a piece of furniture."

"Zachary, chairs are furniture, too, so stop jumping on Daddy's chair. Right now!"

"You're so full of energy tonight, Zack. Why don't you go outside and run around instead of using the family room as a gymnasium?"

"I can't, Mom," Zachary replied. "It's still raining."

Mary looked out the window and saw that the rain was coming down pretty hard. It had been raining for the past four days and her six-year-old son's energy level seemed to have doubled during that time. He really needed to be able to run around in the backyard and burn off some of his excess energy. For a moment, Mary considered dressing Zack in his slicker and boots and sending him out in the rain, but she quickly decided that cleaning up the mud he would track in afterward would be even worse than having him act so "hyper." Besides, it was almost dinnertime.

"Zackie, I need to finish making dinner and I'd like your help."

"Sure, Mom. What do you want?"

"I want you to set the table and then you can help me make some brownies for dessert."

"Yippee! Brownies are my favorite!" Zachary said and immediately got to work setting the table. He carefully laid out the plates, silverware, and napkins as his mother had taught him, and then said, "I'm done, Mom. Can we make the brownies now?"

Mary helped him gather the supplies and mix the brownies. Zachary stirred the mix slowly, taking care not to spill or make a mess on the edge of the bowl. When he was finished, he brought the bowl to his mother, who poured the mix into the pan and slid the brownies into the oven. As she did, she said, "Thanks for doing such a nice job with the table and the brownies, Zachary. I appreciate the help."

"You're welcome," her son replied. "Can I go watch cartoons now?"

"Sure, honey," Mary said. A few minutes later, she called, "Turn the volume down on the TV, Zachary. The whole neighborhood doesn't want to listen to the Flintstones."

Zachary turned the volume down, but just two minutes later, Mary heard the puppy whining and called, "Zack, don't tease Buddy. He's too little to wrestle with you."

"Don't jump, Zachary," Mary said, when she heard her son jumping on the couch again. And so it went, until dinner was over and Zachary was being tucked into bed. "I'm sorry I was so bad tonight, Mom," he said. "Tomorrow, I'll try really hard to be good. I won't run in the house or jump on the furniture even once."

"Zachary, honey, you weren't bad tonight, you just had cabin fever. I know how hard it is to stay cooped up in the house all day. If it's still raining tomorrow, we'll try to go to the recreation center so that you can play basketball or swim or something."

"Really, Mom? That would be great! I love you!"

"I love you, too!" she said. Mary smiled as she tucked her son in and turned off the light. He really was a good boy—it was just exhausting to keep up with him. If only she had half his energy!

When Being Hyper Is "Just a Phase"

The most frequent question parents ask us is "My son is always so 'hyper.' Do you think he's hyperactive?" When we ask them to define *hyper*, they say, "He's constantly on the move," "He's always on the go," or "He can't settle down." Sometimes, the parents just say, "You know, 'hyper'!," as the term has been used so often that it now has an implicit meaning. That meaning often depends upon the person's perspective, however, and "hyper" is used to refer to everything from a normal three-year-old's exuberant activity to the frenetic activity levels seen in children with hyperactivity disorders. The word "hyper" is actually an abbreviation of hyperactivity, which is part of a medical diagnosis: attention deficit hyperactivity disorder (also known as ADHD—described in detail in chapter 13). ADHD is common and affects about 5 to 10 percent of children in the United States, but even so, most hyper children don't have true hyperactivity or ADHD. Their activity level is in the normal range—for their age.

"My four-year-old wears me out! Is he always going to be this hyper?" Activity levels vary by age along a spectrum that is highest in young children and lowest in the elderly. Most of the change in activity levels occurs in the preschool years. If you think about a child of two to three years of age, he is constantly on the move—running from room to room, climbing up and down from chairs, and covering the entire room with toys as he plays. When he's outside, he runs everywhere—even on the hottest days, he won't slow down for more than the second or two it takes to get a drink and give you a sweaty hug. That same child looks quite different when he's seven to eight years old. By then, he can play quietly with games or toys for long periods of time and is able to stay seated throughout a family dinner (with only occasional forays to the bathroom). His activity level can be adjusted to fit the situation—if he's at soccer practice, he can run as hard and long as a three-year-old, but if he's in school, he can sit quietly in his seat and do his schoolwork.

The decrease in energy levels happens at different times for different children. Sometimes, it seems that your child will never "settle down," especially when you've spent the day running after him and are totally exhausted. If you're not sure whether your child's activity level is normal for boys his age, compare his behavior with other children's: how much do they move, how often do they change activities, and how long can they sit still? If the children are younger than five years of age, they probably run more than they walk and fidget more than they sit still. By the time they reach first grade, most girls can sit still for long periods of time and most boys for at least brief periods. Their behavior is more appropriate to the circumstances, although they might still have hyper periods in certain situations, such as when they're excited about a birthday party or overstimulated by holiday excitement. As the children grow and develop, their nervous systems mature and their activity levels modulate—this happens more quickly for girls than it does for boys. No one knows yet why girls' nervous systems develop faster than boys', nor why their overall activity level is ultimately lower, but the differences are striking, particularly in the early grade school years.

"My son is so much more hyper than his sister was at this age." If you watch a typical boy at age six, he appears younger and more active than a girl of the same age. He prefers rough play and outdoor activities to playing quietly or doing craft projects. If he's seated, he's likely to be tipping his chair back and forth at the dinner table, and, like Zachary, he still runs in the house and climbs on the furniture, especially when he's bored, tired, or needs to blow off steam. His ability to modulate his activity levels to fit the situation is less mature than a six-year-old girl's would be and his activity seems hyper and immature in comparison with hers.

These gender differences can worry parents, especially when they have children of both sexes and their son is second-born. The parents build a set of expectations through experiences with their daughter's behavioral development, and then their son doesn't fit those expectations. In comparison with his older sister, he appears to be hyperactive, but chances are he's not. Comparison with other boys his age will help his parents decide if the activity level is really hyper, or if it's merely a function of his age and gender.

"My son never sits still—especially when we're in church or eating at a nice restaurant." Zachary may have been jumping on the couch and running about the family room because he was bored. After all, he'd already spent four days in the house and it was time for him to get out and do something fun! All children get bored at times, and when they're bored, they look for something interesting to do. Large muscle activities, like running, jumping, and wrestling, are an ideal response to boredom because they are so stimulating. However, there are many situations in which such physical activity is inappropriate, like church, school, or a dinner party. If the child can't escape his seat, he begins to move anyway, by squirming and fidgeting in his chair.

If boredom is the cause for your child's increased activity levels, then he should be hyper only in situations in which he isn't sufficiently stimulated, such as watching a boring program on TV, waiting at the dentist's office, or visiting Aunt Tillie in the retirement home. When he's no longer bored, his fidgetiness will disappear—this distinguishes him from the child whose hyperactivity is due to ADHD. The child with ADHD can't remain seated for more than a few minutes at a time, even if he's very interested in an activity. The exception to this rule is video games (like Nintendo and Sega Genesis). Video games provide intense visual, auditory (hearing), and physical stimulation and can hold the attention of all children for hours, even those with ADHD (also see chapter 13).

"My son is so hyper he can go all day without stopping. I just wish I had half his energy." Parents frequently complain, "My child must be hyper—it wears me out just to watch him run around all day." On the other hand, if we asked the children, they might say that their parents are "hypoactive," or lacking in energy. Neither the parent nor the child has abnormal activity levels, they are just at very different points on the developmental continuum. For their respective ages, each has an appropriate activity level, but the two are a mismatch because of their striking differences. The contrasts lead to different preferences for activities and interests. For example, the more-active child might choose to go to the park to play ball while his less-active parents would prefer to stay home and watch a movie; the child prefers to grab a bite of pizza and a sip of soda "on the fly," rather than sitting down to a leisurely meal, and almost all children will choose not to take an afternoon nap—many parents we know would love to take one. Working out compromises that meet both sets of needs is what parenting is all about. There are times when it is appropriate to yield to your child's preferences (for example, when planning a family outing) and times when the parents' priorities come first (at mealtime, for example). As you decide between the conflicting preferences, it is important to remember that your child needs to have physical activity in order to grow and develop in a healthy manner —occasionally, you'll have to take him to the park!

The differences in activity levels can also cause a mismatch in parents' and children's energy levels, particularly in the late afternoon and early evening. The young child has run around all day and is still going strong (much like the Energizer bunny), while his parents' energy has been drained and their activity levels are at a low point. In our homes, we call this period the "gangrene hours" (between 4:30 P.M. and 6:30 P.M.). Because there is such a mismatch between the parents' hopes and desires and the children's needs and expectations, the situation decays rapidly and irreversibly (hence, the name). The children want to play, eat dinner, and spend "quality" time with their mom and dad. In contrast, their parents are exhausted by the day's work and just want to take a brief nap before eating a quiet dinner—alone. Having determined that their fantasy is impossible, the parents promise "to hear all about your day as soon as we sit down to the table" and send the children off to watch television as they start preparing the evening meal. However, the children are hungry and anxious to spend time with their parents, so the TV program can't hold their attention for long. They're soon bored and seeking stimulation (as well as making further attempts to get their parents' attention). The children get louder and more active with each passing minute. Soon, they begin squabbling and fighting, and it's not long before one of them dissolves into tears while the other throws a temper tantrum. When that happens, their parents scream, "You're giving me a headache. Just go to your room and be quiet!"

The gangrene hours can be prevented by a combination of good humor and advance preparation. When the above scenario happened in one of our homes, the three-year-old responded, "I'm giving you a headache? Well, you're giving me a fever!" since she knew that fevers were *much* more serious than headaches and she obviously was the one who was most in need of attention. As we laughed, we also took a minute to relax and give her a hug, and the gangrene hour disappeared. The next evening, we made a conscious effort to ensure that each of us had a snack, a drink of water (dehydration can cause fatigue and subsequent short tempers), and five minutes of peace. Then we worked together to make dinner and, as we did so, listened to some of our family's favorite music, rather than trying to concentrate on stories from school. You will need to experiment to find out what works best for you and your child—it may mean putting off dinner until after you've had a chance to catch up on each other's day or it may be that taking a walk together will be a way for you to unwind and your child to expend some of his excess energy. Prevention is always the best treatment for "gangrene"—stop it before it starts.

When Hyperactivity Is More Than "Just a Phase"

"Robert, this is your brother's big day and I don't want you to steal the show from him by squirming around or whispering during his baptism," Sally said to her seven-year-old son as they prepared to go into the sanctuary of the church.

"I won't, Mom," Robert replied. "I'll sit really still and be as quiet as a mouse."

"Are you sure?" Sally asked. "I'll be busy with the baby, so I won't be able to remind you to keep quiet. Do you think maybe you should go to children's church instead of staying for the ceremony?"

"No, I want to see Mark get baptized. I'm the only big brother he has and he needs me there. I'll be good—I promise!"

"Okay, I'll hold you to it," his mother said, and led the way to the pew that had been reserved for them at the front of the church. Robert sat quietly for less than a minute before he started squirming and fidgeting in his seat. His mother looked over and mouthed the word "One," which was Robert's warning that he had just used the first of his three chances to behave. Worried that he might be forced to leave before his brother's baptism, Robert tried to occupy himself by looking at his Sunday-school paper, but it wasn't very interesting and he got bored quickly. Fortunately, the organ started playing the first hymn and he was able to stand up and move around a little as they sang one of his favorites. When the hymn was over, Robert was still humming the chorus as they resumed their seats. His mother reached over and tapped him on the shoulder. "Shh," she whispered.

"I was just singing the song to myself," Robert replied, in a whisper loud enough to be heard several rows away.

"Be quiet!" his mother said. "Reverend Easton is starting the morning prayer. Fold your hands, bow your head, and listen to what he's saying."

Robert did as he was told, but a few seconds later, he heard a buzzing sound and opened his eyes to see if he could locate the fly. It was right in front of him! Without thinking, he grabbed for it and, as he did, knocked his little brother in the head. Mark started crying immediately and everyone in the church looked up to see what had caused the disturbance. The minister even stopped praying until the baby had stopped screaming. Robert's mother glared at him and said, "Two and a half," which meant that he was definitely out with the next strike —sometimes, he got an extra warning and his mother said "Two" and then "Two and a half," but "Two and a half" always meant that "Three" would come next, so Robert redoubled his efforts to sit quietly.

When the prayer was finished, Reverend Easton announced Mark's baptism and asked the family to come up to the baptismal font. Robert proudly followed his family to the front of the church and stood behind his mother to make sure that he wouldn't "steal the show" from his little brother. Unfortunately, this meant that he couldn't see anything that was going on and so he started pushing his way through the group, trying to get a better view. As he jostled his mother, she reached to protect the baby and, losing her balance, fell against the baptismal font. The water splashed everywhere—onto her, the baby, and the minister, *who recovered quickly and said, "I know you're anxious to see your brother baptized, Robert. But unless you've been ordained without my knowing about it, you need to let me be the one to anoint your brother with the holy water."*

As the congregation laughed, Robert started to cry with embarrassment and frustration. Despite his best efforts, he had blown it again. Oh, why couldn't he ever behave?

"My son is always so hyper—he's impulsive and distractible, too." A child is considered to have hyperactivity if his activity levels are consistently high—this means that he should be noticeably hyper most or all of the time, and in many different situations. When the hyperactivity is accompanied by inattention and impulsivity, it may be due to attention deficit hyperactivity disorder, or ADHD. ADHD and the differences between hyper behavior and hyperactivity are discussed at length in chapter 13.

"My son is so hyper—he always runs away when I ask him to stay put." If a child runs when he's supposed to walk, or gets up out of his seat frequently without permission, it might appear that he is hyper. That is, until you notice that he does everything in opposition to expectations—he always keeps going past the point where he's supposed to stop, but he also stops when he's told to go. He also talks incessantly during quiet times in school, but then refuses to speak when he's expected to answer his teacher's questions. Toddlers and adolescents frequently demonstrate such oppositional behaviors as they begin establishing their independence, but the limit-testing isn't confined to increased motor activity and shouldn't be confused with ADHD. If a grade school child's hyperactivity is intermittent and clearly represents naughty behavior, it may be a sign of oppositional defiant disorder or conduct disorder. Conduct disorder is a serious problem for parents, since the misbehavior is often accompanied by a sullen attitude and disrespect for authority (see chapter 3 for further information).

"My nine-year-old just brought a note home from school saying that he's 'too hyper.'" When a child or adolescent develops hyperactivity after the age of seven years, it can't be due to attention deficit hyperactivity disorder—by definition, the disorder is always present before the age of six years. Several medical conditions can cause symptoms similar to hyperactivity. For example, anxiety disorders result in agitation, which can cause the child to appear quite hyper as he paces about the room, or squirms and fidgets anxiously in his chair (see chapter 19 for a full description). Prescription medications, such as theophylline and prednisone, and over-the-counter medications, such as decongestants and cold preparations, can cause hyperactivity in the older child. Lead poisoning and thyroid diseases can also cause symptoms of hyperactivity, although this would be unlikely. More often, the older child's hyperactivity is a symptom of illicit drug use. Many of the street drugs cause a child to appear hyper, particularly the stimulants, like amphetamines and cocaine, which can produce increased motor activity, excessive talking, and agitation (see chapter 24 for more information about drugs and alcohol). If your child begins to appear hyper and is over seven years of age, he should receive a complete evaluation to ensure that he's physically healthy and that he's not using illicit drugs.

"My son was sick with a strep throat last week and now he's *so* hyper!" Researchers at the National Institute of Mental Health have described recently a collection of symptoms that can be triggered by strep throat infections. The syndrome is named pediatric autoimmune neuropsychiatric disorders associated with streptococcal infections, or PANDAS, and is described in detail in chapter 17. One of the symptoms of PANDAS is hyperactivity (the others are obsessive-compulsive symptoms, separation anxiety, and tics or other abnormal movements). If a school-age child has had normal activity levels and abruptly becomes hyperactive, it may be helpful to have his doctor take a throat culture, even if he hasn't complained of a sore throat (since some strep infections don't cause much fever or throat pain).

Helping Your Child Outgrow a Hyper Phase

What You Can Do to Help
Provide your child with the three Ls of parenting—love, limits, and large muscle exercise. To the active child, the three Ls represent safety, security, and success. Your *love* provides him with a safety net—he can depend on its constancy even when his behavior has tried your patience or left you exhausted. *Limits* define the boundaries of your protection— inside the limits, you have made a commitment to keep your child safe and secure; outside the boundaries, there are no guarantees that you will

be able to fully protect him. Some of the limits are physical boundaries ("Don't go outside the backyard fence"), while others are established by rules and regulations ("Don't climb on the rock pile"). *Large muscle exercise* provides the hyper child with a chance for success. His excess energy is a liability in confined settings or sedentary activities, but it can be an asset in team sports or individual physical activities. Exercise can also be a terrific way for the active child to "burn off some excess energy." It offers one additional benefit as well—providing a base of success upon which the active child can build positive self-esteem, a crucial factor in his long-term success. Large muscle exercise may be as simple as taking the dog for a walk or playing catch in the backyard, or it might be organized sports, such as soccer and basketball, or lessons in ballet, gymnastics, or martial arts. Every child should be doing something active enough to make him sweat every single day for at least one half hour per day.

Increase structure and consistency within your family. Structure provides children with a sense of order, and consistency teaches them about dependability and trust. The structure should not be confining or restrictive, but rather should provide a sense of comfort to the child, particularly when his overactivity causes him to fly through life unsure of where he'll be able to land. You can increase structure for your child by establishing a set daily routine and practicing it consistently. The daily routine will consist of a standardized sequence of tasks, such as getting dressed in the morning, eating breakfast, preparing to leave the house, keeping his desk neat, packing his backpack at school to come home, doing his homework after school, helping around the house, and getting ready for bed. The daily routines are supplemented by various weekly routines, including special family rituals, like going to the deli on Saturday mornings for fresh bagels or taking a hike in the park every Sunday afternoon. These rituals provide your child with more than a sense of safety and security, they also build childhood memories.

Discipline, don't punish, your child. Discipline is the art of training your child to live within the rules of his family and community. Punishment, on the other hand, is a "penalty for some offense, transgression or fault . . . a retribution for misdeeds, with little or no expectation of correction or improvement." It is unfortunate that the two terms are so often used interchangeably, as they are nearly opposites—by definition, there are no negatives in discipline and no positives in punishment. Parents of active children have a particular obligation to learn the art of discipline so that they can teach their children to modulate their behavior in response to the situation at hand. (Chapter 3 includes a list of references that provide further information about appropriate disciplinary techniques.)

Make sure your active child eats a healthy diet and gets enough sleep. A child who is physically active and always "on the go" utilizes a tremendous amount of energy. In order to replace it, he must eat a healthy diet and get enough rest. Almost all children and adolescents (including those in high school) need at least eight to ten hours of sleep each night. To ensure that your child is getting enough sleep, he must have a relatively early bedtime on school nights (8:00 or 8:30 P.M.) and it must be consistently applied, with only minimal relaxation on weekends—9:30 P.M. on Friday night is late enough for most children, because their internal clock will still awaken them at their usual hour on Saturday (and deprive them of the extra sleep).

There is a common misconception that overly active children should not be allowed to get a full night's sleep because it will give them "too much energy." Sleep can refuel a child's body, but it can't be stored in excess—it is similar to your car's gas tank; overfilling is impossible because it just spills out onto the ground. Excess sleep is not the cause of hyper behavior. Quite the contrary, many children are hyper only when they are physically exhausted—their overactivity is the result of decreased inhibition (lack of brakes), rather than a true increase in energy. If parents don't recognize this paradox and help their children settle down for bed, it can be hard for them to fall asleep and may make it more difficult to get them into bed at the established bedtime.

Prevent gangrene (hours). The gangrene hours are the difficult hours between the end of the workday and the beginning of the evening's relaxation. The period immediately before dinner is worst for most families. To avoid "meltdowns" during the gangrene hours, we suggest the following:

1. Make sure your child is well rested. Even grade-school-age children should have a period of quiet time in the late afternoon.

2. Don't let your child get too hungry or too thirsty in the last hour before dinner. Have him drink a glass of water and eat a small healthy snack, such as a few slices of apple or half a banana. You

might even serve the evening's vegetable as the snack—kids love carrot sticks, celery, crisp green beans, and raw broccoli florets, and serving them alone, when children are hungry, is a good way to increase consumption.

3. Make sure you take five minutes to be alone and reenergize yourself (you should also drink a glass of water and eat a small snack if you're "running on empty" by 5:00 P.M.).

4. Provide sufficient stimulation to prevent your child from being bored, but not so much that he gets too "wound up." You might have him help with dinner preparations or use the time to drill spelling words or math problems.

5. Don't worry about the clock—if dinner is served at 6:17 P.M. instead of 6:00, it won't make any difference.

6. Maintain your sense of humor.

Relieve unnecessary worries about your child's activity level by doing cross-comparisons. To find out if your child's activity level is normal and expected for his age, volunteer in your child's classroom, invite his friends over to play (inside), or spend time observing his Scout troop or religious classes. Each of these situations provides you with a different setting in which to observe your child's activity level and compare it with that of other boys his age. If your child's behavior appears to be similar to that of the other children, then it is unlikely that he has hyperactivity. As you make your observations, it may also be useful to assess your child's impulsivity, since impulsive children often appear hyper without having increased motor activity. (Chapter 13 provides a full description of the characteristics of childhood impulsivity.)

What Your Child's Teacher Can Do to Help

Help determine whether or not your child's activity level is in the normal range. Your child's teacher has seen hundreds of children and knows what is normal for your child's age, as well as what is considered to be hyper. Based on her experience, she will be able to tell you whether or not your child's activity level is similar to other children of his age and gender. If she says it is normal, it almost always is normal. If she says that your child is a little hyper, then she should also tell you whether or not the increased activity is interfering with his school performance. If it's not, then you may not need to take action. If she reports that your son is hyper and that it's impairing his schoolwork and peer relationships, then she should also give you an assessment of his inattention and impulsivity. In your discussions, you will want to find out about your child's:

1. Activity level. Is he more active or hyper than the other boys? Does he get out of his seat frequently or perch on the edge of his chair? Does he seem to disturb the other children?

2. Ability to pay attention. Can he concentrate on his schoolwork or is he easily distracted? Does he seem to be listening as the teacher speaks? Does he get the whole assignment or only pieces?

3. Interactions with other children. Is he able to carry on a polite conversation or does he butt in before they finish speaking? Does he wait his turn in line? Is he part of the classroom community or have the other children learned to tune him out?

4. Daily behaviors. Are the behaviors present the majority of the day, and do they cause problems?

If the answers to these questions suggest that your child's hyperactivity is a problem, you should take action. Start by getting a second opinion from another teacher or your child's doctor.

Be informed about expected activity levels. In order for a child to learn to stay in his seat, both developmental maturity and careful, consistent training are required. For children with average activity levels, these usually come together some time between kindergarten and second grade. Experienced kindergarten teachers know that their students aren't yet ready to stay seated for long periods, so they organize their classrooms to encourage mobility and freedom. At the beginning of the school year, they do very few activities that require the children to sit still and work quietly. As the year progresses, they gradually increase the number of quiet activities to the point where the kindergartners may remain seated for two or three consecutive sessions, such as storytime and sharing. First graders remain relatively active and teachers allow them to retain some mobility—the children are frequently away from their desks, working in small groups or on special activities. By second grade, however, most of the students' work is done at their desks and they are typically required to remain seated for much of the day. For children with high activity levels, this can be impossible, and the teacher might allow the active student to move about the room more freely, or use an alternate worksite (for example, at a table at the side of the room) to complete the activity.

Several of the conditions that cause increased motor activity come on later in childhood (e.g., PANDAS, drug use, thyroid disease) and might first be observed in the classroom. Your child's teacher should let you know of her concerns promptly, so that you can begin to watch for similar behavior changes at home.

Provide structure and consistency in the classroom. Structure and consistency are even more important at school than they are at home, since twenty-five to thirty children must all maintain appropriate behavior. Your child's teacher can provide structure by establishing a daily routine on the first day of school and utilizing it consistently throughout the year. Classroom rules and consequences should also be established on the first day, posted in a clearly visible place and then consistently and equitably enforced.

Maintain open lines of communication. In order to facilitate your child's education, you and his teacher should become partners in his education. As partners, you will need to communicate frequently about your child's successes, failures, and changes in his progress or attitude. An assignment notebook can be used as the vehicle for daily communication. At school, the day's assignments are entered by your child and checked by his teacher, who then adds a brief daily progress report. At home, you can use the notebook to ensure that he does all his homework and that he has any supplies needed for a special project the next day. Of course, telephone conferences and in-person meetings are also helpful and spending time as a classroom volunteer is a terrific way to get to know your child's teacher and to build your partnership.

What Your Child's Doctor Can Do to Help

Provide guidance about normal behavior and expected activity levels. Pediatricians are trained to be child development experts. Your child's doctor should be able to tell you what changes to expect in his behavior in the coming year, as well as providing you with resources for use at home.

Assess your child's behavior and determine whether it is normal or hyperactive. Although a checkup is a very brief interaction and a definitive diagnosis of ADHD cannot be made at that time, your child's doctor should be able to provide you with a general impression of the appropriateness of your child's activity for his age level. If you raise concerns, the doctor should follow up with a more complete assessment of your child's activity, impulse control, and attention.

If your child has hyperactivity, determine whether or not he has ADHD. The diagnosis of attention deficit hyperactivity disorder (ADHD) is made by taking a history of your child's behavior at home and in school, and determining whether or not he has problems with inattention, impulsivity, and hyperactivity. If two or more of the symptoms are present, further questioning should help to determine whether or not they are causing problems for your child and if they have been present long enough to be considered ADHD. In making a diagnosis, the pediatrician will need to depend heavily upon your observations and those of your child's teacher. The diagnosis of ADHD is based solely on the clinical history and does not require a physical examination or laboratory tests for confirmation. However, a physical examination is helpful to ensure that your child's symptoms aren't being caused by another medical problem, such as poor hearing or decreased vision. If your child's doctor isn't comfortable with this assessment, then he should refer you to a child psychiatrist, a behavioral pediatrician, or other pediatric specialist for evaluation.

If your child has ADHD, ensure that he gets proper treatment. Some pediatricians have the skills, training, and experience to manage the treatment of a child with ADHD. If your child's pediatrician does not, he should refer you to a child psychiatrist or a behavioral pediatrician who specializes in ADHD treatment. The treatment should utilize a combination of behavior therapy and medications, as described in chapter 13.

Further Reading
Child Development

Gesell, Arnold, Frances L. Ilg, and Louise Bates Ames. *The Child from Five to Ten.* New York: Harper & Row, 1977.

Ilg, Frances L., M.D., Louise Bates Ames, Ph.D., and Sidney M. Baker, M.D. *Child Behavior: The Classic Child Care Manual from the Gesell Institute of Human Development.* New York: Harper Perennial, 1981.

Kutner, Lawrence, Ph.D. *Your School-Age Child.* New York: William Morrow & Co., 1996.

Philadelphia Child Guidance Center, with Jack Maguire. *Your Child's*

Emotional Health: The Middle Years. New York: Macmillan (The Philip Lief Group, Inc.), 1994.

Singer, Dorothy G., and Tracey A. Revenson. *A Piaget Primer: How a Child Thinks.* New York: Penguin Books, 1996.

Parenting

Dinkmeyer, Don, and Gary D. McKay. *The Parent's Handbook: Systematic Training for Effective Parenting (STEP).* Circle Pines, MN: American Guidance Service, 1989.

Elkind, David, Ph.D. *Parenting Your Teenager.* New York: Ballantine Books, 1993.

Gordon, Dr. Thomas. *P.E.T.—Parent Effectiveness Training.* New York: Penguin Books, 1975.

What Do Children Need? Understanding, Doing and Sharing Parenting— Especially the Parenting of a Challenging Child. Kansas City, MO: Health Education Consultants, 1993 (updated 1997).

"My Daughter Is Such a Picky Eater"

Feeding difficulties and obesity

"I don't know what I'm going to do with my Lindsey," Barb said to her friends Kelly and Patty. "She used to have a great appetite, but since she turned four last month, I can't get her to eat hardly anything. Well, except for breakfast—she eats really well then, but at lunchtime, she eats less than half a sandwich and then asks to be excused from the table because she's 'full.' And at dinner, she just picks. I'm lucky if she takes even a small bite of the salad and vegetables and she usually refuses the main course, too—especially if it's something she hasn't tried before."

"She sounds just like my Jonah," Kelly said. "He refuses to try anything new, so he has the same thing for lunch every day—peanut butter and jelly, chips, Oreos, and juice. And for dinner, I have to make him macaroni and cheese every night, otherwise, he won't eat a thing."

"Nothing?" Patty asked. "How old is Jonah now?"

"He's almost six."

"And you still make him macaroni and cheese every night?" Patty asked incredulously.

"Yes, unless we're having pizza or lasagna—he'll eat those, he likes them," Kelly said.

Patty laughed and said, "Girl, you're being taken for a ride. Any child who can eat pizza and lasagna doesn't have a problem with spicy foods or strong tastes, so there shouldn't be any food that he can't handle. Jonah's not picky by nature, he's picky by choice and you're letting him get away with it. Why don't you make him eat what you're eating or go hungry?"

"I couldn't do that," Kelly answered. "He'd choose to go hungry and I couldn't bear for him to go to bed with an empty stomach."

Patty said, "I bet you a week's worth of groceries that he'd only miss supper once, maybe twice, before he started eating whatever you put out for him. Don't sabotage yourself, though, by breaking down and giving him a bedtime snack, because the only way you'll break this bad habit is to teach him that either he eats with the family or he goes hungry. It's his choice, but if he chooses to go hungry, he should know what it feels like to have an empty tummy until breakfast."

"Boy, Patty," Barb said. "You're tough!"

"Yes, I am," Patty replied. "I have to be. When you're raising two kids by yourself, you can't afford to be a short-order cook—it takes too much time and costs too much money to cook two or three different meals. Besides, I don't think it's a good idea for kids to order their parents around. It seems like we should decide what to make for dinner and the kids can decide whether or not to eat it."

"Well," Kelly sniffed, "you raise your children your way and I'll raise mine my way. I'm not sending my son to bed hungry and that's that."

"I'm sorry I brought it up, ladies," Barb said. "Let's change the subject." She hadn't gotten any answers to her questions about Lindsey's picky eating, but she had heard enough to realize that it might have as much to do with parenting as it did with a child's food preferences.

Barb was absolutely right—picky eaters are both born and made. Some children are picky eaters because they are born with a heightened sensitivity to taste or textures. The child's first food refusal might come early in infancy when she refuses to nurse if her mother has eaten garlic or spicy foods that flavor the breast milk. Other children, like Jonah, are described as picky eaters because they refuse to try new foods or to eat at scheduled mealtimes, but their pickiness is related to issues of control as much as it is to food preference or appetite. Most children are not true "picky eaters," but they still may go through periods of picky eating during certain developmental phases or in response to changes in growth rate. Even kids who eat everything, like "Mikey" in the old Life cereal commercials, will pass through a variety of "picky" phases as they grow and develop. The phases are usually short-lived and disappear within a few weeks, but occasionally they persist for several months or longer. During these periods, the children either eat noticeably less than they did before, or they may become more particular about the types of foods that they will eat. Some children appear to eat "nothing" (at least at the dinner table), while others will eat only certain foods, like PB&J sandwiches, cold cereal, pasta, or white foods like mashed potatoes, vanilla ice cream, yogurt, rice, and white bread. (For some reason, we've never had a parent complain that her child eats "only" lima beans, Brussels sprouts, and broccoli!)

Parents often worry that their child's picky eating is a precursor to anorexia, bulimia, or the other eating disorders. However, there is *no* evidence to suggest that picky eating is associated with eating disorders, which are characterized not only by limited food intake, but also by distortions of body self-image and obsessive concerns with food and food intake. (See chapter 23 for a complete description of the eating disorders.) Parents also worry that their picky eater will become malnourished, but children need to eat only small amounts of a variety of foods in order to satisfy the minimum nutritional requirements of childhood. They also need to eat relatively few calories to have enough energy for daily needs. The remaining calories (about one-half of normal daily intake) are converted to energy for growth—so if your child is growing properly, her picky eating is probably not causing serious problems with her nutritional balance. In fact, picky eating has surprisingly few health risks, but it still deserves our attention, particularly since it is so often a source for concern and conflict.

When Picky Eating Is "Just a Phase"

"My child won't eat—she says she's not hungry." Caloric requirements of childhood are determined by the rate at which your child grows. When she's growing quickly, she'll seem to have a "hollow leg" and will eat voraciously; when her growth slows, she'll dramatically decrease the amount of food that she eats. Suddenly, she seems to be a "picky eater" because she's refusing to eat a full serving of meat or vegetables, but she probably eats only small portions of other foods, as well. Children have a good sense of hunger and satiety (sense of fullness) and should be allowed to respond to these feelings. If your child says she's full, she's probably full and should be allowed to stop eating. If you require your child to eat when she's not hungry or to continue eating past the point of fullness ("Clean your plate," "Eat three more bites," or "Finish your meat and drink your milk"), her sense of satiety decreases, which puts her at risk for overeating and obesity.

There are several common causes of picky eating that are easily overlooked. One of these is not leaving enough time for the child to become hungry. For example, if a child eats well at breakfast and lunch, but is "not hungry" at dinner, it may be because she eats her afternoon snack at 4:30 and dinner at 6 P.M., and she doesn't have enough time to develop an appetite for dinner. It's important to allow at least two to two and a half hours between the afternoon snack and dinner to ensure that your child eats well at the evening meal.

Children who drink juice or milk when they are thirsty (instead of water) may also appear to be picky eaters because they have "filled up" on liquid calories. Fruit juice, milk, and soda pop all have very high calorie contents, and if a child drinks five to six glasses of juice or milk during the day, she will have drunk nearly three-quarters of her daily caloric needs. Many pediatricians recommend that children consume no more than one glass of juice each day and two to three glasses of milk, not only to prevent pickiness at mealtimes, but also to avoid excess calories and childhood obesity.

"My child's diet is atrocious—she eats peanut butter and bananas for breakfast, lunch, and dinner." Actually, peanut butter and bananas isn't an atrocious diet, although if it were continued for a long-enough period, the child could develop some nutritional deficiencies. Fortunately, food fads such as these are usually self-limited—especially if parents exhibit appropriate control over the child's food intake. Our advice to this mother would be: "Let your child have peanut butter and bananas for lunch, but don't serve it for breakfast or dinner."

Food fads are expected during a child's preschool years, when her tastes haven't matured, but they may also develop later in childhood, particularly during periods of stress or adjustment (such as starting a new school or after there is a new baby in the home) and may be related to the child's need to regain control over her environment. Even though this sounds quite similar to the proposed cause of bulimia and binge-purge eating disorder, food fads do not appear to predispose a child to developing an eating disorder. If your school-age child develops a food fad, try to figure out why it's happening and help her cope with that stress but, meanwhile, keep control of the situation by ensuring that you serve her a wide variety of healthy foods.

"My child won't try anything new." Most children are reluctant to try new foods, particularly if they have a strange appearance or a strong odor. There is some disagreement about how much of a new food a child should be required to try (three bites? one bite? or "just a taste"?), but all agree that the child should be expected to try the new food. Unless children are exposed to new tastes and textures, their palate cannot mature. Some experts have said that it takes at least twelve exposures before a food becomes familiar, so don't despair if your child is still turning up her nose at your favorite casserole several months from now.

When Picky Eating Is More Than "Just a Phase"

"Mom, can I be excused from the table?" asked Tamara, a slightly built ten-year-old.

"Not until you've finished your milk," her mother, Marilyn, replied.

"I don't want it," Tamara replied. "It's not cold anymore and I hate warm milk."

"Tamara, if you had drunk your milk when it was served, it would have still been cold. Since you didn't, you'll have to drink it warm."

"No, it will make me sick."

"Nonsense," her mother responded. "You're not going to get sick from drinking warm milk."

"I might. Daddy does," Tamara said.

"The temperature has nothing to do with that—Daddy is lactose-intolerant and can't digest milk properly. You've been drinking milk all your life and haven't had any problems, so there's no reason for you not to drink it," Marilyn said.

"But, Mom," Tamara said, "I do get problems from milk, especially when you make me finish the whole glass. I have really gross diarrhea about an hour later and sometimes I get terrible cramps in my stomach."

"Really?" her mother asked. "Why didn't you tell me about this before?"

"I did, but you said it was just the leftovers from the flu. Remember?" Tamara said.

"Of course, I remember," Marilyn said. "But that was just a few days after you'd gotten over that terrible stomach bug—a little diarrhea and queasiness were certainly not unusual."

"That wasn't it, though, Mom," Tamara interrupted. "I can prove that I get sick from drinking milk. Just wait a minute," she said and ran off to her room. She returned a few seconds later with a small spiral-bound notepad and said, "This is my clue diary. We learned all about how scientists solve problems

by comparing their notes on one experiment with those on another. I thought I could do the same thing for my diarrhea—you know, like it was an experiment or something."

"That was very clever, Tamara," her mother said. "What did you find out?"

"I found out that I only get sick when I drink milk. See, every time I've had diarrhea, I've had milk beforehand. I don't get sick after breakfast and I drink orange juice then. Same thing at lunch—I drink a juice box, not milk, and I don't get sick. One day, I had chocolate milk for lunch and I got diarrhea that afternoon, just like when I drink regular milk. I didn't want to count that one, though, because I really like chocolate milk."

"Tamara," her mother said as she looked through the journal, "I think you're right about this. You've had diarrhea every day for the past week and always within an hour or two of having drunk a glass of milk. I wish you would have come to me with this earlier so that I could have helped you, but since you've already done all the background work, we might as well go see your pediatrician and see if he agrees with your 'diagnosis.' Meanwhile, I guess you'd better dump the rest of that milk down the drain—I certainly don't want you drinking something that will make you sick."

"My child is only picky about breakfast. She refuses to eat eggs or drink orange juice." Lactose intolerance and food allergies are relatively common and contribute to picky eating for many children, particularly in the grade school years. The children learn through experience that certain foods will make them sick and they avoid eating them. To their parents, this avoidance looks just like any other food refusal, but it is actually a matter of not being able to eat the foods comfortably, rather than not wanting to eat them. Since the difference between "can't eat" and "won't eat" is often obscured by a variety of other issues, it is helpful for parents to keep their own clue diary in preparation for the doctor's visit. Parents (and children if they are old enough and reliable enough to provide useful observations) should keep track of the foods refused, the reasons given for not eating them, the child's overall appetite at the time, any physical symptoms associated with eating the foods, and so forth. The child's doctor can use the information in the diary to look for patterns that suggest a food intolerance, such as the fact that the child avoids all dairy products or that she develops a rash each time she eats strawberries. Even if a clear pattern emerges, additional testing should be done to confirm that the problem is a food allergy before the child's diet is restricted; otherwise, she may be denied potential nutrients without good cause.

"My child has stopped growing." A slowed growth rate may be an indication that a child isn't taking in enough calories. If a child's growth slows to less than two inches per year, or she stops gaining weight, then she isn't growing as expected. Although it is natural to assume that a picky eater's slow growth is due to her poor food intake, there are many other possibilities, including the fact that children frequently "plateau" and stay at the same weight and height for several months before "shooting up" to their expected size. These plateaus are so common that the standardized growth curves take them into account. The normal plateaus would not last for a full year, however, and are never associated with weight loss. Your child's doctor can compare your child's current height and weight against her previous record. If the picky eating is a problem and she has stopped growing, her height and weight will have moved down a category or two on the growth chart; if it is merely a plateau, she should still be in the same range as previous measurements.

"My six-year-old is so picky about what she eats, and yet she's already overweight." Picky eaters are usually defined by being choosy about what they eat, not by how much they eat. They may even eat more than other children because their parents are concerned that they're "not getting enough to eat" at mealtime and allow them to choose their own snacks —these children often eat two to three times as many calories at snacktime as children whose parents control their snack choices. The children may also refuse to drink plain water and instead quench their thirst with soda pop, juice, or milk—these beverages are another source of hidden calories. In another common scenario, the child is viewed as a picky eater because "it's so hard to get her to eat," when, in actuality, she's making high-calorie deals at the dinner table: "I won't eat my potatoes unless you put more butter on them" or "I'll eat some broccoli if it has cheese sauce on it." In our experience, a child's chances of being overweight are actually increased by picky eating, because she is more likely to choose candy, ice cream, and French fries, rather than an apple, orange, or carrot sticks.

The overweight picky eater is the only one who is at risk for developing an eating disorder. Her picky eating is a sign that she is controlling her own diet at a stage when she lacks the knowledge and maturity to make healthy choices, and her obesity suggests that the foods she chooses are too high in calories (and probably too low in fiber, vitamins, and minerals) and that she may be ignoring her sense of satiety (feeling of satisfaction and fullness). The child may also have poor self-esteem and a poor body image as a result of her obesity—both of which put her at increased risk for developing an eating disorder during adolescence.

The overweight picky eater needs help. She needs her parents to take control of her diet and to choose healthy foods for her meals and snacks. She needs help reprogramming her eating patterns so that she doesn't pick at her meals and gorge on snack foods. She also needs her parents (particularly her mother) to provide a positive role model for healthy eating and positive self-image. The overweight child does not need her parents to put her on a weight-loss diet, since that is usually a "no-win" situation—the diet is unlikely to be successful, but it is very likely to set up battles over her appearance and her food intake, both of which are risk factors for adolescent eating disorders. (See chapter 23 for more details on eating disorders.)

"My child refuses to eat the foods I cook because she's worried about getting fat." Children as young as age seven or eight can develop anorexia nervosa, and the diagnosis should be considered in any child who refuses to eat because of fears of gaining weight. However, anorexia is very rare before adolescence and is not likely to be the cause of your child's picky eating, unless she begins dieting to lose weight or she sees herself as fat when she's clearly not. (See chapter 23 for a full description of anorexia.) In most cases, the child's picky eating is due to one of two things: realistic concerns about a diet that is too high in calories, or excessive concerns about dietary fats. The child may have learned about the food pyramid in school and discovered that fats are supposed to be the smallest component of her diet, so she begins avoiding foods high in fat content. However, she appears picky to her family members because she refuses to eat the vegetables (in butter sauce), meat (fried chicken), and even dessert (fudge brownies with ice cream). If she gets the majority of her information about "healthy" foods from TV commercials, she may be confused between Madison Avenue hype and real nutrition concerns. She may be reluctant to eat any foods that are not labeled "low fat" because they are "bad" for her. The only way to determine why the child is avoiding these foods is to ask her—find out what her concerns are and what her pickiness really represents. If the child's concerns are misinformed, correct any factual errors in her knowledge base and use the discussion as an opportunity to teach her about wise food choices. If her concerns have merit, they can serve as a springboard for establishing a healthier diet for the entire family.

"My child says that she 'has' to eat only certain foods in a certain way or something 'bad' will happen." The picky eater who is preoccupied with food or the way in which she eats her meals may be suffering from obsessive-compulsive disorder, or OCD. If so, her pickiness would not be due to limited food choices but rather to limitations enforced by contamination fears or a compulsive ritual, such as a need for symmetry. If your picky eater is blaming her fussiness on "having to" do things a certain way, then OCD should be considered as a possibility. (Chapter 16 provides enough information to decide if this could be a problem for your child.)

"My child has always been a good eater, but lately she refuses to eat almost everything." Although all children go through stages in which they have increased fussiness and decreased food intake (as described above), a sudden, dramatic reduction in appetite should be a cause for concern, particularly if the child isn't hungry several days in a row, she refuses meals (especially breakfast), or she suddenly loses her taste for certain foods. The most frequent medical cause of such symptoms is hepatitis, a viral infection that usually is associated with jaundice (yellowing of the skin and eyes). Other infectious illnesses, such as infectious mononucleosis ("mono"), also can cause decreased appetite, as can leukemia or other forms of cancer, bowel disturbances such as ulcerative colitis or Crohn's disease, and other chronic diseases. The decreased appetite may also be a symptom of depression, an anxiety disorder, or a recent traumatic event. If your child has a persistent or dramatic change in her appetite, she should be seen by her pediatrician, who can determine which, if any, of these illnesses are the cause of the appetite change and can provide appropriate treatment.

Helping Your Child Outgrow a Picky-Eating Phase

What You Can Do to Help
Plan and serve healthy snacks. Your child needs at least one snack (midafternoon) and may require two or three if she is a "grazer." Since the main feature that distinguishes a healthy diet from one that isn't as healthy is the quality of the snacks consumed, it's important to plan for nutritious snacks that are appropriately timed. The afternoon snack should be relatively small and come at the midpoint between lunch and

dinner (usually around 3:00 to 3:30 P.M.) so that your child is hungry when dinner is served. Your child cannot afford empty calories, so she shouldn't snack on junk foods. If she prefers sweet treats, then her snack might include fruit, chocolate milk, oatmeal cookies, or frozen yogurt. If she likes salty foods, try pretzels, trail mix, crackers, or whole-grain cereal snack mix.

You decide WHAT she will eat, but let her decide HOW MUCH to eat. Your child's calorie intake will vary as she grows and develops—sometimes she'll eat very little, and at other times, she'll eat so much that you'll wonder where she's putting it all. Children are very good judges of their energy requirements and eat as much as they need, but not much more—they rarely eat past the point of fullness. So rather than cajoling your child to "Take just one more bite" or "Finish your dinner so you can have dessert," let her stop when she's full. Start with small portions and let hunger be her guide to second or third helpings. Your child will get sufficient nutrients if she eats a variety of foods and will take in adequate calories if she's allowed to use hunger as her guide.

Make some allowances for her eating style. Your child's style of eating is probably quite different from yours. She has her own favorite foods, her own preferences for seasonings, and may even want to arrange her meals differently—for example, she might want to eat most of her calories at lunch, while you prefer to have your main meal in the evening. To help your child enjoy eating, you should accommodate these differences to the maximum extent possible within the limits of family rules and the requirements of a healthy diet.

First, establish the "unbreakable rules" for your family. These rules should fit your family's needs, and should be followed by all family members (including parents, so don't make rules you don't want to keep!). Examples of unbreakable rules include: breakfast is a requirement on school days, everyone should be present for the family meal, each food that is served must be sampled (one bite), good manners must be observed at all times, no food is to be eaten outside the kitchen or dining room, and so on.

After establishing how your family will eat, it is important to decide what they will eat. It is your job to choose foods that meet your child's nutritional requirements and ensure appropriate calorie intake. Then, within those boundaries, you can work with your child to accommodate her eating style and food preferences. For example, the rule might be that everyone must eat a healthy breakfast, but if your child doesn't like cereal or other traditional breakfast foods, she might have leftover pizza, a yogurt shake, or a sandwich and juice. If your child prefers to eat frequently during the day and to consume only small amounts of food at any one time, then serve her only the entree and a small portion of a single side dish at dinner and spread her vegetables, fruits, and grains out over the day in the form of healthy snacks. Your long-term goal is to help your child establish healthy eating habits and not to have her become rigidly bound to any particular diet regimen.

Eat dinner together as a family. It seems trite to insist upon sharing dinner together as a family, particularly since every politician seeking reelection has claimed that the family dinner is the cure for everything from teenage pregnancy to gang violence. But the family dinner is important, and not only as a vital part of your child's education in appropriate table manners, the art of conversation, and the practice of good nutrition, but also as a time to share joys and concerns and to provide support to one another. As you will see in other chapters in this book, it is also an ideal time for you to take inventory of your child's activities and to assess her state of mind—is she happy and healthy or does she need some special attention?

If suppertime isn't possible for your regular family meal, then make it breakfast each day or a late-evening snack, or a combination of different meals—dinner during the weekdays, brunch on Saturday, and informal supper on Sunday. It doesn't matter when you share the meal, but it is important for it to become a regular daily routine so that your child learns she can count on her family for stability, consistency, and support.

Learn more about nutrition and children's eating patterns. Seek out information about nutrition from the library, your child's school, and her pediatrician. The U.S. Department of Agriculture and your county's extension service also provide information about nutrition and health. Your child's annual physical examination should include a dietary assessment. Use this opportunity to discuss any concerns that you have regarding your child's diet and to obtain information about appropriate portion sizes and special dietary needs.

Teach your child about nutrition and let her practice planning a healthy menu. Once you've learned all you can about nutrition, it's time to teach your child about a healthy diet and let her take some control over her food choices. This should not be a transfer of responsibility (for this may predispose girls to problems with eating disorders, as described in chapter 23), but rather it should be an opportunity for teaching and learning. There are many possibilities—you might let your child help you plan the weekly menu, do the grocery shopping together, or teach her how to prepare some of her favorite snacks. The age at which this can occur depends upon your child's interests and abilities. Some preschoolers are very interested in food and want to help in the kitchen. Discussing healthy snack choices as you pare carrots together can be a wonderful introduction to nutrition. Furthermore, when food serves as a control issue, then planning meals together allows your child to feel more in control, and thus more likely to eat.

Your child might become interested in nutrition only when you begin turning down her requests for junk food and encourage her to choose snack foods that give the highest "return" on her investment of calories. You might pique your child's interest in eating well by creating a nutrition bank, in which your child fills her account each day by satisfying the requirements of the food pyramid—she will learn that junk food doesn't help fill her account and that the calories she spends are truly "empty" ones.

If your child is overweight, don't turn it into an eating disorder. Overweight children don't always grow up to be overweight adults. In fact, they are more likely to grow out of it than to remain obese after adolescence. However, overweight children are at an increased risk of developing eating disorders, in part because of the excessive, negative attention given to their weight. Chapter 23 discusses how mismanagement of childhood obesity can contribute to these disorders; it also provides strategies for preventing the development of eating disorders.

If your child is overweight, it is important for her to establish healthy eating habits and to maintain a positive self-image. One part of this is to have pride in her appearance, so encourage her to use good grooming habits and allow her to choose clothes that she likes and feels comfortable wearing.

Don't let her extra pounds become the focus of family attention. Her diet should be the same as other members of the family, including snacks and desserts, and should consist of healthy foods with reasonable portion sizes and appropriate calorie content. Often, a diet that stabilizes your child's weight is ideal. If her weight stays the same, she will automatically slim down as she grows. If your child wishes to lose weight, and you are willing to support her efforts, then it is advisable to seek consultation from her doctor or a registered dietitian before beginning the diet.

What Your Child's Teacher Can Do to Help

Teach about nutrition and healthy food choices. Teachers can have a tremendous influence over their students' diets by teaching them how to make healthy food choices. The lessons might be based on the nutrients in the food pyramid, the how-tos of reading food labels, or the science of nutrition. The specific content of the lessons isn't as important as the overall message that "You are what you eat" and that it is important to choose foods that provide adequate energy to grow and thrive, and sufficient nutrients to build a healthy body.

Discourage teasing or inappropriate comments about obesity or other figure flaws. Girls as young as seven or eight years old are already self-conscious about their figures and the concerns increase dramatically as they pass through puberty. Teasing can be the trigger that sets off an eating disorder, particularly if the girl has a poor self-image. In the adult workplace, comments about any aspect of a woman's body are considered to be sexual harassment and are not tolerated. This "zero tolerance" policy is well advised for the classroom, too.

Watch for eating problems and excessive thinness. Although teachers don't always eat lunch with their students, they usually have an opportunity to watch the students during classroom parties and snacks. If unusual eating behaviors are noticed, it's important for your child's teacher to share her observations with you or your child. Similarly, if a teacher notices a dramatic change in your child's weight or hears her making negative comments about her appearance, she should make sure that you're aware of the potential for problems. And if you notice unusual eating patterns at home, be sure to ask your child's teacher to closely monitor your child at lunchtime.

Allow sufficient time for lunch and snacks. Rushing through lunch to get out to recess or bolting down the afternoon snack to have more time on the computer is commonplace, but not in keeping with a healthy eating style. Although there is no direct relationship between hurried meals and the development of binge-purge eating disorder, there is ample evidence that eating quickly is associated with excess calorie intake, because it takes about twenty minutes for the satiety center to be activated by the fullness of the stomach.

Provide opportunities for exercise. The main cause of childhood obesity in the United States is underactivity—too much TV-watching and sitting in front of the computer and too little active play. Your child's teacher can encourage her students to play active games at recess and might even initiate a game of freeze tag or red rover in order to help them burn off calories.

What Your Child's Doctor Can Do to Help

Determine whether or not your child's "picky" eating is a problem. Your child's doctor should be alert to excessive drooling and other symptoms that would suggest a neurologic basis for the picky eating. He should also be able to estimate whether or not your child is meeting her energy needs and receiving adequate amounts of vitamins and minerals. If not, he should provide you with recommendations for improving her diet, or refer you to a dietitian for nutritional counseling. The doctor might also recommend occupational therapy if the picky eating is related to heightened sensitivities to taste and texture.

Monitor growth and development. Both slowed growth and early obesity are easily detected if your child's doctor plots her height and weight at each regular checkup. In order to help the doctor obtain the most reliable growth curve, you should schedule her annual physical examination at about the same time each year (such as near her birthday). Your child's height and weight can then be compared with other children her age— for example, if her weight is at the fifth percentile, she weighs less than 95 percent of the girls her age and may be underweight if her height is in the 50 percent range. These comparisons are important, but not as important as your own child's pattern—for example, if she's always been at the tenth percentile for weight and this year has jumped to the 50 percent range, your child's doctor might want to evaluate her diet carefully for excess calories, even though she's still of "average" weight compared with other children.

Assess your child's diet and nutritional status and provide suggestions for improvement. Your child's doctor should take a diet history to determine if your child is meeting her nutritional needs. Often, this is as simple as asking about the number of daily servings your child consumes in each of the major food groups. If she appears to have a problem with her diet, the doctor may take a three-day diet history, asking about meals on a typical school day, a weekend day, and the day before the office visit. This allows him to determine more accurately whether or not her picky eating is causing a nutritional problem.

If your child is a picky eater and is growing slowly, you will want to ensure that her diet is adequate by consulting a registered dietitian (your child's doctor or your local hospital should be able to recommend one). The dietitian will examine your child's diet patterns and provide suggestions for ways in which the caloric content can be increased and the nutritional content improved. She also can suggest ways to improve your child's eating habits.

Assess your child's body image and self-image. Your child should feel good about herself and be proud of the way her body looks. It is important for your child's physician to reinforce this positive self-image and also to provide some advice about expected changes in your child's size and shape during the ensuing year. For example, if your child is on the brink of a growth spurt, her doctor might warn her that her feet, hands, and nose will grow first. If her growth is on the slow side, she should be prepared for being smaller than her classmates in the fall. Your child's doctor can also provide some advice about the range of differences in body shapes and sizes, particularly to preteens as they enter puberty and complete their growth spurt.

Provide wise counsel about childhood obesity. Pediatricians vary widely in their views on childhood obesity and weight management strategies for children. However, all pediatricians would agree that weight management is achieved only when calories in (food intake) equal calories out (exercise, energy expenditure, basic metabolic needs, and growth). The more-difficult questions are whether or not childhood diets are effective and at what age they are appropriate, with many physicians coming down against putting children on diets (too restrictive, too difficult to maintain, too stigmatizing, and too often ineffective). It is hard for children to be on a diet strict enough to lose weight, so some physicians compromise by helping the obese child restrict her calories to a level at which she maintains a stable weight, then as her height increases, she "automatically" slims down. If your child has problems with obesity, you might want to discuss these issues privately with your child's doctor before discussing it in your child's presence in order to avoid potential embarrassment or conflicts.

Recognize eating disorders and provide appropriate treatment or referral. Early treatment for eating disorders can mean the difference between success and failure, so it is important for physicians to recognize an eating disorder in its earliest stages and also to help the teenager's parents become more aware of unhealthy eating styles and the symptoms of the various eating disorders. If the doctor suspects an eating disorder, he may choose to refer the child to a center that specializes in the treatment of eating disorders, since the best results are obtained by a multidisciplinary team.

Further Reading
See chapter 23.

Eisenberg, Arlene, Heidi Murkoff, and Sandee Hathaway. *What to Expect: The Toddler Years.* New York: Workman Publishing Company, 1994.
    Although this book is directed at eating problems of toddlers, the advice for feeding your children applies equally well to all ages.
Satter, Ellyn. *How to Get Your Kids to Eat . . . But Not Too Much.* Palo Alto, CA: Bull Publishing Company, 1987.

"My Son Is So Naughty—
He Never Does
What I Ask Him to Do"

Disobedience, stubbornness, and other behavior difficulties

"Thank you, Jimmy!" Meredith said to her six-year-old son as he handed her a bouquet of flowers he had just picked from the garden. "They're beautiful! Where did you get them?"

"From your garden," Jimmy said.

"Oh, well, I like the flowers very much, but I like them even better in the garden," Meredith said.

"I thought you'd be surprised," Jimmy pouted.

Meredith saw his pout and softened her voice. "I love them, Jimmy. It was very sweet of you to want to surprise me. Thank you!"

A week later, Meredith went out to weed her perennial bed and found that all the blossoms were gone. Suspecting that her son was responsible, she shouted, "James Arthur, get out here!"

"Yes, Mom?" Jimmy said, as he came over and stood next to his mother.

"What did you do to my beautiful flower garden?"

"Nothing," Jimmy said. "I just picked some more flowers to give you as a present. Joanie wouldn't help me find a vase, though, so I put them in the garage to give you later."

"You mean you picked all those beautiful flowers and then left them lying in the garage to rot?" Meredith asked, and then continued sarcastically, "Thank you very much! What a nice present—ruining my flower garden and destroying the flowers, too. Well, just for that, you won't be watching any TV tonight."

"I'm sorry, Mom," Jimmy said. "I'll never, ever do it again. Can I help you fix the garden?"

"No," Meredith said. "I'm too angry with you right now. Go play in the backyard. But be careful of your little sister—she's playing in the sandbox."

"Okay, Mom," Jimmy said contritely and ran off to get his soccer ball.

A few minutes later, Meredith heard her daughter start crying. She ran around the house to find Jimmy squatting in the sandbox, trying to brush the sand out of his sister's face. "Stop it, Jimmy! You'll make it worse!"

"I was just trying to help."

"Just trying to help, just trying to surprise me—everything you 'just try' today gets you into trouble. How would you like to 'just go' sit on the steps for five minutes and think of ways to stay out of hot water?" Meredith said as she wiped the last of the sand from Logan's face.

"I don't want to," Jimmy said.

"Don't talk back to me, young man," his mother said, totally exasperated.

"But, Mom, the sand wasn't my fault," Jimmy pleaded. "I kicked the ball into the tree, and it bounced off a branch and landed in Logan's sandbox. It was an accident."

"It wouldn't have happened if you had been more careful," his mother said. "Now, go sit on the steps for five minutes like I told you before, or I'll make it a ten-minute time-out."

Jimmy muttered under his breath as he walked to the steps, "You didn't tell me before, you asked me before if I wanted to go sit on the steps—and I don't."

"Jimmy, I told you not to talk back to me and I meant it," his mother said. "Go to your room."

"But, Mom, that's not fair," Jimmy protested. "First, you get mad at me for doing something nice for you, then you get mad because I'm trying to help Logan stop crying, and now you're sending me to my room because I was talking to myself about something. It's not fair."

"Life's not fair, Jimmy," Meredith said. "You can think about all the ways that it's unfair as you spend the next half hour in your room. Now go!"

Meredith and Jimmy's interaction represents many of the problems parents face in disciplining their children—establishing reasonable expectations, retaining parental controls, maintaining consistency, and using consequences rather than retribution to improve a child's behavior. Meredith was inconsistent in her response to Jimmy's picking flowers from her garden—one week, she accepted his gift with delight and the next, he got punished for stripping her garden. Jimmy was set up for failure by being encouraged (through positive reinforcement) to do something his mother considered undesirable. He was similarly set up for failure when he was told to "Go play in the backyard" but also to "Be careful" about his sister. At his age and skill level, an accident was inevitable, and yet Jimmy was held responsible for its occurrence. These inconsistent messages and unreasonable expectations left Jimmy confused about how he was supposed to behave. Since he didn't know what was expected of him, he chose to do whatever was most appealing at the moment, figuring that if he was going to get into trouble no matter what he did, he might as well have fun!

Jimmy's behavior was also worsened by the fact that his mother punished him, rather than disciplining him. Discipline means "to teach or train in a manner that shapes, molds, or perfects the mental faculties or moral character" while punishment is "control gained by enforcing obedience or order." Meredith punished Jimmy for stripping the garden and getting sand on his sister, and then escalated the punishments as her frustration grew. The thirty-minute time-out in his room was earned for complaining about his mother's lack of precision. Disrespectful behavior is certainly inappropriate and should not be permitted, but Jimmy was set up by his mother's comments. She had asked him if he wanted to go sit on the steps, rather than telling him clearly, "Jimmy, go sit on the steps for a five-minute time-out—now!"

We chose to open this chapter with a vignette in which the parent shared the blame for the child's inappropriate behavior, because it is too often overlooked as a factor in children's disobedience. Parents inadvertently set up their child to be naughty, by providing positive reinforcement for undesirable behaviors, sending mixed messages, or having unreasonable expectations. Unreasonable expectations often result when parents fail to consider their child's developmental maturity when they give instructions. For example, when five-year-old Junior is told to "behave" at a fancy dinner party, his parents mean for him to use adult manners, sit straight and still in his chair throughout the meal, and speak politely and at an appropriate volume. Junior hears "behave" as: use a fork not my fingers for the goopy stuff, don't run around too much, don't talk about boogers or bathroom stuff at the table, and when I get bored, ask Dad to do the magic trick, instead of trying it myself. Junior's version of "behaving" carries him pretty well through the appetizers and the interminable salad course, but, as might be expected, he's done with his entree about three minutes after it is served and grows tired of behaving himself. Unfortunately, his parents and their friends are tarrying over dinner as they reminisce about the "good old days" and only notice that Junior's slipped away from the table when they hear a crash in the living room. Obviously, if he had followed the "Look, but don't touch" rule, he wouldn't have dropped the antique plate and broken it, but on the other hand, he had been told that he could "help himself" to the appetizers on the plate, which had been left perched on the edge of the table. It's hard to say that Junior's behavior was "bad," even though he broke a well-established (and consistently applied) rule, because there were extenuating circumstances. He had nothing appropriate to do and he was following an adult's suggestion to "help himself." The bottom line is that it was unreasonable to expect a five-year-old boy to behave as an adult for several hours. His parents should have provided him with plenty of quiet activities and decided ahead of time who would be "in charge" of him that evening to take him for a walk or entertain him while the other parent finished dinner or, ideally, left him at home with a baby-sitter, so they could enjoy their evening out without requiring Junior to "behave."

When Naughty Behavior Is "Just a Phase"

"My child won't behave—no matter how much I explain it to him, he won't do what I want." Parents who expect their young children to behave because they've explained why "it's the right thing to do" usually have children who don't live up to their expectations. The child is often too young to comprehend the elaborate explanation given by his parent and he tunes out to everything except the "Okay?" that inevitably follows the soliloquy. The parent thinks she's communicating effectively, but in actuality she's confused the child with the explanation, while simultaneously relinquishing control over the situation.

Grocery stores seem to be a common setting for misbehavior related to overexplanation or over-the-child's-head explanations. For example, Jeffrey's mother wants him to pick the cereal that week so he can practice making decisions, but she also wants him to choose the one that's "good for him," rather than the one he's seen advertised on television (not a reasonable expectation, by the way). She says, "You can choose the cereal this week, Jeffrey. I think that you want this one, Totally Boring Bran, because it's healthy and nutritious, while Kids Gotta Have It is full of processed sugars and artificially colored marshmallows. So, we'll get Totally Boring Bran, okay?" "No!" says Jeffrey, and his mother is stuck. She not only had given him control over the initial choice without ensuring that both options were acceptable to her, but she also confirmed his control over the situation by asking his permission to buy the Totally Boring Bran and he refused. Now, she either goes back on her promise to let him choose or she relinquishes her parental control over his diet and lets him choose a cereal that she doesn't want him to have. Both are equally destructive to Jeffrey's development, as inconsistency and lack of parental controls are at the root of most childhood behavior problems. Suggestions for avoiding these pitfalls are provided at the end of this chapter.

"My child is always so naughty—he won't behave no matter how much we punish him." Punishment is not an effective tool in teaching children how to behave and, in fact, may increase problem behaviors. The best example is the parent who spanks his child for hitting his sister. The father wants to teach his son that it's wrong to hit his sister, but, in fact, he's teaching him that hitting is okay, as long as you're bigger than the other person and in control of the situation. If effective disciplinary techniques were being used to stop the hitting, the parent would establish a rule against hitting (which would apply to everyone in the family) and would also set consequences for infringements of the rule (ten-minute time-out). To be fully successful, the child would be informed of both the rule and its consequences, and they would be applied consistently.

"My child is really showing us what the term 'Terrible Twos' means— but he's four now!" Every parent is familiar with the Terrible Twos, in which a child acts out in a variety of ways as he struggles to establish independence. The Terrible Two-year-old refuses to put on his socks, or spits out his green beans because they're "yucky," or throws a temper tantrum when his mother refuses to buy him Kids Gotta Have It cereal. When the child throwing a tantrum is four or six or eight, we're less prepared for his rebelliousness, but the even-numbered years are often difficult. The pattern is related to the developmental tasks that the children are accomplishing and the names of the stages reflect the most common behaviors—Ferocious Fours, Sassy Sixes, and Awkward Eights. (Note that if the child's first period of acting out came when he was eighteen months or three years old instead of when he was two years old, the odd-numbered years would tend to be difficult since the typical pattern is for an easy year to be followed by a difficult year and then another easy year, etc.)

The Ferocious Four-year-old has a short fuse on his temper and a strong need to "do it myself" even if it takes twice as long. His developmental task is initiative versus guilt (per the noted child psychologist Erik Erikson), and in order to avoid feeling like a failure, he really does need to do it himself, from making his own bed to tying his own shoelaces. The key to avoiding conflicts is to let the child proceed at his own pace and to schedule extra time to allow him to accomplish tasks successfully.

During the Sassy Sixes, the child moves into a period of industry versus inferiority. He feels a sense of mastery over the tasks he's learned and his sassiness is a reflection of his self-confidence. He's always right and has no problem telling you so! However, the six-year-old needs to learn to be respectful of others and to understand the limits of his authority. He should also be challenged to accept responsibility for his behavior—including keeping track of his own homework assignments, using proper phone etiquette when he invites a friend over to play, making amends when he hurts someone's feelings, or suffering the consequences of breaking family rules.

During the Awkward Eights, the child has developmental traits reminiscent of each of the previous periods. He is working on issues of independence and autonomy, which makes him as rebellious or stubborn as a two-year-old. He's also completing tasks related to initiative, which means that he wants to do things himself—in his own way and on his own time (like cleaning his room!). He also may not yet have outgrown his Sensitive Sixes and appears emotionally vulnerable and overly sensitive. When all of these are combined, it leaves the child in the Awkward Eights—not sure who he is or in which direction he wants to go. To avoid unnecessary conflicts, his parents must relax and "go with the flow." They can give him more responsibility and ease up on some of his restrictions in order to show confidence in his maturing abilities, but they must not yet "cut the apron strings," as the eight-year-old needs to know that his parents are providing for his safety and security. One final note: Some experts say that the Awkward Eights are the skirmish that foretells the battles of adolescence, so it's helpful for parents to pay attention to those issues that are difficult for them and use the opportunities to prepare for parenting an adolescent.

"My child has been terribly naughty recently. His teacher sent him home from school again today for misbehaving." Children often act as the barometer of the family's stability. When there is stress in the family, such as marital discord, financial problems, or an ill family member, the child is often the one who signals the coming storms. He senses the tension in the home and is made uncomfortable by it—when he can't get reassurance through positive attention (because his parents are too distracted by their own problems), he seeks negative attention by being naughty. To a distraught child, negative attention is better than no attention at all. This is true not only at home, but also in school and other public settings. A child who is suddenly causing problems in the classroom may be signaling his distress about things at home, or about something that's gone awry in the classroom. Any sudden change in a child's behavior should be investigated—the inquiry often uncovers a second problem even more worthy of attention.

"My child's new friend is a real brat, and my son is becoming one, too." Children are great mimics—they are able to closely imitate one another's behavior, whether it's good or bad. They seem to be particularly prone to picking up other children's bad habits, objectionable language, and disrespectful behavior. Often, "bratty" children are attractive role models because they are outgoing, gregarious, and self-confident. They seem to have all the answers, so children adapt their mannerisms in the hopes that they too will feel in control. Unfortunately, the mimics usually succeed in copying only the disobedient behaviors, and don't acquire the self-confidence that they're seeking. The solution lies in helping the mimic to identify what he values about the other child and encouraging him to emulate those qualities, while discouraging him from adapting the inappropriate behaviors. If your child's behavior is deteriorating as a result of a particular friendship, it is also useful to help your child broaden his circle of friends to include children whose behavior is worthy of copying. Sometimes, it may even be necessary to prohibit your child from playing with the child who is a negative influence—this is well within your parental rights and, more importantly, is part of your parental responsibilities.

"Even though my son is a teenager, he's acting like a two-year-old." Erik Erikson was among the first to notice the similarities between the behavior of the rebellious teenager and the tantrumming two-year-old.

Dr. Erikson concluded that these behavioral similarities were related to the fact that toddlers and teens were both dealing with the same developmental task—establishing an independent identity. The Terrible Teens are characterized by rejection of the parent's ideas and ideals, as well as seeking alternative role models, some of which may be as negative as those he chose earlier in childhood. The teenager also may have difficulty balancing the task of becoming independent against his need for safety and security. This can cause him to act out in negative ways or take risks as he tests the boundaries between the two. The key is to maintain firm limits—allowing your child to test the limits as he establishes his independence, but following through consistently on consequences for infractions (see chapter 10 for further details).

When Being Naughty Is More Than "Just a Phase"

"Mommy, help me!" the eight-year-old screamed from high up in the tree.

"Jeremy, where are you?" his mother, Paula, asked.

"Up here," Jeremy called. "I'm stuck."

"Jeremy, how on earth did you get up there?"

"I climbed up," Jeremy said. "My kite was stuck, so I had to come up to get it."

"Did you ever consider coming in the house and asking me to help you get your kite down?" his mother asked.

"No. Not really," Jeremy said. "I just climbed up and once I was here I realized that I can't reach my kite from here but I can't get back down either. Will you help me get down?"

Paula surveyed the situation and concluded that there was no way that she could climb up high enough in the tree to help her son down. "Stay put, honey. I'm going to have to go next door and see if Mr. Wilson can help."

"Not Mr. Wilson, he'll yell at me."

"He won't be the only one," his mother said, and headed to the neighbor's house.

When Mr. Wilson opened the door and saw Paula's flustered look, he said, "What is it this time, Paula? Jeremy get his head stuck in a drainpipe again or did he break another window?"

"Stuck in a tree, I'm afraid, Mr. Wilson," Paula replied with more humor than she felt. "I don't know what I'm going to do with that boy. I'm afraid he's going to kill himself one of these days—he never thinks before he does something, he just does it. He's like that Nike commercial, 'Just do it'—only when Jeremy does it, he always ends up getting in trouble."

Jeremy's inappropriate behavior is a problem because it is the result of his impulsivity. He always leaps before he looks and runs the risk of hurting himself or someone else.

"My child can't behave—even when he tries his best, he'll leap into action without thinking and get himself into trouble." The impulsive child is a constant source of concern to his parents. He understands the family's rules and accepts the consequences for breaking them, but he never learns from his past misdeeds—he continues to rush into trouble without taking the time to think things through. Learning to "look before you leap" is a developmental task of early to midchildhood. Boys tend to mature later than girls, so it is not unusual for a seven- to eight-year-old boy to still be impulsive, while girls are usually able to consider the consequences of their actions by the age of five to six years.

The child who acts impulsively can't be left home alone because he needs someone there who can protect him from himself. He needs constant supervision and his parents have to be ever vigilant to issues of safety and security. The impulsive child gets an idea and acts on it, so he scrambles up a tree to get his kite down or he lights matches inside a tent of blankets because he wants to get the "full effect" of his pretend camping adventure, or he has his little brother put him in the dryer "to see what it feels like to spin around in there."

Although most children outgrow their impulsivity by age eight to nine, some never outgrow it, and others are very delayed in acquiring the ability to "think first." These children often have distractibility and concentration difficulties, in addition to the impulsivity, and may have hyperactivity as well. If a child has only impulsivity and distractibility, he may have attention deficit disorder (chapter 14); if he also has hyperactivity, then he may have attention deficit hyperactivity disorder (chapter 13). Chapter 13 contains a full description of problematic impulsivity and strategies for dealing with it.

"My child is so stubborn—he's always doing naughty things because he has to do everything his own way." The stubborn child can sometimes be the most difficult child to raise. His unacceptable behavior isn't an "accident" like the impulsive child's. He makes a conscious decision that his way is the right way, and refuses to do it differently—even if it means getting into trouble. He will persist with the behavior despite being told that he'll be punished if he doesn't stop, or after being shown that it's dangerous or harmful. Fortunately, the child who misbehaves out of stubbornness can be taught to behave, because he's conscious of his actions—unlike the impulsive child who acts before he thinks and therefore has no opportunity to amend his behavior. Firm limits, clear consequences, and consistent applications are key to improving the stubborn child's behavior. To avoid a battle of wills, parents should proceed slowly and provide the child with as much control and decision-making as possible.

"My child must have been possessed by the devil. He's become absolutely impossible!" Any time a child has an abrupt deterioration in his behavior, it is a cause for concern. Children seek negative attention when they are frightened for their safety, worried about their security, or concerned about the future. For example, a child who refuses to do his homework or acts naughty at the dinner table may be responding to a failing grade in math class, a parent's alcoholism, or the family's financial concerns. He may have been a victim of child abuse and is acting out the violence that has been done to him (see chapters 7 and 18). The child also may feel emotionally distanced from his parents—to him, negative discipline is preferable to being ignored.

Two medical conditions are known to cause sudden "possession" of a child by bad behavior. In the first case, the sudden misbehavior follows a strep throat infection or scarlet fever, and is associated with obsessive-compulsive symptoms and abnormal movements. This poststreptococcal behavior change is known as PANDAS and is described in chapter 17. The second condition is a rare neurologic disorder in which the child has brief, intermittent episodes of violent, out-of-control behavior known as rage attacks. The rage attacks are similar to epileptic seizures in that they occur without provocation or trigger. The rage attacks don't occur because the child is angry, but rather because of dysfunction in his brain activity which occurs randomly and without warning.

"My child was impossible as a toddler and he hasn't improved at all since then." Conduct disorder, or persistent aggressive and violent behavior, is a serious long-term problem. A child who has conduct disorder does not behave according to the family's rules or society's regulations and customs, and he frequently intrudes on the rights of others. The symptoms common to children with conduct disorder include:
    1. Aggressive behavior. The child bullies, threatens, and intimidates others; initiates physical fights; uses sticks or other objects as

weapons to do harm; is physically cruel to animals or people; and, when older, he engages in violent crimes, such as mugging, armed robbery, or sexual assault.

2. Destruction of property. Deliberate acts of vandalism and destruction of property are common.

3. Dishonesty/theft. Lying frequently and breaking promises, breaking school rules, and breaking into someone else's car or home.

4. Lack of empathy and lack of remorse. The child expresses little empathy or concern for the feelings, wishes, and well-being of others; he does not feel guilt about his actions and does not express remorse for the victims of his harmful behavior. When he's asked if he's sorry about what he did, he answers, "Well, I'm sorry that I got caught."

5. Low self-esteem and difficult temperament. The child has very low self-esteem, which is covered by projecting an image of toughness and bravado; he is easily frustrated, and is frequently irritable and short-tempered.

6. Engages in high-risk behaviors. The child with conduct disorder has more accidents and injuries than other children and frequently engages in risky behavior at a young age, such as smoking, drinking, or using drugs, running away, "joyriding," and sexual experimentation. He is also at an increased risk of suicide because of the risk-taking behaviors and frequent bouts of depression.

7. Lack of conscience. The child's moral development is arrested at an immature stage, which prevents him from developing a sense of right or wrong. The usual phases of moral development are as follows: a preschool child's sense of right or wrong is based upon the limits and consequences imposed by an authority outside himself (his parent); the school-age child bases his sense of right or wrong on the "rules" he has learned from his experiences; the preadolescent is able to interpret these rules in the framework of concern about the feelings of others and his wish to please others; and the adolescent has a clear understanding of good and evil and works toward making the right choice, even when he must choose between "shades of gray" rather than black and white.

The child with conduct disorder is stuck at the eighteen-month to two-year level. He constantly has to be reminded of rules and regulations, because he is always testing the authority behind them. His parents often "give up" in their efforts to shape his behavior and abandon their efforts to set reasonable limits and to apply them consistently. This actually increases the child's inappropriate behavior, as he seeks other "authority" figures, such as the school's principal or the local police department, to establish limits within which he can feel safe. Unfortunately, his only access to those authority figures is through bad behavior—acting inappropriately in school, or breaking the law through vandalism, drug use, or violent crimes. Further, the limits are so far beyond normal estimations of safety that the child is constantly worried about his well-being, which leads to more attempts to find a safe zone within some clearly set boundaries.

The child with conduct disorder needs a comprehensive treatment approach, since there is no one behavioral technique or medication that has been found to be effective for conduct disorder. If you're concerned that your child may have conduct disorder, discuss the possibility with his doctor, or contact the mental health service facility in your community.

Helping Your Child Outgrow His Naughty Behavior

What You Can Do to Help

Use the three Ls of parenting: love, limits, and large muscle exercise. There may be times when you don't like your child's behavior very much, but there should never be a time when you don't love your child, and there should never be a time when he thinks that you don't love him. Unconditional *love* is important for every child, but it is especially important for the child who tends to be naughty, since he is concerned that his behavior will make you stop loving him. Show him and tell him that you love him "no matter what" and prove to him that your love is a constant in his life.

Limits, or family rules, are tremendously important at every age and stage of childhood, including adolescence. Children need the safety and security that limits provide, while their parents need rules to maintain peace and sanity in their home. "Safety rules" are rules that are absolute, final, and must never be violated. These include such things as: always sitting in a car safety seat or wearing a seat belt, wearing a helmet whenever riding a bike, waiting to cross the street until an adult takes your hand, not driving after drinking alcohol/riding with someone who has been drinking, etc. Other rules and regulations are more flexible and might be amended at the parent's discretion. Your child's age, maturity, and degree of impulsivity will influence the types of limits that can be effectively enforced. For example, if your child is an impulsive, overly active four-year-old, the rule might be that he has to sit quietly through the prayer before the family meal, whereas if he is eight years old, he should be able to stay seated throughout dinner.

Large muscle exercise is not as important to a child's upbringing as are unconditional love and clear, consistent limits, but it can help improve his behavior. First, it allows him to "blow off steam" so that he isn't as likely to be overly rambunctious in the house later in the evening; second, it provides him with a physical outlet for his aggression; and, third, it raises levels of endorphins (or "feel good" hormones), which improve his mood and make him feel better about himself.

Increase positive attention—catch him being good. Your child craves attention, and if he doesn't get it by being good, he'll seek it by being naughty, so praising him for his good behavior can actually decrease bad behaviors. Further, it is important for you to provide positive reinforcement (praise and positive attention) for his desirable behaviors, so that he is motivated to repeat them; after he repeats them frequently enough, they become almost automatic, and he'll remember to wash his hands after using the toilet, or to use a napkin rather than his sleeve. It isn't necessary to praise your child for every good thing that he does, but if he's having trouble with one area of his behavior (for example, he makes rude comments or interrupts others), then focus on praising him when he's doing a good job (for example, when he's being polite and waiting his turn).

Discipline—don't punish—your child. Discipline is defined as "training to act in accordance with rules" or "instruction and exercise designed to train to proper conduct and action." Thus, for all children, discipline is a crucial part of their upbringing. Discipline is *not* punishment—punishment is a penalty or negative reinforcement for an undesirable behavior. Psychologists have proven that negative reinforcement is not effective in helping establish new, positive behaviors and is only slightly effective in extinguishing negative behaviors (the extinguished behavior reappears as soon as a positive reinforcement is presented for it). Thus, punishment may reduce an undesirable behavior temporarily, but it will not help your child learn how to behave.

When disciplining your child, always keep the focus of the discussion on his unacceptable behavior, to avoid inferring that it is the child himself who is undesirable. Also, avoid applying negative consequences for your child's misbehavior without making an effort to understand what caused it. Talking with your child about his misbehavior may elicit information about abuse, bullying at school, feelings of insecurity, school failure, or other problems. The need to establish the cause of the disobedience is particularly important for adolescents, although the questions get harder for parents to ask because they concern sex, drugs, and alcohol (see chapter 24). Sometimes, the hardest thing about asking the questions is that we don't want to hear the answers, but since the child needs to tell us, he'll either do it verbally or nonverbally by acting in unacceptable (naughty) ways. If your child can't verbalize a reason for his misbehavior, he should at least be able to identify what he was feeling before he misbehaved.

Don't expect him to do things that he's not yet ready to do. Study the developmental ages and stages of childhood and adolescence so that you know what skills lie within your child's capabilities. Books are an excellent resource, and we've included several at the end of the chapter, but observations can also be quite instructive. Watch your child and children of his age in various settings. What do the children act like at his birthday party? in the park? or at a restaurant? Unless he seems to be more rude and disobedient than the majority of children you observe, there's not a cause for concern.

Communicate your expectations clearly. Once you've established that your expectations are developmentally appropriate, make sure that they are clearly communicated. Too often, parents provide a detailed explanation of why they want the child to behave, but neglect to provide clear instructions for how to behave or why it's important to the child that he behave. Does your child understand what "good" behavior is? Does he know what rules he's supposed to be following and also the consequences of breaking one of the rules? If so, then he'll be able to choose to behave in a way that's satisfactory.

If your child is less than five or six years old, there's little point in providing him with any explanation—just give him a brief instruction and indicate the consequence for misbehavior. For example, "You must wear your helmet every time you ride your bike, or else you won't be able to ride your bike for the next three days." As your child gets older, he can handle more responsibility—this includes remembering family rules and instructions with minimal prompting. For example, if your ten-year-old is going to go roller-blading with his friends, he might be asked to tell you the rules governing his play, and should be able to respond, "I have to wear my helmet and pads at all times or I lose my blades for a month; I have to stay in our driveway or Billy's driveway or I won't be able to play with him the rest of the week; and I need to be home at five P.M. to do the rest of my homework or else I can't watch TV tomorrow night." He knows the rules and consequences and, equally important, he's acknowledged that he knows them, so if he decides to break one, he can't argue, "I didn't know that you wanted me to do that." The list of limitations is also short—only two safety rules and a limit on the time he can spend with his friend. This keeps the focus on what's important and avoids overwhelming the child.

Know who your child's friends are. We usually think of peer groups as an influence during adolescence, but peer pressure actually begins at a much earlier age. As soon as children begin to play together (rather than alongside each other, as they do at two to three years of age), they begin to mimic each other's behavior. Since you'd prefer to have a well-behaved, respectful child, it is important to ensure that your child's friends are well-behaved, respectful children. Invite your child's friends to your home and watch how they play together, listen to their opinions about school, other children, and various activities, and watch how your child and his friend handle problems. Do they bring out the best in each other, or does your child tend to pick up only undesirable behaviors and attitudes from his playmate?

In adolescence, it is important to respect your child's privacy. You shouldn't "spy" on your teen, but it is equally important for you to know who your child is hanging out with and what they're doing/thinking/feeling. You should know who your teen's friends are and you should be able to like and respect them. If not, your teenager may begin to demonstrate behaviors that you find offensive, since he'll be emulating his friends and his friends' parents to a greater extent than he'll be turning to you for advice over the next few years (also see chapter 10). If one of your child's friends causes you concern, talk with your child about the friendship and see if there's some reason why the relationship is of value. If you'd still prefer for him not to associate with the teen, don't forbid him from seeing his friend, but let him know the reasons why it might not be desirable for him to continue the friendship.

What Your Child's Teacher Can Do to Help

Help determine the cause of behavior problems. If your child's behavior deteriorates suddenly and without explanation, contact his teacher to determine if something is going on at school. Often, she'll reveal that the class has just started a new math or social studies unit and that your child is having some difficulties or that your child was recently "outed" by the class clique. Alternatively, your child's teacher may indicate that there's nothing unusual going on in class, but that she too has noticed that he is more withdrawn and moody and is having increasing difficulties with his schoolwork—all of which are signs of a possible episode of depression (chapter 21).

Prevent behavior problems by setting classroom limits. Just as parents must establish firm limits and clear consequences and apply them consistently, so teachers must establish clear classroom limits and use them routinely. As behavior modification programs have gained popularity, classroom teachers are being provided with more guidance on establishing a positive behavior-shaping classroom environment. Typically, the students help write their own classroom rules and establish the consequences for infractions; thus, they are all fully aware of both the rules and consequences, and have agreed to be governed by them. Rewards, such as extra recess time, are offered for examples of good behavior so that the peer pressure in the classroom is directed at positive behaviors, rather than negative ones.

Help your child learn to express anger and frustration appropriately. Your child's teacher can be a great ally in helping you teach your child how to respond appropriately to anger and frustration. His classmates can be counted on to serve as critics of unacceptable behavior (grade school children are very intolerant of rude or selfish behavior and will ignore your child when he's behaving badly), but his teacher can also shape his behavior through positive reinforcement for desirable behaviors.

Role-playing and classroom exercises directed at recognizing and dealing with negative emotions can help your child learn to deal with his anger and to express his frustrations appropriately. Your child's teacher can use the exercises to help him validate his negative feelings and determine why he's angry/frustrated/sad/jealous/etc. She can also teach him to choose the most appropriate way of responding to frustrations. The more often your child practices appropriate reactions to situations like being pushed or having someone cut in front of him in line, the more likely he is to respond appropriately in real-life situations.

Participate in behavior therapy programs, if requested. If you and your child are working on a particular behavior at home and find that it is not being resolved because he's continuing to do it in school, you may want to enlist the help of his teacher. In general, her role should be limited to "catching him when he's being good," although there are times when she will need to do active ignoring or negative reinforcement (loss of a privilege) to extinguish the unwanted behavior (see chapters 5 and 12 for additional information).

What Your Child's Doctor Can Do to Help

Determine whether or not the misbehavior is in the normal range. Your child's doctor is an important resource for information about expected patterns of development, including the phases when naughty behavior is more likely to occur, such as the Terrible Twos, Ferocious Fours, and Sassy Sixes. Your child's doctor should evaluate his behavior—by your history and by observing your child in the office—and help determine whether or not his behavior is in the expected range.

Provide you with a safety outlet to use when your child's naughty behavior threatens to push you over the edge. Child abuse is never planned. It happens when parents are stressed by so many factors and stretched in so many directions that they can't cope with further aggravation. Their child's naughtiness is the final straw that pushes them over the edge and causes them to lash out at the child, either verbally or physically.

If you feel that you are stretched beyond your limits, it is essential that you get help before you strike out at your child. There is no shame in admitting that you need help, but you will feel a great deal of shame if you fail to get help when you need it. Your child's doctor is a good resource, since she knows both you and your child. Other resources include school counselors, teachers, a minister or clergy member, or other professionals. There is also a national child abuse prevention hotline that you can call for help at any time: 800-4ACHILD (800-422-4453).

Help you set limits—particularly for safety rules. You and your child's doctor have the same goal—for you to raise a safe, healthy, well-adjusted (and well-behaved) child to adulthood. Your child's pediatrician will be happy to help reinforce safety rules, such as wearing seat belts and using protective gear when bicycling or roller-blading. The American Academy of Pediatrics has guidelines for providing these safety interventions throughout childhood and adolescence, and your child's doctor can either provide you with pamphlets and other written materials or discuss these safety rules with your child at his routine checkup.

Recognize impulsive behavior and provide evaluation and treatment or referral. Impulsivity is a hallmark symptom of attention deficit hyperactivity disorder (chapter 13), and if your child is excessively impulsive, and also seems to have difficulties with poor concentration and increased distractibility, he may have ADHD. Your child's doctor should be attuned to these symptoms, and if she observes them, perform a comprehensive evaluation to determine if they're problematic. If they are, she may treat your child herself, or refer him to a child psychiatrist for treatment.

Further Reading
See chapter 10 and chapter 11.

Beekman, Susan, and Jeanne Holmes. *Battles, Hassles, Tantrums and Tears: Strategies for Coping with Conflict and Making Peace at Home.* New York: Hearst Books, 1993.

Bodenhamer, Gregory. *Back in Control: How to Get Your Children to Behave.* Englewood Cliffs, NJ: Prentice-Hall, 1983.

Charney, Ruth. *Teaching Children to Care: Management in the Responsive Classroom.* Greenfield, MA: Northeast Foundation for Children, 1991.

Corwin, Donna G. *The Time-Out Prescription: A Parent's Guide to Positive and Loving Discipline.* Chicago: Contemporary Books, 1996.

Eastman, Meg, Ph.D., with Sydney Craft Rozen. *Taming the Dragon in Your Child: Solutions for Breaking the Cycle of Family Anger.* New York: John Wiley & Sons, 1994.

Greenspan, Stanley I., M.D., with Jacqueline Salmon. *The Challenging Child: Understanding, Raising and Enjoying the Five "Difficult" Types of Children.* Reading, MA: Addison-Wesley, 1995.

Peters, Dr. Ruth. *Don't Be Afraid to Discipline.* New York: Golden Books, 1997.

Sears, William, M.D., and Martha Sears, R.N. *The Discipline Book: Everything You Need to Know to Have a Better-Behaved Child—From Birth to Age Ten.* Boston: Little, Brown & Co., 1995.

Silberman, Mel, Ph.D. *When Your Child Is Difficult: Solve Your Toughest Child-Raising Problems with a Four-Step Plan That Works.* Champaign, IL: Research Press, 1995.

Wolf, Anthony E., Ph.D. *It's Not Fair, Jeremy Spencer's Parents Let Him Stay Up All Night! A Guide to the Tougher Parts of Parenting.* New York: Farrar, Straus & Giroux, 1995.

"My Daughter Refuses to Go to School"

Fear of leaving home and fear of attending school

"I don't want to go to school! I don't want to be one of Mrs. Brown's little brown bears!" Abigail wailed, as she dropped to the floor and struggled to pull her hand from her mother's grasp.

"Come on, honey. It'll be fun. You'll have a wonderful day," her mother Sarah said soothingly. "Remember last week when we came to see Mrs. Brown and your new classroom? You loved it! Especially your new desk and all the cute teddy bears your teacher has collected. And remember Mrs. Brown said that you would get to paint today and then she would read Brown Bear, Brown Bear, What Do You See? You love that story. You're going to love kindergarten, too, Abigail. Come on, honey, let's go."

But Abigail didn't move. She just sat on the hallway floor and sobbed. The other children looked a little smug as they hurried past her into the classroom. The mothers were more understanding and smiled knowingly at Sarah as they left their children with Mrs. Brown. Sarah didn't smile back—she was too busy panicking. Why was Abigail throwing a fit? She had done everything that the parenting books had recommended to prevent this situation. She had brought Abigail for a preopening day visit to see the classroom and meet Mrs. Brown, she had helped Abby pick out a pretty new outfit for the first day of school, and they had practiced getting ready for school each day for the past week to ensure that the morning would go smoothly. And it had, until now.

It had been the same way last year. Abigail had been excited about going to school until they actually got to her classroom and then she had refused to go inside. After they repeated this process several mornings in a row, the preschool teachers recommended that Sarah keep Abigail home and "try again next year." Now that Abigail was a year older, Sarah had expected it to be different. Abby was clearly ready for school—she could already write her name, she colored beautifully, and she could even read a little bit. In fact, Abby was so advanced for her age that Sarah had been upset when the school's principal assigned her to the prekindergarten class, rather than to regular kindergarten. When Sarah challenged the placement, the principal explained that all children who were entering school for the first time were placed in the pre-K class, no matter how much of the material they already knew, in order to ensure that "they were ready for school." Today's performance certainly confirmed the principal's concerns—Abby wasn't ready for kindergarten.

Abigail is intellectually ready for school this year, but she isn't yet emotionally ready. Her hallway tantrum is a sign of "school refusal." School refusal is a broad term that covers everything from Abigail's emotional immaturity to a child's oppositional refusal to attend classes. Most school refusal is a sign of a problem phase, although it can occasionally be a symptom of a psychiatric disorder, such as separation anxiety disorder, obsessive worries about using a public rest room, or performance anxieties (worries about taking a test, having to speak in public, or having other children make fun of her). The child might be doing badly in school and fear further school failures, or she may have been physically harmed or threatened by a school bully and refuse to attend school in order to avoid further abuse. In deciding how to handle a child's school refusal, it is important to consider not only the severity of her response, but also the reason for her refusal.

When a Child's School Refusal Is "Just a Phase"
"I'm too young to go to that big, scary school." Abigail's school refusal may have come from fears of entering a strange place, worries about leaving her mother, or both. Fears of the unknown and separation anxieties are both normal, expected stages of a child's development, but both can also cause problems when they are excessive and begin to interfere with the child's functioning. Although the term "separation anxiety" can be used to refer to both expected and excessive separation fears, for the

purposes of clarity, we will refer to normal developmental anxieties about separation as separation difficulties and excessive separation fears as separation anxiety (which is described in detail in chapter 18).

Separation difficulties are a normal, healthy part of a child's development and are a consequence of her growing attachment to her parents. Attachment begins in mid-infancy when a child begins to have a sense of belonging to her parents. This attachment causes her to be saddened by their leave-taking and anxious about the possibility of being deserted —her crying is due to both sadness and anxiety. As the child begins to trust in her parents' return, the separation protests subside. Each of us can remember the first time we left our infant with a baby-sitter and she cried inconsolably as we went out the door. Usually, the crying stopped as soon as the door was firmly shut or shortly thereafter, but some babies aren't able to overcome their separation concerns and continue crying until their parents return, even if it's hours later. The child who has prolonged separation difficulty during infancy is likely to have problems again when she enters preschool or kindergarten. Separation is also difficult if she is young, immature, or bashful. If a child has separation difficulties, she may cry or throw a temper tantrum when it is time to leave home, cling to her mother's side as she tries to say good-bye, or refuse to enter the classroom, as in Abigail's case. Even though these reactions may seem extreme, they are quite normal, as any preschool or kindergarten teacher can tell you.

"My baby's too young to go to that big, scary school." Sometimes a child's reluctance is actually a reflection of her mother's concerns about letting her child start school. The mother may be afraid that her child is too young to be comfortable in school, she may be afraid that her child won't succeed, or she may be fearful that the mother-daughter relationship will change as her child becomes more independent. In this case, the mother unconsciously signals her daughter that she doesn't want her to leave and the child responds by crying or refusing to let go of her mother's hand. Her protests begin only when her mother says, "Are you sure you're going to be okay? It's an awfully big classroom. Maybe I should stay for a little while and help you get used to it. Do you want me to stay?" She has implied much with her questions and now, in order for the child to leave her mother's side, she not only has to overcome her own anxieties about leave-taking, but also her mother's fears about leaving her and, further, she must reject her mother's love and support. Tough situation! Fortunately, most preschool and kindergarten teachers have had enough experience with first-day anxieties to step in and make separations easier for both mother and child.

"My child is so stubborn—she refuses to go to school." If a stubborn temperament is the cause of your child's school refusal, then refusing to go to school is just one of many things that she won't do. As soon as she awakens in the morning, her resistance starts. She refuses to get up and has to be dragged out from between the covers, then she refuses to make her bed, and when required to do so, she does it carelessly and with disdain. Every step in the morning routine is a struggle, from brushing her teeth through getting dressed and eating breakfast to putting on her jacket as she leaves. She should have plenty of time to catch her school bus, but dawdles so long that she misses it once again. When you reluctantly drive her to school, the morning's struggles culminate with her refusal to leave the car and enter the school building.

In this case, the child's refusal to attend school is not due to anxiety, but is rather just one more example of difficult or oppositional behavior (also see chapter 3). It is difficult for the oppositional child to obey orders of any kind and her life is a constant struggle to take control of situations that other children intuitively understand are adult-determined. Often, her resistance is accompanied by a sassy mouth and a defiant attitude, both of which further increase her parents' frustrations. Her parents need to be constantly on their guard against the inappropriate use of punishment, because she really knows how to get under their skin and annoy them.

Obviously, the "cure" for school refusal in this situation is very different from the times that school refusal is a consequence of anxiety. The key to getting the stubborn child to go to school is to allow her to control as much of the leave-taking as possible by allowing her to choose between two alternatives that are both equally acceptable to you. Behavior therapy techniques that are useful for oppositional behavior will also be helpful, as discussed in chapter 12 and the help sections of chapters 2, 3, 5, and 13.

"My child doesn't like school right now—I've got to force her to go." "This section applies to everyone" was the comment of our resident teenager and she's right. Every child has periods when she needs to be encouraged to go to school—she's fighting with her best friend, she's worried about presenting her oral book report, or the math unit is *really* hard and she knows that she'll do badly on the test. Some children have an entire year that is difficult—they don't like their teacher, they're the new kid in school, or they're a junior high school student. Middle school (sixth to eighth grades) is often a difficult time for children because they have so many demands put upon them, both academically and socially. It's hard to stay positive about school when you're worried about flunking your history test and also worried about peers, pimples, and popularity. The only answer is to provide your child with as much support and encouragement as she needs to attend school.

When School Refusal Is More Than "Just a Phase"

"Erin," Marjorie said as she walked into her ten-year-old daughter's room. "I was looking at your report card and saw that your grades are down quite a bit from last year. And what's worse, you've missed fifteen days of school so far this fall—that's three weeks! How could you have missed so many days in the first nine-week quarter?"

"Well, Mom. Remember that I had that stomach bug for a week at the beginning of school, and then I had that really severe headache for a couple of days—you thought it was a migraine or something. And then you took me to the doctor because I had such bad allergies."

"Yes, Erin, I do remember. But I also remember that when you had the allergies, Dr. Lewis said that you could go to school," her mother replied, and then asked, "Did you stay home?"

"Yeah, you let me. Remember? The medicine made me so sleepy that I couldn't wake up the next morning."

"Oh, yes," her mother recalled. "But that was only one day. There have been so many others. Are you sure you were really sick each time or is there something else going on?"

"Like what, Mom?" Erin said.

"Well, is there something about school that is bothering you?" Marjorie asked.

"Everything about school bothers me," Erin said. "I hate it! The kids tease me and call me 'Airhead' instead of Erin. Mindy has a new best friend so I don't have anybody to eat lunch with, and Ms. Brooks calls on me when she knows that I don't know the answer just so she can prove how dumb I am. School is horrible and I hate it!"

Erin paused for a moment, and then said, "But, Mom, I didn't stay home because I hate school, I stayed home because I was sick."

"I guess so," Marjorie said, but she wondered if there wasn't some connection between Erin's absences and her problems at school. Marjorie returned to her study and sat down at her desk to review the times that Erin had missed school during the past few weeks. She found that Erin was right. She had been sick each time with vomiting, diarrhea, or low-grade fevers. She certainly couldn't be faking those symptoms. On the other hand, Erin's illnesses were always gone by midday and they spent the afternoons running errands or watching soap operas together. It was nice to have some company, but maybe that was the problem—maybe she was letting Erin have too much fun when she missed school. Well, if that was the problem, there was an easy solution—she'd keep Erin in bed all day the next time she missed school. After all, if her daughter was too sick to be in school, then she was too sick to go to the mall.

Two days later, Erin again complained of "not feeling good." "Mom, I just threw up again. Can you check my temperature?"

"Yes," Marjorie replied. "Get back into bed while I get the thermometer." Erin's temperature was slightly elevated at 99.6 degrees, so her mother called the school and told them that she wouldn't be in class again that day. Marjorie also called Erin's pediatrician, Dr. Lewis, and arranged an appointment for her daughter.

When Erin was seen by the doctor later that afternoon, Dr. Lewis asked her dozens of questions about her recent illnesses, as well as questions about her friends, school, and family. He also performed a physical examination, took samples of her blood and urine, and handed her a specimen cup in which she was to "save a stool sample, because kids' stomachaches sometimes come from worm infections."

"Stool sample? Worms?!?" Erin said as she drew back from the cup. "I'm not doing that, Dr. Lewis. It's totally gross."

"Yes, it is pretty disgusting," the doctor replied. "But we still need to have a sample to be sure you're okay. I expect that it will be, and that the other tests will also be fine. Your physical examination was completely normal. It doesn't look like there's anything wrong with your body, so it must be something else that's making you sick. Do you think it could be something about going to school that's making you sick?"

"Yes, the teacher, the kids in my class, and the ratty old building," Erin replied jokingly.

"Erin, I'm serious," Dr. Lewis responded. "Disliking school or being worried about something at school can make you sick. It's called school avoidance. You're not faking your symptoms—they're very real. But your body isn't making you sick, your worries are."

School avoidance is the end result of untreated school refusal, and it can occur whenever a child's school refusal becomes so severe that she stops going to class. Often, the child and her parents are unaware that she's missing excessive amounts of school and it goes unnoticed until it's an entrenched chronic problem, as in Erin's case. School avoidance is a cause for concern whenever it happens, but particularly when it begins a year or more after the child enters school. By the time a child reaches first or second grade, she should have mastered the school routine, learned how to deal with her separation anxieties, and established enough friendships to make going to school fun, as well as work.

"My child won't go to school because it makes her too anxious." Anxiety disorders, particularly separation anxiety disorder, are a common cause of school refusal. (Chapter 18 describes separation anxiety disorder in detail.) A child with separation anxiety disorder is not only reluctant to leave her parents in order to attend school, but she is also anxious about being left alone at other times. She becomes distressed when her mother goes to work or her father goes to the store, she can't be left with a baby-sitter, and she may be unable to play alone in the backyard or even to stay alone in her bedroom at night because of her fears.

Children with generalized anxiety disorder frequently develop school-related physical illnesses (see chapter 19). Even when they are happy about attending school, these children tend to have more physical symptoms than other children. The ailments include headaches, stomachaches, nausea, abdominal cramps, and diarrhea. The child's physical symptoms are clearly related to anxiety, as they disappear when the anxiety disorder is treated with medications or behavior therapy. If a child has an anxiety disorder that is mainly related to school activities (such as performance anxiety that is triggered by taking tests or giving an oral report), she is at risk for school avoidance and special efforts must be made to ensure that she attends school each day.

"My child is embarrassed to go to school because she's doing so badly." School failure is a common cause of school avoidance. The children are embarrassed by their poor performance and try to skip school in order to avoid being teased or humiliated. Children occasionally develop school avoidance after being downgraded to the "dumb" reading group or failing an important test. More often, however, the child has a pattern of repeated failures, such as consistently poor grades or problems keeping up with the rest of the class. For the child with learning disabilities, she may become so demoralized by her inability to learn that she gives up (see chapter 14 for more information). At first, the child may withdraw only in her mind—she'll sit and daydream rather than participate in class activities. This puts her behind in her schoolwork and causes more embarrassment, so she withdraws further and refuses to attend school.

For the child with performance anxieties (discussed in chapter 20), school avoidance may be triggered by something as minor as a B− on a test, instead of her usual A+. She is so anxious to be "perfect" that she can't abide even the slightest failure and the B− makes her too uncomfortable to return to school, particularly if one of her classmates teases her about it. School avoidance is also a problem for children with attention deficit hyperactivity disorder (ADHD—chapter 13) and attention deficit disorder (ADD—chapter 14). These children develop fear of failure because of their constant struggles to keep up with the class. Children with ADHD are also frequently scapegoated as a consequence of their hyperactivity and impulsivity and fear embarrassment or humiliation from those symptoms. Sometimes, the attentional problems have gone unnoticed, because the child is very bright and can compensate for most of the ADHD symptoms, but she develops school avoidance secondary to her own feelings of failure or criticisms that she's "not working up to her potential." Since ADHD and ADD are so common, they should always be considered when a child develops school avoidance.

"My child hates school because she has no friends there." School is the place where children have daily opportunities to socialize with other children. Normally, this is good news—the children talk to their friends in the classroom, eat lunch with a best friend at noon, and play with a group of children at recess. They get along well with most of the children in their class and feel that they belong. When this doesn't go as expected and the child doesn't have any friends, then her isolation is even more painful by comparison—she stands alone after class buddies are picked, she sits next to a group of girls in the cafeteria but they shun her, and she waits in vain to be picked for a four-square game at recess. The isolation is so humiliating that she begins to dread going to school and the solitude is so painful that she stops going to school in order to avoid confronting her loneliness.

This kind of social isolation is a risk whenever a child is the "new kid" in school, especially if she is shy or otherwise reluctant about initiating friendships. Being the new kid in school can be particularly tough when the child moves into a small school or a well-established classroom, where the cliques aren't flexible enough to include her. It can also be difficult during particular times of a child's development, such as during second and fifth grades, when children tend to be very clannish, and again in junior high school, when the children are too worried about their own status to take a chance on befriending a new student. To avoid problems associated with starting a new school, it is essential that parents take preventive action. The child should attend summer day camp or participate in recreation programs at the school she will attend so that she can meet some children from the community. It helps to get the class roster so that play dates can be arranged with a few of the children in the class before school starts. The new teacher can also make special efforts to help the child fit in with the rest of the class. The child can be coached on how to initiate friendships and how to handle potential rejections (not every child will become a friend, nor will they want to become friends with every child they meet). This is particularly important for students entering junior high or high school, since the other students won't reach out to welcome a new student, but often will respond positively to her overtures.

Children with behavior disorders (including ADHD) or social disabilities (difficulty understanding social cues) may have difficulty making friends. These children may even be labeled as "weird" or "a loser" and become the class scapegoat. Teachers should be intolerant of such negative peer pressure and take actions to stop it early, but unfortunately they're often unaware that it's happening. In some tragic cases, teachers have actually encouraged the teasing in a misguided attempt to "motivate" a child whom they have labeled as "lazy" or "an attitude problem." Teacher education and frequent parent-teacher communications can avoid such problems (as discussed in chapter 13).

"My child is sick this morning. I can't send her to school." Most children with school avoidance are absent because they have physical symptoms—abdominal pain, headache, vomiting, diarrhea, malaise (feeling lousy without having specific symptoms), and even fever. When a child has frequent physical symptoms, it is always a cause for concern and requires that a physician determine whether or not there is a treatable medical illness underlying the symptoms. There are several clues that may suggest that the symptoms are due to school avoidance rather than a physical illness. These include: symptoms that occur frequently on school days but never on the weekends or during school vacations, improvement during the late-morning hours, and symptoms that are present soon after awakening, but which didn't awaken the child during the night.

Chronic illnesses, particularly those that involve the GI (gastrointestinal) system, may have a clinical picture that is quite similar to school avoidance. Irritable bowel syndrome, Crohn's disease, and ulcerative colitis can all occur in childhood and cause intermittent abdominal pain, fever, and diarrhea. The symptoms may also wax and wane in severity throughout the day, so that the children might appear much sicker in the morning than they do during the rest of the day. If a child is missing school frequently, the first thing that her doctor should do is to make sure that she isn't suffering from a chronic medical illness. This requires that the doctor perform a complete history and physical examination, as well as ordering selected laboratory tests. Of note, migraine headaches can occur in childhood and are often missed as the cause of a child's recurrent headaches unless a neurological workup is also done.

Frequent infections, such as colds, ear infections, and strep throat, are a common cause of frequent absenteeism. Children are sick more often than normal in the first year or two after entering a new school (whether as a kindergartner or by transfer) because they are being exposed to a new set of germs. Each school has its own unique strains of bacteria and viruses and the child will get sick each time she is exposed to one of these new germs until she develops adequate immunity against them. To decrease the frequency of infectious illnesses, it is necessary for your child to develop good hygiene habits, such as washing her hands thoroughly with soap after using the toilet and before eating meals. She should avoid picking her nose, rubbing her eyes, and sharing food, straws, glasses, and other utensils, since germs are usually spread in these ways.

"My child is so tired and wiped out, I can't send her to school this way." Morning fatigue contributes to a surprising number of cases of school avoidance. Lack of sleep is by far the most common cause of excessive fatigue in childhood—the children go to bed too late and get up too early to get enough rest. An eight o'clock bedtime is appropriate for the school-age child because she requires nine to ten hours of sleep each night. Teenagers need at least eight hours of sleep but, with homework and other requirements, usually get only five or six. "Sleeping in" is a frequent cause of missed morning classes for teens, but is not a form of school avoidance. Rather, it is a natural consequence of the mismatch between the teen's biological rhythms and the school's schedule. Chapter 22 provides information about how to help your teenager reconcile her internal clock with the requirements of the school day.

If a child suddenly begins missing a lot of school because of fatigue, she might be suffering from a blood disorder, like anemia or leukemia. If so, she would also appear pale and "wiped out"—tiring more easily when climbing the stairs or exercising. Anemia, or a low red blood cell count, affects nearly one-quarter of teenage girls. Boys can also have anemia, since it can be caused by deficiencies of iron, zinc, or the B vitamins—none of which are found in adequate amounts in hamburger, French fries, soda pop, or pizza. In general, American children and adolescents have such poor diets that a multiple vitamin with iron is a daily necessity, but check with your child's doctor before starting any dietary supplementation.

Depression should also be considered before deciding that a child has school avoidance, particularly when the problem first appears during adolescence. The depressed child is physically exhausted and is also overwhelmed by her apathy and sad mood. She feels lousy in the mornings, especially when she has lain awake half the night, and may rally somewhat by midmorning, particularly if she has been able to get a few hours of uninterrupted sleep. This pattern is identical to that seen in school avoidance, but depression won't respond to the treatments that are used for school avoidance. Depression is discussed in detail in chapter 21.

"My child skips school. I don't know if she's there or not." There are many reasons why children skip school—boredom, school failure, fear of embarrassment, abuse or threat of abuse, peer pressure, and drug and alcohol use. Although almost all children skip school at least once, repeated unexcused absences are inexcusable and must be stopped before they become truancy. In some states, just two or three unexcused absences will trigger an investigation by a truancy officer and chronic truancy is sufficient grounds for sentencing a child to serve time in a juvenile detention facility.

Unfortunately, truancy is more difficult to treat than other forms of school avoidance because it has so many contributing factors, each of which requires its own intervention. Some of these, such as drug use, must be treated successfully before initiating treatment of the truancy or the truancy interventions will fail. Early detection and intervention are once again critical to the success of the treatment, since truancy is an escalating problem. Peer counselors have been helpful in some situations, particularly when the truancy is related to peer relationships or drug use. In most instances, a multidisciplinary treatment team is required, including the child's parents, physician, psychiatrist or psychologist, the school's psychologist, and her teachers.

Helping Your Child Outgrow Her School Refusal

What You Can Do to Help

Make sure that your child is in school every day. No matter what is causing your child's school avoidance, the solution is for her to go to school every day. The only exception to this rule is when she has a contagious disease that she might spread to the other children. Then her doctor should examine her and excuse her absence for a brief, specified period of time.

It is your child's job to attend school and your job to make sure that she gets there. It can be very difficult for you to require your child to do something that is clearly so hard for her, but you must send her to school. You can acknowledge your child's concerns and anxieties, but you cannot allow them to keep her out of school. It may help to remember that the longer she stays at home, the more difficult it will be for her to go back. She will have built up greater anxiety about returning, will be more isolated from her classmates, and will have fallen farther behind in her work. The first time that your child skips school, you must respond—let her know that skipping school is unacceptable, require her to accept the consequences of her actions, and set safeguards in place to prevent future absences. If necessary, you might want to buttress your position by reminding your child that her school attendance is required by law until she reaches the age of sixteen.

Determine the cause of her school avoidance. In order to determine whether your child's school avoidance is an expected part of her development or a symptom of a deeper problem, you will need to obtain information from your child and consult with both her teacher and her pediatrician. You should discuss all aspects of the school day with your child, including not only her classes and classmates, but even seemingly extraneous details, like the weight of her backpack or the bus ride to and from school each day. (There have been several instances in which school avoidance was cured by letting the child ride in a car pool, rather than forcing her to ride the noisy/stinky/fear-inducing school bus. If the car pool works, there will be plenty of time to deal with her school bus fears after she's comfortably back in school.)

When you meet with your child's teacher, you should also discuss all aspects of your child's day, with special emphasis given to your child's reaction to tests and oral presentations, her status within the class, and the quality of her peer relationships. The teacher may have an opinion about your child's reasons for avoiding school—she may have observed signs of school failure, anxiety, boredom, social isolation, or a combination of several factors. Your child's pediatrician should then be able to use all the information you've gathered, in combination with his physical examination, to arrive at the appropriate diagnosis.

If she's scared of the new teacher and classroom, help make them more familiar. When kindergartners refuse to attend school, it's frequently because of anxieties over the newness of the school situation. Your child will overcome these anxieties as soon as she becomes accustomed to the classroom and learns that she can trust the teacher to keep her safe and that she can depend upon the daily routine. Kindergarten teachers will often hold a special open house in which the children can come and play in the classroom, while their parents remain nearby. This allows the child to explore the unfamiliar setting while still under the protection of her parent. To begin to develop a teacher-pupil bond, the teacher might provide the children with a fact sheet about the classroom and the school day, or she might give each child a special name tag to wear on the first day of school to increase that child's sense of belonging.

Transitional objects can help a child adjust to a new school by transferring the safety of the child's home to the classroom. Because it comes to represent home and family, it is important that the transitional object always be there—it shouldn't be irreplaceable or easily lost. Having your child use the last scrap of her baby blanket as a transitional object is a prescription for disaster. If she loses it, it can't be replaced and will be further proof that the universe is unpredictable and dangerous. In contrast, shoes make terrific transitional objects—you and your child can make a special trip to pick them out when she is feeling positive and excited about starting school, and you can bestow magic properties upon the shoes so that they will protect her from harm during the school day, just as they protect her feet from getting hurt or dirty. Best of all, your child can't lose them because she will be wearing them all day. Underwear can serve the same purpose—some brands even come with superheroes to guard and protect the child during the school day.

Predictability is one of the keys to overcoming anxieties about the unknown. It is important for your child to establish a comfortable routine and to be able to count on its sameness. The need for predictability explains why two-days-a-week preschool may cause more difficulties for young children than attending school every day. The children never quite adjust to the preschool routine, so it's always new, different, and somewhat frightening. For most children, these fears are offset by the excitement of doing new activities and being with other children, but for the child with anxiety, they aren't opportunities for fun but merely additional challenges to her safety and security.

Decrease separation anxieties for both you and your child. Just as trust and dependability were the keys to your child's mastery of the unfamiliar classroom, they are also critical to her success in overcoming separation difficulties. She needs to trust that your love continues even when you're away from her and must be able to depend upon the fact that she will be reunited with you after school. Keep the leave-taking brief and positive, tell her you love her, and clearly communicate your expectations that she will be safe and happy in school. For example, you might say, "Have a great day, Abby! I love you very much and I'll see you when you get home after school." On the other hand, if you say, "Do you want me to go into the classroom with you, Abby? I could go in for a minute just to make sure you're going to be okay," it implies that you're worried about the classroom or the teacher, and that she should be worried, too. If you're concerned about how your feelings will affect your child's first day of school, you should plan to meet with your child's teacher ahead of time and seek her help in making the leave-taking easier. The teacher should be happy to coach you on the most effective ways to say good-bye, and also to give your child extra support during those first difficult moments.

Your child's leave-taking will be made easier if you explain little and expect much. Don't gush about how much she'll love her teacher or how wonderful her classroom will be or she'll begin to doubt your sincerity (and the safety of her classroom). Similarly, don't tell her how much you'll miss her or how brave she is—she's not going off to war, she's going to work. She has a job to do and people to help her do it, so your expectation should be that she will succeed. Many times, your confidence is all that is required to help your child gain mastery over her fears.

Eliminate the source of her fear. If your child has had a bad experience (being teased, bullied, or abused) and she is afraid to return to school for fear of being victimized again, you must be able to assure her honestly that she'll be safe when she returns. This means that the teasing must be stopped, the bully curtailed, or the abuser removed from your child's surroundings. You will need to enlist the help of your child's teacher and principal to ensure that your child is safe. Sometimes, school personnel are reluctant to take action because they fear retaliation or litigation from the abusive child or her parents. However, it is their responsibility to ensure your child's safety and security during the school day, so persevere until you've gotten an appropriate response. Start with your child's classroom teacher and enlist her advocacy on behalf of your child. If that isn't sufficient, or she isn't responsive, then turn to a counselor, the school's psychologist, or the principal. They should be willing to help, not only to benefit your child, but also to prevent other children from being victimized in the future. In rare instances, the local school response is not satisfactory and it is necessary to go to the district superintendent or the school board. This circumstance is very rare, but if it's required, you should not hesitate to take any action necessary to ensure that the situation is resolved quickly and your child is able to return to school without fear.

Teach her to overcome her fearfulness. Your child's doctor should confirm that her fearfulness is in the normal range before you undertake any treatments at home. If it is "just a phase," a behavior therapy technique known as imagination training can be very helpful in overcoming fearfulness. In imagination training, the child is taught to imagine a pleasant scene or a happy memory (distraction), to place herself in the scene and relive the moment of happiness (relaxation), and, when she feels comfortable, to return from the daydream and use one of the behavior therapy techniques she has learned to help her take control of the situation (empowerment).

Dr. Jeffrey Brown describes several specific techniques of imagination training in his book *No More Monsters in the Closet: Teaching Your Child to Overcome Everyday Fears and Phobias*. The techniques include:

The Finger Circle—the child makes a circle with her thumb and middle finger to keep all the good strength inside and make her more powerful, thus allowing her to try new things and achieve mastery over the situation;

The Take-along Friend—the child creates an imaginary friend who provides support, encouragement, and protection in any stressful situation; and

The Magic Carpet or Cloud-copter—the child can be whisked away instantaneously if she is in danger, thus allowing her to try new situations without worrying about possible misfortunes.

Each of these techniques provides the child with a means of simultaneously facing her fears and controlling her anxiety. Because they are relatively easy to learn and can be used unobtrusively, they are perfect for the school-age child who needs help in overcoming her separation difficulties, performance anxieties, or fears about new situations.

Make going to school easier and more fun than staying home. Erin's mom discovered that she had been rewarding her daughter for staying home from school—without conscious thought, she had allowed her daughter to trade the work of school for the fun of shopping at the mall. When Marjorie discovered her error, she decided on the right solution: make staying home from school less enjoyable than going to school. If your child is sick enough to stay home from school, she is sick enough to remain in bed all day (at least until dinnertime). She should spend her day working on missed schoolwork, reading ahead in her textbooks, and practicing math facts or spelling words. Watching TV, listening to the radio, and playing music should be limited to after-school hours. After-school plans should be canceled and telephone time should be limited to one brief conversation to get her homework assignment. These restrictions are not punishments for staying home, but rather an attempt to ensure that you aren't providing any positive reinforcements for missing school.

What Your Child's Teacher Can Do to Help
Make the unfamiliar familiar and ease transitions. Teachers can decrease first-day anxieties and prevent some cases of school refusal by making sure that their classroom is warm and inviting and that they are, too. Preschool, kindergarten, and first grade teachers should be particularly skilled at establishing a welcoming environment and helping their students over-

come fears about the strange new classroom. They should also help the child and her parents overcome separation difficulties by helping the child enter the classroom and teaching parents how to say good-bye most effectively. By the end of the first day, an experienced teacher will already know which children need to be drawn out, which need to be left alone until they're ready to speak, and which she will have to help wait for their turn. Having the teacher respond to each child in her class on their own terms is also crucial to the child's successful adjustment to school.

Provide parents with information about normal and worrisome separation difficulties. Teachers are experts in child development and can provide anticipatory guidance about what you should expect from your child during the upcoming school year. Your child's teacher can tell you whether your child's adjustment is within the normal range or is excessive. If you suspect that your child is having a problem, contact her teacher and ask to discuss the situation. Come to the interview with a list of prepared questions: Are other children having similar difficulties? Is this behavior expected at this age or is it unusual? If it is common to children her age, what can be done to make it easier for her to get through this developmental phase? If it's not in the normal range, is it a serious concern and what can be done to help her? Also ask the teacher to suggest sources of further information. She should either provide you with reading materials or refer you to specific books in the library for answers to your more general questions.

Watch for problems that can lead to school avoidance. It is important for your child's teacher to remain vigilant to school adjustment problems throughout the school year. Performance anxiety can worsen as the child's desire to please her teacher and her classmates increases. Similarly, negative peer interactions may not develop until later in the school year. School avoidance is actually more common during the second semester because of increasing academic pressures and the entrenchment of cliques and closed social groups.

Your child's teacher should communicate her concerns to you as soon as she notices a problem. If it's a minor concern, such as an abnormally low grade on a test, then she might send a note home with the student. If it is of greater concern, like declining overall performance, frequent absences, or lack of friends, then she should discuss it with you over the phone or in person.

Eliminate teasing and intimidation from the classroom and playground.
Once again, vigilance is key. Your child's teacher should observe her
classroom with an eye toward spotting social problems. Teasing and social
ostracism are usually not subtle and will be noticeable if the teacher is on
the lookout for them. If your child is being teased or harassed, then her
teacher should not only provide her with support and reassurance, but
also take appropriate disciplinary action against the bully. The teacher
should then be vigilant for retaliation, since the major goal is to assure
your child's safety and security.

It should go without saying that the teacher herself must be respectful
of her students and avoid teasing or humiliating any child. Because teachers are such powerful authority figures to their students, it is impossible
for a teacher to tease a student "just in fun" and not have it hurt the
child's feelings. Her words carry the weight of official truth, and even
when she assures your child that she was "just teasing," she can't undo the
damage done by publicly labeling her as "a slowpoke" or "a chatterbox."

Help your child overcome her difficulties. To help your child overcome
her separation difficulties, her teacher might arrange to have her come to
class a bit earlier than the other students, so that she can help her adjust
to the classroom or provide extra support during the separation.

Your child's teacher might also need to provide your child with extra
support and encouragement throughout the school day. As with parental
interventions, the teacher should explain little and expect much. It is
enough to say, "Julie, I'm sure you know the answer to that question.
Take your time and think about it before you answer," rather than "Julie,
this is a really hard question, but if you try hard enough, I bet you can
come up with the answer." By expecting success, teachers often can help
their students achieve success. To avoid unduly stressing a child who is
overly anxious, the teacher might need to modify her daily schedule or
the teaching plan—for example, if your child has performance anxiety,
her teacher shouldn't require her to take a big test and give an oral
presentation on the same day. She should also volunteer to implement
any behavior therapy plans within the classroom.

What Your Child's Doctor Can Do to Help

Provide anticipatory guidance. As experts on child development, it is
important for pediatricians to teach parents what to expect at each stage
of development. Your child's doctor should provide you with some guide-

lines at each annual visit. In addition, he should provide you with specific guidance based on his knowledge and experience of your child. For example, if the doctor's developmental evaluation shows that your child isn't ready to start school, he should explain why it will be difficult for her to start school at this time. Or if he finds your child to be shy or withdrawn, he should tell you why he considers this behavior to be outside the normal range, and also what problems this might create and how to avoid them.

Consider school avoidance in the diagnostic workup of multiple school absences. Sometimes, as in Erin's case, school avoidance is well established before anyone notices that the number of school absences is excessive. The child may have been seen by her doctor several times for a variety of symptoms without the doctor realizing that she's missing a lot of school. To avoid this, pediatricians should take note of recent illnesses each time they see a child for a sick visit and use a record-keeping system that allows them to track illnesses over time. When the child is brought to the doctor for evaluation of her multiple absences, it is important that the physician specifically consider school avoidance. If not, the excessive absences could be easily dismissed as "There's a lot of that going around" or "She's just having a bad year." Although the latter statement is correct, the doctor has missed the reason why.

Perform a comprehensive evaluation of the child with multiple school absences. Even when school avoidance is considered to be the most likely diagnosis, it is still imperative for the doctor to take a careful history, perform a complete physical examination, and order appropriate laboratory studies. There are a great number of diseases that can appear similar to school avoidance and they shouldn't be missed.

Provide support and encouragement. Your child's doctor should understand that school avoidance is not a conscious decision and that no one is at fault. He may need to reassure your child that her symptoms are real (even if their cause isn't physical), and mediate any parent-child conflicts that have arisen from this difficult situation. In some instances, the doctor can provide support by playing the role of enforcer—the doctor is the one to send the child to school if he finds no physical reason for her to stay home. Because the parents don't make the final decision, they don't have to feel guilty about sending their child off to school when she doesn't feel well.

Recognize school avoidance and provide appropriate treatment or referrals. Most pediatricians will refer children with school avoidance to a child psychiatrist experienced in the treatment of anxiety disorders. A multidisciplinary team and combination therapy (medications, behavior therapy, psychotherapy, and family therapy) may provide for the best outcome. Even though he may have only a minor role in the therapy, your child's physician should remain involved throughout the course of treatment.

Further Reading
See chapter 14 and chapter 18.

Brown, Jeffrey, M.D. *No More Monsters in the Closet: Teaching Your Child to Overcome Everyday Fears and Phobias*. New York: Prince Paperbacks, 1995.

Oppenheim, Joanne. *The Elementary School Handbook: Making the Most of Your Child's Education*. New York: Pantheon Books, 1989.

Schaefer, Charles, and Theresa Foy DiGeronimo. *Helping Children Get the Most Out of School: How to Instill Essential Learning Skills in Children Ages 6–13*. Northvale, NJ: Jason Aronson, 1990.

"My Six-Year-Old Still Sucks His Thumb —Is It Really Just a Bad Habit?"

Thumb-sucking, nail-biting, knuckle-cracking . . .

"Danny, get that thumb out of your mouth," Steve said.

"Okay, Dad," Danny replied, as he pulled his thumb out of his mouth and wiped it on his shirt.

"Danny, I thought that you were going to stop sucking your thumb," his father said.

"Pretty soon," Danny said.

"But when we talked about this last month, you said that you wanted to quit then. We even made a star chart to help you. Now, you're saying you're not ready. What happened?"

"I changed my mind," Danny replied and sounded annoyed as he continued, "I'm not bothering anybody, so why are you so worried about it?"

"Because thumb-sucking is a bad habit. You've had it since you were a baby and I think you're old enough to break it," Steve said.

"I will break it—before my birthday next month. Seven-year-olds don't suck their thumbs, you know!" Danny said and smiled.

Steve smiled, too, as the tension between them had been broken. "Okay, son," he said. "We'll wait until you turn seven, then."

Bad habits are so common that it's hard to think of someone who doesn't have at least one habit, and most people have several. Thumb-sucking, nail-biting, skin-picking, nose-picking, head-banging, rocking, knuckle-cracking, hair-twirling, and hair-pulling are the most common habits in childhood and adolescence. Some of the behaviors are barely noticeable, while others can be quite annoying, but all are defined as bad habits because they are unwanted behaviors that persist despite repeated efforts to stop them. Research surveys have shown that about 10 percent of children aged six to twelve years suck their thumbs and over 50 percent bite their fingernails. Many children "outgrow" these behaviors and break the habit by adolescence, but over 35 percent of college students report that they still bite their fingernails.

The cause of childhood habits is unknown, but they may develop as a result of a young child's need for comfort and security. Thumb-sucking is one such example—sucking one's thumb is a natural substitute for nursing and provides a release for the sucking reflex, as well as rekindling the feelings of satisfaction and security associated with nursing. If we accept that explanation, however, we are still left wondering why it continues so long. The continuation of thumb-sucking past the point of need, and the development of knuckle-cracking and other behaviors later in childhood, suggest that bad habits may be learned behaviors. Psychologists see the habit as an unconscious, stereotyped behavior that has become habitual through repetition. Thus, the child can only stop the habit by unlearning the behavior—he must increase his awareness of the behavior and consciously prevent himself from engaging in the habit.

When a Habit Is "Just a Phase"

"My four-year-old still sucks his thumb." Bedtime is a particularly stressful time for children and bedtime habits or rituals are very common in children between the ages of two and six. The bedtime rituals often incorporate self-soothing habits, such as thumb-sucking, hair-pulling, rocking, and head-banging (the child bangs his head rhythmically against the wall or headboard—the repetitive motion is thought to be similar to being rocked in a cradle). Sometimes, the young child will have several habitual behaviors—he may suck the thumb on one hand and pull his hair with the other hand, while rocking back and forth in his bed. The habits provide comfort and assurance to the child and should definitely be ignored by the parents until he outgrows them (or the habits become a problem, as discussed later in the chapter).

"My child bites his fingernails and I just hate the way his nails look."
Habits are defined as bad habits when they cause problems for the child
—not when they bother his parents. If your child is unaware of his
nail-biting and doesn't mind the appearance of his fingernails, then the
nail-biting is just a habit and it doesn't require attention—even if you
hate it! Parents can talk with their child about the reasons why the habit
is undesirable, but they can't make him accept that it's "bad." Until he
does, he won't be motivated to participate in efforts directed at breaking
the habit and the attempts won't be successful.

**"We moved last month and now my six-year-old has started sucking his
thumb again."** Childhood habits are frequently reactivated when the
child is under stress. Just as adults bite their fingernails or crack their
knuckles when they are anxious, children also turn to these habits as a
source of comfort and reassurance. The habits also serve as a distraction
—if the child's concentrating on picking at a scab, his attention is at
least temporarily diverted from worries about his grandmother's terminal
illness or the impact that his new baby sister will have on his life.

When Bad Habits Are More Than "Just a Phase"

*"Stand still, Brittany! I want to fix your hair before Grandma gets here—you
know how she grumbles when you don't look your best," Tina said to her
ten-year-old daughter, Brittany.*

*Brittany held still for a few minutes as her mother combed her hair. Suddenly,
Tina said, "Brittany! You've got a bald spot on your head."*

"What? Where?"

*"A bald spot about the size of a nickel. Right here on the top of your head.
How did it get there?"*

"Don't ask me—you're the one who found it."

*"Brittany, don't be disrespectful. Are you sure you don't know anything
about this?"*

"Yep, I'm sure. Now can I go to my room?"

*Mrs. Powell got busy with the preparations for her in-laws' visit and forgot
all about the bald spot until she took Brittany in for her annual checkup. "Dr.
Westin, could you please check Brittany's scalp? She had a little bald patch on
the top of her head a couple of weeks ago and I'd like to know what it is."*

*Dr. Westin examined Brittany's scalp and found the bald spot was now about
the size of a quarter. As the doctor continued his exam, he noticed that Brittany*

had very thin eyebrows and only a few outside lashes on her upper lids. "Brittany, I see that you not only have a bald spot on your head, but you're also missing some of your eyelashes. Have you been pulling them out?"

Brittany looked both surprised and embarrassed as she replied, "Just a little. How did you know?"

"The combination of a bald spot with even edges and missing eyelashes is almost always due to trichotillomania—that's a fancy medical word for pulling out your hair and eyelashes. For some people, hair-pulling is just a bad habit—they do it without even noticing it; but others pull in response to an urge or sensation that makes them feel like they have to pull. Do you get a special feeling before you pull, Brittany?" asked Dr. Westin.

"No, not really," Brittany said.

"Does your hair-pulling bother you?"

"Well, only because it's such a stupid thing to do and lately I've started worrying that one of the kids at school will notice that I'm missing a bunch of eyelashes and will think I'm weird. So, I've been trying really hard to quit, but I can't. I must be lacking willpower or something."

Dr. Westin replied, "I'm sure you're not lacking in willpower, Brittany. Not being able to stop even though you try really hard suggests that your hair-pulling is related to trichotillomania. Lots of people can stop pulling only when they have help from a therapist. I'll finish up my exam and then we'll talk about whether or not it makes sense for you to get some help with your hair-pulling."

"My child says she 'has' to pull her hair—is it still a habit?" Trichotillomania (pronounced *trick-oh-till-oh-mane-ee-ah*) is a medical disorder characterized by compulsive hair-pulling in response to tension or anxiety. Hair-pulling can also occur as a symptom of obsessive-compulsive disorder (see chapter 16) or it can be "just a habit." If the hair-pulling is a symptom of trichotillomania, it should be accompanied by three other symptoms: (1) the child feels an overwhelming urge to pull, which increases in intensity until the hair is pulled; (2) if the child resists the urge to pull, she becomes anxious; and (3) when "just the right hair" is pulled, she feels a sense of relief. If your child has hair-pulling that is associated with these three symptoms, then it deserves prompt attention, not only because this type of hair-pulling is always distressing to the child, but also because it is more easily treated when therapy is begun early.

In adolescence, trichotillomania is a secretive disorder because the teens recognize the senselessness of their hair-pulling. Often, the teenager will deny pulling her hair because she thinks that it is "crazy" or "stupid."

As a parent, you can help her admit to the hair-pulling by letting her know you understand that trichotillomania is a medical condition, not a sign of weakness or a lack of willpower. In some cases, however, even an accepting attitude is not sufficient to overcome the teen's reticence and the evaluation must include a scalp biopsy to demonstrate that the hair loss is due to pulling, rather than alopecia (hair loss resulting in baldness). Further information about trichotillomania is available from the Trichotillomania Learning Center, 1215 Mission Street, Suite 2, Santa Cruz, CA 95060; telephone: 408-457-1004.

"My child is so embarrassed by his habit." If your seven-year-old sucks his thumb while watching TV and is reluctant to visit a friend or go on a sleepover for fear that he'll be caught and teased, then his thumb-sucking is a "bad habit" and it is appropriate to help him break it. Even if the habit itself isn't embarrassing, your child may be concerned that the habit's aftermath (such as short, stubby fingernails or bald spots from hair-pulling) may bring him embarrassment—this is also a situation deserving of attention. In each of these instances, the child considers his habit to be "bad" and wants to break it—behavior therapy techniques will have a good chance of success in such a motivated child.

"I'm worried that my child will get sick because of her habit." There are at least four habits that are "bad" because they have potential medical complications:

1. Thumb-sucking past the point at which the child has permanent teeth. This can cause misalignment of the teeth by the pressure of the thumb.

2. Nail-biting that includes trauma to the cuticle or skin around the nails. Trauma to the nail bed and infections can result.

3. Skin-picking (such as adolescents who pick at their pimples). This can cause infections and scarring.

4. Hair-pulling associated with eating of the hair. Ingested hairs can cause blockage of the stomach or intestines.

Even in cases in which the habit is potentially harmful, the behavior therapy rule still applies—the habit won't be broken by behavior therapy unless the child wants to stop. Therefore, if your child's habit is a potential health risk, you must help him understand why the habit is undesirable and help him become motivated to break it.

"My child sucks his thumb when he's nervous or tense." Any of the common childhood habits could be a symptom of an anxiety disorder, as they are all self-soothing behaviors. Thumb-sucking and nail-biting are the two that are seen most often in association with the anxiety disorders. If your child is fearful, excessively shy, or has other symptoms that would suggest he has an anxiety disorder, treatment of the anxiety disorder may also help eliminate the bad habit. (See chapters 18 through 20 for full descriptions of the anxiety disorders.)

"My child is totally preoccupied with his skin-picking. Sometimes he spends hours stuck in front of the mirror." There is a great deal of overlap between childhood habits and the compulsive rituals of obsessive-compulsive disorder (OCD—see chapter 16). Skin-picking and nail-biting are common childhood habits, but are also seen as symptoms of OCD. If the behavior is a symptom of OCD, then it should cause the child distress (in terms of discomfort when prevented from doing the behavior) and interference (because of time lost to performing the behavior). For example, a child's knuckle-cracking would be just a habit if it occurred only when he didn't need to use his hands, but if he couldn't finish his math test because he had to crack his knuckles eight times after each problem, then it might be a symptom of OCD.

The length of time that the symptoms have been present can also distinguish between habits and OCD. If the behavior is a habit, it will usually have been present for much of the child's life, while OCD comes on later in childhood and is usually more complex—the child has several symptoms, not just an isolated behavior, such as knuckle-cracking or nail-biting.

"My child has so many nervous habits, I can't count them all." A tic is a repetitive behavior that occurs involuntarily, but can be partially controlled by the child—the child isn't aware that he's doing it, but when it's brought to his attention, he may be able to stop it for at least a short time. Thus, tics are quite similar to habits and it can be difficult to decide whether a child's unwanted behavior is a tic or a habit—in fact, nose-picking is listed as both a habit and a tic, as is excessive spitting. The distinction between tics and habits can be made by looking for other motor or vocal tics (see chapter 15); if they are present in roughly the same frequency and intensity as the behavior in question, it is likely to be part of a tic disorder. If the behavior occurs in isolation, or is limited to certain situations (such as watching TV or falling asleep), then it is more likely to be a habit.

Helping Your Child Outgrow His Bad Habit

What You Can Do to Help

Do nothing and wait for your child to outgrow it. Often, the best thing that you can do for your child's unwanted habit is to do nothing—just ignore it as much as possible and wait for your child to outgrow it or to ask for help in overcoming it. This wait-and-see approach won't make the bad habit go away any sooner, but it can make your family's life much easier, particularly if your child doesn't see his habit as a problem. "Waiting it out" can be frustrating to parents, but remember that even the most heroic efforts on your part won't be successful if your child isn't interested in breaking the habit. If you try to force him to stop, you'll set up a never-ending cycle of nagging and negativism—it's not worth it because it just won't help.

Limit the habit to certain places at certain times. Sometimes, it's impossible to ignore the bad habit—for example, if your son cracks his knuckles constantly or picks his nose at the dinner table. In such instances, it is important to establish some rules to ensure that the habit doesn't bother the other members of the family. The rules are not intended to make your child break the habit, but rather to diminish its negative impact. It is reasonable to expect your child to practice good hygiene (washing his hands after touching his nose), to use good table manners (no nose-picking, knuckle-cracking, or nail-biting at the table), and to respect other family members' rights (such as enjoying a movie or TV show without having to listen to incessant knuckle-cracking). Thus, we would advocate setting firm limits on where the behavior is tolerable (e.g., in your child's room) and where it is not (at the dinner table) and then to enforce these rules consistently.

Avoid punishment, teasing, and name-calling. Habit disorders are outside your child's control and should never be ridiculed or punished. Since your child can't control his thumb-sucking or nail-biting, he isn't being naughty or defiant when he starts sucking his thumb again within seconds of your reprimand and he shouldn't be punished. Negative comments are also inappropriate—not only are they ineffective in helping your child break his habit, but they may actually increase its frequency by increasing his level of stress.

Negative remarks can also damage your child's self-esteem, particularly if they come from you. Obviously, you can't protect your child from teasing at school or elsewhere, but you can keep him safe in your own home by preventing teasing by his brothers and sisters. When you comment on his habit, avoid saying things like "If you weren't such a baby, Tommy, you wouldn't still suck your thumb" or "Picking your nose again, Marilyn? You're disgusting—go get a tissue." These comments are hurtful because they attack the child directly—Tommy is told that he's a baby and Marilyn that she is disgusting. The habit may be undesirable, but that shouldn't be a reflection on the child himself.

When your child is ready, help him break the habit. Birthdays and other anniversary dates are a good time to discuss your child's bad habits with him, in order to determine whether or not he's ready to work at stopping the habit. Just as Danny focused on turning seven as the time when he would be "ready" to stop sucking his thumb, many children attach special significance to their birthdays and are motivated to do what it takes to be a "big boy" by their birthday date. Christmas, Thanksgiving, and other family holidays might also be a motivating factor, particularly if you are planning to visit relatives. Keep the discussion low-key to avoid pressuring your child into making a commitment he doesn't want to have to keep. Remember that "breaking the habit" must be your child's decision.

If your child decides that he's ready to stop, he will need some help, and behavior therapy is the most effective means of breaking bad habits. Behavior therapy is based on the theory that habits are learned behaviors that can be unlearned through practice. A behavior therapy program that is based on positive "rewards" for desirable behaviors is most effective.

Star charts. One of the simplest behavior therapy techniques is the star chart, in which the child receives a star for not doing the behavior for a specific period of time. For example, if your child wants to stop sucking his thumb, he might earn a star for each night he falls asleep with a "dry thumb." After he has earned ten stars, he can cash them in for a previously agreed-upon reward, such as a trip to McDonald's or watching a movie. As your child is accumulating stars, it's important for you to praise his successes lavishly and only minimally acknowledge his relapses (for example, by pointing out that he earned a star yesterday and that you're sure he will again tonight). After your child has successfully earned two rewards, the interval required to earn a star can be lengthened and/or the reward level raised to twenty stars (or a period of about three weeks). When three or four charts have been completed, the habit is usually under control and the star charts are no longer necessary.

Habit reversal. The habit reversal technique was originally developed by Dr. N. H. Azrin and Dr. R. G. Nunn in 1977 and has been widely used since that time to treat a variety of bad habits. The technique is more complicated than a star chart, but can still be done at home and is preferred for nail-biting and hair-pulling because of its greater likelihood of success. The basic components of habit reversal are outlined below (hair-pulling is used as the example, but the technique is equally effective for all the habit disorders):

1. *Find an alternative.* Have your child choose a behavior, such as clenching his fist or tapping his thigh, to replace the hair-pulling. Practice this behavior four times every ten minutes for one hour each day until it becomes automatic.

2. *Increase awareness.* Your child should watch himself in a mirror as he goes through the motions of pulling his hair. Have him pay close attention to when and where the physical motion starts and stops, as well as the "point of no return," at which the behavior becomes automatic and he no longer can control it.

3 and 4. *Identify triggers and habit-prone situations.* Have your child keep a diary of the thoughts, feelings, behaviors, activities, and places that are associated with the hair-pulling (e.g., 1:00 P.M. —bored and tired, watching TV; 3:00 P.M.—no special feelings, doing homework; 8:00 P.M.—worried about test tomorrow, getting ready for bed, in front of mirror).

5 and 6. *Habit prevention and interruption training.* Practice the substitute behavior for a full three minutes whenever the hair-pulling might occur (e.g., while watching TV, doing homework, getting ready for bed, etc.), as well as any time he pulls his hair.

7. *Positive alternatives.* Practice a positive and related alternative to the habit (e.g., brushing his hair). Do this daily.

8. *Practice the substitute in front of a mirror.* Several times each day, have your child pretend to reach for a hair to pull and substitute the new behavior for the hair-pulling.

9. *Keep a record of progress.* Note the circumstances surrounding both successful substitutions and hair-pulling lapses, including the

setting and situation, your child's mood, the number of hairs pulled, time spent, etc. Your child should also keep track of his larger successes, such as ways that the habit is becoming less bothersome. For younger children, a star chart can be used as a progress record.

10. *Social support.* Reward your child's successes and encourage him during his lapses. Frequent encouragement from parents and other loved ones is crucial to a child's success.

What Your Child's Teacher Can Do to Help

Prevent teasing and name-calling. Usually, it is not necessary to involve your child's teacher in the management of his bad habit. Busy teachers don't have time to monitor each child's habits, particularly since they are so common. However, if your child has been teased by one of the students in the class, or he is concerned about being ridiculed by his classmates, then it might be useful to discuss the habit with the teacher and ask her to remain vigilant to negative comments.

Help with behavior therapy. Behavior therapy is usually limited to the home situation. However, if your child is interested in using behavior therapy for his nail-biting and most of it occurs during school hours, then it is appropriate to inform the teacher about the behavior therapy and on occasion to enlist her assistance. Schedule a meeting for you, your child, and his teacher to discuss ways in which the teacher might help monitor and prevent the behavior without raising undue attention. A special signal, such as the teacher tapping her lips with a pencil or her fingers, could be used to call your child's attention to the behavior, and if that isn't sufficient, she could say, "Danny, stop." It would be up to your son to respond immediately or risk the negative consequence of having the teacher announce that he should stop biting his fingernails. One behavior therapy study found such negative reinforcement to be 99 percent effective for nail-biting. It should always be last on the list of alternatives, however, so that your child will have a chance to break the habit without threat of embarrassment.

Let parents know if the habit is a symptom of another problem. When a habit isn't really a habit, but rather is a symptom of a disorder like generalized anxiety disorder or obsessive-compulsive disorder, your child's teacher may be the first to know. She might notice that your son's knuckle-cracking occurs only when he's taking a math test and not when he's writing in his journal—this could be a symptom of performance anxiety or it might be associated with an OCD counting ritual. If your child's "habit" was actually a symptom of a tic disorder, his teacher might notice that it is accompanied by excessive eye-blinking or throat-clearing. She should take note of these associations and inform you of her observations and their potential meaning so that you can seek the proper medical attention.

What Your Child's Doctor Can Do to Help

Determine whether or not there are medical complications of the habit. Your child's doctor should be consulted if your child has hair-pulling, skin-picking, severe nail-biting, or prolonged thumb-sucking. Ask the doctor whether or not your child is at risk for medical complications. If not, then you can relax and ignore the habit until your child is ready to stop. If there are potential complications, then the doctor should explain these to the child and help him understand why it is important to break the bad habit.

If the habits are actually rituals, diagnose obsessive-compulsive disorder (OCD) promptly. Your child's doctor should consider the possibility that your child's bad habits are actually compulsions (behavioral rituals) from obsessive-compulsive disorder (OCD). Chapped hands (from excessive washing), heaped-up scars (from picking), and excessive concerns about germs (such as a six-year-old asking for an AIDS test) are a few of the signs of OCD that your child's doctor can pick up on his own. In addition, if you suspect that your child has OCD, discuss it with his pediatrician *before* the appointment so that the doctor can ask the appropriate questions. Many children have told us that they knew their OCD was real when we were able to describe their symptoms for them. Your child's doctor can also utilize a questionnaire, called the Yale-Brown Obsessive-Compulsive Checklist, to help determine whether or not his symptoms are related to OCD. (See chapter 16 for a full description of the diagnosis and treatment of OCD.)

Provide treatment for habit disorders and trichotillomania. Treatment of the habit disorders is successful only if your child is interested in stopping the behavior; if he's not, then there's no point in seeking professional help. However, if he wants to break his habit and hasn't been successful in his own attempts at behavior therapy, then a therapist might be helpful. Your child's pediatrician should be able to provide you with recommendations for clinicians experienced in behavior therapy.

Medications are *not* indicated for the treatment of bad habits, but may be useful for the medical disorder trichotillomania. The medications used to treat trichotillomania are the same as those used to treat obsessive-compulsive disorder: clomipramine (Anafranil), fluoxetine (Prozac), fluvoxamine (Luvox), paroxetine (Paxil), and sertraline (Zoloft). (These medications are discussed in detail in chapter 12.) Medications have been reported to improve hair-pulling in about 60 to 75 percent of adults with trichotillomania, but the response rates in children and adolescents are unknown. Combination therapy, which utilizes both medications and behavior therapy, is preferred by most clinicians (when a qualified behavior therapist is available), as it appears to help nearly 80 percent of adults with trichotillomania.

Further Reading
See chapter 15 and chapter 16.

Anders, Jeffrey, and James W. Jefferson. *Trichotillomania: A Guide*. Pamphlet available from the Obsessive Compulsive Information Center, Dean Foundation, 8000 Excelsior Drive, Suite 302, Madison, WI 53717-1914; 608-836-8070.

Azrin, N. H., and R. G. Nunn. *Habit Control in a Day*. New York: Simon & Schuster, 1978.

Heitler, Susan M., Ph.D. *David Decides About Thumbsucking: A Motivating Story for Children, an Informative Guide for Parents*. Denver, CO: Reading Matters, 1985.

6

"My Eight-Year-Old Still Wets the Bed"

Bed-wetting (enuresis)

"Mom! Mom! Can you come help me?" George called upstairs to his mother. "I can't find the laundry detergent."

His mother hurried down the basement staircase, saying, "George, the detergent should be right there on the shelf."

As she came into the laundry room, she said, "There it is, George. Right in front of you. How could you miss it?"

"Uh, well, actually, I knew it was there, Mom. I just wanted you to help me start the washer," George explained. "Allison's going to be up soon and she'll start teasing me if she sees the wet sheets."

"Oh, George. Another accident? Well, don't worry about it. And don't worry about your sister, either," his mother reassured him. "Your dad and I had a talk with Allison about her teasing. She promised to lay off."

"Well, she hasn't teased me yet this week. But it's only Tuesday. Besides, she doesn't really have anything to tease me about anymore. I only had wet sheets twice last week."

"George, that's terrific! That's so much less than last month. There must have been something about turning seven years old that's making your bed-wetting disappear."

"Yeah, I think it was my birthday wish that did it. Either that, or the fact that I've been sleeping with my lucky penny. Daddy found it for me. He taught *me a rhyme to say as I put it under my pillow at night: 'Have a penny just for luck, and all the night you'll be dried up.' "*

George looked so serious that his mother didn't dare laugh as he repeated the rhyme. Besides, he was having more dry nights recently. Who knew? Maybe it was the lucky penny.

Bed-wetting is the most common condition described in this book, with over 20 percent of five-year-olds (one in five kindergarten students!) still wetting the bed most nights. Enuresis *(en-you-ree-sis)* is the medical name for bed-wetting, and doctors describe two types: primary and secondary. Primary enuresis is the common, chronic type of bed-wetting in which children have never had full nighttime bladder control. In contrast, secondary enuresis is bed-wetting that occurs in a child who has had at least several months of dryness before beginning to wet again. Children with primary enuresis may have an occasional dry night, but they usually wet the bed each night. In essence, they aren't yet toilet-trained for nighttime. In contrast, when a child has secondary enuresis, he has been toilet-trained normally, but begins having nighttime wetting again six months or longer after achieving nighttime dryness.

Encopresis *(en-coe-pree-sis)* is the term used to describe stool-soiling. It is used only to describe children who were previously trained and then started having accidents with stooling outside the toilet. Some children have stool-staining of their underpants because they fail to wipe their bottoms thoroughly after a bowel movement—that is not encopresis. Encopresis is a bowel movement that occurs when the child is not sitting on a toilet. It can be voluntary (conscious defecation in inappropriate places—for example, a child who has anxiety about using a public rest room might choose to defecate in his pants, rather than sit on a public toilet) or involuntary (unintentional stool release, which might occur after prolonged bouts of constipation or other gastrointestinal problems). Encopresis is never part of a child's normal development and should always receive immediate attention from the child's physician.

When Bed-Wetting Is "Just a Phase"

"My four-year-old still wets the bed." Nighttime dryness is more difficult to obtain than daytime dryness, so bed-wetting is normal in all young children who have not yet been completely toilet-trained. In order to stay dry at night, a child must be able to do two things: awaken when he senses a full bladder and avoid letting go of his urine before awakening. This is a complex process that requires maturation of both the nervous system and the urinary bladder muscle. The nervous system must be able to send the message about the full bladder to the brain and allow the child to awaken in response to the command. Children who don't have these impulses require either outside assistance, such as an alarm system (like a bell and pad), or a "wait and see" attitude—there is nothing that can help a child's nervous system mature more quickly. Similarly, bladder muscle tone depends upon developmental maturity. Babies have very little muscle tone—they wet their diaper every time their bladder becomes the least bit distended. Eventually, they begin to wet less and less frequently, as bladder muscle tone increases. Bladder maturation is slower in boys than in girls, so boys achieve nighttime dryness at a later age, and have more bed-wetting than do girls. Eventually, every child's bladder control matures to the point of overnight dryness.

The average age to achieve nighttime dryness is three, but this means that one-half of all three-year-olds aren't yet reliably dry at nighttime. Even in kindergarten, about one in five children (20 percent) still wet the bed nightly; by age six, the rate is one in ten (10 percent), and by age twelve, it's about three out of one hundred (3 percent). Occasional bed-wetting is even more common. Between 5 and 10 percent of school-age children have occasional accidents, so if your child still wets the bed from time to time, you can reassure him that he is not alone!

"My husband wet the bed until he was twelve. Does that mean our son will, too?" One of the best predictors of nighttime dryness is the age at which a child's parents were dry. If your spouse was completely trained by age six, but you didn't achieve dryness until age ten, your child may continue to wet the bed until he's about ten years old. This is because children inherit developmental genes from their parents (in much the same way that they inherit eye color or height), and these genes determine the rate at which the nervous system and bladder mature. There is no way to influence these developmental genes, so once again, it's a matter of waiting for the child's body to mature before expecting nighttime dryness.

When Bed-Wetting Is More Than "Just a Phase"

Carolyn listened sadly as Joey spoke to his best friend: "No, I can't come over to your house tonight—my mom has something for me to do."

As soon as Joey hung up, Carolyn turned to him and said, "Joey, I don't have any plans for you tonight. Why did you tell Eddie that you couldn't sleep over at his house?"

"You know why, Mom," said Joey. "If I sleep over at his house, then he'll know that I still wet the bed and everybody at school will find out. I'd die if anyone knew that I still wet the bed—I'm ten years old, for Pete's sake!"

"I'm sorry you're so embarrassed about this, Joey. Do you want me to call Dr. Thomas and see if he can help?"

"No, that would be almost as bad—I really don't want anyone to know. I still have that bell and pad thing we got last year, maybe I could just try it again."

"That sounds like a good idea," his mom said. "Let's give it two weeks, and if you're still having a problem, I'll schedule an appointment with Dr. Thomas."

The bed-wetting alarm did help Joey slightly. He was dry for two nights in a row—the first time in over a year that he hadn't soaked his sheets every night. But by the second week, he was back to his usual pattern of wetting the bed every night shortly after 2:00 A.M.

Joey was really upset. Other kids could have sodas after dinner and still stay dry all night, but he couldn't. Other kids could wake up when they had to go, but he couldn't—he only woke up when his sheets were soggy and cold. It just wasn't fair!

"My son is so embarrassed by his bed-wetting." Even though bed-wetting is *very* common, your child may feel he is the only one who has this "babyish" problem. If he is seven years of age or older, and he is having significant problems as a result of his bed-wetting, then you may want to seek treatment for him. If he has had frequent bed-wetting all his life, then he will eventually grow out of it, but treatment may help him to be dry more quickly.

"My five-year-old was dry every night for over a year, until we brought his baby sister home from the hospital." Emotional stress is a common cause of secondary enuresis, usually as a result of developmental regression, but on rare occasions because of a loss of bladder control. Any emotional stress, such as hospitalization or death of a loved one, can be associated with bed-wetting. In children of all ages, bed-wetting can occur during times of family strife or when there is an impending divorce or marital separation. It is also common for younger children (ages four to six) to develop bed-wetting after the birth of a new brother or sister. If your child has been dry for an extended period, and then begins wetting the bed again, it is helpful to examine his life at home and at school to see if you can find a precipitant. A visit to his pediatrician is also in order, to ensure that the cause is stress, rather than one of the several medical conditions that can cause secondary enuresis.

"My nine-year-old just started wetting the bed again—he's also complaining that it stings when he goes to the bathroom." Urinary tract infections or bladder infections are common in childhood, particularly among girls. Anything that irritates the urethra (opening to the urinary tract) can increase a child's risk of getting a bladder infection; this includes such things as bubble baths and sitting in a wet bathing suit. The presence of a urinary tract infection can be detected by means of a history and physical examination, urinalysis (showing protein or white blood cells in the urine), urine culture (demonstrating bacterial contamination), and, if necessary, a blood test to detect the presence of an increased white blood cell count. If the infection is in the kidneys, rather than in the bladder, it is sometimes harder to discover the problem, and making the correct diagnosis may require several urine samples or more specialized tests.

Treatment of the urinary tract infection with antibiotics will usually relieve the bed-wetting. Occasionally, however, the infection decreases the tone of the bladder so that the bed-wetting continues even after the infection is cleared. In that case, exercises to increase bladder muscle tone will help restore nighttime dryness. Your child can increase his bladder tone by holding on to his urine, even after the bladder is completely full. The longer he can hold it, the more exercise the bladder gets. In addition, bladder tone can be increased by starting and stopping the urine stream several times as the child voids.

"Recently, my son's started getting up in the night to drink a glass of water and use the bathroom. Sometimes, he wets the bed, too." Diabetes, or high blood sugar, can cause bed-wetting in an older child (secondary enuresis) because of increased urine production. Diabetes is a serious medical illness that can be life-threatening if untreated, but can be well controlled by careful regulation of the blood sugar through insulin therapy. The symptoms of diabetes include: increased thirst and hunger, increased urinary frequency, secondary enuresis, weight loss, fatigue, decreased energy, abdominal pains and vomiting, fruity breath odor, and/or fainting. The onset of diabetes in children is usually abrupt and it always requires immediate medical attention.

"I'm worried about my son—he's always been so awkward and clumsy and now he's started wetting the bed again." Very rarely, enuresis is the result of a birth defect, such as absence of the bladder sphincter muscle or a deformity of the spine known as spina bifida. Usually, children with such birth defects have primary enuresis—they never achieve nighttime dryness and frequently aren't able to obtain daytime dryness, either. In some cases of spina bifida, however, the child toilet-trains normally, but as he grows, he develops secondary enuresis because the spinal cord has become entrapped in the abnormally shaped spine. The entrapment causes progressively severe symptoms, including bed-wetting, daytime accidents, and encopresis (stool-soiling), as well as problems running or jumping. In order to make sure your child doesn't have spina bifida, he should have a comprehensive physical and neurological examination. If the examination is abnormal, the doctor may order an MRI scan of the spine in order to rule out this rare, but medically critical, abnormality.

"Every time my son has a nightmare, he wets the bed." Bed-wetting is associated with several different sleep disorders, including excessively deep sleep and parasomnias (abnormal sleep events). These disorders are discussed in chapter 22. If your child's bed-wetting is related to a sleep disorder, he may have other symptoms, such as excessive daytime sleepiness, difficulty awakening in the morning, nightmares, night terrors, or sleepwalking.

Children who have an abrupt onset of bed-wetting may be having seizures or epileptic fits in their sleep. These are quite rare, but should be considered if a child develops secondary enuresis, particularly if the child is known to have epilepsy, or if the bed-wetting is associated with a new onset of drowsiness or abnormal behaviors during the daytime.

"My daughter fell off her bicycle and then she started wetting the bed again. Is there any connection between the two?" Physical trauma rarely causes enuresis in boys; but in girls, even mild traumas, such as slipping off the seat of a bicycle or landing hard while doing the splits, can result in increased urinary frequency, decreased bladder control, and bed-wetting. For these reasons, as well as those listed above, any child with secondary enuresis deserves a complete medical evaluation by an empathic physician. It is important to consider the possibility of sexual abuse whenever a child develops secondary enuresis, as the physical and psychological traumas of sexual abuse can cause loss of bladder control. (See chapter 18 for a complete discussion of sexual abuse.)

Helping Your Child Outgrow His Bed-Wetting

What You Can Do to Help

Accept that bed-wetting "just happens." The most important thing that parents can do to help their child is to accept that the bed-wetting is not his fault and remain patient until he eventually outgrows it. Your child isn't bad or stubborn or weak-willed when he wets the bed—he's just the victim of an immature nervous system. When you view the bed-wetting as a physical symptom, rather than a willful disobedience, it takes the pressure off both you and your child—neither of you has to find a solution to this problem because it's not under your control.

Provide your child with much-needed emotional support. Even if you are able to accept your child's bed-wetting as a medical problem, he may not be able to do so. It is hard for children to believe that the enuresis is completely outside their control—they see themselves as weak or bad because they aren't able to stop wetting the bed. At the very least, it is embarrassing to be a "bed wetter" and, as we saw in Joey's case, it can undermine a child's self-confidence and his ability to interact freely with his friends and peers. Joey's mother handled the situation perfectly—she let Joey know that she would be helpful to him in any way that she could, but she also reminded him that his bed-wetting was not a problem for her or other members of the family.

Let your child take control of his bed-wetting problem. Keep the problem confined to those with a "need to know," allowing your child to maintain as much privacy as possible. Make sure that your child's bed-wetting isn't discussed in the presence of his brothers or sisters, and that they aren't allowed to tease him about it. As soon as your child is old enough (age six to eight), allow him to assume responsibility for changing his own wet linens and doing his own laundry. He will have an easier time doing this if you use a plastic cover over the mattress and a drawsheet (available at hospital supply stores and some pharmacies) or other protective covering in the middle of the bed, so that he has to change only minimal bedding. It also may be helpful to have him restrict his fluid intake in the evening in order to minimize nighttime production of urine. However, make sure he drinks plenty of water during the daytime—not only to stay well hydrated, but to help him stretch his bladder capacity. Your child can practice holding his urine during the daytime to increase his bladder capacity. Have him try once or twice each day to delay urination for fifteen to twenty minutes or until his bladder feels very uncomfortable. To avoid the development of daytime accidents, make sure he practices this exercise only when a bathroom is immediately available.

Have your child train himself to get up and use the bathroom during the night. You can help your child learn to self-awaken by providing him with an alarm clock and having him set it to go off approximately a half hour before he usually wets the bed each night. When the alarm sounds, he should get up, go to the bathroom, and then reset the alarm for several hours later. This must be your child's choice and his responsibility, so that he truly learns how to wake up to void. There is some disagreement about whether or not self-awakening is all that helpful, so if your child doesn't want to set the alarm clock, he doesn't need to do it. Everyone agrees that it is *not* helpful for you to set your own alarm and help your sleeping child into the bathroom to use the toilet—all you will do is reinforce his bed-wetting by teaching him to void during his sleep.

Consider using an alarm system if your child is age seven or older. A bed-wetting alarm, such as the bell and pad device, can be used with children who are at least seven years of age. As the name implies, these alarms utilize a sensor (the pad), which sets off an alarm (the bell) when wet by the child's urine. There are a number of modifications on this system—some models are truly a bell and pad, while others have a small alarm system sewn into special underpants, or they resemble a miniature beeper, which is worn inside the underwear and vibrates or audibly alarms when the child begins to void. All alarm systems are based on the theory that awakening a child as soon as he begins to void will help him learn to recognize a full bladder and to awaken before voiding. The alarm systems are quite effective—as many as three-fourths of the children who use them will stop wetting the bed. To avoid long-term disappointment, however, your child should know that many children (20 to 40 percent) resume bed-wetting after they stop using the alarm; again, this is not a failure on the child's part, it just means that his body and brain aren't fully trained yet. Bed-wetting alarms cost between $40 and $60 and are available through most pharmacies, as well as by mail order or through your doctor's office.

What Your Child's Doctor Can Do to Help

Determine whether your child's bed-wetting is primary or secondary. Since secondary enuresis can be a symptom of a variety of medical disorders, it is always necessary to have your child evaluated by his pediatrician if the bed-wetting comes on after an extended period of nighttime dryness. If your child is six or seven years old and hasn't had at least six months of dry nights, then he is more likely to have primary enuresis. A visit to your child's pediatrician is still a good idea, so the doctor can examine your child, check his urine, and determine that there is no medical basis for the bed-wetting.

Teach your child about enuresis so that he understands it's not his fault. Your child's physician can offer tremendous reassurance to your child by teaching him about bed-wetting. The doctor should explain about bladder maturation and the time that it takes for the nervous system to mature, as well as helping him understand and accept that he has to "wait to outgrow it."

Provide recommendations for effective behavior therapy methods. Your child's pediatrician should be able to provide you with referrals to community sources of bed-wetting devices. The bell-and-pad devices are particularly reliable and cost-effective.

Teach your child to use self-hypnosis. Self-hypnosis has been reported to be very helpful for bed-wetting. In one report, over three-fourths of the children treated with self-hypnosis obtained nighttime dryness and two-thirds maintained it for at least six months after the study ended. Treatment of enuresis with self-hypnosis involves direct hypnotic suggestions coupled with mental imagery. For example, the child might be taught how to relax, stare at a simple object, and repeat, "When I need to urinate, I will wake up by myself, go to the bathroom all by myself, urinate in the toilet, and return to my dry bed. When I wake up, my bed will be dry and I will be happy." In one study, this technique helped thirty-one of forty children achieve dryness and improved self-confidence for all forty children.

Hypnosis can work fairly quickly. After a few sessions with a hypno-therapist, the child will be able to use self-hypnosis to maintain dryness. Some pediatricians and child psychiatrists are trained in hypnosis techniques, but usually your doctor will refer you to a therapist who specializes in hypnosis.

Prescribe medications to help stop the bed-wetting. Medications may be indicated for primary enuresis when the bed-wetting is troublesome to your child and traditional methods (such as the alarm system) have failed. At present, there are two medications that are known to be helpful: DDAVP and imipramine.

DDAVP (or desmopressin acetate) is a synthetic hormone that mimics the effects of vasopressin, a naturally occurring hormone that decreases the amount of urine made by the kidneys, so that the bladder doesn't become as full and there is no need for nighttime voiding. DDAVP isn't helpful to all children—if they make enough vasopressin on their own, the DDAVP offers no additional benefit. However, for many children, DDAVP decreases urine production to a point where they can achieve nighttime dryness. Side effects are very rare with DDAVP treatment and are limited to a stuffy nose and mild headache. As with all hormonal treatments, however, it is important to discuss the risks and benefits of treatment with your child's doctor before using DDAVP.

The second drug, imipramine (Tofranil), is used in low doses for persistent cases of enuresis. Imipramine, a tricyclic antidepressant, is more effective than DDAVP in helping children achieve long-term dryness, but it also has more side effects (see chapter 12 for a complete description). The slight increase in effectiveness seen with imipramine may not be worth your child having problems with dry mouth, constipation, or abdominal pain. Imipramine appears to improve bladder muscle tone, as well as changing the child's sleep patterns so that he is more likely to awaken before wetting. In boys who have both enuresis and attention deficit hyperactivity disorder (ADHD), imipramine may be the preferred treatment, because it helps the enuresis and the ADHD simultaneously. (See chapter 13 for a description of ADHD treatment.)

Further Reading
Mack, Alison. *Dry All Night: The Picture Book Technique That Stops Bed-wetting.* Boston, MA: Little, Brown & Company, 1989.

"My Daughter Is Afraid
of the Dark"

Childhood fears

"Leave the light on, Mommy. Please. And leave the door open so that I can call you if I need you," seven-year-old Megan pleaded as her mother tucked her into bed.

"The light on?" her mother said with surprise.

"Yes, I want to have my light on and the door left open," Megan said.

"That's a change. You've always wanted it to be really dark in your room. If I left the hallway light on for your brother, you'd shut your door to keep out the light."

"That was before I got scared of the dark," Megan explained.

"Scared of the dark?" her mother repeated. "Since when did you become afraid of the dark?"

"Since a couple of nights ago, when you and Daddy were down in the basement and some strangers started talking to you, and then, all of a sudden, there was a big bang and the strangers stopped talking and it got really dark. I couldn't see anything and I couldn't hear anything, either. I was so scared that I thought I was going to die!"

"Megan, why didn't you come and get me?" her mother asked. "Or call for me to come take care of you?"

"I did call for you, Mom," Megan said. "That's what I've been trying to tell you about. I started to look for you, but everything was so dark, so I got back in bed and called for you to come. But you never did, so I thought something happened to you. Those strangers had been talking about 'getting even' with somebody right before they got quiet."

"Getting even?" her mother said. "Oh, Megan, that was on the radio. There weren't strangers in the house. Your dad and I were listening to an old radio play while we worked in the rec room. The voices that you heard were just the radio actors saying their lines."

"Then why did they stop talking all of a sudden?" Megan asked.

"Because the electricity went out," her mother explained. "A transformer blew up at the substation and our whole neighborhood lost power. That's why it got so dark and quiet all of a sudden. As soon as we found a flashlight, your daddy and I came in to check on you, but you were all curled up under your covers and it looked like you were fast asleep. I never dreamed that you were wide awake under there, much less that you were scared half to death. Why didn't you say something?"

"I was hiding because I thought that you were the bad guys. But later I called for you and you didn't come."

"I'm sorry, Megan, I just didn't hear you," her mother said. "It must have been terrible to be so frightened and not have us come help you. I promise that it won't happen again. I'll check on you every few minutes until you fall asleep to make sure you don't need anything and we'll leave the hallway light on all night for you."

"Thanks, Mom," Megan said. "I love you."

"I love you too, sweetheart," her mother said as she finished tucking Megan into bed. "Now, go to sleep and dream only good dreams. Your daddy and I will listen to some music tonight—no more radio dramas!"

Although Megan's fear of the dark is unusual in that the trigger is so readily identified, it is not an unusual fear for a seven-year-old child. The most common fears at that age are those that concern the child's safety and security, such as fear of strangers, animals, the dark, storms, death, and being separated from her parents. Between the ages of three and eight, many children fear the dark, as well as having concerns about their own safety and that of their parents. For some children, the fears begin early in childhood when they are experiencing separation difficulties (see chapter 4). For other children, like Megan, the fears don't appear until six to eight years of age, when the child is beginning to establish her own identity.

Fears are so similar among different children that they appear to have been lifted from a single TV or movie script. For example, many children report being afraid that a thunderstorm will come up "out of the blue" and produce a tornado that destroys the child's home and separates her from her family. The scenario is so uniform, and so familiar, that it seems as if the children must all be recalling the opening scene from *The Wizard of Oz*. However, the children had never seen the movie or read L. Frank Baum's book, and it appears that Mr. Baum was either drawing upon his own childhood memories or he had firsthand knowledge of the universal nature of childhood fears—the themes are a reflection of the developmental challenges facing all children.

When a Child's Fear Is "Just a Phase"

"My child says she's afraid of ————." A child begins to have fear as soon as she is old enough to understand that her parents are not all-powerful and that she can't be protected from every injury and disappointment. Surveys show that all grade-school children have at least one fear, and most have several, including fears of sleeping or staying alone, animals (especially large dogs), "bad" people, monsters, ghosts, storms, the dark, and being injured or having someone they love get hurt or killed. In the preteen years, some of these fears fade (e.g., monsters and ghosts), and are replaced by concerns about school performance, physical appearance, and peer relationships (also see chapter 8). Other fears, such as those concerning physical injury and parental separation, remain into adolescence. The preschool-aged child worries that a nameless, faceless monster will come and take her away. As the child grows older, she may have worries about the specific ways in which she will be hurt or a particular person who will cause her harm. The child may also begin to incorporate events outside her family into the concerns—for example, she might hear a news report about a girl in another state who has been kidnapped or murdered and fear that she'll be next. To prevent this from escalating into full-blown separation fears, it is important to discuss the rarity of such events and to provide reassurance about the ways in which you can protect your child against a similar occurrence.

At the age of seven or eight, children begin to understand that death is a permanent separation that affects everyone. This leads to fears that the child's parents will die soon and leave her alone. This fear is difficult to counter because of the universal and unpredictable nature of death, but a calm, supportive attitude and appropriate reassurance are usually sufficient to overcome it. The fear would be considered a problem if the child was preoccupied with her parents' death or if symptoms of anxiety accompanied her concerns (chapter 18).

"We moved recently, and now my child is afraid to be left alone in the house." It is normal for children to experience increased fearfulness following a move to a new home, change in schools, death in the family, or other traumatic event. These stresses pose a potential threat to the child's safety and well-being, and fear is elicited whenever we are exposed to a potentially dangerous situation. The fear subsides as the child learns that her new environment is safe and secure, or she becomes more confident that her parents won't abandon her in this strange place. The process takes time because the child must first learn through experience that her new surroundings are not dangerous, and then she must unlearn the fear response through repeated practice. In order to avoid overwhelming her ability to cope with the situation, the child shouldn't be asked to take on too many challenges at one time—for example, she shouldn't be left home alone in the new house until she's comfortable being there with her parents.

"My child has always been overly fearful, but it doesn't really bother her." Certain children (about one in ten) are predisposed by their temperament to be fearful. They overreact to sudden movements and loud noises and are frightened much more easily than other children—these are the toddlers who shriek with fear, rather than surprised delight, when the jack-in-the-box pops out of his house. Dr. Jerome Kagan at Harvard University found that the fearful children have an overly sensitive nervous system and overreact to frightening situations—jumping at the slightest noise, running away from potential threats, and screaming when someone startles them. The children have an exaggerated fear response, but they don't have excessive fears—they are not fearful unless they're confronted with a threat or challenge. The absence of fearfulness in safe situations is what distinguishes the child with a fearful temperament from one with an anxiety disorder (chapters 18, 19, and 20).

The child with an oversensitive fear response will often avoid situations that trigger the response, in order to avoid feeling uncomfortable. This is not a conscious decision, but rather an unconscious response to the discomfort she feels. The term "behavioral inhibition" is used to indicate that the child's behavior is inhibited by her avoidance—she is reluctant to try new things, meet new people, or enter strange places. Some children have mild behavioral inhibition and avoid only truly dangerous or "scary" situations (such as roller coasters, haunted houses, and horror movies), while others are so sensitive that they avoid all potentially stressful situations, including meeting new people. (See shyness and behavioral inhibition in chapter 9.)

"My child is afraid of having a nightmare—they're so real to her." Occasional nightmares are common among grade-school children. The nightmares are thought to be a reflection of the child's current fears and challenges, just as an adult's dreams are thought to represent her unresolved conflicts and unfulfilled wishes. As the children mature, the content of their dreams and nightmares changes. Young children often have nightmares about scary monsters chasing them or being lost in a dark forest, while older children dream about being trapped in a scene from a scary movie or having a bully beat them up. Adolescents have nightmares in which they miss an important test or deadline, or they are left standing alone and naked in the dark. Although the details of the dreams change over time, the nightmares all share a common anxiety-producing theme —the danger is imminent, the child is powerless against it, and there is no hope that she'll be rescued.

The fear experienced during a nightmare is very real—the child's breathing quickens, her heart beats more rapidly, and she feels anxious and upset. Often, she'll awaken from the nightmare crying or calling for help. When this occurs, provide her with reassurance that she's safe and that the dream wasn't real.

When Childhood Fears Are More Than "Just a Phase"

"Mom, can I sleep in your bed tonight?" asked eight-year-old Carrie.

"Why? Is something wrong with your room?" her mother, Elaine, responded.

"Yeah. Ever since Mr. Green took down the fence, the porch light shines into my room and makes these creepy shadows. They give me bad dreams," Carrie said. "Besides, I hardly ever get to see you anymore—you're always at the hospital or at Grandma's house."

Elaine pulled her daughter onto her lap and said, "Carrie, you know that I have to go to the hospital and get chemotherapy every week or the cancer will come back. And I have to stay at Grandma's house for a couple of days before I feel well enough for Aunt Trudy to drive me home. But even when I'm not here, I'm thinking about you all the time and missing you bunches. I love you, honey."

"I love you too, Mom," Carrie said, and then, noticing her mother's tear-filled eyes, she continued, "Don't be upset, Mommy. I won't sleep with you tonight. I'll just leave my door open and then I can't see the shadows."

"Honey, I'm not upset. I'm not even really crying," Elaine said. "I'm just thinking about how proud I am of you and how brave you are. I can't think of anything better than cuddling in bed with you tonight. We'll make it a pajama party—just like old times."

Elaine fell asleep with her daughter in her arms, only to be awakened a few hours later by Carrie's frightened cries: "Help! Help! It's going to get me!" Seeing that her daughter was dreaming, Elaine shook her and said, "Carrie, Carrie, honey, wake up! You're having a nightmare."

"Mommy. Help me! There's a terrible monster in here," Carrie said, still half asleep, but staring wide-eyed into the corner.

"No, there's not, sweetheart. It's just us—see?" Elaine said soothingly as she turned on the bedroom light.

"Oh, Mommy, it was so scary. The monster came and took you away and I couldn't find you anywhere. And the monster was just about to eat me!" Carrie said.

"What a terrible dream!" her mother replied, still holding her daughter tightly.

Carrie looked up at her mother and said, "I have the same dream every single night. That's why I don't like going to sleep—it's too scary! Sometimes, I even start thinking about it in the daytime."

"Oh, you poor baby," her mother said. "Dr. Fisher explained this to us, remember? In your last therapy session, he told us that you might start having nightmares because of your worries about my cancer. The nightmares are just the way your brain tries to figure out its worries. We'll schedule an extra therapy session with Dr. Fisher as soon as we can. But, meanwhile, maybe we can help you feel better by making up a happy ending for the dream."

Carrie said, "I already do that. I pretend that the monster comes when I'm alone in the backyard, but as soon as I scream, you come running out to save me."

"That's a great idea!" Elaine said. "Now, let's make it even better. We're having a picnic together in the backyard when the monster comes. He's not coming to steal you, he's just trying to get our hot dogs. But I bop him on the nose with the barbecue tools and you squirt him with the ketchup so that he runs away."

Carrie laughed and said, "I can just see us doing that. The monster wouldn't have a chance if he tried to take our hot dogs!"

"Right!" Elaine said. "So you know that I wouldn't let anything else happen to you. I promise I'll keep you safe. Now, do you think you can go back to sleep?"

"Yeah, I am getting a little sleepy," Carrie said and snuggled under the covers again.

As Elaine held her daughter, she thought about how fortunate they were to have found a child psychiatrist like Dr. Fisher. He had given her all the tools she needed to deal with Carrie's concerns and another crisis had been averted. She hoped that since her cancer had gone into remission, there wouldn't be many more.

"My child is afraid to fall asleep at night because she has such scary dreams." Separation anxieties are often played out in nightmares similar to Carrie's—the child is under attack, and her parents can't be found to help her. Nearly every child will have at least a few such dreams, because fears of being orphaned are common to all children. Although occasional nightmares are an expected occurrence during childhood and adolescence, frequent or persistent nightmares are not considered to be normal. If a child is having nightmares three or four times per week, or she has the same nightmare repeatedly, it may be a sign of excessive stress or a symptom of an anxiety disorder (see chapters 18 through 20). The child's parents should try to determine the source of her anxiety; if they're unsuccessful, then her doctor should be consulted.

"My child is afraid to leave my side—she won't even let me go into the bathroom by myself." Separation anxiety disorder (chapter 18) is characterized by the child's excessive fears about her parents' safety. The child fears that she will be separated from her parents or her home and that she won't be able to return. She will usually be fine when her parents are present, but in their absence, she not only feels nervous and tense, but may also have physical symptoms, such as headache, stomachache or rapid heartbeat, sweating, trembling, and numbness or dizziness. In severe cases, the child worries about her parents' well-being even when she is sitting right beside them.

"My child is suddenly so afraid of the dark that she's started sleeping on the floor next to my bed." A school-age child who has a sudden, dramatic increase in nighttime fears, or an abrupt onset of separation difficulties, may have PANDAS (pediatric autoimmune neuropsychiatric disorders associated with strep infections). The fearfulness is unusually abrupt in PANDAS—the child is fine one night, and the next she is unable to fall asleep by herself because of her anxieties. These nighttime fears are accompanied by nightmares, motor or vocal tics, and obsessive-compulsive symptoms, and, as the name implies, occur as a consequence of strep throat infections. Chapter 17 contains a full description of the symptoms of PANDAS.

"My child is so afraid that she'll get hurt, she refuses to learn to ride a bicycle." Children who are fearful by temperament may be reluctant to take risks or try new things, but with sufficient reassurance, they are able to take on almost all challenges. When a child's fears make her anxious or upset, or get in her way—by limiting her social relationships, interfering with activities at home or at school, or prohibiting her from trying new things and taking the risks necessary to accomplish developmental tasks—then the fears are excessive. Excessive fears may occur in response to stressful situations, such as moving to a new house or losing a loved one, or they can be a symptom of generalized anxiety disorder. When fears arise from generalized anxiety disorder, they are present most of the time each day for at least six months and cause both anxiety and interference (see chapter 19).

"My child is terrified of insects [or dogs, or horses, or heights, or closed spaces, or ———]." Excessive fears about a specific thing, such as heights or insects, are called phobias. Phobias are often triggered by an unpleasant incident or a stressful encounter, such as a near fall or a bee sting. To be classified as a phobia, rather than a normal childhood fear, the child must experience both distress (anxiety) and interference—either as a direct consequence of her response to the feared object or as a result of her avoidance of situations in which she might be exposed to the thing she fears. For example, a child might become phobic about dogs after being knocked down by a large German shepherd. The fear generalizes to all dogs and she becomes upset and anxious whenever she has to be near a dog, even one that is obviously harmless. The child will begin to avoid situations in which she might be accidentally confronted by a strange dog, such as playing in the park or riding her bike on unfamiliar streets. However, when she is in a safe environment, such as in her house or school, she has no difficulties. Many phobias can be managed by limiting accidental exposures and providing reassurance and support for necessary encounters, but sometimes treatment, such as desensitization therapy or behavior modification, may be required (see chapters 12 and 18 for complete description).

"My child is so afraid of germs that she washes her hands twenty times a day." When a child's fears are about specific things, such as germs or other contaminants, and she performs special rituals, such as washing her hands, in order to decrease the anxiety that she feels, she is exhibiting symptoms commonly seen in obsessive-compulsive disorder (OCD). The obsessions of OCD are discrete, irrational fears (for example, fear of catching AIDS by touching an elevator button) that persist for extended periods of time and preoccupy the child's attention in a variety of settings and circumstances. The obsessions are linked to compulsive rituals, such as hand-washing, cleaning, repeating, checking, and arranging things "just so" in the closet or on her desk. OCD is not often confused with normal childhood fears because the two sets of concerns are so different. (See chapter 16 for a full description of OCD.)

"My child was sexually abused by our neighbor, and now she refuses to leave my side." Sexual abuse is so offensive that we find it difficult to conceive of its happening to any child, much less to someone that we know and love, but it does happen—far too often. Sexual abuse is defined as any kind of sexual contact with a child—it includes allowing a child to view pornographic materials or taking photographs or videos of the child for obscene purposes, exposure of the child's or adult's genitals, inappropriate fondling of the child, forcing the child to touch or fondle the adult's genitals, mouth-to-genital contact, anal penetration, or sexual intercourse. The abuse is usually not limited to a single episode, but involves multiple incidents over an extended period of time, often continuing into adolescence.

The victims of sexual abuse are boys and girls of all ages, with girls aged eight to twelve years at greatest risk. There are more than 150,000 new cases of sexual abuse reported each year, with at least twice as many cases going unreported. It is estimated that millions of Americans have been victims of sexual abuse—in some studies, as many as one in four adult women recall an inappropriate sexual encounter during childhood. But the most alarming statistic is that the abuse is perpetrated by a family member or other known person in 85 percent of the cases. The abuser is less likely to be a stranger than he is a neighbor, friend, baby-sitter, teacher, coach or Scout leader, relative (cousin, uncle, grandfather), step-parent, older sibling, or father. Clearly, the threat of sexual abuse is not just from "stranger danger" and we need to warn our children against all inappropriate touching, as well as encouraging them to report any uncomfortable encounters as soon as they occur.

Children who are sexually abused are often afraid to reveal the abuse, either because of threats from the perpetrator or because they feel ashamed about their role in the abuse. In these instances, the child's behavior often provides clues—she becomes afraid of a particular person or place and especially of being left alone with the person; she develops new awareness of sexual words or body parts; she acts "sexy," she mastur-bates excessively, or tries to engage other children in sexual play; she is unduly anxious about a doctor's physical examination; she draws unusu-ally frightening or sad pictures (particularly with excessive use of red and/or black); she develops symptoms of depression or anxiety; or she becomes excessively clingy or unusually withdrawn from her family. The child may tell a friend or classmate about the abuse, or she may hint about it to trusted adults. If a child reveals that she has been sexually abused, it is important to believe her and to take action to protect her from further harm. False accounts of abuse, or false memories, are rare (less than 3 percent of the cases of reported sexual abuse are found to be without basis). Furthermore, the reports can be investigated without negative impact, while ignoring a child's report of sexual abuse increases her vul-nerability to physical and psychological problems, such as infections, pregnancy, loss of trust, depression, anxiety disorders, and post-traumatic stress disorder. Other factors that can worsen a child's prognosis include: threats of violence, invasive abuse, long-term abuse—particularly when it continues into adolescence—and a close relationship between the child and the abuser. Sexual abuse by a father or stepfather is particularly traumatic, and both intensive individual psychotherapy and family ther-apy are necessary in order for the child to begin to heal. Overcoming the effects of childhood sexual abuse is possible however, particularly if the child's family is loving and supportive and helps to convince her that she is not at fault and will be protected from further harm.

Helping Your Child Outgrow Her Fears

What You Can Do to Help

Recognize whether your child's fears are within the normal range or are excessive. Become familiar with the fears commonly experienced by children at your child's age and developmental stage. If your child is a "young" six-year-old, she might still have concerns common to five-year-old children, such as fear of animals, the dark, and "bad" people, but she shouldn't continue to fear loud noises or large machines, since those fears usually disappear by age four. Your child may have one fear or several, but none should cause her excessive concern, nor should they interfere with her daily activities. To decide whether or not her fears are problematic, have her tell you about them. What kinds of things make her feel afraid? Are her fears related to a specific person, place, or situation? Does she think that the fears make sense? Is she in control of the fears or are they too frightening for her to handle? Do they bother her? Do they get in her way? As she talks, your child will tell you whether she is comfortable with the fears, or whether they are a source of concern to her. If her fears are bothering her (causing her distress) or getting in her way (causing interference), then they are outside the normal range and it's possible that she has an anxiety disorder that requires treatment. (See chapter 12 for additional clues about distinguishing phases from anxiety disorders.)

Be sympathetic to your child, not to her fears. Your child's fear is real, but her fears aren't based in reality, so it is important to acknowledge the anxiety that she feels without validating the fears themselves. For example, if she is afraid of the dark, she could use a night-light for comfort, but not to "keep the monsters away." Similarly, if she is afraid of thunderstorms, you can provide reassurance and support during a storm, but don't increase her anxieties by making up fables about thunder being the sound of angry gods stomping across the sky. Instead, teach her how to read a barometer so that she knows when a storm is approaching or help her research thunderstorms so she understands the true nature of thunder and lightning. Information and understanding are the tools needed to master her fears, no matter what their source.

Talk to your child about her nightmares. If your child's dreams are contributing to her fear of the dark, discuss the nightmares with her.

Talking about the details of the dream will allow her to alter the story's ending so that she's in control—in her nightmare, a scary monster might have threatened to steal her away, but as she retells it, she'll recall that she called you and that you came and saved her.

Help your child confront her fears. Fears often decrease, and sometimes disappear completely, when the child confronts them and sees that they are without basis. Obviously, this isn't done in a single step, or the child would be overwhelmed with anxiety, but instead it is done gradually, in many small steps, with support and reassurance along the way. For example, if your child is afraid of the dark, she is actually afraid of many different things; primary among them are unseen threats to her safety and separation from her loved ones. Confronting these fears simultaneously is impossibly difficult because each of them is so frightening by itself, but tackling each of the fears separately makes it possible for the child to master them. To overcome her fear of the dark, she might practice staying alone in her room with the light on for increasing lengths of time until she is quite comfortable with her solitude, and also might practice getting used to the darkness—with you beside her for protection. As you sit with her in the dark, make a game of naming the noises that you hear—she will begin to realize that the noises are no more sinister in the dark than they are in the light. When your child is comfortable with the darkness and with staying alone in her room, she is ready to combine the two by staying alone in a darkened room.

Help your child overcome her fears. The technique described above— gradual, stepped exposure to the child's fears—is actually a form of behavior therapy. Other techniques are equally useful. One of our favorites, imagination training, was developed by Dr. Jeffrey Brown and is described in detail in his book, *No More Monsters in the Closet.* The key elements of successful imagination training are control, safety, relaxation, and reward. Your child is the one who is always in control because she uses her imagination to move through the steps of exposure to the thing she fears. She is safe because she knows that she can get out of the stressful situation whenever she feels uncomfortable and can escape as soon as she chooses to leave. Relaxation helps prevent the physical discomfort that often accompanies anxiety-provoking exposures. It is difficult for children to master the art of relaxation, so Dr. Brown suggests that you help your child relax by performing the exercises with her before teaching her how to do the exercises alone. The reward in imagination therapy is the child's mastery over her fears—she will feel a tremendous sense of accomplishment each time she successfully confronts her fears. If she falters along the way and fails to complete a step, remind her of the progress she has already made toward the goal and encourage her to "try again" with a slightly smaller step. When she reaches the final level, not only has she conquered the fear, but her anxiety is gone and she feels great!

Protect your child from the fear of sexual abuse. A child should be instructed from an early age that her body belongs to her and only to her, and that she is the only one who decides whether or not someone touches her. Between the ages of three and five years, she should learn about her "private parts" (those parts covered by a two-piece bathing suit for girls and swim trunks for boys) and should know the proper names for all body parts. She should also know that any touching that makes her uncomfortable is wrong and that she can say "No" or "Stop"—even to an adult. Let her know that you will support her decision, even if it's embarrassing to have her refuse Great Aunt Tilly's bosomy hug or an invitation to sit on Grandpa's lap as they watch TV together.

Once your child enters school, it is important to discuss safety away from home and the difference between "good touch" and "bad touch." You should encourage her to talk about scary experiences, and, again, it is important to let her know that you will believe her and protect her, even if she tells you something you don't want to hear. The peak age at risk for sexual abuse is between eight and twelve years, so it is particularly important to keep the lines of communication open during this period.

Teach your child how to stay safe in all types of situations. During late childhood and early adolescence, she is oblivious to warnings of impending danger and also beginning to experience the false omnipotence of adolescence—a combination that puts her at risk of discovering too late that she's not in control of the situation. Role-playing is an excellent way to help her practice staying safe or getting safe when she's home alone, at the mall with friends, in school after-hours, at a party where alcohol is being served, and so forth. The exercise is also an excellent opportunity for you to reinforce that you will protect her—no matter what she's done.

For adolescents, the issue becomes sexual rights and responsibilities. Your teenager has a responsibility to protect her health and fertility, and the right to determine whether or not she wants to be sexually active.

"Date rape" is an increasing problem, and your child should know that she always retains the right to say no to sexual contact, even if: he's really cute or popular, he tells her he won't go out with her again, he threatens to tell lies about her, he says he'll "die if he doesn't get relief," or he's "spent five hundred dollars on dinner, a tux, and a limo to take her to the prom." Women's centers and rape prevention centers offer special courses for teenage girls that are designed to increase their sense of autonomy and control, to teach them how to say "No!" effectively, and to provide them with basic self-defense training.

What Your Child's Teacher Can Do to Help

Be informed about normal fears of school-age children and recognize excessive fears. The informed teacher can be a valuable resource as you try to decide whether or not your child's fears are excessive. Teachers have the opportunity to interact with their students in a variety of settings, such as the classroom, cafeteria, and playground; as well as to observe them in various circumstances, including interacting in class discussions and presenting oral reports in front of the class. Your child's teacher may have observed that she never leaves the asphalt-covered portion of the playground and discover that she has a phobia about bees, or she might notice that your child is reluctant to participate in class activities and that she always answers questions in a soft whisper (one sign of social phobia and selective mutism—chapter 20). If your child's fears are excessive, her teacher should inform you of her observations and the reasons why she feels that your child's fears are outside the normal range.

Respect the child's fears and prevent teasing and ridicule. Your child's teacher should show respect for her students and should also require the students to show respect for each other. Therefore, she will not tease or belittle a child for being fearful, and she won't allow teasing by the pupils in her classroom.

Encourage the child to confront her fears, but avoid producing unnecessary fears. Depending upon the nature of your child's fears, her teacher may be able to provide her with opportunities to confront an aspect of her fear, and thereby gain mastery over it. These opportunities must be planned carefully and coupled with supportive encouragement from the teacher in order to ensure success. For example, if your child has a fear of public speaking, it might be impossible for her to memorize a poem and recite it in front of the class, but her teacher might modify the assignment to allow her to read a poem from note cards so that she can concentrate on keeping her voice loud enough to be heard. The next assignment might require her to look up at the audience three times during the presentation or to memorize the first three lines of the poem.

Your child's teacher should strive to make the classroom environment both supportive and challenging. She should establish a predictable classroom routine, provide adequate instruction and review, and "push" her students to reach slightly beyond their comfort level to achieve their maximal potential. Just as a child overcomes her fears by gradual exposure to increasingly difficult challenges, she will learn best by building incrementally and stretching beyond what's easy and comfortable. When a student seems overwhelmed by the material, however, the teacher should reestablish a secure base of knowledge and encourage the student to "try again" with more manageable units of study.

What Your Child's Doctor Can Do to Help

Prepare you for your child's fearful stages. Information is not only key to your child's mastery of her fears, but it is also crucial to your success in keeping her fears from escalating out of control. Your child's doctor should be an expert in child development and should educate you about your child's approaching developmental tasks and the fears that are commonly associated with those challenges. He should provide you with guidelines for distinguishing between normal and excessive fears at each age.

Recognize phobias and anxiety disorders and provide for appropriate treatment. If your child is distressed by her fears, or they're causing difficulties for her at home or at school, then her doctor should refer her to a child psychiatrist for a comprehensive, psychiatric evaluation. Child psychiatrists have training and experience in childhood anxiety disorders (chapters 18 through 20) and can determine whether the fears stem from a simple phobia and will respond well to behavior therapy, or whether they are a symptom of a more complex condition, such as separation anxiety disorder, and will require treatment with a combination of medication and behavior therapy.

Help safeguard your child against sexual abuse by providing information and instruction. Your child's doctor should take an active role in teaching your child about her personal safety. He should respect her privacy and demonstrate his respect for her ownership of her body. At least a few minutes of the annual checkup should be devoted to age-appropriate discussions of sexual abuse prevention. The content of the discussions will change, as detailed above, but one thing should remain constant—before beginning his examination, the doctor should inform the child that he will touch her private place only because it is necessary for the medical examination. As the child gets older, the doctor should request permission to perform the exam and should allow the child to remove her own underwear.

Recognize sexual abuse and provide appropriate treatment. As the doctor talks to your child and performs his examination, he should be vigilant to signs of sexual abuse. If the doctor suspects sexual abuse, or if your child reports that she's been abused, her doctor is legally required to report the abuse and morally obligated to protect your child against future abuse by activating the child protection system.

Further Reading
Childhood Fears
Chapters 18 through 20 discuss anxiety disorders in childhood.

Brown, Jeffrey L., M.D., with Julie Davis. *No More Monsters in the Closet: Teaching Your Children to Overcome Everyday Fears and Phobias.* New York: Prince Paperbacks, 1995. This is an especially good book.

Feiner, Joel, M.D., and Graham Yost. *Taming Monsters, Slaying Dragons: The Revolutionary Family Approach to Overcoming Childhood Fears and Anxieties.* New York: Arbor House, 1988. This is also a very helpful book.

Garber, Stephen W., Ph.D., Marianne Daniels Garber, Ph.D., and Robyn F. Spizman. *Monsters Under the Bed and Other Childhood Fears: Helping Your Child Overcome Anxieties, Fears and Phobias.* New York: Villard Books, 1993.

Golant, Dr. Mitch, with Bob Crane. *Sometimes It's O.K. to Be Afraid! A Parent/Child Manual for the Education of Children.* New York: RGA Publishing Group, 1987.

Schachter, Dr. Robert, and Carole S. McCauley. *When Your Child Is Afraid: Understanding the Normal Fears of Childhood from Birth Through*

Adolescence and Helping Overcome Them. New York: Simon & Schuster, 1988.

Warren, Dr. Paul, and Dr. Frank Minirth. *Things That Go Bump in the Night: How to Help Children Resolve Their Natural Fears*. Nashville, TN: Thomas Nelson, 1992.

Sexual Abuse Prevention

Adams, Caren, and Jennifer Fay. *No More Secrets: Protecting Your Child from Sexual Assault*. San Luis Obispo, CA: Impact Publishers, 1981.

———. *Helping Your Child Recover from Sexual Abuse*. Seattle, WA: University of Washington Press, 1992.

Benedict, Helen. *Safe, Strong and Streetwise: Sexual Safety at Home, on the Street, on Dates, on the Job, at Parties and More*. Boston: Little, Brown, 1987.

Colao, Flora, and Tamar Hosansky. *Your Children Should Know: Teach Your Children the Strategies That Will Keep Them Safe from Assault and Crime*. Indianapolis/New York: Bobbs-Merrill, 1983.

Resources for Concerns About Child Abuse, Including Sexual Abuse

National Child Abuse Hotline, 800-4ACHILD (800-422-4453). Counselors will answer questions and provide referrals.

National Clearinghouse on Child Abuse and Neglect
P.O. Box 1182
Washington, D.C. 20013
703-385-7565

National Committee for Prevention of Child Abuse
332 South Michigan Avenue, Suite 1600
Chicago, IL 60604-4357
312-663-3500

"My Son Worries Too Much"

Childhood anxieties

"Mom, are you going to die?"

"Yes, Tim—everybody dies someday," his mother answered.

"I mean today. Are you going to die today?" Tim asked.

"No, of course not. Why would you ask such a question?"

"Because I love you and I don't want you to go away—I want you to stay with me forever."

"I love you, too, Tim," his mother quickly replied. "And I'll be with you for a long, long time, so you don't need to worry about it. Why are you having these thoughts anyway?"

Tim replied, "Because I was watching this movie where the mother got killed in a car accident and the two little kids had to do everything themselves. The mom came back as an angel to try to help them, but they couldn't see her or hear her and they never knew she was there. It made me feel sad."

"I'm sure it did, Timmy-bear," his mother said as she gave him a hug.

"Mom, you promised not to call me that baby name anymore," Tim protested as he squirmed out of her arms.

"No, I promised never to call you Timmy-bear in front of your friends. But I can still use your nickname here at home, especially when you need some extra loving."

"Yeah, but if you keep calling me Timmy-bear here at home, you might *forget and say it in front of my friends and I'd die of embarrassment," Tim concluded—without realizing just how completely his new worry had supplanted the earlier concerns.*

Tim's pattern is typical of the grade school child's pattern of worries—they encompass a wide variety of concerns, are accompanied by only mild anxiety, and are easily relieved by reassurance. The content of Tim's worries is also typical—issues of safety, security, performance (particularly tests and grades in school), and public presentation (appearance, "fitting in," etc.) are common during childhood and adolescence. Worries differ from fears in that they are less intense, they often concern past events as well as possible future occurrences, and they have a "rational" or reality-based nature—for example, a child might worry about how he will perform on a math test for which he's unprepared, but if he had performance fears, he would fear failure even when he knew the material well.

The content of the worries is influenced by the child's developmental stage—younger children tend to worry more about safety and security, while older children focus on issues of school performance and public image. In addition to these developmental differences, there are differences in the extent to which children worry—some children are seen as "not having a care in the world," while others "carry the worries of the world" on their shoulders. Both inborn (temperament) and environmental factors (e.g., stress-related worries) determine a child's place on this spectrum, as is discussed below.

When a Child's Worrying Is "Just a Phase"

"My child has always been a worrier." About one child in ten has a temperament that predisposes him to excessive worrying. From the time that he can talk, the child is fretting about one thing or another. He worries that he's not good enough or smart enough, that it's going to rain or it's not going to rain, that he's caught a chill or he's overheated. There is nothing too trivial for this child to worry about and usually he worries about everything he says, does, and experiences, although occasionally he'll focus his concerns on a particular category of worries, such as his safety or his grades in school. The worried child may be described as "old before his time" because he worries about things that are typically of concern only to adults, such as leaky roofs and having enough money to pay the bills. The worries are always present, but they aren't really a problem for the child because they don't cause distress (in the form of anxiety or dread) or interference (with concentration or activities). If they did, the worries would be classified as generalized anxiety disorder (described in chapter 19), rather than as a part of the child's temperament.

The worried child is also predisposed by temperament to be excessively careful and cautious—he doesn't like to take unnecessary risks. He is uncomfortable with uncertainty and needs extra reassurances about his safety and security. Once he has been reassured, he is able to take on most challenges and risks, unlike the shy or anxious child who remains unable to "take a chance" (as described in chapter 19).

"My sister and her husband recently divorced and now my child is worried that we'll be next." Any stressful situation can cause worrying —an impending divorce, the death of a grandparent, or even starting school in the fall. As adults, many of us can remember feeling anxious each fall as we entered a new classroom and met our new teacher and classmates—these "first day jitters" are a very common trigger for worries, particularly during the middle school years when peer approval is so important. The first day jitters are exaggerated if a child moves to a new town or starts a new school—not only does he have to adjust to a different classroom, but also to new school procedures, a foreign student body, and strange cafeteria food. Children will normally worry about these circumstances for several days or weeks before school starts, and the worries may continue for a few weeks after school has started. To avoid unnecessary worries, the child should be given a chance to familiarize himself with the school and to be introduced to some of his teachers before the first day of school.

"My child is so worried about what his friends think of him." Concerns about peer approval and "fitting in" usually begin in fifth or sixth grade and peak during the middle school years (seventh through ninth grade). During this period, the child is struggling with issues of individuation and turns to his peers for help in establishing his identity. His parents begin to appear to play only a secondary role as he becomes less interested in their opinions and values and more interested in those of his peers. This shift in attention is deceiving. Parents are still playing a primary role in the teen's life—he will continue to seek their approval, and will count on them to set appropriate limits (albeit less restrictive than in previous years) and help him avoid potential disasters. When parents don't fulfill this role, the teen is forced to worry about issues of safety and security, as well as other age-related issues, and may become overwhelmed by his concerns, thereby increasing his risk of developing depression or problems with alcohol or drug use (see chapters 21 and 24, respectively). Even with appropriate parenting, the adolescent period is fraught with worries—the teenager worries about bad hair days, pimples, or having a big nose (as the teen's face matures, his nose grows more quickly than other parts of his face and looks "huge" and out of place for a period of time); about "fitting in" with the crowd and yet "being my own person"; about doing well in school—but not too well; and about his first sexual relationship. Each of these issues is an appropriate cause for concern, but needn't become a focus of worrying if the teen receives appropriate information and reassurance. Thus, continued communication between parent and child is essential and, despite the teen's outward attitude, it is welcomed as a source of comfort.

"My child is so worried about his SAT scores and whether or not he'll be accepted to college." Sometime during his sophomore or junior year of high school, the teenager's attention turns away from concerns about the present to making plans for the future—preparing for graduation, choosing a college or trade school, and deciding who he wants to be and what he wants to do with the rest of his life. Since so many of the variables are unknown and those that are known are outside the teen's control, the adolescent can only worry about their outcome. These worries are normal if they remain focused on specific concerns and do not cause the adolescent distress (in the form of accompanying anxiety) or interfere with his ability to study and socialize. If a teen complains of feeling "stressed out" or he begins to isolate himself by avoiding activities and social interactions, then his worries may be excessive and require special attention.

When Worrying Is More Than "Just a Phase"

Anne had just poured herself a second cup of coffee when her nine-year-old son, Jason, walked into the kitchen and asked, "Mom, do I have to go to school today?"

"Of course, you have to go to school," Anne replied. "You have a math test today."

"I know. But my stomach hurts and I woke up at four-twenty-four this morning and couldn't get back to sleep."

"Four-twenty-four?" Anne asked curiously.

"Yes, precisely four-twenty-four A.M.," Jason replied. "That's two hours and thirty-six minutes before my alarm goes off, but I couldn't go back to sleep because I was so worried about my math test. I know I'm going to do terrible on it. I'll probably get an F."

"Jason, every time you take a test, you worry about failing it, and then you do very well. Why don't you just skip the worrying and do your best?"

"I wish I could," Jason said. "I hate worrying—it makes me feel horrible. But it's not that easy. It's not like I can control it or anything. Worrying is like breathing—you can hold your breath for a couple of minutes, but then it just starts back up again. Worrying is the same way—I can stop for a minute or two and then I start worrying again. In fact, I could probably hold my breath longer than I could go without worrying. Want to time me?"

"No." Anne laughed. "I don't think that would help. But it might help you feel better if we figured out why you're so concerned about this test."

"I'm worried because I might forget how to do fractions," Jason said. "Then, I'll miss all those questions and Mrs. Anderson will think I'm a dummy."

"No, Jason," his mother replied patiently. "You won't forget how to do fractions. And even if you did, Mrs. Anderson wouldn't think you were a dummy—she knows you too well and I'm sure she thinks you're one of the smartest kids in her class. If you fail this test, she'll blame herself, not you. But you're not going to fail—I'm sure you'll do just fine."

"I hope so," Jason said and sat down at the table to eat his breakfast.

When he was finished, his mother drove him to school. As he opened the car door, Anne said, "Good luck on your exam, Jason!"

"Thanks, Mom. But I don't really need any luck," Jason said. "I know I'll do fine on the test—I was just worried that I might fail it."

Anne didn't have a chance to ask her son what he meant before he slammed the car door shut. But as she drove to work, Anne thought about his comment —how could Jason know that he would do well on the test, and yet be so preoccupied with worries that he gave himself a stomachache?

How can worries be so real, and yet have no basis in reality? No one has an explanation, but children recognize this incongruity and complain that their worries "aren't really important, but they still bother me." The observation is quite accurate and reflects the dual components of a worry. Anxiety, the emotional part of a worry, arises from one part of the brain, while thoughts are produced in a separate area of the cerebral cortex. Because the two areas operate independently, the anxiety is often out of proportion to the content of the cognitive thought—the child is "worried about nothing" and can recognize the senselessness of his concerns, but cannot control his feelings of anxiety.

"My child worries constantly—sometimes he worries so much he makes himself sick." Generalized anxiety disorder is characterized by chronic, excessive worrying about the past, the present, and the future (see chapter 19 for a full description). The worries produce distress (anxiety and physical complaints), and also interfere with the child's ability to concentrate or to participate fully in school or social activities—these features distinguish generalized anxiety disorder from normal childhood worrying. Any time a child has physical symptoms, such as headaches or stomachaches, in association with his worries, the worries are excessive. If these symptoms occur only on rare occasions, they are probably not a cause for concern. But if they happen at least once a week or are present for several days in a row, then the worries and physical complaints should be evaluated to make sure that they are not symptoms of generalized anxiety disorder.

"My child worries about being separated from me—even if I just go into the next room." If a child's worries are limited to concerns about being taken away from his parents or about his parents' safety, and they are severe enough to make him anxious, then he may have separation anxiety disorder (described in detail in chapter 18). The child with separation anxiety disorder might appear to be worry-free in the presence of both his parents, but his worries would become more obvious as the distance between himself and his parents increased.

"My child worries about what people will think of him—he won't even eat in a public restaurant because he's so terrified that he might embarrass himself." All children worry about what others think of them, particularly during the middle school years. But when the worries begin to interfere with the child's ability to participate in social activities or to function in a variety of social settings, then the worries are outside the normal range. Excessive worries such as these are the hallmark of social phobia (see chapter 20 for a complete description). Children with social phobia are afraid of being scrutinized by others and worry about becoming the center of attention, so they avoid situations in which people could look at them, laugh at them, or otherwise cause them to be embarrassed. Most children have symptoms only when they are out in public, but others continue to have worries about social interactions even when they are in the safety of their own home. When that happens, the social phobia is more difficult to distinguish from generalized anxiety disorder —the distinction is made by determining whether or not the child has worries in addition to his social concerns.

"My child worries about strange things—like having something sticky on his hands, or catching AIDS from a light switch." When a child's worries are persistent, focused, and/or very specific, he may be exhibiting the irrational fears of a phobia (such as a fear of heights or fear of insects), or he may be having obsessive worries related to obsessive-compulsive disorder. In both OCD and phobias, the child has fears, not worries, and he experiences distress and interference, thus separating these concerns from normal childhood worries. The obsessions and phobic fears also differ from normal worries in their persistence of focus—the content of normal childhood worries varies according to the circumstances of the child's life, but obsessions and phobias remain focused on a specific concern regardless of life events (see chapter 16 for more information).

Helping Your Child Outgrow His Worrying

What You Can Do to Help

Recognize that your child is worrying too much. It is often difficult to identify a child's worries as excessive because they have become such a customary part of the parent-child interaction. To recognize the full extent of your child's worries, it is sometimes necessary to step back from the situation and ask some key questions: Does my child express a large number of concerns or ask for frequent reassurances? Do the worries fall into a particular category or are they about a wide variety of issues? Is he reluctant to try new things or to meet new people? Does he have unwarranted concerns about his grades in school or his ability to get along with his peers? Does he have trouble falling asleep because of worrying? Does he make himself sick with headaches or stomachaches? Is there a likely cause for his worries, such as an overly strict teacher or a recent death in the family? If not, is the worrying new (developmental phase or anxiety disorder) or is it part of a lifelong pattern of behavior (temperament)? If the answers to these questions suggest that your child may have excessive worrying, it is important to check the accuracy of the "diagnosis" with his pediatrician and/or teacher.

Don't dismiss or belittle your child's worries. To avoid damaging your child's self-esteem (and potentially increasing his worries), it is important to treat both your child and his worries with respect. Your child may recognize that his worries are senseless or unwarranted, but they are still a source of real concern to him, so don't belittle their content as "silly" or "crazy." Instead, help him in his efforts to ignore or suppress the worries and focus his efforts on more positive thoughts. Don't tease him about being a "baby" or a "wimp" for having excessive worries, because those names label him (not the worries) as the problem. Don't allow others in the family to tease or belittle him, either.

Provide your child with reassurance—in appropriate amounts. Reassurance is necessary and appropriate for childhood worries. It helps put the concern into perspective, and sometimes eliminates the worry completely. Your child may be able to provide his own reassurance by reasoning through his worry, and, in some instances, your role would be to help him "talk it out" and find his own solution. For example, if your son came to you seeking reassurance that he's tall enough for the basketball team, you might ask him to tell you how he measures up to the other boys in his class, or whether being tall is actually requisite for playing basketball (some guards are quite short in comparison to the centers, but make up for their lack of height with quickness and agility).

If your child can't provide his own reassurance, then you should help him cope with his worry by responding directly to his concern. Don't expand the concern beyond its specific scope by generalizing the problem or recalling similar, previous worries—in the example above, it isn't necessary or helpful to reassure the grade school boy that "not only are you tall enough to play basketball this year, but I bet you'll be tall enough to make the college squad." Your child is unlikely to believe the second half of your statement and since he can't believe your prediction, he becomes less certain about the accuracy of the first half of the statement as well.

Providing the worried child with the right amount of reassurance is essential—too little and he won't be able to confront the stressful situation successfully, too much and he'll worry that his concerns have validity.

Keep your own worries out of the discussion, and to the extent possible, remain emotionally neutral as you discuss your child's concerns. If money is tight, for example, and your child is worried about not getting a birthday present, don't compound his worries by sharing your own concerns about the family's poor finances, but instead let him know that his birthday will be happy because of the special things that you have planned. By responding to his underlying concern and then redirecting the discussion, you can provide him with the necessary reassurance without raising false expectations.

Provide your child with the information he needs to avoid unnecessary worries. Preparation is often the best weapon against worrying. In general, children respond best to stressful situations when they are fully informed—the less that is unknown, the less the child has to worry about. Parents who try to keep an impending divorce a "secret" to spare the child from worrying are rarely successful, since it is impossible to hide the fact that "something's wrong" and the child imagines it as something even worse than divorce. Rather than hiding the problem from the child, it is more helpful to tell him the truth and to provide him with reassurances about his safety and security, as well as a reminder that he is loved by both his parents.

What Your Child's Teacher Can Do to Help

Provide an independent assessment of your child's worries. Your child's teacher is an expert in the spectrum of normal worries and the types of concerns common to the school-age child. Talk to her about the nature of your child's worries. If she tells you that your child's worries are "well within the range of normal," then you can be reassured that the worries are common to children in that developmental stage. If you have seen worries at home that your child's teacher has not observed in school, it may be because your child's worries are limited to issues outside the classroom or because he hides his symptoms while he's in school, but ask her specifically about your child's concerns. Similarly, if your child's teacher has observed that your child is worrying excessively, she should inform you of her concerns and also any stressors within the classroom that could be contributing to the worries.

Prevent unnecessary worries. Your child's teacher can decrease his worries by providing a supportive classroom environment and by decreasing the unknowns in his life. She should establish a predictable classroom routine, avoid "pop" quizzes (unless they have no impact on the final grade), and ensure that each of the students is adequately prepared for tests and oral presentations. If she notices that your child is particularly worried about an upcoming exam or assignment, she should provide him with reassurance about his ability to meet her expectations or suggest ways in which he can be sure that he's fully prepared.

Recognize symptoms of the anxiety disorders. Your child's teacher should be able to distinguish between normal "stage fright" and excessive performance anxiety, as well as recognizing differences between the child who wants to do well and the one who's afraid that he won't be "good enough." Because the anxiety disorders—such as performance anxiety and generalized anxiety disorder—involve every sphere of your child's life, his teacher will probably be aware of his doubts and worries, as well as his excessive need for reassurance. If she suspects that your child has an anxiety disorder, she should inform you immediately of her concerns and be prepared to suggest sources of help within the local community.

What Your Child's Doctor Can Do to Help

Warn you in advance to expect worries during particular developmental phases. Your child's pediatrician can help you prepare for many of your child's worries by providing you with information about upcoming developmental milestones. The doctor should discuss management of separation difficulties and stranger anxiety at the kindergarten checkup; nightmares and school performance in first or second grade; and peer relationships and issues of individuation in fifth or sixth grade. If you are well prepared, you will be better able to help your child handle his worries and prevent them from mushrooming into more difficult problems.

Be aware of the differences between normal worries and anxiety disorders. Your child's doctor should be aware of the difference between normal worries and the symptoms of the anxiety disorders. She should also be familiar with the full spectrum of worrying styles from the most laid back to the most uptight. At each annual checkup, your child's doctor should assess the extent and nature of your child's worries and determine whether or not they fall within the normal range.

Recognize anxiety as a cause of physical ailments. Worried children often have an excessive number of stomachaches, headaches, and other physical symptoms. An astute pediatrician will take note of the frequency of these complaints and be suspicious that they are psychosomatic in origin (psychosomatic means physical symptoms caused by the mind, not "made up" or imaginary symptoms—they are not under the child's control and are every bit as real as strep throat or an ear infection). Once a psychosomatic illness is suspected, the doctor can determine its cause and prescribe appropriate treatments, but if she doesn't consider the possibility, a proper diagnosis cannot be made.

Provide treatment for excessive worries or refer your child to a qualified specialist. If your child's worries are a symptom of an anxiety disorder, his doctor should refer him to a child psychiatrist for evaluation, or recommend treatment with behavior therapy or medications (see chapters 18 through 20). If your child's pediatrician advises treatment, make sure that you understand why she is making the recommendation and what benefits she expects your child to receive. If you're not comfortable with the prescribed course of therapy, ask your child's doctor to help you obtain a second opinion. It is always appropriate for you to seek confirmation of her diagnosis and treatment plan.

Further Reading
See chapter 18.

Hart, Archibald D., Ph.D. *Stress and Your Child: Know the Signs and Prevent the Harm.* Dallas, TX: Word Publishing, 1992.

Jarratt, Claudia Jewett. *Helping Children Cope with Separation and Loss.* Boston, MA: Harvard Common Press, 1994.

Medeiros, Donald D., Barbara J. Porter, and I. David Welch. *Children Under Stress: How to Help with the Everyday Stresses of Childhood.* Englewood Cliffs, NJ: Prentice-Hall, 1983.

Mendler, Allen N., Ph.D. *Smiling at Yourself: Educating Young Children About Stress and Self-Esteem.* Santa Cruz, CA: Network Publications, 1990.

Wilson, Miriam J. Williams, R.N. *Stress Stoppers for Children and Adolescents.* Shepherdstown, WV: Rocky River Publishers, 1987.

9

"My Daughter Is Too Shy"

Shyness and introversion

"Samantha, say hello to Mrs. Gates," her mother prompted.

"Hi," Samantha mumbled as she looked at a spot on the floor near the teacher's feet.

"Hello, Samantha," Mrs. Gates responded. "It's nice to meet you. I'm very glad that you'll be in my class this year. Are you all ready for school?"

Samantha shook her head yes, but didn't say anything, so Mrs. Gates continued, "Do you have your school supplies?"

Samantha nodded her head again, and Mrs. Gates said, "That's terrific. I'm glad that school's about to start, but also kind of sad that summer's almost over. I had such a nice vacation. How about you? Did you take a vacation this summer?"

Samantha once again nodded her head without raising her eyes to look at Mrs. Gates.

"Where did you go, Samantha?" Mrs. Gates asked.

"The beach," her mother answered as Samantha continued to look at the floor. "Samantha and her brother spent half the time in the water and the other half looking for shells. She brought back a huge grocery bag full."

"How lovely!" Mrs. Gates said. "I'd like to see them, Samantha. Maybe you can bring a few of them for show-and-tell next week."

"Okay," said Samantha, almost audibly.

"Good! I'll look forward to it," Mrs. Gates said. "Now, I'd better go meet some of the other students and their parents. Do you have any questions before I go?"

Samantha shook her head no and took a step closer to her mother, who said, "Thank you, Mrs. Gates. It was nice meeting you this afternoon."

"Nice to meet you, too," Mrs. Gates said. "See you next week, Samantha." Samantha looked up and smiled shyly as the teacher turned away.

If Samantha was a first grader, the interaction above would have been well within the range of normal—most five- to seven-year-olds are initially shy with strangers, particularly those in positions of authority, such as a teacher or coach. But if Samantha was entering fifth grade and had been a pupil in the school in previous years, her reticence and her reluctance to make eye contact would be signs of shyness. Shyness, like other childhood behaviors, is defined as much by the child's age and developmental stage as it is by the behavior itself.

When Shyness Is "Just a Phase"

"Lately, my child's been pretty shy around strangers—she warms up once she gets to know you, though." Shyness arises from stranger anxiety, which is a natural consequence of the child's growing attachment to her parents. Stranger anxiety first begins in infancy, peaks at about fifteen months of age, and continues until at least three to four years of age and sometimes longer. When children have stranger anxiety, they are wary of all strangers—both adults and children—and are hesitant not only about meeting their preschool teacher, but also about joining a group of children playing in the park (also see chapter 4). By the time they reach kindergarten, 85 to 90 percent of children have outgrown their stranger anxiety and are no longer shy about interacting with children their own age, but may continue to exhibit shyness with older children and adults. These occasional periods of shyness are likely to continue into adulthood. In a study conducted at Stanford University, only 1 percent of the ten thousand respondents reported "never having been shy," while over 97 percent reported being shy "in certain circumstances," such as starting school or a new job, meeting a VIP, or joining a new club. In some instances, the shyness is related to stranger anxiety; in others, it's a function of the importance of needing to create a good impression or being accepted by the group. The increased shyness seen among junior high school students is usually related to the latter concerns.

"My child has always been shy—I am, too, so I guess she comes by it naturally." Shyness tends to run in families—shy parents have shy (or introverted) children and outgoing parents have extroverted children. It isn't clear whether the family patterns are due to inherited personality traits, modeling (learning by example), or a combination of the two. Research done by Dr. Jerome Kagan and his colleagues at the Harvard Infant Study Center suggests that some children's shyness is inherited as part of a complex set of biological variables—the children are born with a shy temperament. As infants, these children are more fretful and difficult to soothe than other babies, and when they reach toddlerhood, they are more shy and fearful than their peers. In grade school, the children remain quiet and introverted, and tend to be overly cautious at play and in social settings. The 10 to 15 percent of children who are in this shy, anxious group stand in sharp contrast to children at the opposite end of the spectrum, who are characterized as sociable, gregarious, and bold.

Kagan found that the two groups of children could be distinguished not only by their behavior, but also by key biological differences. The first group was described as "behaviorally inhibited" because they avoided new or stressful situations, were reluctant to take risks, and tended to retreat from challenges. They also had unique patterns of biological reactivity— heart rate, blood pressure, and breathing patterns all showed exaggerated responses to simple physical challenges, like going from a sitting to a standing position. When the children were exposed to a stressful situation (such as being left alone in an exam room for a short period of time), their heart rate and blood pressure rose even more dramatically. These changes suggested that the children had an overactive sympathetic nervous system—the system that is responsible for the "fight or flight" reaction. The fight or flight reflex is an automatic, preprogrammed series of biological changes that allow us to respond to danger with increased strength (to fight) and speed (to take flight). The fight or flight reflex was crucial for the survival of our ancient ancestors, but for the behaviorally inhibited child, it represents a source of potential discomfort—a racing heart, agitation or "jumpiness," and increased anxiety. To avoid discomfort, the child avoids stressful situations, such as going new places or meeting new people, and thus she becomes "behaviorally inhibited." For most children, this translates into a shy, reserved temperament, but for some, it means that they are at increased risk for developing an anxiety disorder (such as social phobia, which is described in detail in chapter 20).

"I never thought my child was shy, but her teacher says she didn't say a word until the second week of school." New experiences are always stressful—whether it's the first day of school, the first night at sleep-over camp, or the first practice with a new soccer team. The uncertainty of not knowing whom the child will meet, what he will do, or whether or not it's safe to be in this new place causes tension that increases the activity of the sympathetic nervous system. This sympathetic overactivity is similar to that of the behaviorally inhibited children and the "first-timers" respond to this sympathetic overactivity in much the same way —they become shy and reserved in order to avoid situations that might trigger the fight-or-flight response.

Once the child becomes familiar with her surroundings, her nervous system returns to its normal activity levels and she can resume her usual, unguarded patterns of behavior. For a child entering kindergarten, it often can take a month or more to become completely familiar with the classroom and to feel comfortable with her new routine. During this period, she will exhibit classic symptoms of shyness, including not speaking in public. If the child is still not speaking after being in the classroom for several months, or if she were in second grade rather than kindergarten, then her silence would not be in the normal range.

When Shyness Is More Than "Just a Phase"

Rosemary rushed to the school as soon as the nurse called to tell her that her daughter, Michelle, had fainted in class. When she arrived, she was relieved to find Michelle sitting in a chair, reading a book. "Michelle, how are you feeling? Are you all right?"

"I'm fine, Mom," Michelle said. "I just got dizzy and fainted."

"What happened?" Rosemary asked.

"Well, while I was waiting to give my book report, I started feeling really scared. I didn't want to stand up in front of the kids and make a fool of myself. The more I thought about it, the more scared I got and that made me start to feel sick. You know how much I hate to do book reports and especially when Mrs. Axel is being picky—she told Peter today that he didn't give enough details, and since he always gets A's, I figured I didn't have a chance. Mrs.

Axel would give me another C for 'not talking loud enough and not having good eye contact.' Well, anyway, while Emily was giving her report, my mouth got really dry, and my heart started beating so loud that I thought everyone could hear it. I felt like I had to throw up, too. But before I could ask to go to the bathroom, Mrs. Axel told me that it was my turn. I couldn't ask to be excused then, or everyone would laugh at me, so I just went up front to give my report. My hands were sweating so much that they made my cards wet and that must have taken all the water out of my body, because my mouth got so dry that I couldn't talk. Then, I started getting really dizzy and the next thing I remember is waking up on the floor."

"That's terrible!" her mother said. "How do you feel now?"

"Fine," Michelle said. "I'm not sure how I'll feel when I have to go back to class tomorrow, though. I'm worried that all the kids will laugh at me for being such a wimp."

"Mrs. Axel will make sure that no one laughs at you, so you don't have to worry about that. But I'd feel better if we knew why you fainted, so I'm going to take you over to the emergency clinic and have them check you over."

"Oh, Mom," Michelle whined. "Do we have to go to the clinic? I feel fine now!"

"Yes, Michelle, we have to. Now, put your coat on and get going."

The doctor at the clinic listened to Michelle's account of the fainting episode, checked her heart and lungs, and then took her pulse and blood pressure twice—once when she was lying down and again when she was standing up. "Everything looks fine at this point," he said. "Sometimes, children faint because their blood pressure is too low, especially when they're standing up, but Michelle's is right in the middle of the expected range. Based on what you've told me, I think she fainted from performance anxiety. That's a type of stage fright or social phobia in which the children become so anxious about public speaking that they have an anxiety attack, complete with sweating, dry mouth, nausea, rapid heartbeat, and dizziness. Sometimes, the nervous system becomes so overstimulated that the child even faints. I think that's what happened to Michelle."

"Anxiety attack? Performance anxiety?" Rosemary said. "Michelle, did you feel anxious enough to make you faint?"

"I guess so," Michelle replied. "I hate book reports because they make me so nervous. That's why I said I didn't want to do them anymore. It's not like I'm lazy or something. It's just that every time I have to stand up in front of the class, I feel so scared that it makes me sick. I'm just lucky that I haven't fainted before—or thrown up in front of the whole class."

"Well, now that you have, you can get some help," the doctor said. Turning to Rosemary, he continued, "There are several helpful treatments available for social phobia and performance anxieties. Michelle will need to see a child psychiatrist for an evaluation—I can make the referral, or you can have Michelle's pediatrician recommend someone. All that matters is that she gets started with therapy soon. The sooner she gets treatment, the better her chances of a full recovery."

"We'll start right away, Doctor," Rosemary said. "Thank you! I had no idea that Michelle could get scared enough to make herself faint."

Social phobia is an excessive fear of any social situation in which embarrassment or excessive public scrutiny might occur. Social phobia is related to shyness, but can take many forms, ranging from stage fright or performance anxiety such as Michelle's, to fear of using public rest rooms ("Someone might hear me pee") and fear of eating in public ("I might choke and everyone would be staring at me"). A child might have social phobia about one situation, such as speaking in front of a large group, or about many situations, such as initiating a conversation, participating in a small group discussion, speaking to authority figures, attending parties, dating, and so forth. Obviously, the more situations that are feared, the greater the chances that the child will have problems. Social phobia is diagnosed when the symptoms cause the child distress or interfere with her ability to function. (See chapter 20 for a full description of the diagnosis and treatment of social phobias.)

"My child is so scared about meeting new people, she makes herself sick." If a child dreads meeting new people, or becomes anxious thinking about certain social situations, she's too shy. Similarly, if she's so shy that she feels nauseous or light-headed about a social interaction, her shyness is excessive. Normal shyness is not associated with distress or interference —the child may feel nervous as she meets someone new, but the nervousness doesn't cause any real distress and it passes away quickly. Similarly, normal shyness doesn't limit the child's activities—she may be reluctant to enter the new classroom, but she does it. The excessively shy child, in contrast, is so fearful of the social interaction that she avoids it, even if it means missing a birthday party or a trip to the amusement park with another child's family. If your child is missing out on opportunities for fun because she refuses to try new things or to meet new people, then her shyness is outside the normal range and deserves further attention.

(See chapter 20 for a full description of the symptoms and treatment of excessive shyness.)

"My daughter has always been very quiet around strangers, but now her teacher has noticed that she won't speak in class either." A child who speaks normally at home, and is unable to speak in public, may have selective mutism (see chapter 20 for a detailed description). If a child has selective mutism, she has perfectly normal speech at home, or when only close friends or family members are present, but she is completely mute in public settings—even to the point of being unable to order an ice cream cone or to tell her mother that she needs to use the rest room. For years, it was thought that the children were just stubborn and were refusing to speak, but we now know that a child with selective mutism is unable to speak in public for fear of having someone hear her voice. Research has shown that selective mutism is an anxiety disorder with many similarities to social phobia, including a good response to both medication and behavior therapy.

"My child never really warms up to anyone—she's not even very affectionate with us." Some children are unable to "warm up" to people, even when they have known them for a long period of time. These children might be described as unsociable, rather than shy. They don't appear to enjoy the company of others and are as reluctant about spending time with relatives and family friends as they are about meeting a stranger. The children have a social skills disability that limits their ability to interact with others. Social skills disabilities are similar to learning disabilities in that the child isn't able to process information correctly—in this case, she can't "read" facial expressions and emotional responses properly. The social skills disability is present from birth and will be present throughout the child's life. The child with a social skills disability doesn't make friends because she doesn't know how to build a relationship, she doesn't interact appropriately because she can't learn from previous encounters, and she doesn't reach out to others because she doesn't know that she should. If the disability affects all aspects of the child's social interactions, it is known as pervasive developmental disorder (or PDD). The diagnosis and treatment of PDD is described in detail in chapter 16.

"My child has become so shy and withdrawn, she no longer has any friends." When a child moves to a new town or starts a new school, she may be too shy to make new friends, but normal shyness and social phobia do not interfere with a child's ongoing friendships. The child who is reluctant about meeting new people will often have a narrow circle of friends, but she won't be friendless. Even an adolescent who develops social phobia during junior high school or later won't withdraw from her current friendships, she'll merely have difficulty meeting new people. If a child becomes reclusive when she has previously been socially interactive, it may be a normal stage of development or it may be a symptom of excessive stress, depression, or drug use. (Chapter 10 provides detailed information about social isolation.)

Helping Your Child Outgrow Her Shyness

What You Can Do to Help

Provide her with a variety of opportunities to be sociable. Shyness is overcome by repeated social interactions—even first-time meetings can become less stressful when they are practiced enough to become commonplace. For many children, overcoming shyness is like Dr. Dolittle's "Push Me–Pull You"—it's not enough to be pushed into settings in which they are expected to socialize, they must also be pulled into the interactions through curiosity, interest, or invitation. Provide your child with a variety of opportunities for social interactions—dance lessons, martial arts classes, reading groups at the local library, play groups of various sizes, Sunday-school classes, soccer and other team sports, Scout troops, and others. These activities allow your child to practice her social skills without putting her in the spotlight or requiring her to carry on a conversation with a stranger (the most difficult task for a shy child to master). Hands-on science classes and community service projects (such as picking up trash along the roadside or working in a soup kitchen) are particularly good at building social skills, because they require little conversation and yet require the child to speak frequently: "Please pass me the ————" or "Look at that!" The shy child may want to invite a friend or classmate to accompany her—not only will she be able to model her behavior after the classmate's, but the pair will be more comfortable in facing social interactions together and their relationship will be strengthened as a result of the shared experience.

Help her practice being more outgoing. Encourage your child to take advantage of the opportunities that you have provided. Have her identify one or two goals ahead of time, and help her practice achieving them: "Stephanie, what could you do to make a friend today?" "What will you say when you meet your new coach?" Since shyness decreases as the situation becomes more familiar, it is helpful to practice the interaction ahead of time. Use your family meal to help her practice the art of conversation. Teach her to listen carefully to what the other person is saying, since this will help take the pressure off her. You should also practice introductions at home so that she's well prepared for this important, but intimidating, social ritual. Have her practice saying hello politely and loudly enough to be heard (but not too loud) and make sure that she looks directly at the other person during the meeting. Eye contact is a form of confrontation and is particularly difficult for shy children; once again, practice makes it easier, if not perfect.

Don't force her to be friendly, but don't encourage her shyness, either. It is often hard to tell if your child is refusing to participate in a social encounter because she is unwilling (it's hard or she doesn't want to do it) or she's unable to interact. The key to handling this situation is to expect, rather than to require, your child to successfully engage in the social encounter. If you expect her to be successful, you will provide her with the encouragement she needs, but she won't be forced to participate in an interaction that's too uncomfortable for her. It's important to reduce your level of expectations during times of increased shyness. Your child may become more shy and reserved at times of increased stress, such as when she is the "new kid" in school, or during challenging phases of development, such as junior high school. These occasional retreats help prepare her for future successes and are an expected part of your child's development.

Set a positive example. Most children with excessive shyness have parents who are also shy. If you're uncomfortable meeting new people or speaking in front of others, your child may have picked up on this discomfort and inferred that such situations are inherently dangerous. In order to help her overcome her shyness, you don't need to become an extrovert, but you do need to decrease your level of discomfort with social encounters. Like your child, you will become more comfortable in social settings by taking advantage of new opportunities to increase your social skills and then practicing for success.

What Your Child's Teacher Can Do to Help

Recognize excessive anxiety related to public speaking or social interaction. Teachers have a particular advantage in determining whether or not a child's quietness is really selective mutism or her shyness is social phobia —they see a lot of children of the same age. Draw upon her experience if you have doubts about the "normality" of your child's behavior. If she shares your concerns, then it is time to get help for your child; if she doesn't, then your concerns will be alleviated.

Provide a positive, supportive environment for her students. Your child's teacher should be sensitive to her shyness and should provide her with additional support and encouragement during social interactions. For example, if your child is having trouble making new friends, her teacher might arrange for her to work with a small group of children on a special project, or pair her with the same child repeatedly so that she has a chance to "warm up" enough to pursue the friendship. The teacher should recognize that oral reports are particularly difficult for shy children and must be approached in stages—in first grade, for example, your child might be expected to stand in front of the class and tell her classmates the name of an object that she brought for show-and-tell, but she wouldn't be required to talk about it. As she grows more comfortable with her classmates, she'll be able to tell them a few more facts about her show-and-tell and eventually deliver a three- to five-minute oral report with confidence (if not full comfort).

Provide opportunities for improving social skills. Your child's shyness will decrease once she becomes familiar with a person or situation, so it is helpful for her to practice social interactions until they become second nature to her. For example, if she is to be introduced to the principal or a special adult guest, her teacher should practice the introduction with her ahead of time, so that when the real introduction occurs, she'll already know the procedure. Dealing with only one "stranger" at a time is less likely to trigger excessive shyness.

Teachers can provide a variety of opportunities for children to practice their social skills, including not only meetings and greetings, but also small group discussions, large group discussions, and formal presentations, such as book reports or oral presentations of special projects. These practice sessions are essential, but they are also quite intimidating and your child may not yet be ready to handle the pressure. Alternatives to formal oral reports, such as videotaped presentations, should be permissible, particularly in the primary grades (first through third).

Inform parents about excessive anxiety related to oral presentations.
Because social phobia and selective mutism are both situation-dependent, it is possible for parents to be unaware of their child's disorder. If your child's teacher observes that your child has difficulty with certain social situations, she should check with previous teachers to see if this is a new situation, and then speak to you and your child about her observations.

What Your Child's Doctor Can Do to Help

Provide information and guidance about shy phases. Your child's doctor should be familiar with the times that shyness is expected, such as developmental phases dealing with separation (toddler, preschool, and adolescent years) and periods of major change in your child's life (moving, starting school, etc.). These shy periods are managed more easily when they are anticipated and you are prepared. Discuss your child's developmental shyness with her doctor, including strategies for dealing with it effectively.

Recognize social phobia and related disorders and provide appropriate treatment or referrals. Many children are excessively shy or quiet in the doctor's office—it's a scary place! But an experienced physician will be able to determine whether or not a child has social phobia by his observations and behavioral assessment. If your child has excessive shyness, her physician should provide appropriate treatment or he should refer her to a child psychiatrist for assessment and treatment, as discussed in chapter 20.

Refer patients with selective mutism or social phobia to qualified therapists. Selective mutism and social phobia are not common in childhood, so finding a qualified therapist can be difficult. Your child's doctor should ensure that the therapist he recommends is qualified to treat children and experienced in the treatment of childhood anxiety disorders. Often, your child's doctor will refer her to a child psychiatrist for evaluation and treatment and will depend upon the child psychiatrist to make any additional recommendations needed for behavior therapy.

Further Reading

See chapter 20.

Berent, Jonathan, with Amy Lemley. *Beyond Shyness: How to Conquer Social Anxieties*. New York: Simon & Schuster, 1993.

Golant, Dr. Mitch, with Bob Crane. *It's O.K. to Be Shy! A Parent/Child Manual for the Education of Children*. New York: RGA Publishing Group, 1987.

Zimbardo, Philip G., and Shirley Radl. *The Shy Child: A Parent's Guide to Overcoming and Preventing Shyness from Infancy to Adulthood*. New York: McGraw-Hill Book Co., 1981.

"My Son Won't Have Anything to Do with Me"

Social isolation and withdrawal, particularly during adolescence

"Do you remember the good ol' days when our son Randy used to live here?" Michael asked his wife, Sherry.

"Live here?! What are you talking about? Randy's only fifteen—last time I checked he still lived here," Sherry said.

"No, he just sleeps and eats here. I'm talking about when he was actually part of the family. You know, joined in on the dinner conversations, hung out with us on weekends, even went out in public with us occasionally," Michael said. "But we hardly ever see him anymore. Or at least I don't. He never talks to me. These days, I consider myself lucky to get a 'Bye, Dad' as he runs out the door to be with his friends. He doesn't spend any time with me either. We used to watch football together every Sunday afternoon—I really enjoyed that. I thought Randy did, too, but now he just watches a couple of plays from the doorway, and then goes into his room and shuts the door. One of these days, I might just follow him in there and make him hang out with me for a while—I miss him."

"I know you do, Mike," Sherry replied. "I miss him, too. But I think this is all just part of adolescence. The speaker at the last parents' meeting said that teens are supposed to be reclusive, and that this kind of behavior is perfectly normal. She said teenagers need to 'cut the apron strings' so that they can begin to establish an identity for themselves. They spend less time with their parents, care less about our opinions and more about those of their friends, and they *even become embarrassed to be seen with us in public. It's all part of the process. From what I heard at that meeting, Randy's going easy on us. One woman got up and talked about having to wait for her son three blocks away from the school so that his friends wouldn't see them together."*

Michael laughed and said, "Randy wouldn't dare do that—he knows he'd walk the rest of the way home, too."

"Precisely my point," Sherry replied. "Randy's balancing it the best that he can, so let's cut him some slack. He's a good kid and if this is what he has to do to grow up, then we have to let him do it."

Michael said, "I guess so. This must be the stage your folks warned us about when Randy was eight and we were complaining about his incessant chattering at the dinner table. They said there would come a day when we would have to use a crowbar to pry any conversation out of him."

"I'd forgotten about our son's talkative phase," Sherry said with a smile. "Well, like that one, this too shall pass."

"Hmm," Michael said. "And then what??"

A teen's withdrawal from his family and the family's activities is normal and expected during the adolescent years. The example above is fairly typical for a healthy teenager's relationship with his family—Randy obviously loves and respects his family, so that even as he's separating from them, he remains connected: making sure the Sunday routine hasn't changed by hanging out in the doorway for a few minutes, showing up for family dinners (even if he doesn't actively participate in the conversations), and recognizing that his parents won't tolerate dropping him off some distance from his school. He is safe within the boundaries of the family's limits, which give him the safety and security he needs to test his own limits and become independent from his parents.

When a Child's Isolation Is "Just a Phase"

"My son acts like we're poison and he'll die if he gets too close to us."
One of the first tasks of adolescence is to separate from one's parents. This must be accomplished before the teen can begin to work on his other developmental tasks: to build new and meaningful relationships, seek economic and social stability, and develop a personal value system. The teen separates from his family by isolating himself both psychologically and physically (hence the closed door to his room). He takes on a new name ("Matt" instead of "Matthew"), dresses by a new peer-determined dress code, and speaks a language that is filled with references

to TV shows and popular songs that are appealing only to teens. He will rebel against the family's values and his parents' opinions, as all teens do —the only question being whether or not he'll do it in a safe way (hair style, clothes, music, etc.) or in a way that puts him at risk (alcohol, drugs, staying away from home, unprotected sex, driving dangerously, and others). Since he will value his parents' opinions less as time goes by, anticipating this stage is crucial—rules and limits need to be firmly established *before* the child becomes a rebellious adolescent. Safeguards should also be in place, such as ensuring that the teen knows how to protect himself from danger and how to enlist his parents' help when he needs it (for example, having a "no questions asked" policy for picking him up wherever he is, no matter what he's done, rather than compounding any problems by having him drive while intoxicated or high).

As the teen separates from his parents, he will begin to notice their imperfections and to focus on their shortcomings rather than on their strengths. This is a natural consequence of the separation phase as the teen seeks (unconsciously) to justify his rejection of his parents. He becomes increasingly critical of their appearance and behavior and is embarrassed by their presence. He avoids being seen with them in public, particularly if he'll be interacting with his friends or their parents. (It's ironic to note that while the typical teenager is worrying about his parents embarrassing him in front of his friend's parents, his friend is worried about his own parents being a source of embarrassment!) If the teenager has to be seen with his parents, he'll try to "fix them up" at home beforehand: "Mom, you're not going to wear that ugly purple dress tonight, are you?" or "Dad, when you meet my science teacher, Mr. Huntley, don't tell him that stupid joke about the solar system. It's too lame for someone as smart as Mr. Huntley. Oh, and don't tell your fishing story either—Mr. Huntley thinks fishing is for losers." Mr. Huntley and other adults take on an increasingly important role in the teen's life, as he rejects his parents' views and begins to establish his own values and ideals. He tries out new identities and ideas by modeling adults whom he respects: Mr. Huntley's views on fishing become more important than his father's; his best friend's mother thinks that ketchup belongs only on hamburgers, not on meat loaf or scrambled eggs so he stops putting ketchup on his eggs; and his civics teacher believes that "Candidate X is better than Candidate Y" so the teen prefers Candidate X. He and his friends also share ideas and become near clones of one another. This allows him to see what his new identity looks like and also provides him with a sense of belonging, since he suffers from loneliness during the process of separation and individuation, even though he is the one who is distancing himself.

"My son has always liked his own company best—he's not really shy or antisocial, he just likes being alone." Some children are "aloners." They aren't unlikable or antisocial, so they're not "loners," and they're not lonely, because they're comfortable with their solitude. Their temperament is such that they like being by themselves—they were born to be alone. This is not to say that they don't form meaningful attachments, because they do. Unlike children with autism or pervasive developmental disorders, these children can make friends and are able to show affection to their family members (although they are often more reserved about demonstrating affection than the other children in the family).

The "aloner" makes friends slowly and carefully, but he is able to have meaningful friendships. He will tend to have only one friend at a time, and if the friend moves away, the child might choose to eat alone for several months before forming another friendship. The solitary child chooses his friends carefully, usually looking for someone who shares his interests (books, computers, and the like) and who respects his privacy, since he places such great importance on it. As a teenager, the "aloner" wouldn't understand the need for peer modeling and would be reluctant to change his appearance or behavior in order to fit in with the other adolescents. This, in combination with his reclusiveness, might make adolescence a difficult period for the aloner, depending upon his level of maturity. If he is developmentally advanced, he will be comfortable enough with his identity to enjoy his solitude and use it productively; if not, his isolation could lead to depression. (See chapter 21 for a full description of depression and its symptoms.)

"My son has no friends this year. I don't know what happened—he used to be so popular." Waxing and waning popularity is common in childhood—one year, a child might have a dozen friends (both boys and girls) in his class and the next year he has none. This is the result of the children's developmental differences, varying interests, and changing class assignments—some years the mix is better than others. A child might be slightly behind his classmates in his interests one year, or slightly ahead. Both can contribute to difficulty in making friends in the classroom. Or a boy may have had only girls as friends in first or second grade and finds it has become unacceptable to have "girl friends" when he reaches second or third grade. That year, he may be lacking in friendships. If the child is friendly and sociable, or even if he's shy and reserved but has had previous friendships, his temporary lack of friends is not a cause for concern.

"My son is only happy when he's alone in front of the computer." Nearly every child goes through phases when he withdraws from his family circle in order to pursue a special interest—for example, the child might spend all his spare time shooting baskets as he tries to improve his free-throw shot, or he might develop an all-consuming interest in music and spend hours listening to his stereo or composing his own songs. Surfing the Internet is becoming an increasingly popular solitary activity, and there are concerns about where children should be allowed to go and what they should be allowed to see on the Internet. As with other solitary activities, parents should know what their child is doing when he's spending hours at his computer and why it is holding his interest so completely.

When a Child's Isolation Is More Than "Just a Phase"

"Rose, have you seen Ted?" Pat asked his wife late one Sunday morning.

"Not since last night," Rose replied. "He said he was going to stay with a friend for the weekend. Butch or Jim or something."

"You don't know where he is?" Pat asked.

"No, I don't," Rose snapped. "I'm tired of trying to keep track of him all by myself. You're no help at all. If you're not working late, you're out drinking with your buddies. And then you get up at noon and start ranting and raving about our missing son."

"I'm sorry, Rosie," Pat replied. "I did stay out too late last night, but it's been a long time since I've seen my college buddies. We started drinking and talking, and talking and drinking, and pretty soon they were closing down the bar. I totally lost track of time. I'm sorry."

"It's okay," Rose said tearfully. "I'm not actually upset about your going out, I'm worried about Teddy. He's been home even less than you have this week, and the reason I don't know where he's staying is that he wouldn't tell me last night. He just muttered 'Later' and left."

"That's not like him," Pat said. "He's always been pretty careful to tell us where he was going and who he was going to be with—especially if he was going to be gone overnight."

"I know," Rose answered. "He's changed so much these past couple of months. He won't have anything to do with his sisters or me. He's dressing strangely and acting differently. He even has different friends. I've seen them a couple of times when he brought them over, but I haven't really met them. They went straight to his room and started playing that horrible Marilyn Manson CD. If I didn't know better, I'd think he was on drugs."

"How do you know he isn't?"

"He can't be, Pat. He just can't be taking drugs."

Obviously, Ted could be using drugs. Every child in the United States is at risk for drug use, because drugs are present in every community and are available to every child and adolescent. No child is immune to the temptations of smoking cigarettes, drinking alcohol or using drugs, and nearly every child will try at least one of the three. Since there is no way of knowing who will get "hooked" through this casual experimentation, drug use should always be suspected when an older child's behavior changes for the worse. The dramatic changes in Ted's appearance, behavior, and interests, and particularly his isolation from friends and family, are strong signals that he is using drugs. A complete list of warning signs of drug and alcohol use is provided in chapter 24, which also discusses prevention and intervention strategies. A list of parenting guides is provided at the end of this chapter to help you keep your child sober and drug-free.

"My son is so sullen and withdrawn, he hasn't said more than three words to me in a month." Although teenagers are frequently described as moody and difficult, in truth, they're not—at least, not for very long. Any time a teen has a prolonged period of negativism, whether it's a sullen attitude, or sadness, hostility, or isolation, it is a cause for concern. Irritability and isolation can be the only symptoms of depression in teenagers (especially among boys). Depression is very common in adolescence and should always be considered when a child or adolescent becomes socially isolated. A detailed description of the symptoms and treatment of depression is provided in chapter 21.

"My son is so alone—he's never been able to make friends, but I'm not sure that it bothers him." The child who has never been able to make friends and doesn't show real affection for his parents may have pervasive developmental disorder or PDD. The disorder is a special type of learning disability that prevents the child from learning how to show affection, establish relationships, or communicate effectively. Often, the child with PDD will also have a narrowed range of interests and activities and may appear to be "rigid" or stubborn. There is a broad spectrum of severity within PDD, and some children have very mild deficits (specific social skills disabilities such as not having much empathy) while others have severe impairment in several areas, such as can occur in autism. The symptoms and management of social skills disabilities and PDD are described in chapter 16.

Helping Your Child Outgrow His Isolation

What You Can Do to Help

Provide opportunities for your child to make new friends. School relationships define the majority of friendships, because that's where children spend most of their time. However, if your child's classmates aren't interested or available, then he should be encouraged to look outside his class. For example, one of his friends from the previous year might be in another class but have the same lunch period or recess and the friendship could be renewed in the cafeteria or on the playground. You can also make arrangements for your child to have his friends over after school or on weekends.

Recognize problem behaviors and seek help early. If your child seems to prefer to be alone, observe his interactions with his peers and with family members. If your child seems "cold" or "stiff," he may have a social skills disability. Consult chapter 16 for information on making the diagnosis and obtaining help for his symptoms.

Although adolescence normally is filled with short periods of isolationism, prolonged social isolation is not normal, nor is it normal for a teen to be sullen or hostile. You should expect your teen to want to be alone frequently, but not to be lonely (isolation associated with sadness) or a loner (prolonged periods of isolation). If you're concerned about your child's isolation, talk to him about it. You may also want to speak with his doctor or his teachers to determine whether or not his isolation is a potential problem or if it falls within the expected range.

Prepare for adolescence before your child is a teenager. Adolescents need to separate from their parents and this separation can compromise communication during adolescence, particularly if you aren't comfortable with your child expressing opinions contrary to yours. Lay the groundwork for good communication well in advance of your child's adolescence by showing your willingness to discuss difficult topics and to respect his opinion, even if you don't agree with it.

Start early to protect your child from drugs and alcohol. Education is the best protection against drug and alcohol use, and it must start while your child is in grade school. Not only will he be less receptive to the message when he's a teenager, but he may already have been exposed to cigarettes, alcohol, and other drugs. The references at the end of the chapter provide a variety of methods for educating your child about the dangers of drug use. Read them, choose the method that is most comfortable for you, and discuss this issue with your child soon.

What Your Child's Teacher Can Do to Help

Provide an impartial assessment of your child's social skills. Since your child's major social interactions occur at school, his teacher is often in the best position to judge his social skills. She can also provide you with important information that you can't assess at home, such as: Does he have friends? Does he make friends easily or does he have difficulty "warming up" to other children? Is he more solitary than other children? If so, is it in the normal range (an "aloner") or is she concerned that he's lonely or socially isolated? Has something happened in the classroom that could explain his social isolation? Or is this a pattern that has been present in previous years and is now a cause for concern?

Be aware of the developmental tasks of adolescence and help teens accomplish them. Middle school and senior high school teachers are experts in adolescent behavior, but are sometimes less informed about the developmental tasks of adolescence and put unnecessary pressure on teens. Your child's teachers should be aware of the tasks facing him and help him to achieve the necessary goals, rather than creating situations that make it more difficult for him to grow and develop.

Recognize her status as a role model and behave accordingly. As teens turn away from their parents as role models, they frequently turn toward teachers for guidance and consultation. Your child's teacher can be a great help to him if she takes her role seriously and provides him with both good advice and a positive example to follow.

Make her classroom a drug-free zone. Your child's teacher should help to educate your child about the risks of drug and alcohol use, as well as suggesting ways that he can refuse to experiment with these substances. School systems are becoming increasingly sophisticated in their drug abuse prevention programs, and should now include cigarettes and alcohol on the list of banned substances.

Your child's school should have a "zero-tolerance" policy toward drugs. Prohibitions against possession or exchange of any type of drug are the only way that the school system can prevent drug use and dealing of drugs. There are occasional stories in the media poking fun at the principal who suspends a girl for giving a Midol or a Tylenol to her friend, but that is what zero-tolerance means—clear limits against drug exchange, clear consequences for the infractions, and no exceptions to the rules (otherwise, the students would learn to keep a legal drug in one hand as they pass the illicit substance with the other). In most school systems, the students and their parents have to sign off that they have read the school's drug policy at the beginning of each new school year, so there need be no excuses granted for a student not knowing about the policy.

Recognize signs of drug and alcohol use and intervene appropriately. Teachers have the opportunity to observe their students' behavior over an extended period of time, as well as in comparison with other children of the same age. If your child's behavior changes, his schoolwork deteriorates without explanation, or he begins missing or sleeping through class, his teacher should take note of this and make sure that you are aware of her observations.

If your child seeks help from his teacher for a substance abuse problem, she has an obligation to intervene—usually, by arranging for him to see the school counselor or psychologist. She may also refer him to the youth services division of the community mental health center, or to one of the intervention/treatment programs that are sponsored jointly by the schools and the local police department. In some states, minors are eligible for confidential drug/alcohol treatment. If your child requests that his problem be treated confidentially, his teacher is obligated to maintain his privacy and cannot inform you of his substance abuse problems.

What Your Child's Doctor Can Do to Help

Identify inappropriate isolation and social skills deficits. Your child's doctor should ask about developmental milestones at every visit until the age of five or six years. An important part of this evaluation is an assessment of his social skills development. If your child's doctor notices that he's delayed in these milestones, she should investigate further. The doctor should also be attuned to the verbal and nonverbal communication skills of your child. All children are somewhat shy in the doctor's office, so she will be accustomed to having young children who are reluctant or unwilling to speak. But if the doctor notices that your child doesn't maintain eye contact or make use of nonverbal communication, she should perform a more comprehensive evaluation. In addition, if you have concerns about your child's emotional development, you should point them out to his pediatrician, since the office visit may not provide an opportunity for her to observe that particular area of development.

Provide parents with a road map of adolescence. Your child's pediatrician can help you respond appropriately to your teen's behavior by providing you with information ahead of time about the normal tasks of adolescence. For example, knowing that your child needs to separate in order to establish his own identity will make it easier to understand why he challenges your opinions so frequently, and why he prefers to spend time with his peers, rather than with you. Your child's doctor should tailor her advice to your child's particular developmental course—your teenager may also find it helpful to hear about the developments that he can anticipate.

Maintain confidentiality. Your teenager must begin to take responsibility for his own body and his health and must learn how to do so. His physician may indicate that she wants to speak with him alone, in addition to interviewing the two of you together, and she may perform the physical examination with a nurse, rather than a parent, in the room. She will inform you that the doctor-patient relationship is changing and that she will need to respect your teen's medical privacy—if he tells her something that he doesn't want you to know, she won't tell you, unless it's a life-threatening situation. Because your child's physician also recognizes the importance of the parent-child relationship, she will often help your child to tell you about any troublesome health problems, so you can provide him with the appropriate assistance and support.

Provide complete medical care and teaching. Your child's doctor should begin early to instruct him about the dangers of cigarette smoking, drug use, and underage drinking. Your child can't hear the message too often and, further, the physician may succeed where you cannot, either because she carries the weight of medical authority, or because your child continues to listen to her views for a longer period during adolescence.

Your pediatrician should educate your child about his body throughout childhood and adolescence, but particularly during his late teen years as he prepares to leave home. She should make sure that he knows how to do a testicular self-examination (or breast self-examination for a young woman). She should also teach him the principles of good health— variety in his diet, daily aerobic exercise, six to eight glasses of water (not soda!) each day, seven to eight hours of sleep each night, and avoidance of the four deadly Ss: sun, stress, STDs (sexually transmitted diseases), and substances of abuse (alcohol and drugs).

Recognize cigarette, drug, and alcohol use and provide appropriate treatment. Pediatricians are often just as reluctant as a child's parents are to admit that his physical complaints are related to drugs and alcohol, but the doctor must not deny the possibility of substance abuse. She should be vigilant to the warning signs of alcohol and drug use, and willing to intervene if she finds them. Your child's physician should be aware of the reputations of the local drug and alcohol treatment programs and should help facilitate your child receiving the best treatment for his problem.

Further Reading
See chapter 22 and chapter 24.

Asken, Michael J., Ph.D. *Dying to Win: Preventing Drug Abuse in Sports.* Minneapolis, MN: Community Intervention, 1990.

Domash, Leanne, Ph.D., with Judith Sachs. *"Wanna Be My Friend?": How to Strengthen Your Child's Social Skills.* New York: Hearst Books, 1994.

Levant, Glenn. *Keeping Kids Drug Free: D.A.R.E. Official Parent's Guide.* San Diego, CA: Laurel Glen Publishing, 1993.

Main, Ronald C., Ph.D., and Judy Zervas. *Keep Your Kids Straight: What Parents Need to Know about Drugs and Alcohol.* Blue Ridge Summit, PA: McGraw-Hill, 1991.

Nowicki, Stephen, Jr., Ph.D., and Marshall P. Duke, Ph.D. *Helping the Child Who Doesn't Fit In*. Atlanta, GA: Peachtree Publishers, 1992.

Schwebel, Robert, Ph.D. *Saying NO Is Not Enough: Raising Children Who Make Wise Decisions About Drugs and Alcohol*. New York: Newmarket Press, 1989.

Strasburger, Victor, M.D. *Getting Your Kids to Say "No" in the '90s When You Said "Yes" in the '60s*. New York: Simon & Schuster, 1993.

Wilmes, David J. *Parenting for Prevention: How to Raise a Child to Say No to Alcohol/Drugs*. Minneapolis, MN: Johnson Institute Books, 1988.

"My Daughter Is in Such a Bad Mood These Days"

Excessive moodiness

"What!?!" shouted Clarissa, a fourteen-year-old high school freshman.

"Clarissa, there's no reason to scream at me," her mother, Claire, said. "I simply asked where you were so that I could come talk to you. I'm going out to the store and I wanted to know if you'd like to come along or if you need anything."

"You wouldn't buy it, anyway," Clarissa said.

"What?"

"Lip gloss and eyeliner."

"How can I buy lip gloss for you, Clarissa?" her mother asked.

"See, I told you. You never buy me anything."

"I didn't say that I wouldn't buy it. I asked you how I could buy it. All I meant was that I can't imagine picking out the right lip gloss for you. Why don't you come along with me?"

"Because I don't want to go to the store, I'm tired and Hillary's supposed to call in a little while. Besides, I've got homework to do."

"I thought you did your homework as soon as you got home from school. When you were watching MTV and I asked you about it, you said it was all done."

"So I lied, so sue me," Clarissa said with annoyance.

"Clarissa! That comment was uncalled-for and rude. Certainly not something I'd expect to hear from someone who wants me to do her a favor," Claire said with increasing impatience.

"I'm sorry, Mom," Clarissa replied. "Will you get me the eyeliner, please?"

"Clarissa, I don't think I can pick that out either. Why don't you just get it this weekend?"

"Because I want to wear it tomorrow night to Steffie's party."

"You're not going to Stephanie's party, Clarissa. We discussed this yesterday. Her parents aren't going to be home, so you can't go to the party."

Clarissa whined, "But I've got to go. Everybody's going to be there."

Claire was tempted to say, "Well, if everyone was jumping off a bridge, would you jump too?" but she settled for "No, Clarissa. Not without proper chaperones there."

When she realized her mother wasn't going to change her mind, Clarissa changed from a whining child to an enraged harpy and hissed, "I hate you! You're old-fashioned and mean and I hate you for ruining my life."

"Clarissa, you are not to speak to me that way. Go to your room."

"You can't send me to my room."

"I certainly can. You're being rude and I won't tolerate it. And if you continue to talk back to me, you'll be grounded for the next two weeks."

"Who cares?" Clarissa snapped back. "I can't go to Stephanie's party anyway."

Claire responded with equal annoyance, "Not just grounded for going out—you'll lose telephone and TV privileges, too. If you don't want to spend the next two weeks totally grounded, I'd advise you to go to your room right this minute and be ready to apologize when I get back from the store."

Clarissa stomped up the stairs, muttering under her breath.

As Claire listened to Clarissa slam her door shut, she murmured, "Lord, give me strength. Strength and patience enough to get through the next few years."

Adolescence is often a difficult time for parents—and for their teenagers. Teens face a series of demanding physical and psychological challenges—hands and feet that are too big, bodies that are constantly changing, a never-ending barrage of developmental tasks, and unexplained moodiness. The fact that mood swings are normally increased during adolescence doesn't make it any easier for parents to tolerate their teen's ill humor when it occurs. The adolescent's parents must help her learn how to handle her bad moods in a socially acceptable manner, since the adolescent must master this task before moving on to the next one—establishing an intimate relationship. In order to mature, the teen must be taught to express her anger and frustration, not by pouting or throwing a temper tantrum, but in a way that allows for discussion and compromise. For example, it would have been acceptable for Clarissa to say, "Mom, I really wanted to go to Stephanie's party and I'm mad that you won't let me go." Then, Claire could have responded, "I know you're disappointed, but unchaperoned parties are dangerous and I'm not going to change my mind about Stephanie's party. You said that your friends were all going to see a movie first—why don't you go with them and then come home instead of going on to the party?"

The other lesson in adolescent mood swings is that a normal teen's moods always swing back to normal. Although it may seem as if the teenager is "always" in a bad mood, in reality, she isn't. Most of the time, she is fairly happy and is pleasant company. She's more "prickly" than she was during childhood, but, otherwise, she's the same person that she was at ages ten to twelve. If not, her moodiness is outside the normal range.

When Bad Moods Are "Just a Phase"

"My child is so sensitive, the slightest thing can put her in a bad mood." Just as temperament defines sociability and activity levels, it also can define a child's moods and reactions—responses fall along a spectrum between carefree and sober, happy and somber, and impervious to criticism or easily insulted. If the child has a temperament that makes her sensitive to criticism, she might be in a bad mood more frequently than other children because she's always responding to some perceived insult or slight. If she is pessimistic by temperament, she views the world through dark-colored lenses and her negative moods are a reflection of this perspective. Temperamental traits cannot be changed, but their negative impact can be minimized, as discussed in the help section at the end of this chapter.

"My child has been so moody ever since my mother died." Children, like adults, must go through a period of bereavement or grieving whenever they suffer a loss. Unlike adults, they don't always know the right words to say to express their grief and they don't always act as if they're grieving—they may be irritable and cranky, rather than sad, and do impulsive or naughty things, rather than crying or being sober. Adolescents may also react to losses in socially unacceptable ways—appearing not to care when a loved one dies or saying that they're "glad" the person is gone. The teens are not callous and unfeeling, they're just confused by the mixed emotions they feel and tend to speak more openly about their anger and denial than do adults. It is not unusual for a teen to publicly declare that she's glad her grandmother died because "she was so old and cranky" but then to weep for hours in the privacy of her own room.

"My teenager is so irritable and moody that I'm not sure we'll both survive her adolescence." Adolescents are universally described as moody and difficult, but it's unclear whether or not they deserve this reputation. Studies done by Dr. Daniel Offer at the University of Chicago found that the normal teenager actually has very mild mood swings. She tends to be positive about life, generally happy, and willing to try new things. This is not the picture, however, that her parents have of her. They see the teenager as more unhappy and negative than she was as a child. The discrepancy appears to lie in the difference between how the teen perceives herself and what she portrays to those around her. The healthy teen portrays a negative self-image because she is experiencing mood swings that she can't predict and can't understand. She experiences disappointment more keenly and so she has more frequent (and more intense) periods of unhappiness than she did when she was a child, but these periods are short-lived and do *not* take up the majority of her time. When she does have a bad mood, it shouldn't last more than a day or two. If her bad moods persist for several days or longer, she may be suffering from depression. (See chapter 21 for a full description of the symptoms and treatment of depression.)

"My daughter has PMS-like mood swings—they seem to come more than once a month, though." Hormones are clearly associated with mood changes. Thyroid dysfunction is a well-known cause of depression, testosterone is a factor in increased aggressiveness, and studies have finally proven what has long been suspected—that estrogen and progesterone both have a profound effect on mood stability. During adolescence, these hormones are all in a constant state of flux. Unlike adult males, adolescent boys don't have a predictable cycle of testosterone release—their testosterone levels can spike at any time. Adolescent girls have a similarly chaotic picture and it is not uncommon for them to have "PMS" several times each month until their female hormones are driven into a predictable cycle by the onset of ovulation (this usually occurs one to two years after the girl's first period). True premenstrual syndrome is rare in adolescence, however, because the teen's cycles aren't well-enough established to provide the cyclic hormone changes that cause the PMS symptoms.

Although hormone surges can help explain an adolescent's excessive moodiness, they are not an explanation for out-of-control behavior or persistent bad moods. The normal pattern is for the teen to be happy much of the time but to have a more sensitive trigger to her anger and sadness than she did during childhood. For example, a healthy teen might get angry at her parent and storm out of the room, slamming the door as she leaves, but, an hour or so later, she returns contrite and apologetic, or she resumes her usual interactions with her parent as if nothing had happened. The troubled teen would get angry with her parent and leave the room in sullen silence or with shouts of "I hate you," and would not return. She might lock herself in her room for the whole evening and leave for school the next morning without speaking to her parent, or she might storm out of the house and go to a friend's house for the night, without telling her parent where she's staying. Excessive anger or persistent sadness are not normal and must receive attention since they are signals of, among other things, depression (chapter 21), sleep problems (chapter 22), and drug or alcohol use (chapter 24).

"My teenager never gets enough sleep. It's no wonder she's so irritable all the time." Many teens suffer from "adolescent insomnia" as a result of having too little time for sleeping when they're sleepy. Teens need eight to nine hours of sleep each night, but their sleep clock is delayed, so they don't get sleepy until 11:00 P.M. or later. Most junior and senior high schools start dreadfully early to accommodate school bus schedules or after-school activities, and the teen must get up at 5:30 or 6:00 A.M. to arrive at school on time. Therefore, to get the eight or nine hours of sleep she requires, she would need to be asleep by 9:00 P.M., but she can't fall asleep until after midnight and so she accumulates three hours of sleep debt each school night. To make up for the missing sleep hours, she might sleep all day Saturday and/or Sunday, but if this isn't possible, her sleep debt continues to grow. Chronic sleep deprivation is "normal" in adolescence only because most teens have it. It is not healthy and is associated with symptoms such as fatigue, sleepiness, decreased attention span, and feeling "hungover" or "jet-lagged" during the day. Irritability and excessive moodiness are also common. Correcting the sleep debt and restoring sleep balance can eliminate these symptoms, as described in chapter 22.

When Bad Moods Are More Than "Just a Phase"

"That's it, Leo! We're through—I never want to see you again," Jennifer shouted through her tears, as she slammed the telephone receiver down and ran to her room.

Her mother, Dolores, waited a few minutes before following her down the hallway and calling through the door, "Jennifer? Are you okay, honey?"

"Go away!" Jennifer replied. "I don't want to talk to you."

"Are you sure?" her mother asked. "Sometimes it helps to talk things over."

"Not this time," Jennifer said. "Nothing you can say or do will help."

"It can't be that bad, honey," Dolores said. "I'm sure I can help if you'll just talk to me about it. But if you'd rather not discuss it right now, that's okay. I'll be in the kitchen if you change your mind and want to talk."

As Dolores resumed her dinner preparations, she thought about how much her fifteen-year-old daughter had changed over the past few weeks. Jennifer was no longer the fun-loving, easygoing girl she had been when school had started in the fall. She had dropped out of most of her after-school activities, including quitting the swim team even though she had worked so hard to earn a place on the varsity squad. She had dropped many of her friendships, too. Her boyfriend, Leo, had been the last holdout and Dolores suspected that Jennifer had started the fight today so that she would have an excuse to break up with him. She had done the same thing with her best friend, Allison, earlier in the week. Jennifer just didn't want to spend the energy to have a relationship these days. She was so moody, too. One day she was up and the next she was down—only lately, the down days were stringing together for weeks at a time. The more Dolores thought about it, the more she realized that Jennifer hadn't seemed happy for over a month.

"My child is so depressed." Depression is a very common problem among adolescents. Some studies have shown that as many as one in ten teenage girls and about one in twenty teenage boys are suffering from depression. The symptoms can mimic normal adolescent moodiness, except that they are much more intense and prolonged. If a teenager has persistent black moods, she is sad more often than she is happy, or she is excessively tearful, she may be depressed. Chapter 21 provides a detailed description of the symptoms of depression, as well as information about the latest treatments for this common condition.

"My child is grumpy as a bear all winter—she doesn't snap out of it until the middle of March." Seasonal affective disorder, or winter blues, can occur in children, although it doesn't become a common problem until adolescence, when about one in twenty teens will have symptoms of irritability, increased appetite (especially for carbohydrates and sweets), weight gain, difficulty concentrating, and school failure. Winter blues is described in chapter 22 with the sleep disorders because one of its primary symptoms is excessive fatigue and increased sleepiness.

"My child's bad mood lasts for weeks, and then suddenly she'll be higher than a kite." Bipolar disorder (manic-depressive disorder) is a psychiatric illness that is characterized by periods of depression and periods of euphoria (excessively happy or expansive mood) or irritability (see chapter 21). The major features that distinguish this disorder from normal adolescent mood swings are the duration (length of time that the symptoms last) and the degree of impairment. Normal mood swings shouldn't cause any interference for the teen, while the excessive mood swings seen in bipolar disorder impair her school performance, or interfere with social relationships and activities at home. The bad moods also last longer than just a few hours if the teen is suffering from depression or bipolar disorder —the increased irritability or sadness and tearfulness may persist for several days in a row, at least, and often for weeks at a time if the condition is not treated.

"My child bites my head off whenever she's worried about something —she acts like it's my fault that she has a math test in the morning." Children who get moody when they are confronted with a difficult situation, such as taking a test or staying alone at night, may actually be exhibiting symptoms of an anxiety disorder, rather than depression. The anxious child might become irritable and snappish as her tension increases, or she might become isolated and withdrawn as she tries to calm her anxieties. If the moodiness is coming from an anxiety disorder, the child will have additional symptoms—such as excessive worrying, difficulty separating from her parents, or obsessive concerns about contamination. Obsessive-compulsive disorder is discussed in chapter 16 and the other anxiety disorders are described in detail in chapters 18 through 20.

"My child has such unpredictable mood swings—on weekends, she acts like a complete stranger." Alcohol abuse and drug use are major causes of excessive adolescent moodiness. Both substances can turn a happy, easygoing child into one who is excessively moody and unusually "touchy" or volatile. Drugs and alcohol can also cause dramatic personality changes, as well as social isolation. Any time an older child or teenager has a sudden deterioration in her behavior, parents should suspect a problem with drugs and/or alcohol. A complete description is provided in chapter 24.

Helping Your Child Outgrow Her Moodiness

What You Can Do to Help

Patience, tolerance, and a positive attitude. Normal adolescent mood swings require both patience and tolerance. You must be patient with the teen's moody phases, because they may last for several years, and tolerant of her new rebelliousness, because she will learn to handle her bad moods appropriately only if you allow her to discover acceptable ways to express herself. Discussions, negotiations, and efforts at compromise should be encouraged, while inappropriate responses (such as pouting and whining) should be ignored, and unacceptable behavior (such as rude or mean-spirited remarks and aggressive outbursts) should be discouraged by establishing consequences for the behavior, such as removal of a privilege. (See chapter 3 for more information about management of inappropriate behaviors.)

In addition to being patient with your teen, you must also help her to learn to be patient and tolerant with herself. She will have periods when she doesn't like herself very much. She may recognize that her behavior is unreasonable or her mood swings are excessive, but won't know how to control them. She needs help in moderating her emotional responses and modulating her behavior. This is possible only when she's taught to be patient and tolerant.

A positive attitude can help both of you get through adolescence more easily. When your child is being negative about herself or her situation, help her to reframe the circumstances in a positive way. This is a form of cognitive-behavior therapy (CBT), a technique that has been found useful not only for the treatment of depression, but also for preventing negative thoughts (see chapter 12 for a full description of CBT). Cognitive-behavior therapy appears to work by changing the child's response patterns from negative to positive ones—consistent reinforcement of positive thoughts and reframing of negative thoughts increase positive thinking and decrease depressive responses.

The three Ls—love, limits, and large muscle exercise. Your adolescent child needs the three Ls just as much as she did when she was a toddler.

Love. Your love must be given freely and without conditions. Your teenager may act in unloving and unlovable ways, particularly when she is dealing simultaneously with excessive mood swings and separation issues; her unacceptable behavior can be rejected, but your teenager should never be. When she acts in unloving ways, it is because she feels bad about herself, and you must convince her, by words and deeds, that she is worthy of your love. If she screams, "I hate you," it may be tempting to scream back, "Well, I hate you, too!" But you mustn't. As her parent, you must stay in control and avoid saying things that will hurt her. Words spoken in anger by a parent are often internalized by the teen, because she doesn't yet have the maturity to separate meaning from content. If you say you hate her, she will feel the rejection, even if she is able to understand that you only said the words because you were angry.

Limits. Your teen's moodiness must be tolerated because it is not within her voluntary control, but her response to the bad moods can be controlled and she should be expected to minimize its impact on others. It is important to set clear limits, defining both acceptable and unacceptable ways of expressing anger and disappointment, and then to adhere to these rules consistently. For example, if your child is feeling irritable, she can excuse herself and go to her room until she feels better, but she cannot scream at her younger brother, turn off his favorite TV program, and play the stereo at top volume so that she can "calm down by listening to my favorite song."

Limits on behavior are also important during adolescence. Teenagers are more likely to go "astray" when their parents aren't consistent about enforcing family rules. Inconsistencies send mixed messages to the teenager and encourage her to behave inappropriately in the hope that this will be one of those times when her parents "forget about the rules." For example, if a teen's parents establish consequences for whining, such as not letting her go to the movies if she asks inappropriately, but then give in and buy her a phone after she whines about it for a month, she's only learned to be very persistent about her whining.

Large muscle exercise. It may surprise you to learn that large muscle exercise is still necessary for your teen, but it is actually more important during adolescence than at any time since your child was a toddler. Large muscle exercise, such as running, playing ball, swimming, or other aerobic exercise, will increase the amount of endorphins ("feel good" hormones) that are present in the brain. As the level of endorphins increases, the adolescent feels better both physically and psychologically—an exercise "high." With regular exercise, this improvement in psychological outlook can persist for several hours and helps to prevent the development of negative moods.

The three Rs—respect for you, respect for herself, and responsibility for her actions. Self-respect and respect for others are the hallmarks of successful teenagers. Although self-respect can't be taught, it can be increased through encouragement and decreased through discouragement (contrary to popular folklore, self-respect is an inherent property of children and cannot be created—teachers can help children recognize its worth, but cannot bring it into existence). It is just as important for you to encourage your child's positive self-image and discourage any inappropriate negative self-assessment as it is to help her create a positive outlook on life.

The teen also needs to be taught to take responsibility for her actions. If she destroys property, she must replace it or repair it. If she hurts someone, she must make amends. If she insults you or someone else, she must apologize. Learning to say that she's sorry is a very important task of adolescence. If your teen doesn't learn to apologize (and to accept apologies from others), she won't be able to sustain a long-term, intimate relationship.

What Your Child's Teacher Can Do to Help

Provide a basis for comparison. Your child's teachers can serve as unbiased observers of your child's behavior and can help determine whether or not the mood swings are problematic. In addition, her teachers can provide valuable information about the impact of her moodiness— whether or not it interferes with her school performance or her ability to interact with her peers.

Eliminate unnecessary school pressure. Teachers should be encouraged to view their students positively in order to help the students view themselves that way. Adolescence is not an appropriate time for teaching through negative reinforcement. Teachers should avoid creating situations in which their teenage students will fail, such as creating a pop quiz as a punishment for the class being unprepared with an assignment, or failing half the class on a midterm because they didn't follow directions precisely. Teens learn best through repetition and positive reinforcement, and your child's teachers should recognize this.

Notify parents when problems are observed. If your child's teacher observes that she has more than one or two days in which she is apathetic about her schoolwork, isolated from her peers, or overly sensitive to criticism, she should let you know, so that you can ensure that she gets help promptly if she's suffering from depression or anxiety.

What Your Child's Doctor Can Do to Help

Help you to anticipate adolescent mood swings. Your child's physician should help you anticipate the problems that you'll face during adolescence and help you lay the groundwork for dealing with them. He should ensure that you are familiar with the developmental tasks of adolescence and their impact on your teen's behavior well before your child enters her teenage years.

Recognize problems with excessive moodiness. You may have difficulty deciding whether or not your child's mood swings are excessive. Because of his experience and training, your child's doctor should be able to provide an independent, unbiased assessment about the "normality" of your child's moodiness and, if the mood swings are excessive, to determine their cause.

Provide appropriate treatment or referrals for excessive mood swings. If your child's moodiness is excessive, her pediatrician should help to determine the cause and suggest possible remedies, including the possibility of changing the approach you are taking to parent your teen. If the moodiness is a symptom of depression or an anxiety disorder, the doctor should be prepared to treat the disorder or offer referrals to appropriate therapists.

Further Reading
See chapter 21 and chapter 24.

Seligman, Martin P., Ph.D., with Karen Reivich, Lisa Jaycox, Ph.D., and Jane Gillham, Ph.D. *The Optimistic Child: A Revolutionary Program That Safeguards Children Against Depression and Builds Lifelong Resistance*. Boston, MA: Houghton Mifflin, 1995.

Adolescence

Craig, Judi, Ph.D. *"You're Grounded Till You're Thirty!" What Works and What Doesn't in Parenting Today's Teens*. New York: Hearst Books, 1996.

Dinkmeyer, Don, and Gary D. McKay. *Parenting Teenagers: STEP— Systematic Training for Effective Parenting of Teens*. Circle Pines, MN: American Guidance Service, 1990.

Elkind, David, Ph.D. *Parenting Your Teenager*. New York: Ballantine Books, 1993.

Fleming, Don, Ph.D., with Laurel J. Schmidt. *How to Stop the Battle with Your Teenager: A Practical Guide to Solving Everyday Problems*. New York: Prentice Hall, 1989.

Giannetti, Charlene C., and Margaret Sagarese. *The Roller-Coaster Years: Raising Your Child Through the Maddening but Magical Middle School Years*. New York: Broadway Books, 1997.

Phelan, Thomas W., Ph.D. *Surviving Your Adolescents: How to Manage and Let Go of Your 13–18 Year Olds*. Glen Ellyn, IL: Child Management, Inc., 1993.

Wolf, Anthony E., Ph.D. *Get Out of My Life (But First Could You Drive Me and Cheryl to the Mall?): A Parent's Guide to the New Teenager*. New York: Noonday Press, 1991.

Girls' Special Needs

Gadeberg, Jeanette. *Raising Strong Daughters*. Minneapolis, MN: Fairview Press, 1995.

Pipher, Mary, Ph.D. *Reviving Ophelia: Saving the Selves of Adolescent Girls*. New York: Ballantine Books, 1994.

Part II

Problems That Are More Than "Just a Phase"

"I'm So Worried About My Child's Behavior—This Can't Be 'Just a Phase'"

Introduction to part II

"He's fine, dear," Tom said to his wife, Diane.

"No, Tom, he's not," Diane whispered through her tears. "Brian's not fine. There's something wrong with him. I just know it. You're not home with him all the time, but I am and I'm telling you—there's something that's just not right!"

"You're obviously upset about this and we need to talk, but not here. I don't want the kids to hear us," Tom said as he put his arm around his wife and led her to the privacy of their bedroom.

"What's bothering me is that you don't see any of this!" Diane blurted out as soon as the door was closed. "How can you be so blind? Brian's not 'fine.' He's not happy. He doesn't talk to us, he doesn't spend any time with his friends or his brothers anymore, and he has no interests other than his computer games."

"Lots of kids are into computers," Tom said. "I'm sure it's just a phase— he'll grow out of it soon."

"I don't think so, Tom," Diane said. "This has been going on too long for it to be 'just a phase.' Besides, it's getting worse. Just today, Brian's teacher sent a note home saying that he was failing social studies. Our brilliant Brian— failing a class!?! It's just not like him."

"Maybe you're right," Tom said thoughtfully. "Maybe it _is_ more than just a phase. But if it is, what do we do?"

Is it "just a phase" or something more serious? Can we ignore it and wait for it to go away, or should we do something? If we should intervene, what do we do and whom can we turn to for help? As parents, we struggle to answer these questions correctly, worrying that if we don't find the right answers, we will have missed an opportunity to help our child recover from his problems. However, the thought of our child having any illness, particularly a psychiatric disorder, is so troublesome that we try to ignore the possibility and blame the behavior on a "passing phase," as Tom did, in the hopes that the phase will disappear as mysteriously as it came and leave no trace of its passing. In truth, however, psychiatric disorders are quite common and are frequently found to be the cause of a child's behavior problems. Community-based surveys have shown that anxiety disorders affect 13 percent of children ages nine through seventeen (one child in eight), depression about 6 percent (one in fifteen), and attention deficit hyperactivity disorder about 5 percent (one in twenty). Some children have more than one disorder, so the total number of children affected is less than if each of the figures were added together, but childhood psychiatric disorders still affect about one child out of five (21 percent). They occur so commonly that they must be considered whenever a child's behavior falls outside the expected range of development—whenever the problems are more than "just a phase."

It's More Than "Just a Phase," But Is It a Psychiatric Disorder?

Psychiatric disorders are separated from problem phases by three distinguishing features: duration, difficulties, and distress. *Duration* is the amount of time that the symptoms are present—both in terms of the number of days or weeks that the symptoms persist and also the amount of time each day that the child has difficulties. In a phase, the troublesome behavior is generally present only a small proportion of the time, while symptoms of psychiatric disorders are more persistent and occupy the majority of the child's waking hours. For example, if a child seems anxious about going to school each morning, but she doesn't exhibit anxiety about it in the afternoon or evening, her anxiety is probably just a phase, which will resolve after a month or two. On the other hand, if she's preoccupied with her worries about school even when she's home, and her anxieties show no sign of lessening after the first month, they are more likely to be symptoms of an anxiety disorder. The disorders vary in the length of time that is required to meet the severity criteria for diagnosis—depression is diagnosed after two weeks of persistent sad moods, while generalized anxiety disorder is diagnosed only after six months of continuous symptoms. Obviously, however, if your child is having problems with anxiety, you wouldn't wait six months to seek help. Chapters 13 through 24 describe the duration criteria for each disorder, as defined in the American Psychiatric Association's *Diagnostic and Statistical Manual* (also known as *DSM-IV*).

The second severity measure is *difficulties*, an assessment of how much the child's symptoms get in his way—do they keep him from doing things that he likes to do, accomplishing tasks that he needs to accomplish, or fulfilling his obligations at home or at school? Difficulties, like distress, are defined from the child's perspective, but they usually are identified by the parent's observations or those of his teacher or physician. For example, a child might not see that his poor school grades and frequent reprimands are a result of his hyperactivity and impulsivity. Sometimes, even his parents can become "blind" to the symptoms because they have been present so long or started so subtly. This is particularly common with anxiety disorders. It can be hard to detect the difference between a child's anxious temperament and the onset of worries that are causing him to lose sleep or to do poorly in school. Difficulties can also be hard to detect because of the child's inherent strengths and coping skills—for example, the child may be so smart that he gets all A's on his report card, even though he has to study twice as hard as the next child because of a hidden learning disability. When considering whether or not a child is impaired by his symptoms, his unique strengths must be considered—the question is whether the child is performing at expected levels for his capabilities and not is he doing "average" work (as described in chapters 13 and 14 in the discussions about attention deficit disorder and learning disabilities).

If your child's behavior problem is persistent, bothers him in some way, or is interfering with his ability to function at home, at school, or with his peers, then it is worthy of attention. The chapters in the next section of the book describe specific examples of problem behaviors and provide checklists for determining whether or not your child might meet diagnostic criteria for a specific disorder. The chapters also provide information about behavior problems that don't meet diagnostic criteria for a particular psychiatric disorder, but still require intervention. Whichever pattern is a closer fit to your child's behavior, it is important to know that:

• The symptoms are real. They are not your fault, nor are they your child's fault. They are symptoms of a medical illness, just as wheezing and shortness of breath are symptoms of the medical illness asthma.

• The symptoms are recognizable. Sometimes, however, they are subtle enough to go unnoticed unless the child's parents specifically look for them. Observations by the child's teacher or physician can also be very helpful in bringing the problem to proper attention.

• The symptoms are treatable. Medications and psychotherapies provide relief to the majority of children who suffer from psychiatric illnesses. In some disorders, the symptoms are nearly gone following successful treatment, while in others, they are reduced to a more manageable level.

It's More Than "Just a Phase," So Now What Do We Do?

As soon as it is clear that your child's problems are more than "just a phase" and may be symptoms of a psychiatric disorder, your question changes from "What is going on?" to "How do I help him?" That question is accompanied by even more questions demanding immediate answers: What treatments are available and appropriate to my child's condition? Who can provide the therapy? Which treatment works best? Are there side effects? What can I do at home to help my child get better? The answers to these questions vary among the different disorders, so each chapter in the second part of the book provides specific guidelines for treatment, and also suggests ways in which you can help your child cope with his disorder. In order to avoid redundancies, we will present a general description of the most commonly used treatments here, and limit the individual chapters' discussions to those aspects of therapy that are unique to the disorder.

Psychological Treatments

The psychological therapies useful for the treatment of children's psychiatric disorders include psychotherapy, behavior therapy, and cognitive-behavior therapy. *Psychotherapy* includes not only traditional psychodynamic therapy or "talk therapy," but also play therapy, art therapy, family therapy, and group therapy. In each of these, the therapist's goal is to help the child identify the similarities in the problems he's experiencing and to understand why they occur. When the child has identified the cause of his negative responses, he is able to modify his behavior and respond in a more positive manner. For example, if a teenager saw himself as socially isolated, the therapist might help him identify missed opportunities for establishing relationships and then look for a common theme in the interactions—what is it that caused him to withdraw? What can he do to prevent similar situations in the future? What changes can he make in his behavior to improve his social relationships? By answering these questions with the guidance of the therapist, the teen changes his response pattern to one that encourages, rather than discourages, friendships. Psychotherapy is used as a primary treatment for mild depression and for several anxiety disorders, and is also useful as an "adjunctive" or helping therapy in disorders in which medication and/or behavior therapy is the primary treatment, but there are psychological issues to be addressed.

Family therapy is used frequently as an adjunctive therapy. In family therapy, the child and his parents attend the therapy sessions together. Sometimes, the child's siblings are included and at other times they are not. Most family therapy sessions are aimed at improving family communication and finding ways for the family to work together to solve their problems. Because childhood psychiatric disorders aren't caused by family problems, they can't be improved by family therapy, so it's never used as a primary treatment. However, it can play an important role in helping the child to recover from his disorder—for example, by reducing stress within the family, which had been aggravating his symptoms or impeding his recovery. Family therapy is used most frequently in the treatment of eating disorders, such as anorexia and bulimia, because these disorders are particularly vulnerable to family-related stresses.

Group therapy is useful as an adjunctive treatment for adolescents. Teenagers tend to respond better to solutions offered by their peers than they do to those suggested by an adult, so the therapist works "behind the scenes" (by asking questions or calling on a particular person within the group) to help the group find their own solutions to common problems. For example, a teenager in a drug abuse treatment program might participate in a number of group therapy sessions focusing on avoiding future drug use. Not only would he benefit from hearing new ideas about ways that he can enjoy life while staying sober, but he would also receive feedback on his own ideas, which would reinforce his new, positive viewpoint. Mixed groups, in which adolescents are included who have a variety of psychiatric anxiety disorders, depression, or illnesses, such as

ADHD, are also useful, since many of the issues requiring attention are common to all teenagers, regardless of diagnosis.

Behavior therapy can be used as a primary treatment for a number of childhood psychiatric disorders, including separation anxiety disorder and obsessive-compulsive disorder. The advantages of behavior therapy are obvious: no unpleasant drug side effects, the possibility of long-term symptom control without continued medication use, and, in a few instances, complete symptom resolution. Behavior therapy is based on the theory that all behaviors (including emotional responses, like anxiety) are learned and can be unlearned through conscious practice and changing the pattern of reinforcements so that positive behaviors are rewarded and negative behaviors are ignored. For example, if behavior therapy was being used to treat a young child's separation anxieties, she might be rewarded with a special treat if she waved good-bye to her parents without crying, but ignored if she cried or begged her parents to return to her side. To avoid overwhelming the child, behavior therapy should be done gradually and in small steps, particularly when the child has long-standing fears or severe anxiety.

Exposure-based behavior therapy is directed at uncoupling the association between the source of the fear and the emotional response. The child is exposed to her fears (such as dirt or other contaminant if she has obsessive-compulsive disorder, or imagining a night alone in her room if she fears the dark) and is encouraged to focus on her physical and psychological responses. She learns that the anxiety she feels is only temporary —it abates almost as quickly as it rises, and she discovers that the physical distress is not that uncomfortable. Many of the difficulties associated with the anxiety disorders come about because the child is so fearful of feeling anxious that she avoids all situations that might produce anxiety. Exposure therapy breaks that cycle. In addition, the child learns that she can control her anxiety by exposing herself to increasingly difficult situations.

In obsessive-compulsive disorder (OCD), exposure therapy is usually combined with a special behavior therapy technique known as response prevention. *Exposure with response prevention therapy* is unique to OCD and is discussed in chapter 16.

Relaxation therapy teaches the child how to relax "on cue" and is helpful in blocking the physical symptoms associated with anxiety. Thus, relaxation therapy is most useful to the child who has nausea, sweating, trembling, or a racing heartbeat in conjunction with her anxiety. The goal of relaxation therapy is to decrease the body's response to the mind's perception of stress—the child practices controlling her breathing, and tensing and relaxing various muscle groups, so that if she feels herself becoming tense in response to an impending crisis, she can voluntarily relax those same muscle groups. Relaxation therapy may not be suitable for preteens because it requires a certain degree of physical maturity to master the muscle control.

Parents should be involved in their child's behavior therapy, but they shouldn't do the therapy for him, since the child must be the one who learns the new behavior (just as having a parent do his homework or practice the piano for him wouldn't be very useful). The extent to which parents are involved depends upon their child's particular set of symptoms —some children require only an occasional reminder that it's time to do their behavioral homework, others have symptoms involving their parents (such as separation anxiety or compulsive rituals) and the parents must practice giving only positive responses to the behavior. The child's therapist will evaluate his symptoms and develop an individualized behavior therapy plan which will include guidance about how and when the parent's participation is helpful in the child's recovery.

Cognitive-behavior therapy combines key aspects of behavior therapy with techniques that are designed to change the child's unhealthy pattern of thinking (cognition). Cognitive-behavior therapy can be very helpful in the treatment of children with depression and/or anxiety disorders. The child's symptoms are seen as the outcome of a series of inappropriately reinforced responses—the child's negative views and behaviors have been reinforced while his positive ones have been neglected. Cognitive therapy is used to help the child become aware of his negative thoughts (depressed or anxious thoughts) and their destructive impact, and then to replace the negative thoughts with more accurate, positive, or constructive ways of thinking. There are a variety of techniques that can be used in cognitive-behavior therapy, including a multiple-choice strategy in which the child chooses the best alternative and explains why it's preferable to the other two choices, or a pro-and-con technique in which the child is challenged to explain possible outcomes of two opposing ways of thinking or behaving. For example, a child might be presented with a situation in which she receives an invitation to a birthday party and then asked to explain what would happen if she went to the party or if she refused the invitation. The therapist works with the child to help her understand that the positive consequences of attending the party would be preferable to remaining socially isolated.

Medications

The medications used most often to treat childhood psychiatric disorders are all known as "antidepressants." The name arose because the medications were first developed to treat depression. However, they are useful in a variety of other disorders, including separation anxiety disorder (chapter 18), panic disorder and generalized anxiety disorder (chapter 19), obsessive-compulsive disorder (chapter 16), and the eating disorders (chapter 23). There are three general classes of antidepressant medications: the selective serotonin reuptake inhibitors (SSRIs), the tricyclic antidepressants, and the monoamine oxidase inhibitors (MAOIs). In children and adolescents, the SSRIs have become the drug treatment of choice because of their safety and effectiveness. The tricyclic antidepressants have more side effects than the SSRIs, but are still used often because of their well-established track record as an effective treatment for depression and anxiety. The monoamine oxidase inhibitors are not generally used in children because a special diet is required during MAOI therapy and they have several potentially serious side effects.

The main concern with medications is their side effects. Fortunately, the SSRIs have very few and most children have little or no problems during treatment. Further, the side effect profile of each of the SSRIs is different, and if one medication has too many side effects, another can be found in which there is little or no downside to treatment. To keep side effects to a minimum and ensure that the child's dose is at an optimum level, the doctor should start the medication at a very low dosage and slowly and carefully increase the amount until the child begins to experience unpleasant side effects or he starts to get better. *Start low and go slow!* is the cardinal rule of all types of drug therapy.

Selective serotonin reuptake inhibitors (SSRIs). The SSRIs are the first choice for several psychiatric disorders, including depression, selective mutism/social phobia, and obsessive-compulsive disorder. The medications have become the "treatment of choice" because they are usually helpful and have few side effects. SSRIs work by increasing the amount of serotonin (a brain messenger chemical) available to the nerve cells— this helps to correct the chemical imbalance that is causing the child's symptoms and decreases the severity of those symptoms. Since all the SSRIs work through the same mechanism, their side effects are quite similar, but because each drug's formula differs slightly from the others, it is possible for a child to get benefit from one SSRI but not another. Several SSRIs have been approved by the Food and Drug Administration

(FDA) for treatment of children; they are: sertraline (Zoloft), which can be used in children as young as six years of age; fluvoxamine (Luvox), for children eight and older; and fluoxetine (Prozac), for adolescents and older children. Paroxetine (Paxil) is another SSRI that is sometimes used to treat children, although it is not specifically indicated for that use.

One important difference among the SSRIs is the half-life of the drugs, or the amount of time that the drug stays in the child's body after the medication has been stopped. Fluvoxamine (Luvox), sertraline (Zoloft), and paroxetine (Paxil) vary slightly in the amount of time that it takes for them to be flushed from the system, but, in general, they are gone within the first forty-eight to seventy-two hours. Fluoxetine (Prozac) has a very long half-life of five to seven days, and it can take fourteen days or longer for the medication to be cleared from the body. Thus, with fluoxetine (Prozac), the *Start low and go slow* rule is particularly important. If a child develops unpleasant side effects, they may persist for a week or more after the medication has been discontinued. It's better to avoid the discomfort of unwanted side-effects by being patient and increasing the dosage in small increments—fortunately, fluoxetine (Prozac) is available in a liquid form, so the dosage can be adjusted to very precise levels.

Side effects of the SSRIs are usually mild and resolve after a few weeks. A number of side effects were reported during the clinical trials, but most were present in equal numbers in the group taking a placebo (sugar pill), suggesting that the side effects may not have been caused by the medication. If a child develops side effects from the SSRI, he might experience one or two of the following: nausea, stomachache, weight loss, headache, excessive sweating, nervousness, and difficulty sleeping. The sleep difficulties include trouble falling asleep or staying asleep, and changes in the sleep pattern that result in less-restful sleep (the child wakes up feeling tired). If waking up too early in the morning is a problem, the child's doctor might want to decrease the dosage slightly or divide the dose so that a portion of the day's medication is taken in the morning and the rest in the early afternoon. If the medication causes the child to have difficulty falling asleep, the doctor might decrease the dose or have him take it first thing in the morning. All of the side effects will diminish over time, so if they are mild, the child might be encouraged to "stick it out" for a few days and wait for them to disappear. If they are truly bothersome, however, the dosage of medication should be decreased. If that doesn't help, another medication should be tried.

Tricyclic antidepressants have been used for over forty years and are of benefit to more than 70 percent of the patients who take them. They are particularly useful for depression and generalized anxiety disorder. The tricyclic antidepressants include: imipramine (Tofranil), desipramine (Norpramin), amitriptyline (Elavil), amoxapine (Asendin), nortriptyline (Pamelor), and doxepin (Sinequan). Clomipramine (Anafranil) is a tricyclic antidepressant that has special benefits in obsessive-compulsive disorder and is discussed in chapter 16. The tricyclics have been widely studied in children, in part because of their role in treating bed-wetting (see chapter 6), and have been found to be safe, as well as effective. A few years ago, the medical community became concerned about the continued use of tricyclic antidepressants after there were reports of sudden cardiac deaths in children following high-dose, long-term treatment. Several studies have now shown that the association was a statistical fluke and that there is no reason to blame the tricyclic medications for the heart problems. However, your child's physician will still want to check an electrocardiogram (ECG) before starting treatment in order to make sure that your child doesn't have an underlying heart problem that could be made worse by the medication.

The dosages of the tricyclic antidepressants vary depending upon their formulation, but should be administered in amounts comparable to 3 mg/kg or less of imipramine. Some psychiatrists use higher doses (as high as 4 to 5 mg/kg) and have found them also to be safe and effective, but this requires frequent monitoring of the ECG. In general, "pushing the limits" on the dosage of a tricyclic antidepressant isn't advisable and shouldn't be done until more data are obtained from controlled studies.

Tricyclic antidepressants have more side effects than do the SSRIs because they affect several different brain chemical systems. Children typically have one or more of the following symptoms: blurred vision, headache, constipation, weight gain, difficulty sleeping, rapid pulse, and blood pressure changes (either too high or too low, with low blood pressure occurring more commonly among children). Many of the side effects are temporary and decrease after a couple of weeks of treatment at a stable dosage, but some side effects, such as constipation, weight gain, and dry mouth, remain a problem throughout the treatment. It should be noted that stopping a tricyclic medication abruptly can be very uncomfortable, as the cholinergic system "rebounds" and causes profuse sweating, abdominal cramps, and muscle aches (the child will feel as if he's got a bad case of the flu).

"To use medications or not—that is the question!" Parents are often concerned about treating their child's illness with medications. As physicians, we are also cautious about using medications and prescribe them only when the benefits outweigh the risks, such as when there is no equally effective psychotherapy available or the child's symptoms are so severe that combination therapy (psychotherapy plus medication) is a necessity. In order to feel comfortable with the therapy prescribed and to ensure that your child receives optimum treatment, you must be an active participant in the decision-making process, helping your child's physician to weigh the risks and benefits of each therapy for your child. However, you must also be able to trust the doctor to make the final decision, since that is his responsibility, just as your child's pediatrician chooses the antibiotic to treat his pneumonia or the orthopedic surgeon decides whether your child's broken bone is put in a cast or repaired in surgery. In all of these situations, there is an implicit partnership between the parent and the physician, and each has an equally important role to play in the treatment process. The physician must use his medical knowledge and training to prescribe the best therapy possible and the parents must use their knowledge, skills, and experience to ensure that the treatments are accomplished—whether it means attending psychotherapy sessions, completing behavior therapy assignments, or giving the medication exactly as prescribed. Your child should also be an active participant in his therapy. Not only does it improve his long-term outcome, but it also helps him to regain control of his life and to feel better in the short term as well.

Further Reading

Backman, Margaret, Ph.D. *Coping with Choosing a Therapist*. New York: Rosen Publishing Group, 1994.

Harris, Scott O., Ph.D., and Edward N. Reynolds, Ph.D. *When Growing Up Hurts Too Much: A Parent's Guide to Knowing When and How to Choose a Therapist with Your Teenager*. Lexington, MA: D. C. Heath & Co., 1992.

Reaves, John, and James B. Austin, Ph.D. *How to Find Help for a Troubled Kid: A Parent's Guide to Programs and Services for Adolescents*. New York: Henry Holt, 1990.

Also Helpful:

Carter, Rosalynn, with Susan Golant. *Helping Someone with Mental Illness*. New York: Times Books, 1998.

Koplewicz, Harold, M.D. *It's Nobody's Fault: New Hope and Help for Difficult Children and Their Parents*. New York: Times Books, 1996.

Resources

American Academy of Child and Adolescent Psychiatry
3615 Wisconsin Avenue, N.W.
Washington, D.C. 20016
202-966-7300
http://www.aacap.org/
Contact for Facts for Families pamphlets.

Association for the Advancement of Behavior Therapy
305 Seventh Avenue, 16th Floor
New York, NY 10001–6008
Phone: 212-647-1890
Fax: 212-647-1890
http://server.psych.vt.edu/aabt/

Center for Mental Health Services
Office of Consumer, Family, and Public Information
5600 Fishers Lane, Room 15-81
Rockville, MD 20857
301-443-2792

Federation of Families for Children's Mental Health
1021 Prince Street
Alexandria, VA 22314
703-684-7710

National Alliance for the Mentally Ill—Children and Adolescents
    Network (NAMICAN)
200 North Glebe Road, Suite 1015
Arlington, VA 22203
800-950-NAMI or 703-524-7600

"I Know My Son Is Hyper—
But Is He Hyperactive?"

Attention deficit hyperactivity disorder

Matthew celebrated his seventh birthday on the Saturday after Labor Day. As he blew out the candles on his birthday cake, he fervently wished, "Please, please, let me do well in school this year, and please help me fit in with the rest of my class!" Matthew desperately hoped that this year he would be the right size—and behavior—for his class. His September birthday had kept him out of kindergarten when he was five years old, so he was much bigger than the other kindergartners when he started school the next year and never really fit in with the other children in Mrs. Richardson's class. Matthew thought maybe they were scared of him because he was so much bigger than they were, but that didn't explain why the few friends he had made had stopped liking him by Thanksgiving. He wasn't sure what he had done to alienate them—maybe he'd taken their place in line, or spilled paint on their picture, or lost their pencil when they loaned it to him. Maybe he hadn't done anything and it was because his teacher was always reminding them that he was a problem case: "Hush, Matthew, it's not nice to interrupt," "Stay in your seat, Matthew, or we'll start calling you Pepe, the Mexican jumping bean," or "Stop playing with that, Matthew, it's bothering the other children. They're all coloring nicely. Why aren't you?" The answer to that one was easy—he had already finished coloring his picture and now he was bored! But Mrs. Richardson didn't seem to want to help him find anything fun to do. She just wanted him to sit down and be quiet. And he hated having to sit down and be quiet.

Yes, all things considered, kindergarten had been a really bad year. And so far, first grade hadn't been much better. In fact, Matthew thought it might even be worse. It was much harder to pay attention to his new teacher, Ms. Cooper, because she talked so long, and harder still to stay seated at his desk for the whole morning. He couldn't keep up with the rest of the class, either. When they started learning how to do a math problem, he was still trying to find his workbook, and when they moved on to reading, he was finishing up his math problems. He had no friends in his class yet and, even worse, some of the kids had started calling him "Cheater" because he had taken their place in line a couple of times. That was why he had made his birthday wish—he really wanted things to get better.

Matthew's mom overheard his wish and was concerned by both her son's words and his obvious distress. As soon as they were alone after dinner, she asked, "Matthew, why did you make a wish to fit in better at school?"

Matthew blurted out, "Because I'm tired of being a dumbo. I'm tired of always being in trouble for not paying attention and for not thinking things through first. And I'm sick and tired of being picked on for stuff I don't even know that I do, like getting out of my seat or cutting in line. I don't want to be me anymore. I just want to be a normal kid, not a big, stupid cheater."

His mother was stunned. "Matthew, I never knew you were having so many problems. No wonder Ms. Cooper called and asked to see me. I'll make an appointment with her this week. I'm sure if we work together, she and I can help you fit in better at school. I'm sure we can help you get your wish."

Matthew did get his birthday wish. His mother arranged for a school conference with Matthew's new teacher, Ms. Cooper, who suggested that Mrs. Richardson also attend. At the meeting, Mrs. Richardson and Ms. Cooper took turns sharing their concerns about Matthew. They told similar stories: that he was frequently out of his seat and had trouble waiting his turn in line, that he was easily distracted from his work, and that he caused disruptions in the classroom. They provided examples of how Matthew's inability to concentrate and pay attention was impeding his schoolwork, particularly in math and reading, and how his impulsivity made him do things that irritated and alienated the other children. The teachers also reported that Matthew was much more active than other boys his age—even when he was sitting in his seat, he seemed to be moving constantly. The two of them concluded by saying that they thought Matthew had attention deficit hyperactivity disorder, or ADHD.

When the teachers finished, Matthew's mother replied, "You know, this doesn't really come as a surprise to me. Everything you've said is similar to what I've seen at home. Matthew doesn't pay attention very well and he is a very *active boy. He always has been. In fact, I called him Thumper when I was pregnant because he moved around so much. He runs when he should walk and walks when he should be standing still. And he hates to have to sit down, even at the dinner table. You know, now that I think of it, I bet he's never stayed seated throughout an entire meal. He jumps up from the table to get something that he wants from the pantry, but forgets what it was before he gets there. When he comes back, he doesn't really sit down, he just kind of perches on the edge of his chair—like any second he might fly off again. He's impulsive, too, just as you described—he does things first and thinks about them afterward. But I always thought that he was just a little young for his age and would grow out of it. What did I miss? When did he cross the line between hyper and hyperactivity?"*

What Is Attention Deficit Hyperactivity Disorder?

Attention deficit hyperactivity disorder, or ADHD, as it is more commonly known, is a neuropsychiatric (brain) disorder that causes inattention, impulsivity, and hyperactivity. If a child has inattention and impulsivity, but does not have hyperactivity, he is said to have attention deficit disorder without hyperactivity, or ADD (ADD is described in detail in chapter 14). The attention deficit disorders are reported to be among the most common medical disorders affecting children. As many as one in twenty children (5 percent) have ADHD—which means that there will likely be at least one child with ADHD in every elementary school classroom. Most of these children will be boys, as ADHD is found four to nine times more frequently in boys than in girls. Attention deficit disorder without hyperactivity (or ADD) is seen slightly more often in girls, but it's still two to three times more frequent in boys.

There are three overlapping theories about what causes ADHD. The first suggests that ADHD is caused by structural abnormalities in the brain, or "faulty wiring." It is thought that the child's behavior is unmodulated or uncontrolled because certain parts of the brain are not properly connected to each other and cannot communicate effectively. The second, related hypothesis is that ADHD is caused by an abnormality in the brain's messenger chemicals (or neurotransmitters). The medications that are most helpful for ADHD all act on the same chemical systems and the dramatic improvements that they produce suggest that the drugs may replace the missing neurochemicals and allow the cells within the brain to function more efficiently. The final theory holds that ADHD is the result of a developmental delay. This theory is based on observations that the behavior of a child with ADHD is entirely appropriate for a two- to four-year-old child. The problem is that his behavior doesn't mature at the same rate as he grows up; it is stuck at the two- to four-year-old level, and by the time the child is in grade school, his behavior is no longer in the normal range. The fact that most children outgrow ADHD by the time they reach high school lends credibility to this theory. However, some experts have suggested that children with ADHD don't really outgrow their disorder, but rather "overgrow" it by compensating for their inattention and impulsivity. Further, at least 20 percent of the children with ADHD will continue to have symptoms into adulthood. When ADHD continues into adulthood, it is called attention deficit hyperactivity disorder—residual type, or ADHD-RT (or ADD-RT, since most adults no longer have hyperactivity). For people with ADD-RT, the impulsivity, distractibility, and concentration difficulties continue to cause problems throughout their lives.

Does Your Child Have ADHD?

Your child may have hyperactivity/impulsivity if he has six or more of the following symptoms more often than not.

Hyperactivity
- Fidgets with hands or feet, or squirms in seat.
- Frequently leaves seat in classroom or gets up from dinner table.
- Runs about excessively or climbs in inappropriate situations.
- Usually has difficulty playing quietly.
- Is "on the go" or acts as if "driven by a motor."
- Talks excessively.

Impulsivity
- Blurts out answers before question is finished.
- Has difficulty waiting for his turn.
- Interrupts or intrudes on others.

Your child may have inattention if he has at least six of the following symptoms more often than not:

Fails to pay attention to details and makes careless mistakes.
Has difficulty staying focused (or sustaining attention) on tasks or activities.

Doesn't follow through on instructions or complete tasks and assignments.

Has difficulty organizing tasks and activities.

Avoids or dislikes schoolwork or homework that takes sustained mental effort.

Loses materials necessary for tasks and activities (e.g., pencils, pens, soccer ball).

Is easily distracted.

Is frequently forgetful.

Doesn't seem to listen when spoken to directly.

1. Was each symptom that you identified for your child present more often than not? (For example, he almost always squirms in his seat and only occasionally sits still?)
2. Did these problems start before the age of seven years?
3. Have the symptoms been present for at least six months?
4. Does he have trouble at home and at school?
5. Do the symptoms cause him significant problems? (For example, poor grades, frequent disciplinary actions at home and at school, etc.)

Your child may have ADHD if you answered yes to questions 1 through 5 *and* your child had at least six of the hyperactivity/impulsivity symptoms *and* at least six of the inattention symptoms.

Your child may have ADD if you answered yes to questions 1 through 4, *and* your child had at least six of the inattention symptoms, *but* less than six of the hyperactivity/impulsivity symptoms.

How Do You Know If Your Child Has ADHD?

Symptoms of ADHD are present from a very young age and are usually apparent by the time the child enters preschool. The symptoms must be present before the child reaches the age of seven in order for a doctor to make the diagnosis of ADHD. When boys with ADHD are young (ages three to five), their symptoms may be dismissed as age-appropriate behavior. But, even then, side-by-side comparisons with boys who do not have ADHD will reveal important differences. The child with ADHD has a shorter attention span, higher activity level, and less impulse control than other children. Even during the preschool years, he may appear "immature" or prefer to play with younger children. By the time he reaches kindergarten, the differences will be more obvious and usually even a brief period of observation will be sufficient to note the child's poor attention, impulsivity, and hyperactivity. Of course, not every forgetful, impulsive, or overly active child has ADHD. The diagnosis is made only when the symptoms are chronic, present in *two* domains (school and home), and cause significant problems. The symptoms change over time, and may look different in different situations, so that a child may look quite hyperactive as he jumps about in the Sunday-school pageant, but his impulsivity may be less obvious because the carefully scripted activity helps restrain his behavior.

The diagnosis of ADHD is made only when the symptoms are present *more often than not*. This means that the child who occasionally fidgets and squirms, but usually sits still, does not have hyperactivity. Similarly, if he has only occasional inattention or impulsivity, these would not be considered to be symptoms of ADHD. Since making the correct diagnosis is essential to getting the proper help for your child, it is important for you to recognize the types of behaviors that result from hyperactivity, impulsivity, and inattention. Inattention is discussed in detail in chapter 13 and you should consult it for information about those symptoms.

Hyperactivity

The child with hyperactivity never stops moving. He's constantly "on the go," acts like he's "got a motor inside him," and causes people to say, "He makes me tired just to look at him." The young child with ADHD dashes through the house at lightning speed, often whooping and hollering as he runs. When you ask him to slow down, he walks for two or three steps before he takes off running again. When he's older (age eight and up), he may not run as frequently, but he's still constantly in motion. When he's standing, he's weaving about or bouncing up and down, and if he's seated, he appears to be very restless—bobbing his head up and down, tapping his feet, and shifting back and forth. Sitting next to him in a movie theater is like sitting next to a jack-in-the-box. He's up and down from his seat constantly and, even when seated, squirms about or perches on the edge of the chair. He's also out of his seat at the dinner table, in church, and at sporting events. When reprimanded, he will try to "sit still" but is truly incapable of doing so. Even when he's playing statues or freeze tag, he's unable to stay still for more than a few seconds.

The child with ADHD should appear agile because of the quickness of his movements, but often his motions are so big and jerky that he appears to be quite clumsy, particularly since he's constantly bumping into things, spilling his drink on the floor, or tipping backward in his chair until it topples over. This makes mealtimes particularly difficult, since the child with ADHD is almost always causing a disturbance of some sort.

Because the child with ADHD is constantly on the go, he is intolerant of sedentary activities. Reading, playing games, or watching TV are "boring" to a child with ADHD. Video games, on the other hand, are able to hold his attention because of their high stimulation levels—the visual patterns are bright and constantly changing, and the games require rapid motor responses, so that he constantly has to stay "on guard."

The child with ADHD talks incessantly. He frequently monopolizes the conversation by telling long, never-ending stories. The stories are so poorly organized that they never seem to get to the point, and by the time he's finished, no one (especially him) can remember what he was trying to say. On top of that, his volume control seems to get turned up louder as the day goes by—by evening, he's talking so loudly that he could be standing at the far end of the house and still be heard clearly. Requests to "speak softly" can't be accommodated for long because the child isn't able to modulate his speech any more effectively than he can control his motor activity.

Impulsivity

The child with impulsivity acts without considering the consequences of his actions—he "leaps before he looks." Because he doesn't "think first," he's always getting himself into uncomfortable or dangerous situations, and has more than his share of accidents and injuries. He gets an idea and acts on it immediately, whether it's climbing on the roof "to see the view from up there" or taking the new VCR apart to see how it works. He rushes to "help" and ends up making a mess as he knocks the pitcher from his mother's hand or rummages for a screwdriver in the bottom of his father's toolbox. His impulsivity prevents him from considering the consequences of his actions, so he calls "I get the backseat" and knocks his little sister over as he pushes his way into the minivan or slams her fingers in the car door as he tries to shut her out of the car. The child with ADHD often interrupts other children in the middle of a conversation or when they're playing a game, and then is surprised and hurt when he gets a negative response. If he's physically large and acts impulsively, the child gets a reputation for being a "bully"; otherwise, he's considered by the other children to be "rude" or "a naughty boy." This can cause problems with social isolation, as discussed in chapter 10.

The impulsive child can't wait for anything—especially his turn to speak. He finishes your sentences for you, answers questions before they're asked, and interrupts a story to tell how he thinks it should end. His impulsivity also causes him to speak before thinking about the appropriateness of his remarks, so he frequently insults others, uses swear words, or makes off-color remarks. Although these comments may have been "blurted out" impulsively the first time, it is important that negative consequences be applied so that they don't become commonplace (see parent helps at end of chapter).

If It's Not ADHD, What Else Could It Be?

If your child has hyperactivity, impulsivity, and inattention to a degree that causes problems for him, *and* has "always been this way," then chances are that he has ADHD. However, there are a few things that can mimic ADHD symptoms.

Normal Behavior

Young boys are supposed to be active and "on the go" (see chapter 1 for a complete discussion). One key difference is that healthy boys can settle down for at least brief periods if necessary, but the child with ADHD cannot decrease his activities to appropriate levels even for a short time. Another difference is that normal on-the-go behavior usually diminishes to more manageable levels by first grade, while ADHD does not. Since children develop at different rates, some will lag behind their peers and may appear hyperactive and impulsive because they have retained their early childhood activity patterns. If immaturity is the cause for the behaviors, they should be diminishing by age seven or eight, just at the time that ADHD becomes most noticeable.

Boredom is another common cause of normal hyperactivity and impulsivity (as described in chapter 3, it can also result in problem behaviors). To distinguish between boredom and ADHD at home, examine the patterns of inappropriate behavior—if it's due to ADHD, it will be present most of the time; if it's boredom, it will be limited to only the "downtimes."

Oppositional/Defiant Disorder

Children with oppositional behavior may look very similar to those with ADHD. They will push their way to the front of the line, get up out of their seat, cause distractions, and get into trouble frequently. The difference is that these children's behavior isn't the result of impulsivity or hyperactivity, but rather an inability to follow rules and regulations. Further, these children wouldn't meet the criteria for ADHD because they wouldn't have symptoms of inattention. Oppositional behaviors are discussed in detail in chapter 24.

Hyperactivity/Impulsivity After Age Seven

The diagnosis of ADHD is made only if the symptoms were present before the age of seven. Several disorders can cause symptoms of inattention, impulsivity, and hyperactivity, but since they typically begin after the age of seven, they should not be confused with ADHD. These disorders include depression (chapter 21), which may cause a child to appear restless and/or inattentive; anxiety disorders (chapters 18 and 19), in which the children may appear hyper, irritable, and impulsive; and PANDAS (chapter 17), a newly discovered syndrome in which strep throat infections trigger obsessive-compulsive symptoms and tics, as well as impulsivity, hyperactivity, and attention problems. Substance abuse (chapter 24) is one of the most common causes of impulsivity in older children and adolescents, and can also cause hyperactivity if stimulants are being abused.

Treatment of ADHD

The treatment of ADHD is aimed not only at decreasing symptom severity, but also at minimizing the impact of the inattention, impulsivity, and hyperactivity. Therapy should be multidisciplinary and should include the child, his parents, physician, and teacher and, in some cases, a school psychologist or child psychiatrist. The treatment should be multifaceted, involving simultaneous educational, psychological, and medical interventions to address the three main symptoms. Educational interventions should include, among others, classroom assistance and a structured environment, as described in chapter 14 and the help section at the end of this chapter. Psychological treatments include family and individual psychotherapy, as well as behavior therapy. Stimulant medications are the mainstays of medical treatment. While many physicians will prescribe medications alone for the treatment of ADHD, we prefer to combine medications with behavior therapy because the combination offers greater benefits than either treatment alone. Behavior therapy provides an organizing framework that minimizes the effects of the child's inattention and impulsivity, while medications decrease activity levels to the normal range, and also significantly decrease symptoms of inattention and impulsivity.

Medications

In 1937, Dr. Charles Bradley of Harvard University noticed that Benzedrine, a stimulant that was being prescribed for another purpose, was helping hyperactive children to settle down. This effect was a strange contradiction—stimulants were able to quiet an overstimulated (hyperactive) child, yet they were given their name because they stimulate the central nervous system. Scientists now know that for children with ADHD, the stimulant medications actually help the inhibitory part of the brain to function better—they make the brakes stronger, rather than revving the motor up faster. The "brakes" help the child to ignore distractions and narrow his focus, as well as decreasing symptoms of hyperactivity and impulsivity.

We realize that some parents may be reluctant to have their child take medication for ADHD. As discussed in chapter 12, the decision to use medications for a child's treatment is never an easy one. However, some of the concerns about stimulant medications for ADHD are not based on scientific facts, but rather on a spate of articles in the press that have blamed Ritalin (one of the stimulant medications) for everything from teenagers' irresponsible behavior and drug abuse to societal ills (sample headline: U.S. SCHOOLS ARE DRUGGING OUR CHILDREN INTO SUBMISSION). These stories receive a lot of attention and raise a lot of questions, but have little substance. The truth is that the stimulant medications are very safe (they have been used in the United States for over twenty-five years without problems) and they are of great benefit to hundreds of thousands of children in this country. The medications provide substitutes for the neurochemicals that a child with ADHD lacks, which allow him to function normally, just as insulin allows the child with diabetes to live his life more normally. If your child has been properly diagnosed as having ADHD, then drug treatment is not only appropriate, it is probably essential.

Stimulant medications. The stimulant medications include methylphenidate (Ritalin), pemoline (Cylert), dextroamphetamine (Dexedrine), and a dextroamphetamine/amphetamine combination (Adderall). These four medications are the mainstays of drug treatment for ADHD because they are by far the most effective treatments available for decreasing hyperactivity, improving attention, and reducing impulsivity.

Methylphenidate (Ritalin) has been used for several decades to treat ADHD and is quite effective, improving symptoms for over 90 percent of children at proper dosages. Ritalin is a short-acting medication whose benefits are first seen within about thirty minutes of taking the dose and continue for one to four hours. The starting dose is usually 5 mg taken two or three times per day. The child and his parents will be able to tell within a day or two of starting the medicine whether or not it will be helpful. If it is, then the dosage schedule can be adjusted to maximize the beneficial effects during the school day and minimize side effects (the maximum recommended daily dose of Ritalin is 60 mg/day). Most children take the medication after breakfast, after lunch, and during the late afternoon. A slow-release formulation of Ritalin is occasionally used, particularly for children who have "rebound" hyperactivity between medication doses.

Dextroamphetamine (Dexedrine) and dextroamphetamine/amphetamine combination (Adderall) are also very effective in the treatment of ADHD. The amphetamines offer an advantage over Ritalin in that they remain effective for longer periods of time, but still may require multiple doses each day. This poses the potential disadvantage of increasing the child's sleep difficulties. If he is experiencing insomnia, one of the other stimulant medications may be preferable. Dextroamphetamine therapy is started at 2.5 to 5 mg/day and slowly increased to the point at which the child's symptoms are maximally improved, but he has minimal side effects.

Pemoline (Cylert) is also a stimulant medication, but it is used infrequently to treat ADHD. Its decreased popularity is due to the fact that pemoline has been reported to cause problems with liver function in rare instances and periodic blood tests are necessary while taking the drug. Further, although pemoline is as effective as Ritalin and Dexedrine, it takes longer to begin to take effect (several weeks, rather than a day or two). However, pemoline has one significant advantage over the other two stimulants in that it is taken only once each day.

The side effects of all the stimulants are quite similar. The most frequent side effects are decreased appetite and sleep disturbances. The majority of children have only a mild decrease in appetite, which can be overcome by adjusting the timing of the dosages to minimize the anorexic effects at meal-times—for example, having the child take the morning dose after breakfast and the noon dose after lunch, and giving the late-afternoon dose after the child has eaten his snack, but as long before dinner as possible. Unlike adults, who will eventually adjust to the appetite suppression of stimulant medications, children may continue to have a decreased appetite throughout treatment. If a child's food intake is markedly decreased and he isn't able to eat enough to gain weight appropriately, he may need to take periodic "drug holidays" (for example, on weekends or during school vacations) to allow him to catch up on his growth.

Other side effects of the stimulant medications include trouble falling asleep or staying asleep (the child will awaken at midnight or 2:00 A.M. and have difficulty going back to sleep), and, infrequently, fatigue, headaches, or stomachaches. It is possible for a child to experience mood changes in association with the stimulant medications, ranging from tearfulness or irritability to full-blown depression. These occur rarely, but if a child is experiencing a change in mood as a result of his stimulant medication, it should be stopped and an alternative found.

Stimulants are the most effective way to treat ADHD in adolescents, as well as in younger children, but some physicians are reluctant to use these drugs during adolescence for fear that they will lead to drug abuse. In general, these fears are unfounded. At the prescribed dosages, none of the stimulant medications will cause addiction or dependence in a child or adolescent with ADHD. Further, because of the teen's makeup, he doesn't feel "high" or "up" when he takes Ritalin or Dexedrine, so there's no temptation for him to overmedicate. However, the drugs are abused by others, which means that the child with ADHD might be at an increased risk for unhealthy behaviors, such as trading his Ritalin for marijuana or cocaine. To avoid these potential risks, some physicians recommend that parents retain control of the stimulant medications, rather than allowing the teenager to take his own medicine unsupervised. Other physicians prefer to switch to one of the second-choice medications.

Antidepressants. Antidepressants, particularly the tricyclics imipramine (Tofranil) and desipramine (Norpramin), are often prescribed for ADHD. They are not as effective as the stimulants, but for children who cannot or should not take stimulant medications, they can be helpful. The tricyclic antidepressants are described in detail in chapter 12.

Buproprion (Wellbutrin) has been somewhat successful in treating the inattentiveness and irritability associated with ADHD. The serotonin-reuptake-blocking drugs (or SSRIs—described in chapter 12) have also been used to treat ADHD. This may not be appropriate, since in our experience, the drugs may help the child's impulsivity and related behavior problems, such as mood swings and irritability, but they don't help his inattention or hyperactivity.

Clonidine (Catapres) and guanfacine (Tenex), which work on a different biochemical system than do the stimulants, are used in children with ADHD to help control some of the behavioral symptoms. The drugs are not as successful as the stimulants in treating inattention or hyperactivity, and therefore they are not usually a first choice for ADHD. However, clonidine and guanfacine can be used in addition to stimulants (to obtain additional symptom improvement) or when stimulant therapy is not advisable (such as in a teenager with a history of drug addiction).

What You Can Do to Help Your Child Overcome His ADHD Symptoms

Use the three Ls—love, limits, and large muscle exercise. The three Ls are essential to the well-being of the child with ADHD (see chapter 1 for a full description). The first L, *love*, must be unconditional—your child doesn't have to earn it or deserve it, it's just there. He must be able to depend upon it, so your love shouldn't be used as a bargaining chip ("Do your best today, Matthew, and I'll love you even more") or a threat ("Mommy won't love you anymore if you don't sit down and finish your dinner"). The child with ADHD frequently has low self-esteem and feels guilty for being "so bad," so he worries that you couldn't possibly love him through his many faults. Tell him this isn't the case. Show him and tell him frequently that you love him and that you always will, no matter what he might do to upset you.

Limits are important for helping your child feel as if he fits in—to your family, his classroom, and his community. If a child has ADHD, he lacks an internal organizing framework. He doesn't have a clear sense of the correctness of his behavior. Rules and limits provide him with external guidelines—stopping him before he gets into danger and warning him when he's teetering close to the edge of impropriety. It takes the child with ADHD a long time to learn the rules and even then he will forget them or act impulsively and ignore them. These repeated infractions are tiresome, but consistency and repetition will prevail eventually.

Children with ADHD need to have an opportunity to "blow off steam" or expend their excess energy through *large muscle exercise*. Your child should do some aerobic exercise, such as running, jumping, and climbing, every day, particularly in the after-school hours. The unstructured playtime might be complemented by participation in a group sport, such as soccer or basketball. It's important to pick a sport or activity that your child enjoys and at which he can be successful.

Increase structure and provide consistency. It is essential that you provide clear limits for acceptable behavior, increase external structure (through behavior therapy techniques, among others), and establish consistency in your family's routine. Chapter 14 provides detailed explanations of how to use structure and consistency to strengthen your child's abilities to organize, prioritize, and strategize.

Avoid situations that are difficult for your child. Restaurant meals are torture for the child with ADD, particularly if he has hyperactivity. The best option is to hire a baby-sitter so that he can avoid the one and a half hours of confinement. If that isn't possible, take him outside or to the restaurant's lobby to let him roam while waiting for your food to arrive or for others to finish their meal. Depending upon your child's level of hyperactivity, it may be possible for him to sit still for fifteen or twenty minutes while you eat your food—practicing this at home ahead of time can help him succeed.

Kid-proof your environment. The combination of hyperactivity and impulsivity can be a dangerous one. When a child with ADHD feels compelled to climb, he won't stop to consider whether or not it's safe, he'll just take off up that pile of rusted scrap metal. Even if you fully safeguard your home, it isn't a good idea to leave your child with ADHD alone and unsupervised for more than brief periods of time. Check on him every few minutes to make sure that he's still playing safely, even if you have a fenced-in, kid-proofed backyard.

Use time-outs to help your child regain self-control, not as a punishment. Brief time-outs can be very useful in helping the child with ADHD to regain control, but they are not an effective means of discipline. Telling a child with ADHD to "sit in the corner for ten minutes and think about what you did" is like telling your newborn to contemplate the universe—impossible! The child's attention span is measured in seconds, not minutes, and he will quickly forget what he's doing in the corner, much less what he's supposed to be thinking about. Also, the child's muscles are in biological overdrive from his hyperactivity and this makes it physically impossible for him to sit still for ten minutes. Thus, we recommend short time-outs (less than two minutes each), which are directed at allowing your child to regain control: "Sit down on that stool by the counter and calm down. I'll be back in one minute to get your side of the story [or to talk with you about what happened just now]."

Make sure your child gets enough sleep and a proper diet. The child with ADHD finds it difficult to fall asleep at night, so he tends to procrastinate around bedtime. However, because he is constantly on the go, he often requires more sleep than other children and it's very important that he goes to bed on time each evening. (Not only will he get sufficient rest, but having a strict bedtime provides structure and consistency!)

Proper nutrition is essential for good health and particularly when a child has ADHD. We recommend a regular, balanced diet, rather than a special ADHD diet. There has been a great deal of debate about whether or not dietary changes are helpful for ADHD. Most of the recent evidence suggests that they probably are not. However, special diets, like the Feingold diet, remain popular for ADHD because they do appear to help some children. The Feingold diet is a restriction diet, in which foods are limited to just a few categories. This diet may help children with ADHD who also have undiagnosed food allergies because it has eliminated the food that is causing the child to have problems with attention or hyperactivity. Another feature of the Feingold diet is its rigidity—the child has to eat particular foods at specific times, which establishes a consistent, predictable pattern for the family's daily routine. Since structure and consistency are key parts of the treatment of ADHD, the diet may work through the behavioral changes, rather than by any property of the food itself. If you try one of the special ADHD diets and your child seems improved, then it may be worth continuing. If you try the diet but don't see any effect, then don't use it—you haven't deprived your child of anything useful. If you decide not to try a special diet, that's okay, too—at this point, behavior therapy and medications have been proven effective for ADHD, diets have not.

Form a partnership with your child's teacher. You will need to work closely with your child's teacher in order to ensure his success at school. She will want to meet with you as soon as she observes symptoms of ADHD. You should feel free to discuss all of your concerns with her—chances are that she's already seen the same thing in her classroom. If your child already has a diagnosis of ADHD, you should arrange a meeting with his teacher as soon as school opens in the fall so that you can plan ways to ensure that he has a successful year.

When your child's teacher becomes aware that he is having problems with inattention, impulsivity, or hyperactivity, she should arrange for him to have a comprehensive educational assessment measuring his academic strengths and weaknesses. This may reveal that your child has specific learning disabilities (as discussed in chapter 14) as well as ADHD. When the evaluation is complete, the teacher will want to meet with you to discuss your child's individual educational plan (or IEP), which will spell out the special services your child will receive. If he is going to stay in a regular classroom all day, his teacher may need a teacher's aide or other assistance in order to provide your son with the special attention he requires and still meet the needs of her other students. You can act as an advocate for both your child and his teacher by insisting that she receive these additional resources.

Occasionally, a child will be diagnosed with ADHD merely because his teacher has sent a note home saying that she thinks the child is "inattentive, impulsive, and hyperactive" and should be taking stimulant medications for his ADHD. Often, as in Matthew's case (described in this chapter), the teacher's diagnosis is correct. However, if the teacher's observations don't match your own experience with your child and/or they aren't consistent with his previous teachers' reports, then the first step should be a parent-teacher conference to discuss the discrepancies, rather than an appointment with your child's doctor.

Further Reading

Hallowell, Edward M., M.D., and John J. Ratey, M.D. *Answers to Distraction*. New York: Bantam Books, 1994.

———. *Driven to Distraction: Recognizing and Coping with Attention Deficit Disorder from Childhood Through Adulthood*. New York: Simon & Schuster, 1994.

Ingersoll, Barbara D., Ph.D., and Sam Goldstein, Ph.D. *Attention Deficit Disorder and Learning Disabilities: Realities, Myths and Controversial Treatments*. New York: Doubleday, 1993.

Silver, Larry B., M.D. *Dr. Larry Silver's Advice to Parents on Attention Deficit Hyperactivity Disorder.* Washington, D.C.: American Psychiatric Press, 1993.

Taylor, John F., Ph.D. *Helping Your Hyperactive/Attention Deficit Child,* rev. 2d ed. Rocklin, CA: Prima Publishing, 1994.

Wender, Paul H., M.D. *The Hyperactive Child, Adolescent, and Adult: Attention Deficit Disorder Through the Lifespan.* New York: Oxford University Press, 1987.

Books on Parenting

Alexander-Roberts, Colleen. *The ADHD Parenting Handbook: Practical Advice for Parents from Parents.* Dallas, TX: Taylor Publishing Co., 1994.

Boyles, Nancy S., M.Ed., and Darlene Contadino, L.S.W. *Parenting a Child with Attention Deficit/Hyperactivity Disorder.* Los Angeles, CA: Contemporary Books, 1996.

Copeland, Edna, and Valerie Love. *Attention Please! A Comprehensive Guide for Successfully Parenting Children with Attention Deficit Disorders and Hyperactivity.* Atlanta, GA: Specialty Press, 1995.

Goldstein, Sam, and Michael Goldstein. *Hyperactivity: Why Won't My Child Pay Attention?* New York: John Wiley, 1992.

Resources

Attention Deficit Information Network (AD-IN)
475 Hillside Avenue
Needham, MA 02194
617-455-9895

Attention Deficit Resource Center
1344 East Cobb Drive, Suite 14
Marietta, GA 30068

Children and Adults with Attention Deficit Disorders (C.H.A.D.D.)
499 Northwest 70th Avenue, Suite 308
Plantation, FL 33317
305-587-3700
http://www.chadd.org

National Attention Deficit Disorder Association
P.O. Box 972
Mentor, OH 44061
E-mail: Natladda@aol.com
Website: http://www.add.org
Phone: 800-487-2282 or 216-350-9595
Fax-on-Demand System: 313-769-6729

"My Daughter Studies All the Time, But She Still Gets Failing Grades"

Attention deficit disorder and learning disabilities

Margaret walked into the house with a dejected look on her face. She handed her mother a test paper and said, "Don't yell at me, Mom, but I got an F on my math test."

"An F! Oh, Margaret, honey, how could you fail that test? You've been studying so hard every night, and have been doing so well on your homework assignments. I only have to help you a little bit—the rest you can do on your own now."

"Math's really hard for me, Mom, and I hate it! Grandpa says that I shouldn't worry about it, though, because everybody knows that girls can't do math very well."

Margaret's mother shook her head in dismay. Usually, she tried to ignore her father-in-law's antiquated opinions, but this was just too much. "Margaret, your grandfather is wrong. It is very important for both boys and girls to do their best in all their school subjects, especially math. I think I'd better make an appointment with your teacher, Ms. Sternberg, to talk about your math grades. Are there any other subjects that are giving you problems?"

"English is pretty hard right now—we're learning how to do outlines and I'm having trouble remembering everything."

"Outlines can be hard," her mother said. "I'll check with Ms. Sternberg to see if she has any suggestions for how to make them easier."

Ms. Sternberg welcomed Margaret's mother to her classroom and then said, "I'm sorry about Margaret's math test. You know, I'm glad you called and asked to see me because I've become increasingly concerned about your daughter's progress. She tries so hard, but she just can't seem to get it. I don't know if she's not paying attention, or she doesn't understand the concepts, or perhaps it's a combination of the two. Her scores on the math achievement test were twenty points lower than her math IQ—anything greater than a fifteen-point difference is suggestive of a learning disability."

Ms. Sternberg continued, "Margaret also has some problems paying attention and seems to get distracted easily. Those could be signs of attention deficit disorder, or ADD. The two problems go together fairly often, and would make it harder for Margaret to keep up with the class—especially in math. With your permission, I'd like to arrange for her to be evaluated by the school psychologist to see if she has a learning disability. The tests will also help determine whether or not she has ADD, although Margaret's pediatrician or a child psychiatrist will need to make the diagnosis, since it's a medical condition. If Margaret has a learning disability, we'll need to establish an IEP, or an individualized education program, for her so that she can get special services from the school. I'm very confident that we can help your daughter improve her math grades, and, more importantly, make sure that she reaches her full potential."

Ms. Sternberg was right to suggest that Margaret might have a learning disability and attention deficit disorder. The two disorders often occur together and can have a major impact on a child's ability to learn. Learning disabilities are caused by deficits in one or more of the four areas that are involved in processing information: attention, visual perception, language processing, and muscle coordination. Attention deficit disorder (ADD) is one of two attentional disorders; the other, attention deficit hyperactivity disorder (ADHD), is discussed in detail in chapter 13.

What Is a Learning Disability?

Learning disabilities affect about one in five children in the United States, making them one of the most common neuropsychiatric disorders of childhood. Learning disabilities appear to arise from a "miswiring" of the brain, in which sections of the brain can't communicate with each other efficiently, or process information properly. At the present time, there is no cure for learning disabilities and no known means of decreasing the severity of the disorder. However, educational interventions and psychological treatments have progressed to the point where even children with severe learning disabilities can enjoy academic success—including graduating from college or receiving an advanced degree.

The core deficits (attention, language processing, visual perception, and muscle coordination) affect a variety of skills: academic skills like reading, writing, spelling, and arithmetic; language and speech skills, such as listening, talking, and understanding; and motor-sensory integration skills, including coordination, balance, and writing, among others. Children frequently have impairments in more than one of these areas, and will often have problems in several spheres of learning. Academic learning disabilities are diagnosed when there is a severe discrepancy between achievement and intellectual ability in one or more of the following areas:

1. Listening comprehension
2. Oral expression (speech and talking)
3. Basic reading skills
4. Reading comprehension
5. Written expression
6. Mathematics calculations
7. Mathematics reasoning

To determine that a child has a learning disability, it is necessary to administer at least two tests—a test of intelligence (IQ test) and a standardized test of academic achievement (reading, writing, and/or arithmetic). Usually, additional tests are required to show which specific areas are causing problems. Parents can request testing for learning disabilities if they are concerned about their child's ability to learn, and the school is obligated by law to provide at least a test of intelligence and an achievement test. Teachers can also suggest that testing be done if they have observed that the child's performance is consistently inferior to her intellectual capabilities. However, any such evaluation can be undertaken only with the parents' written permission.

There are several definitions of learning disabilities. Most school systems define it as at least a fifteen-point difference between the child's achievement test scores and her IQ test scores (i.e., achievement lower than IQ). Once the diagnosis has been made, the school is obligated—by the Individuals with Disabilities Education Act (IDEA)—to provide educational accommodations and modifications. These accommodations are tailored to the individual student's needs and comprise the individual education program (IEP), which is the child's contract with the school system. Once an accommodation has been spelled out in an IEP, the school system is bound by federal law to provide it. Examples of accommodations include: allowing extra time to complete written work, using a tape recorder to record lectures, providing access to a computer, assigning study partners to help with particular tasks or activities, allowing the student to answer test questions orally rather than in writing, or giving the student excerpted reading materials. In addition, the law specifies that public school students with disabilities are legally entitled to remain in school through age twenty-one, so in most instances, colleges and universities are also obligated to honor the terms of the IEP.

If you suspect that your child has a learning disability, we suggest that you schedule a meeting with your child's teacher and the school's psychologist or principal. Explain your concerns and ask whether or not the teacher has made similar observations. If not, you may want to ask for screening tests to be done anyway to allay your anxiety. If your child's teacher shares your concerns, then you should decide together upon the best course of action, which would usually begin with a comprehensive evaluation and development of an IEP. A list of references is included at the end of this chapter for additional information about this process. We particularly recommend *Learning Disabilities: A to Z—A Parent's Complete Guide to Learning Disabilities from Preschool to Adulthood,* by Corinne Smith and Lisa Strick.

What Is Attention Deficit Disorder (ADD)?

Attention deficit disorder (ADD) is one subtype of attention deficit hyperactivity disorder (ADHD). As their names suggest, the two types are distinguished by the presence (ADHD) or absence (ADD) of hyperactivity. (ADHD is discussed in detail in chapter 13.) Attention deficit disorder affects about one of one hundred girls and one in fifty boys, but is frequently missed, particularly if the child is bright enough to compensate for her disorder. The core features of ADD are difficulty concentrating, distractibility from the present, failure to pay attention to the future, and poor executive function—children lack the ability to prioritize, organize, and strategize.

One of the hallmarks of ADD is a report card that says, "Suzy needs to focus more on her work and daydream less," or "She hasn't applied herself this quarter," or "Suzy's not working up to her full potential." The teacher's remarks are a response to the difference between Suzy's poor performance and her tremendous potential, as measured by a high IQ or the occasional instances in which she stays focused and does superb work on an assignment. Sometimes, the missed symptoms are so severe that the child with ADD is labeled as "lazy" or "an attitude problem" because her teacher assumes she's purposefully doing poor work.

Does Your Child Have Attention Deficit Disorder (ADD)?

Your child may have inattention if she has at least six of the following symptoms more often than not:

1. Fails to pay attention to details and makes careless mistakes.
2. Has difficulty sustaining attention or staying focused on tasks or activities.
3. Doesn't follow through on instructions or complete tasks and assignments.
4. Has difficulty organizing tasks and activities.
5. Avoids or dislikes schoolwork or homework that takes sustained mental effort.
6. Loses materials necessary for tasks and activities (e.g., pencils, pens, soccer ball).
7. Is easily distracted.
8. Is frequently forgetful.
9. Doesn't seem to listen when spoken to directly.

1. Was each symptom that you identified for your child present the majority of the time?
2. Did these problems start before the age of seven years?
3. Have the symptoms been present for at least six months?
4. Does your child have trouble both at home and at school?
5. Do the symptoms cause her significant problems (like poor grades or missed assignments)?

Your child may have ADD if she has at least six of the inattention symptoms, *and* you answered yes to each of the five questions above.

She may have ADHD if she also has hyperactivity/impulsivity as described in chapter 13.

How Do You Know If Your Child Has Attention Deficit Disorder?

A diagnosis of ADD is made only when a child has had symptoms of inattention for at least six months and the symptoms are causing problems both at home and at school. The specific symptoms of ADD vary among individuals, but some general patterns have emerged over the years that are common to many children with ADD.

General Patterns

Forgetful, careless, and forever losing something. The child with ADD has problems maintaining focus on an activity and often forgets what she's doing or makes careless mistakes. For example, she might cheerfully volunteer to unload the dishwasher, but she doesn't remove the glasses from the top rack or she leaves the still-full silverware basket sitting out on the counter. Her phone messages are notorious for lacking crucial details, like the name of the person who called or one of the seven digits in the telephone number.

The child with ADD is constantly searching for something that shouldn't be lost. Getting out the door in the morning seems to take hours—she has to gather up the contents of her backpack from various parts of the family room (and then go back for the homework assignment that had made its way into the dining room); she can't find her hat or coat, and has to search the entire house for her musical instrument. When she finally gets into the car, she'll have to go back for something she forgot. And she isn't ever able to find her cleats for soccer practice, even though she's sure she brought them home last week. When the child with ADD gets to school, she's likely to discover that she's forgotten her lunch. Her teacher sends notes home that say the child "needs to take her time" or "try harder next time." Her handwriting is rushed and messy and her grades in math are lower than expected because she makes careless mistakes and forgets to check her work.

Easily distracted. The child with ADD is unable to maintain her attention in the face of distracting sights, sounds, and even smells. She goes to the refrigerator to get butter, but sees some bread on the counter and brings that back to the table instead. She hears a song on the radio as she's getting dressed and forgets to take off her pajamas before putting on her clothes or neglects to change her underwear. She daydreams a lot and returns to the task in front of her only because of the teacher's constant reminders to "focus"—however, the noise of the classroom and the movement of the other children make that impossible.

The child with ADD is easily bored and flips from channel to channel on the TV set (not diagnostic by itself, Dads!) or wanders from the room halfway through her favorite show. However, animated cartoons and video games, like Nintendo and Sega Genesis, may hold her attention for several hours in a row. This apparent paradox was explained by a recent medical study that found that video games provide exactly the kind of stimulation that a child with ADD requires—rapidly shifting, high-contrast visual input coupled with intermittent motor activity (pressing the control buttons). Some educators are now taking advantage of this discovery to offer math and reading instruction in a video game format.

Doesn't follow instructions or finish tasks as assigned. The child with ADD starts something and forgets to finish it or, worse, forgets that she's had it assigned. She mows the front yard, but forgets to do the back yard. The next week, she weeds half the garden and then wanders off, leaving the garden tools outside to be ruined in the rain. Her homework is half done or she forgets to turn it in, and she almost always forgets to put her name and homeroom number on the paper. Furthermore, she doesn't read the directions and so gets a C on her math quiz despite having every problem correct.

The child with ADD may have an attention span that is so short she doesn't listen effectively. She doesn't hear the teacher's instructions or her parent's request to go clean her room. In particular, she has trouble following multistep instructions. For example, if you tell her, "Go to your room, pick up your clothes and put them in the hamper, change the sheets on your bed, and straighten the top of your dresser," she will hear only "Go to your room." So when giving instructions to a child with ADD, it's important to KISS her: Keep It Short and Simple!

Poor planning and poorly organized. Children with ADD have poor executive functioning skills. This means they can't prioritize, organize, or strategize. Since the child with ADD doesn't know where to start or what's most important about a project, she can't organize it effectively, so she sits and daydreams while the other children in her class excitedly plan their projects. Then, when the rest of the class is halfway done, she'll look around the room and take clues from what she can see of the other children's work. This is effective for very few projects, since in most instances, the details she can't see are what hold the project together (like the glue in papier-mache) or earn the good grade (like systematic research of the subject, a neatly written report, etc.).

At home, her bedroom is a total mess because she has no idea how to clean it. As you look at the room, you see that she needs to pick up her dirty clothes and put them in the hamper, throw out the old candy wrappers, put her shoes and books away, and straighten her desk and dresser. When the child with ADD looks, all she sees is chaos. She doesn't know where to begin or how to start, so she flops down on her bed and turns on the CD player. An hour later, her room is still a mess and she doesn't remember why she's there.

If It's Not ADD, What Else Could It Be?

Age-Appropriate Behavior
Most children spend at least part of each day daydreaming, or sitting in class wishing that they were outside at recess, rather than concentrating on their lessons. These are absolutely normal behaviors, when the daydreaming is limited in both amount and frequency. If the child is found often to be daydreaming or engaged in unfocused thought, ADD should be considered.

Boredom
An understimulating environment (such as a tedious lecture delivered in a subdued monotone) can interfere with the concentration of even the most focused person. For children, understimulation can occur both at school and at home (for example, during the long, drawn-out days of summer vacation), but ADD would be considered only when a child is inattentive the majority of the time. Some highly intelligent children appear to have ADD because they are understimulated in most situations. However, they would be able to concentrate well when they were intellectually challenged; the child with ADD would not.

Sleep Deprivation
Children who are tired and sleepy will have trouble concentrating, difficulty paying attention, and may appear "spacey," like the child with

ADD. If the symptoms are due to sleep deprivation, however, the child will also appear tired—rubbing her eyes, yawning excessively, or fighting sleep. Sleep deprivation is a major problem for adolescents, whose daily rhythms are "out of sync" with the school day (as described in chapter 22).

Drugs or Alcohol

Alcohol and most of the street drugs interfere with a child's ability to pay attention. To distinguish the effects of drugs from the symptoms of ADD, parents should observe their child's behavior at multiple times during the day and in multiple settings. ADD symptoms remain relatively constant throughout the day, while drug use is associated with shifts between "highs" and "lows." Further, the symptoms of drug use would be of more recent onset and would represent a change in the child's behavior (as opposed to ADD, which is present from early childhood).

Psychiatric Disorders

All of the psychiatric disorders can cause problems with attention and concentration. Some disorders, like pervasive developmental disorder (see chapter 16), are present from birth and have inattention as a core feature, so they share symptoms in common with ADD; however, these disorders have additional symptoms, such as lack of affection and communication difficulties, which are not present in ADD (see chapter 14). Psychiatric disorders which begin later in childhood or during adolescence can also cause difficulties with attention and concentration. Depression (chapter 21) interferes with a child's ability to think clearly— not only would she have difficulty paying attention, but her thinking might also be slowed down and "fuzzy." Generalized anxiety disorder (chapter 19) is associated with attention problems because the child is worrying, rather than paying attention to her lessons. Obsessive-compulsive disorder (chapter 16) not only has the anxiety-related inattention, but also distractibility, caused by obsessive thoughts that intrude upon the child's focus.

Fetal Alcohol Syndrome

Alcohol has a profound negative impact on the developing brain—it can cause learning disabilities, ADD and ADHD, mental retardation, and fetal alcohol syndrome. Children with fetal alcohol syndrome have a variety of problems, including a unique facial appearance, decreased intelligence, and behavior problems. Cocaine and other drugs used during pregnancy (and perhaps while breast-feeding) can also damage the baby's brain. There are now published reports of a recent nationwide increase in the rates of ADHD and ADD; this increase may be related to the widespread use of cocaine during the late 1980s and early 1990s. If you used drugs or drank alcohol during your pregnancy, it is important to share this information with your child's doctor, as it may help him target your child's evaluation toward these types of problems.

Vision and Hearing Problems

All children with attention problems should be screened for vision and hearing problems because they are a common cause of "inattention" and are often present before the age of seven. In this instance, the apparent inattentiveness is actually a failure to pick up clues from the environment, not a result of difficulties with concentration. For example, if your child is nearsighted, she may not see the assignment written on the blackboard, and if she is partially deaf, she may not be able to catch all the words in her teacher's oral instructions; both of which could lead to missed assignments, "forgotten" instructions, and other symptoms mimicking ADD.

Treatment of ADD

There are three equally important components of ADD therapy—psychological, medical, and educational interventions. Behavior therapy is the major component of the psychological treatment of ADD and is discussed in this section. Educational interventions are very important in ADD therapy, but are quite specific to the individual child's needs and so are beyond the scope of this discussion. If your child has ADD, we recommend that you schedule a consultation with your child's teacher and school psychologist to discuss specific ways that your child can be helped through educational interventions. Stimulant medications are the most effective medical intervention and are discussed in detail in chapter 13.

Psychological Treatments—Behavior Therapy

The goal of behavior therapy is to allow the child to function effectively at home and at school. The specific behavioral techniques that will be utilized depend upon the child's areas of dysfunction. For example, if she's failing math class because she doesn't turn her homework in on time, the behavior therapy would focus on the elements needed to get her worksheet and math book home, her homework completed, and the assignment handed in the next morning. If the child needs to avoid careless mistakes, a star chart or other reward-based behavior therapy program could be utilized (see chapter 3), with rewards given for neatness, evidence that she checked her answers, and/or following instructions. Although the individual behavior therapy regimens will have a great deal of variety, all successful programs for ADD treatment will be designed to do three things: increase structure, decrease distractions, and improve organization.

Increase structure. Rules and structured daily routines provide an external framework around which the child with ADD can begin to organize her life, while repeated practice of the desired behaviors builds an internal system of automatic responses or "fixed action patterns." Fixed action patterns are behaviors that have been repeated so many times they have become automatic. A fixed action pattern is always completed successfully once it is started, because the child doesn't have to remember the individual steps in the process. Brushing your teeth is a good example of a fixed action pattern—you do it in the same order each time and aren't fully aware of any of the steps involved. To turn a daily routine into a fixed action pattern, it is necessary to practice it over and over in exactly the same sequence. For example, if a child with ADD needs help with her morning routine, she could practice the individual tasks, such as making her bed or getting dressed, until they became fixed action patterns, and also practice the entire morning's routine until it became a larger fixed action pattern. Since fixed action patterns are only established if the routine is done the same way each time, and the child with ADD will have difficulty remembering the steps in the routine, her parent must supervise the practice sessions. Once she can do the entire routine perfectly on three consecutive mornings, the child will no longer need supervision, but a reminder of the morning routine should be posted in a highly visible place so that she can check that she has completed her morning ritual successfully.

Decrease distractions. The child with ADD is unable to filter out external stimuli, making it impossible for her to ignore the lawn mower next door or the kids playing down the street, even when she's trying her best to concentrate on her homework. Any extraneous sound, sight, or smell will distract her. Thus, she needs a quiet, isolated place to work. In some homes, a corner of the dining room is ideal—it is isolated from the other family areas and has space enough for a small desk (turned toward a blank wall), which can be stocked with all the supplies needed to complete the homework assignments. In other homes, the child's bedroom or a basement rec room can house her homework center. The most important features are good light, quiet surroundings, and neutral walls free of pictures and posters.

At school, your daughter should be protected from distractions as she takes tests and tries to work on "thinking" exercises, like math problems. She might utilize a workstation that is located in a back corner of the room, facing away from the other children and away from the windows. But for lessons taught from the front of the room, she should sit as close to the teacher as possible to decrease the number of potential distractions within her visual range.

Improve organization. Because the child with ADD has deficits in her executive functions and lacks the ability to organize, prioritize, and strategize, she is overwhelmed by systems that we don't even notice. Packing her backpack, straightening her desk, and cleaning her room are very difficult tasks for the child with ADD, unless she is provided with external clues for organization. In the case of the child's backpack, it might mean adding extra pockets (clearly labeled with the title of the book that belongs inside) or using colored folders for her homework—one labeled "Take to School" and the other "To Take Home"; when she completes her homework, she puts it into the "Take to School" folder. The child's room needs to be thoughtfully laid out and free of clutter—the dresser should be near her closet so that she can finish dressing without traveling back and forth across the room, her desk should be located out of sight of any window, and books and toys should each have their own place. Her closet should be organized so that everything has a place and the sections are clearly labeled. She can then take responsibility for putting her clothes on the appropriate shelf or slipping her shoes into the proper cubby.

Children with mild ADD can be trained to become better organized by teaching them the steps involved in routine activities, as well as the sequence in which the steps are organized. The child should be the one to describe the steps required to set the table or get ready for bed, instead of having her parent tell her the order in which it should be done. Similarly, with school projects, the child should be encouraged to "see the steps" involved, with considerable guidance from her parent. Once she begins to understand that everything we do has its own organization, it's easier for her to break large, complicated projects down into manageable units and organize those separately.

What You Can Do to Help Your Child Overcome Her ADD and Learning Problems

Recognize that your child is having problems learning. Often the best help that a parent can provide to a child is to recognize that she has a problem. If your child's school performance is less than you'd hoped, or she seems to have problems paying attention, talk to her teacher and find out if she thinks she's performing at capacity. If not, work with your child's teacher to obtain an evaluation. In addition, schedule an appointment with your child's doctor to make sure that she sees and hears properly, and that she doesn't have symptoms of ADD.

Make sure she's listening when you speak. To ensure that your child is listening, teach her to answer "Yes, Mom" when you call her name and then start each conversation by saying her name, even if she's standing right next to you. Engage her eyes and have her look directly at you while you're speaking. If you're giving her particularly important information, it may help to "get in her face" by holding her chin, her gaze, and her attention simultaneously—take her gently by the chin and tip her face up so that she is looking directly at you and hold her by the chin while you speak. When you've finished speaking, have her repeat your words back to you to ensure that she's gotten the entire message correct.

Repetition, repetition, repetition! Repetition is the key to success in ADD. Have your child repeat her lessons until she's learned them, repeat household routines until they become automatic, and repeat any instructions she's given to make sure that she has them correct. Repeating serves not only to help her pay attention (it is hard to drift off when you're repeating an instruction), but also to cement the instructions in her memory—by using both her ears and her voice as recorders.

Match the task to her attention span. Breaking tasks down into smaller units will increase your child's chances of success. By subdividing the tasks into manageable units, you allow her to focus for brief periods of time and then to return to the task after a brief respite. For example, if your child has a two-page paper to write, she might be asked to write the first paragraph and then take a short break before writing the second. If she can't write a complete paragraph neatly, she can do it a sentence at a time.

Provide external structure and organization. A place for everything and everything in its place. If you teach your child where to put her belongings and then consistently require that she puts them there, she eventually will learn that her coat belongs in the closet, her hat on the hook inside the door, and her boots on the drip mat. A similar system can be implemented at school, utilizing her assignment notebook as a reminder of what she's supposed to bring home each night and her organized backpack as a check that she has it. Eventually, through consistency and repetition, she will get to the point at which she will have the things that she needs, where she needs them, when she needs them. For example, at night before she goes to bed, she should check her assignment notebook and see what she's supposed to bring the next day, assemble it and the rest of her school "stuff," pack her backpack and set it by the door through which she leaves the house in the morning. Sports clothes and supplies should have their own special place in her room or the hallway closet, and when she comes in from practice, her cleats and soccer ball go directly into their storage place and don't get dropped somewhere else along the way. Important papers are kept in one place and one place only —they are never removed by the child without specific permission.

Become partners with your child's teacher. You and your child's teacher have the same goals for your child—to have her learn as much as possible and to enjoy learning as much as possible. Because ADD and learning disabilities cause similar problems at home and in school, it is essential that you work with your child's teacher to solve the problems in similar ways. The two of you should establish consistent guidelines and expectations, communicate frequently, and provide each other with support and encouragement—the parent-teacher team is stronger than either individual alone.

Help your child find new ways to learn. Alternate learning strategies are particularly important for the child who has both ADD and a learning disability. For example, if a child has inattention and memory problems, she may find it impossible to sit down and memorize a list of twenty spelling words. But if you let her take a piece of sidewalk chalk and write ten of the words on the driveway and then draw pictures to illustrate them as she shouts out their spellings, she'll happily do those ten and the second half of the list as well. As you're thinking of creative ways to help your child learn, remember to draw upon her strengths. If she's good at memorizing, turn math problems into memorization exercises. If she's better at figuring out riddles, state them as word problems. You could even help her learn addition and subtraction facts by letting her have a lemonade stand—one day, her lemonade is 6 cents a glass and the next it's 8 cents or 15 cents. Make sure that you and your child's teacher are working in partnership on this one, as she will have many ideas for fun, age-appropriate alternatives.

Provide your child with lots of love and positive attention. Chapters 1 and 13 discuss the importance of the three Ls—love, limits, and large muscle exercise for children with attentional disorders. Love and support are particularly important to the child with ADD or learning disabilities. She may feel that she is stupid because she has gotten such poor grades at school, or she may be frustrated by her learning disabilities or communications problems, or she may have been teased by the other children in her class for needing special resources. Providing your daughter with extra love and attention can help her regain her self-esteem, as well as providing her with a sense of safety and security.

Further Reading

Fisher, Gary, Ph.D., and Rhoda Cummings, Ed.D. *When Your Child Has LD (Learning Differences): A Survival Guide for Parents*. Minneapolis, MN: Free Spirit Publishing, 1995.

Greene, Lawrence J. *Learning Disabilities and Your Child: A Survival Handbook*. New York: Ballantine Books, 1987.

Rossner, Jerome. *Helping Children Overcome Learning Difficulties*. New York: Walker & Co., 1993.

Silver, Larry B., M.D. *The Misunderstood Child: A Guide for Parents of Children with Learning Disabilities*. Blue Ridge Summit, PA: Tab Books, 1992.

Smith, Corinne, Ph.D., and Lisa Strick. *Learning Disabilities: A to Z—A*

Parent's Complete Guide to Learning Disabilities from Preschool to Adulthood. New York: Simon & Schuster, 1997.

Smith, Sally L. *No Easy Answers: The Learning Disabled Child at Home and at School.* New York: Bantam Books, 1995.

Vail, Priscilla L. *Smart Kids with School Problems: Things to Know and Ways to Help.* New York: Penguin Books, 1987.

For Children with Learning Disabilities

Dwyer, Kathleen M. *What Do You Mean I Have a Learning Disability?* New York: Walker & Co., 1991.

Fisher, Gary, Ph.D., and Rhoda Cummings, Ed.D. *The Survival Guide for Kids with LD (Learning Differences).* Minneapolis, MN: Free Spirit Publishing, 1990.

Levine, Melvin D. *Keeping a Head in School: A Student's Book About Learning Abilities and Learning Disorders.* Cambridge, MA: Educators Publishing Service, 1990.

Robey, Cynthia. *When Learning Is Tough: Kids Talk About Their Learning Disabilities.* Morton Grove, IL: Robert Whitman & Co., 1994.

Resources

Resources for attention deficit disorder are listed in chapter 13 with ADHD resources.

Educational Resource Information Center (ERIC)
Council for Exceptional Children
1920 Association Drive
Reston, VA 22091-1589
800-328-0272

International Dyslexia Association (or Orton Dyslexia Society)
Chester Building, Suite 382
8600 LaSalle Road
Baltimore, MD 21286-2044
410-296-0232
http://ODS.org

Learning Disabilities Association of America (LDA)
4156 Library Road
Pittsburgh, PA 15234

412-341-8077

Learning Disabilities Association of Canada
252 Chapel Street
Ottawa, Ontario, Canada K1N7Z2
613-238-5721

National Center for Learning Disabilities
381 Park Avenue South, Suite 1420
New York, NY 10016
Phone: 212-545-7510
Fax: 212-545-9665
www.ncld.org

National Information Center for Children and Youth with Disabilities
P.O. Box 1492
Washington, D.C. 20013-1492
800-695-0285 or 202-884-8200

Parents of Gifted/Learning Disabled Children
2420 Eccleston Street
Bethesda, MD 20902
301-986-1432

Children with learning disabilities have special rights under federal and state laws. To find out about these rights, contact the Director of Special Education at your state's Department of Education or contact:
U.S. Department of Education, Office of Special Education or Rehabilitative Services
Clearing House of Disability Information
330 C Street, S.W., Room 3132
Washington, D.C. 20202-2500
800-688-9889

"My Son Has So Many Little Nervous Habits—Like Blinking Too Much and Clearing His Throat"

Tic disorders and Tourette disorder

"Andy, is there something in your eye?" Linda asked her eight-year-old son as they sat together watching TV.

"I don't think so," Andy replied.

"Then why are you blinking so much?" his mother continued.

"I'm not blinking."

"Yes, you are," Linda said, "and you keep coughing and clearing your throat. Do you think you're coming down with something?"

"I don't know, maybe," Andy said. "But I don't feel sick. I just have this funny feeling in the back of my throat and coughing this way helps to get rid of it."

"Well, instead of making that horrible noise," Linda said, "why don't you get a drink of water? That should make the tickle go away and it would be a lot easier on your throat—and on my ears."

Andy went to the kitchen for a drink of water and his throat-clearing was much less noticeable when he returned. Linda didn't hear Andy clear his throat at all the next day and she thought it might finally have disappeared, until Angie, Andy's second grade teacher, called.

"Linda, I'm calling you about two things. The first is that I'd like you to make cupcakes for our Valentine's Day party."

"No problem. I'd be glad to," Linda volunteered. "Do you need me to do anything else?"

"No, thank you. I already have enough help with the party," the teacher replied. "But I did want to talk to you about your son for a moment. Have you noticed that Andy has tics again?"

"Ticks?" Linda replied. "How could he have ticks in February?"

"Not the kind of ticks that are bugs," Angie responded. "T-i-c-s, tics or nervous habits. Andy blinks his eyes almost constantly, and every few minutes, he shrugs his shoulders as he stretches his neck. He's also got a throat-clearing tic—it's so loud and so forceful that I'm worried he's going to dislodge his tonsils. Haven't you noticed it?"

"Yes, of course we've noticed it, especially the throat-clearing," Linda replied. "But we thought it was due to allergies."

"Well, I'm not a doctor, so I can't tell you for sure," Ms. Brooks said. "But my brother had a tic disorder when he was young and some of his tics were identical to those that Andy has. Andy doesn't seem to notice his eye-blinking, but a few of the students have commented on his throat-clearing, so I know he's aware of that. If it's coming from allergies, then maybe he should be on medication. In either case, I think he should be seen by his doctor, don't you?"

"Yes, of course. I'll make the appointment right away," Linda replied.

Andy's pediatrician, Dr. Wilson, was able to see him the next afternoon. After Linda described the throat-clearing and the little nervous habits they had noticed at home, Dr. Wilson asked, "How long ago did the tics start?"

"I really can't remember. We never thought much about them before. Now that I know they're tics, I've been trying to remember when they first started. I think it was probably some time between kindergarten and first grade," Linda said. "Andy's eye-blinking definitely started first and I know he didn't have it in preschool because the teachers would have brought it to our attention. It's hard to tell about kindergarten—there was a lot going on that whole year, and they could have been missed. Andy definitely had them last year. We all noticed his throat-clearing and his teacher sent a note home suggesting that he get his eyes checked because he blinked so much. We took him to an optometrist, but the exam was completely normal."

"I'm not surprised," Dr. Wilson responded. "Andy probably suppressed the eye-blinking tic during the examination, and unless he's having the tic, there's nothing to see." The doctor asked some additional questions about the timing and nature of Andy's tics and then did a comprehensive physical examination.

"I don't see any evidence of allergies, Linda. Based on what you've told me and the fact that Andy's physical examination is so normal, I think that he has a tic disorder. During the few minutes that we've been together, I heard the throat-clearing and coughing tics and saw five different motor tics—eye blinks, shoulder shrugs, nose twitches, finger-tapping, and some facial grimaces. Since Andy has both vocal tics and motor tics and the tics have been present in various combinations for over a year, they qualify for a diagnosis of Tourette syndrome," Dr. Wilson said.

Linda looked horrified, so the doctor quickly continued, "Please don't worry! The term 'Tourette syndrome' is merely a means of classifying the nature and duration of the tics—it doesn't tell us anything about the severity of the tics or the expected course. Since the label 'Tourette syndrome' is so frightening, I usually avoid it and stick with the generic term, 'tic disorder.' In either case, what we need to focus our attention on is minimizing the frequency and intensity of the tics, so that Andy isn't embarrassed by them."

What Are Tics and What Is Tourette Syndrome?

Tics are brief, intermittent movements (motor tics) or sounds (vocal tics) that erupt suddenly and rapidly and recur repeatedly. Tics are very common in childhood—estimates suggest that between 10 to 20 percent of boys and 2 to 10 percent of girls will have a tic for at least a short time during their grade school years. Tics are divided into simple and complex types, depending upon whether the tic involves one muscle group or several. Simple motor tics include eye-blinking, wrinkling of the forehead, nose-twitching, pursing of the lips, sticking out the tongue, facial grimaces, shoulder shrugs, and simple movements of the arms or legs. Complex motor tics occur when several muscle groups contract in sequence—examples include jumping, kicking, hopping, turning, touching, tapping, and retracing of steps. Smelling, kissing, and licking tics can also occur and can involve people or objects; in severe cases, the child might lick the ground or kiss a stranger as part of a complex tic.

In young children, the tics frequently occur without warning and the child may be unaware that he has any abnormal movements, even when they are obvious to others. In older children and adolescents, the tic is often preceded by a feeling of increasing tension or physical discomfort, such as an "itch" or "tickle"; this sensation is known as a premonitory urge and can be used to distinguish tics from other abnormal movements. The premonitory urge warns the child that he is about to have a tic and he can use voluntary efforts to suppress the tic or to disguise it as a part of a voluntary motion—for example, he might hold his breath rather than uttering a swear word or combine a shoulder shrug tic with the appropriate facial expression to make it appear intentional. Because tics can be manipulated in this way, some physicians describe them as "unvoluntary" or against the person's conscious will, rather than involuntary, or automatic. However, they are usually considered to be involuntary because they occur without conscious thought and often without the child's awareness.

The premonitory urge (or pre-tic urge) is just one of the sensory symptoms seen with tics. Sensory hypersensitivity (also called tactile-sensory defensiveness) is another. When a child has sensory hypersensitivity, his skin is unusually sensitive to touch and texture. The child is bothered by the tag on the collar of his T-shirt, the roughness of the fabric in his jeans, or the way that socks feel on his feet. Some children become uncomfortable if the two sides of their body feel differently—so they wouldn't want to wear a watch on just one wrist or have one sock slip down and the other stay in place. At the present time, no one knows why sensory hypersensitivity develops, nor why it occurs so often in children with tic disorders, although some scientists have speculated that the uncomfortable sensations may be a "sensory tic" that is triggered by rough textures or constricting clothing.

Many children with tic disorders have at least one other neuropsychiatric disorder, such as learning disabilities (chapter 14), attention deficit hyperactivity disorder (ADHD, chapter 13), or obsessive-compulsive disorder (chapter 16). When present, these conditions are often of greater concern than the tics and even when they're not, their presence may complicate treatment of the tic disorder. For example, stimulant medications (such as Ritalin or Dexedrine) have a reputation for "causing" or worsening tics in children with Tourette disorder, and physicians are sometimes reluctant to treat a child's ADHD with stimulants if he also has a tic disorder. However, recent studies have demonstrated that the stimulant medications don't cause tics, but may cause a temporary increase in the severity of the tics—if the medication is continued, the tics return to their pretreatment level after a few weeks.

Does Your Child Have a Tic Disorder?

1. Does he have brief, abnormal movements (motor tics), such as eye-blinking, facial grimaces, or shoulder shrugs, many times a day, nearly every day?
2. Does he make unnecessary noises (vocal tics), such as coughs, grunts, throat-clearing, or sniffing, many times a day, nearly every day?

3. Have the tics been present for at least two weeks?
4. Have the tics been present for more than one year?
5. Does he have only one type of tic (for example, eye-blinking)?
6. Do the tics vary in location, number, and severity over time?

If you answered yes to questions 1 or 2, yes to question 3, and no to question 4, your child may have a transient tic disorder.

If you answered yes to questions 1 or 2, yes to questions 3 and 4, and no to question 6, your child may have a chronic tic disorder.

If the answer to question 5 is yes, he may have a chronic single tic disorder.

If the answer to question 5 is no, he may have a chronic multiple tic disorder.

If you answered yes to questions 1, 2, 3, 4, and 6 and no to question 5, your child may have Tourette disorder.

How Do You Know If Your Child Has a Tic Disorder?

In order to tell whether your child has a tic disorder, you need to watch and listen specifically for the presence of tics. First listen for abnormal noises and watch for tics in your child's face and neck, next turn your attention to his shoulders and arms, then to his torso and finally to his legs and feet—watching for brief, abnormal movements in each group of muscles. You may have to observe your child in several different settings and at different times during the day to detect mild tics, since the movements tend to come and go throughout the day. Many children have their worst tics in the evening, when they're tired, or immediately after school as they compensate for having suppressed the tics during the school day, but some children report that their tics are most severe when they first awaken. The tics may be hard to detect if the child disguises them by incorporating them into voluntary movements or suppresses them during your observations; thus, it is helpful to also watch for tics while your child watches TV or plays a video game.

If your child has motor or vocal tics, he has a tic disorder. Saying that a child has a "tic disorder" is the same as saying that he "has tics" and tells you nothing about the severity of the tics or the prognosis for the future. Even the different categories of tic disorders tell you little about the child's symptoms—they merely define the length of time that the child has had tics (transient—less than one year, or chronic—longer than one year) and the number of tics present (single versus multiple). Tourette syndrome is also just a label that defines the type (both motor and vocal tics), duration (more than one year), and pattern of the tics (moving about the body with a waxing and waning course). There is nothing in the definition of Tourette syndrome that defines it as a severe tic disorder or that predicts a poor prognosis—indeed, most children with Tourette syndrome will outgrow their tics by the time they reach high school.

As with other neuropsychiatric disorders, tics can cause the child distress and difficulties in his daily functioning (see chapter 12). The distress associated with motor tics is usually linked to embarrassment about the "peculiar" nature of the movements, particularly when the tics are so intense that they are noticeable to the casual observer. Vocal tics are most embarrassing when they are loud, inappropriate (like a Bronx cheer or swear words), or interfere with the child's speech. The tics may cause the child to be ostracized by his peers or to become the victim of teasing and ridicule—both cause tremendous distress and threaten the child's self-esteem. Tics can cause difficulties by intruding on a child's movements, speech, and/or thoughts. For example, a child might concentrate so hard on suppressing his tics that he doesn't hear the teacher give the homework assignment. Occasionally, motor tics interfere with a child's fine motor skills and make it difficult for him to write. Vocal tics can interfere with speech fluency and make it difficult for the child to speak clearly, or render him afraid to answer the teacher's questions or to participate in conversations with his classmates.

If It's Not a Tic Disorder, What Else Could It Be?

A Medical Condition

There is a close overlap between tics and symptoms of several different medical illnesses, and these disorders should be considered whenever one suspects that a child has tics. Allergies can cause repetitive throat-clearing, sniffing, and coughing; if the vocalizations are the result of allergies, there should be a seasonal pattern or a history of worsening after exposure to particular allergens. Eye-blinking might be associated with light sensitivity or nearsightedness, and the child's vision should be checked before eye-blinking is labeled as a tic. Some children have skin conditions that cause excessive itchiness and they have excessive scratching in response to it. In general, medical illnesses can be distinguished from tic disorders by the presence of additional physical symptoms or abnormalities seen during the physical examination.

Another Neurological Condition

When both motor and vocal tics are present, the diagnosis of a tic disorder should be made easily, since there are no other neurological conditions that cause both. If the child has only abnormal movements, a long list of neurological disorders must be considered—these include dystonias, myoclonus, choreoathetosis, akathisia, dyskinesias, and excessive startle syndromes. The conditions are not as serious as their intimidating names would suggest, but they do deserve attention. Since each disorder has its own characteristic presentation, a physician will be able to rule out many of these conditions by performing a neurological examination.

Obsessive-compulsive disorder

When a complex motor tic is preceded by a strong urge to perform the behavior (premonitory urge), it can be very hard to decide whether the movement is a motor tic or a compulsive ritual of obsessive-compulsive disorder, or OCD (described in chapter 16). The distinction is particularly difficult because tics and obsessive-compulsive symptoms occur together in the majority of children—over two-thirds of children with OCD have tics and 50 to 75 percent of children with Tourette disorder have obsessive-compulsive symptoms. Further, tics and compulsions overlap considerably in their presentation. Touching, tapping, counting, repeating, and symmetry concerns (needing to have things "even" or "equal") are all common tics, but are also compulsions commonly seen in OCD. The distinction between tics and compulsions is usually made by examining the pattern of the repetitive behavior, evaluating the child's other symptoms (do they look more like tics or compulsions?), and determining whether the preceding urge is a sensory feeling (tic disorder) or a thought (OCD). It is important to identify the tic/compulsion correctly because tics respond best to one type of treatment and OCD to another. Sometimes, however, the distinction cannot be made and the behavior is labeled as a compulsive tic. Then, the child's treatment will depend upon his other symptoms.

PANDAS, or pediatric autoimmune neuropsychiatric disorders associated with strep infections

If a child's tics started abruptly, or they seemed to explode in severity after the child had a cold or strep throat infection, then he might have PANDAS, a subgroup of tic disorders that appear to be triggered by strep throat infections (described fully in chapter 17). Children with PANDAS have tics and/or OCD that began at a very young age (usually ages five to eight) and has an episodic course of severity—the symptoms come and go periodically. Strep infections trigger a relapse that may last for several weeks or months, but if the child isn't exposed to another strep infection, the tics will decrease to low levels or sometimes disappear entirely. Prevention of the strep infections may decrease symptom severity, so it can be important to determine whether or not your child's tics are related to PANDAS (see chapter 17 for more information).

Treatment of Tic Disorders

The first and most important decision to be made in the treatment of tic disorders is whether or not the child's symptoms require therapy. Treatment is usually reserved for children with severe tics or those in whom the tics are causing distress or interference. For a child with tics of mild to moderate severity, in whom there are no signs of distress or interference, therapy is not required. But if the tics embarrass the child or interfere with his schoolwork or peer relationships, then they should be treated —even if they aren't very frequent or intense.

Psychological Treatments

Treatment options are quite limited for tic disorders. Behavior therapy is not helpful for the long-term management of tic disorders, although children may benefit from learning relaxation techniques, since tics tend to worsen during periods of stress and excitement. Psychotherapy is also not useful for the treatment of the tics, but may be helpful to the child who is having psychological difficulties related to his tic disorder.

Medications

Since the psychological therapies are not very helpful in the treatment of tic disorders, medications are usually required. The decision to use medications should not be entered into lightly because of the potential for side effects from the drugs, but it should also not be delayed unnecessarily, since the medications can offer the child significant relief.

Neuroleptics. There are two neuroleptics that are used to treat tic disorders: haloperidol (Haldol) and pimozide (Orap). Both drugs have been used for long periods of time—haloperidol for over thirty years and pimozide for ten years—and both medications are very effective, with improvements seen in about 75 percent of patients. A recent study compared the two drugs and found that pimozide (1 to 6 mg/day) was better than haloperidol (at 0.5 to 3 mg/day) in reducing tics, perhaps because the children had fewer side effects. In many clinics, pimozide is now recommended as a first-choice treatment for tic disorders.

Haloperidol and pimozide are thought to decrease tics by blocking the effects of dopamine in the basal ganglia. Unfortunately, dopamine blockade is associated with a risk of tardive dyskinesia, a potentially irreversible movement disorder characterized by facial grimaces, mouthing movements, and writhing motions of the hands or feet. The condition appears to be dose-dependent and is quite rare at the dosages used to treat Tourette disorder. The risk of tardive dyskinesia can be minimized by using the lowest dose possible, even if it means that some tics remain.

Side effects of neuroleptic treatment include: sedation, fatigue, weight gain, depression, memory lapses, poor school performance, aggressive outbursts, and neurological symptoms such as muscle rigidity, slowing of movements, and akathisia (agitation, increased movement, and a feeling that the child "has to move"). The neurological side effects can be decreased or prevented by treating the child with another medication at times when the dose of neuroleptic is being increased. Pimozide can also cause electrocardiographic (ECG) changes, which may be associated with alterations in heart rhythms. Before starting your child on pimozide, his doctor should make sure the ECG is normal and should continue to check the ECG periodically while the child is on medication.

Risperidone (Risperdal) is a new neuroleptic medication that does not appear to cause as many side effects as haloperidol and pimozide. The drug isn't the first choice for the treatment of tic disorders because clinical experience with risperidone is limited, particularly in children. One recent study has shown that risperidone is useful in decreasing tic severity, causing only sedation as a side effect (although it should be noted that risperidone may also carry the risk of tardive dyskinesia). Two other neuroleptics, sulpride and tiapride, have been used successfully in Europe to treat tic disorders, but aren't yet available in the United States.

Other medications. Clonidine (Catapres) was developed for the treatment of high blood pressure but has been found to decrease the frequency and intensity of tics in up to 50 percent of children. Although fewer children will improve with clonidine, many doctors will try it first because it offers some distinct advantages: no risk of tardive dyskinesia or other neurological side effects, and improvement in behavioral symptoms, such as hyperactivity, inattention, and poor frustration tolerance. Side effects of clonidine treatment include sedation, dry mouth, irritability, insomnia, headaches, and, at higher doses, dizziness and hypotension (low blood pressure). Clonidine is associated with a withdrawal syndrome, characterized by anxiety, increased tic frequency, and irritability. Problems with daily withdrawal can be avoided by taking the medicine more frequently or administering the clonidine as a patch. To avoid a withdrawal syndrome when therapy is to be discontinued, the dosage should be decreased slowly and gradually.

New medications that have similar effects to clonidine are being developed and tested. The new medications should offer better specificity, which means that they should have the same benefits as clonidine with fewer side effects. One of these drugs, guanfacine (Tenex), was tested in a small group of children with ADHD and was found to help both tics and inattention, without causing sedation. Guanfacine is gaining popularity and is sometimes tried first in the treatment of tics because it has so few side effects.

Helping Your Child Overcome His Tic Disorder
Recognize the tics and get confirmation that your child has a tic disorder. The key to recognizing tics is to watch for motor tics and to listen for vocal tics. If you suspect that your child has tics, start recording your observations so that you will be able to tell your child's doctor about the frequency, intensity, and nature of the abnormal movements and vocalizations. It is particularly important to notice the timing of the tics, since throat-clearing that occurs only in the fall or spring may be a symptom of an allergy rather than a tic.

Realize that tics are not under your child's control, even if he can suppress them. Parents tell us, "It doesn't make sense, his teacher says he can control his tics all day at school, but then he says he *has* to do them at home—I don't believe it." Actually, that is exactly what is happening. The child expends a tremendous amount of energy in suppressing his tics at school (or whenever he's in public view) and is tired at the end of the day. In addition, suppressing tics increases the urge to tic, and by the time he gets home, the urge is too strong for him to control. It is important for you to realize that the increase in tics at home is not a form of disobedience, but rather an acknowledgment that your home is a safe and private place for your child to "give in" to his disorder. He should never be punished for his tics because they are not under his control.

Help your child have positive self-esteem. Tic disorders threaten a child's self-esteem in many ways, but particularly in his feelings of social competence. Children with tics are frequently clumsy in their social interactions and find it difficult to make friends. In addition, their tics are an easy target for teasing and ridicule. You can help your child overcome his social difficulties by arranging for play dates, doing role-playing exercises, or allowing him to take a social skills training class. Enlist the aid of your child's teacher, Scout leader, soccer coach, and other adults to help your child have only positive social interactions. Make sure that these adults don't have any misunderstandings about the nature of his tics; give them suggestions for ways in which they can help your child, such as setting a good example in response to the motor and vocal tics, decreasing unnecessary stress, and preventing teasing from other children.

Prevent your child from being teased or ridiculed. Every child deserves a safe, nonthreatening environment at home and at school. For a child with a tic disorder, this means that you and his teachers need to take an active role to prevent teasing and ridicule. Tics are often seen as a source of amusement to other children, particularly if the child has vocal tics that include blurting out bad words—unfortunately, when a child becomes upset about being teased, the frequency of his tics increases, which leads to even more teasing. Teasing can be stopped by education as well as by direct intervention. Our patients report that their classmates stop teasing them (and also prevent others from teasing) after the tic disorder has been fully explained. If your child's teacher doesn't feel comfortable providing this explanation, your pediatrician or a member of the local Tourette Syndrome Association could be invited to address the class.

Be vigilant for ADHD and learning disabilities. Attention deficit hyperactivity disorder (ADHD—chapter 13) occurs in about 40 percent of boys who have Tourette disorder and nearly 25 percent of those with other tic disorders. Learning disabilities (chapter 14) are even more common and occur in about one-half of the children, although less than one-fifth are identified by the school systems. You should be in close communication with your child's teacher about his progress. If he exhibits signs of a learning disability or attention deficit disorder, he should have an educational assessment, as described in chapter 14.

Learn about tic disorders and help your child understand them as fully as possible. You and your child should both become experts on tic disorders. The more information your child has, the better he will be able to cope with his disorder, and the more informed you are, the better prepared you will be to help him. The Tourette Syndrome Association (see Resources) is an excellent source of information for you and your child, and also for your child's teacher and physician.

Further Reading

Bruun, Ruth D., M.D., and Bertel Bruun, M.D. *A Mind of Its Own—Tourette's Syndrome: A Story and a Guide*. New York: Oxford University Press, 1994.

Dornbush, Marilyn P., and Sheryl K. Pruitt. *Teaching the Tiger—A Handbook for Individuals Involved with the Education of Students with ADD, TS or OCD*. Duarte, CA: Hope Press, 1995.

Fowler, Rick. *The Unwelcome Companion—An Insider's View of Tourette Syndrome*. Cashiers, NC: Silver Run Publications, 1995.

Haerle, Tracy, ed. *Children with Tourette Syndrome: A Parent's Guide*. Rockville, MD: Woodbine House, 1992.

Hughes, Susan. *Ryan: A Mother's Story of Her Hyperactive Tourette Syndrome Child*. Duarte, CA: Hope Press, 1990. Call 800-321-4039 to order books by Hope Press.

———. *What Makes Ryan Tick: A Family's Triumph Over TS and ADHD*. Duarte, CA: Hope Press, 1996.

Seligman, Adam Ward, and John S. Hilkevich. *Don't Think about Monkeys: Extraordinary Stories Written by People with Tourette Syndrome*. Duarte, CA: Hope Press, 1992.

Shimberg, Elaine Fantle. *Living with Tourette Syndrome*. New York: Simon & Schuster, 1995.

Resources

Tourette Syndrome Association, Inc.
42-40 Bell Boulevard
Bayside, New York 11361-2820
Phone: 718-224-2999
Fax: 718-279-9596
E-mail: tourette@ix netcom.com

"My Child Is Plagued by Scary Thoughts and Silly Rituals"

Obsessive-compulsive disorder and related disorders

"Mom, help me! I'm stuck."

Steeling herself for what she might find, Joanna ran quickly up the stairs to her eight-year-old daughter Ashley's room. The last time she had been summoned, it was a plumbing emergency—Ashley had used an entire roll of toilet paper as she tried to wipe herself clean and had plugged up the toilet. The time before that, Joanna had found her daughter at the sink, washing and rewashing her hands, sobbing with frustration because she knew that her hands weren't really dirty, but unable to stop washing them until they were "perfectly clean." This time, Ashley was standing in the middle of her bedroom with her jeans tangled around her ankles. She had gotten stuck as she struggled to remove them without touching the hem—the hem that might have been contaminated by brushing against her dirty shoes. If Ashley touched it, she would be contaminated and she would have to wash again. That would be really awful—it would take forever to finish and she still wouldn't be really clean.

Joanna sighed deeply and helped her daughter undress. She started to help Ashley get dressed again so they could get to the doctor's office on time, but first Ashley ordered Joanna to go wash her hands—they had touched the "dirty" pants and might contaminate her. When Joanna returned from the bathroom, she pulled a new outfit from the closet and tried to help Ashley put it on. But Ashley screamed that it was dirty and that she couldn't wear it. The next outfit was dirty, too, and the next one, and the next—they had touched the floor, or her clothes, or the bedspread. The dirt seemed to be spreading by invisible leaps and bounds. The rules of what was clean and what was dirty kept changing, and no matter how careful Joanna was (and no matter how many times she washed her hands), the new garment would always be too dirty for her daughter to wear.

It was clearly torturous for Ashley. She was crying inconsolably and shaking with fear. But it was difficult for Joanna, too. She so desperately wanted to help her daughter, but no matter how hard she tried, she couldn't perform the ritual correctly. Ashley was soon screaming at her, "Stop being so clumsy! You keep getting my clothes dirty" and "You're so mean! You contaminated that skirt on purpose. Well, you can't make me wear it."

Joanna tried to reason with Ashley—explaining that the clothes were clean and safe: "See, it's spotless. It didn't touch a thing. Besides, even if it did, it wouldn't have gotten dirty." But the explanations didn't help—every outfit was refused. When there were no "clean" clothes left, Joanna was finally able to escape for a few minutes to go get some fresh laundry.

Once in the safety of the laundry room, Joanna allowed herself to break down for a moment. As she cried, she wondered what had happened to her daughter. The screaming, tantrumming banshee in that room wasn't her Ashley. Ashley was such a happy, easygoing child—always respectful, well mannered, sensible, and independent, but most of all, a little girl who loved playing outside and getting really dirty. No, the girl in there wasn't her daughter. But who was she? What had happened to her Ashley? Was she sick? Crazy? Possessed? She hoped their pediatrician, Dr. Roberts, could figure it out—he had agreed to see them later that afternoon.

Joanna was finally able to get Ashley dressed by bringing fresh laundry to a "clean" section of the family room and allowing Ashley to pick her clothes directly from the laundry basket. Then, she put on Ashley's socks and shoes, washed her hands before putting on their coats, and led her daughter to the car —making certain that Ashley didn't come close to anything "dirty." Once they were safely settled into the car, Ashley said quietly, "Thank you, Mom—I was really freaking out in there and you saved my life." Joanna was so relieved by this moment of normality that she almost gave her daughter a big hug, but she stopped herself just in time, fearing that touching the car door handle had made her dirty in Ashley's eyes and they would have to go through the whole contamination–hand-washing–clothes-changing ritual again.

When Dr. Roberts interviewed Ashley, it became clear that the fear of being dirty had started suddenly and inexplicably. Ashley told him that she had first noticed it a few weeks earlier, after a field trip to the zoo in which her teacher had cautioned them repeatedly to "Wash your hands carefully and get rid of all germs before eating your lunch. Zoos are very dirty places, you know, and you don't want to get sick." Ever since then, Ashley had been having worries about becoming sick because of animals' germs. At first, only the zoo and stray animals were contaminated. That wasn't much of a problem—her family didn't go to the zoo and she could just avoid places where strays might be lurking. But when she began to feel that her dog, Skippy, was contaminated, it became a very big problem. Ashley really loved Skippy, and now she couldn't pet him or even be near him. Worse, he went everywhere in the house—he laid on the couch, he slobbered all over the kitchen floor as he ate his food, and he did his business in the backyard. The whole house was contaminated, so she stayed in her room most of the time and she started washing her hands more often in order to protect herself.

At this point in Ashley's story, Dr. Roberts interrupted her to ask, "But surely you know that Skippy's germs can't really hurt you? That your house isn't really dirty?"

"Part of me knows that," Ashley replied, "but part of me is really, really scared. And the part that is scared is in control. I used to be able to tell it to leave me alone, but now I can't!"

Dr. Roberts asked a few more questions before saying, "I think Ashley is suffering from obsessive-compulsive disorder. She needs to begin treatment with a child psychiatrist as soon as possible."

Dr. Roberts was right—Ashley did have obsessive-compulsive disorder (or OCD). The fears, the avoidance, and the elaborate rituals were all symptoms of OCD. Obsessive-compulsive disorder affects children and adults of all ages. It can come on suddenly, as in Ashley's case, or it can begin slowly and gradually. Each child has a slightly different set of symptoms (described below), but all share a common knowledge that their obsessions and compulsions don't make sense—that the symptoms are stupid, crazy, or unnecessary.

What Is OCD?

Obsessive-compulsive disorder is a biologically based psychiatric disorder in which children are plagued by worrisome thoughts (obsessions) and time-consuming rituals (compulsions). Children know that what they are thinking or doing is nonsensical, but they cannot stop—they cannot regain control. Often, they feel guilty about their obsessive thoughts or their compulsive rituals. Their parents feel guilty, too, concerned that somehow they caused their child's obsessions or compulsions through something that they did or something that they failed to do. But neither the parent nor the child is to blame. Doctors now know that OCD is not the result of harsh toilet-training or a child's stubbornness, but rather the result of dysfunctions in key brain chemicals. These chemicals are supposed to act as the brain's messengers—carrying bits of information from one cell to another and from one area of the brain to another. When they aren't working properly, the messages can get lost, scrambled, or repeated. If the message is lost, the child may doubt his own senses and find himself checking and rechecking that he turned off the light, or rearranging the contents of his desk drawers hundreds of times in order to be sure everything is there, or repeatedly questioning, "How can I be sure that the sky is really blue?" If the message is mixed up, the child may have frightening images that feel like waking nightmares or troublesome obsessive thoughts (like worries about germs and contamination). If the message is repeated excessively, the child may have "mental hiccups" in which he constantly repeats thoughts, words, behaviors, or physical movements—including both tics (see chapter 15) and compulsive rituals.

Does Your Child Have OCD?

1. Is he troubled by excessive worries, particularly about dirt, germs, or other dangers?
2. Does he repeat the same questions over and over again? Or constantly seek reassurance?
3. Does he seem to have difficulty concentrating?
4. Is he washing his hands excessively? Or taking extra showers or changing his clothes more frequently?
5. Does he "check" repeatedly? Reread or rewrite homework assignments?
6. Does he have to repeat things a certain number of times or until they are "just right"?
7. Does he arrange things in a certain order or become upset if something is misplaced?
8. Do the symptoms bother your child—make him anxious or upset?
9. Do the worries or behaviors get in your child's way, interfering with his activities at home or at school?

Your child may have obsessive-compulsive disorder if you answered yes to any of the first seven questions as well as questions 8 or 9.

How Do You Know If Your Child Has OCD?

The hallmark symptoms of OCD are obsessions (bad thoughts) and compulsions (repetitive rituals). Obsessive-compulsive disorder is diagnosed when a child has obsessive-compulsive symptoms for more than an hour each day and experiences the symptoms as unwanted and intrusive. Typically, she will be able to tell you that the thoughts don't make sense and that they are crazy or silly, but if she is quite young (or if the symptoms are chronic or severe), she may only be able to tell you that she'd "rather not have to have these thoughts anymore" or "I don't want to waste so much time washing my hands."

Obsessions

Obsessions are thoughts, ideas, or images that are distressing, frightening, or so constant that they become bothersome or annoying. Frequently, the obsessions are so persistent or "loud" that they interfere with the child's ability to pay attention—she might even have difficulty reading a paragraph or carrying on a conversation because the obsessive thoughts get in her way. Our patients have told us that they usually can recognize the thoughts as silly or irrational, but that they can't control them: "It's like this one part of my brain goes crazy and keeps repeating the same thing over and over again. The rest of my brain is screaming, 'Shut up! Shut up!,' but the crazy part won't listen." Common obsessions include:

Worries about dirt, germs, or other contaminants. The children are excessively concerned about becoming "dirty" or "contaminated." They may fear that they have germs that they can give to others, or that they will catch germs from other people. Common contaminants include: AIDS, blood, germs in public bathrooms, dirt, bugs, and animals. If the child has a fear of being contaminated by his stool or urine (or of contaminating others), he may use excessive amounts of toilet paper as he tries to wipe himself "clean"—sometimes even plugging the toilet, as Ashley did. Or he may refuse to wipe. Some parents have reported that they still have to help their seven-year-old child wipe himself. The child may be afraid to use a public rest room, or even to use certain toilets at home.

Often, the first sign of a contamination fear is avoidance—staying away from the dirty item or the contaminated place, refusing to tie his shoes or use a public rest room, or quitting the football team because he might get dirty. Sometimes, however, even when a child has fairly severe obsessional fears about dirt and germs, he will be able to keep playing sports. This baffles his parents—how can he get filthy playing soccer, but refuse to take out the garbage for fear that a speck of dirt will get on his clothes or that he'll catch something by touching the garbage can lid? No one knows why these inconsistencies occur, but they frequently do. It is not a willful choice on the child's part. It is a result of the irrational nature of obsessions and compulsions.

Worries about harm coming to yourself or another person. These fears include everything from burglars and kidnappers to hailstorms and tornadoes. The child may fear that he will be hurt or killed, or that his loved ones (especially his parents) will be injured or separated from him. The obsessions can be vague and difficult to put into words, or too frightening to verbalize, so it may be difficult to get the child to tell you about these fears. Some children react to such obsessional fears by asking for reassurance. They might ask the same questions over and over again, hoping that one of the answers will finally convince them that they are safe; while others may refuse to leave their parent's side for fear that they will be hurt or that their parent will be.

Fear of doing something embarrassing. The child with OCD may fear that he will wet his pants in school, or suddenly shout out a bad word in a church service, or otherwise embarrass himself. It may be particularly difficult for a child to admit that he has these fears, because he knows they don't make sense and feels embarrassed about having them. Admitting that he has them would also be embarrassing, so he keeps them a secret.

Sexual thoughts or impulses. These are rare in children who haven't yet entered puberty, but become increasingly common as children mature. Sexual obsessions are distinguished from normal adolescent sexual preoccupations by the fact that they are unwanted, disturbing, and are resisted by the child. Adolescent boys frequently develop obsessive concerns about homosexuality. These are often linked to another obsessional fear, such as contamination fears or fears of harm (for example, a boy might fear catching AIDS from a homosexual encounter). Some teens fear that they will do something sexually inappropriate (such as exposing themselves). But these fears are *not* acted upon. People with OCD torture themselves over their potential for inappropriate actions, but obsessive thoughts do not lead to such behaviors.

Fear of blasphemy or of being evil; excessive religious concerns. These obsessions are often the most painful and debilitating because they are so all consuming. To get a sense of what it must be like, imagine trying not to think about God as you read the rest of this paragraph—your obsession is that you are not worthy of God's love and therefore must not think about Him. If you think about God even once, you are bad and have to do a penitence. You must do the penitence perfectly, in order not to displease God, as well as to try to make it up to Him for being so blasphemous as to utter his name—even though you only said "God" silently in your head. Now, you've just said "God" again, so you must do even more penitences (the number increases each time you show weakness). But as you say your penitence, you become anxious and begin to wish that God would help you, but that only proves that you're weak and tempted by the Devil. Only God can overcome the Devil. . . .

How many times did you think about God as you read the paragraph? If you were suffering from religious obsessions (also known as scrupulosity), that paragraph might have taken you several hours to read. And "God" wouldn't have been the only word to trigger your obsessional anxiety—other words would have also been "bad," such as words with a *t* in them (because the *t* looks like a cross), certain names (because you know a minister or rabbi with that name), colors (purple for Easter, red and green for Christmas, blue and white for Hanukkah, etc.), and other words with connections so convoluted that they no longer make sense. Each obsessional thought produces unbearable anxiety, which may trigger another thought.

Intrusive thoughts, nonsense sounds, or music. These obsessions are the most like the "mental hiccup" described by Dr. Judy Rapoport, in her book *The Boy Who Couldn't Stop Washing*. Snatches of songs, nonsense phrases, or other verbal or nonverbal noises keep repeating over and over again, just like a needle stuck on a broken record.

Preoccupation with certain numbers, colors, or words. When the preoccupation with numbers, colors, and words is an obsession, it goes beyond a superstitious interest in a particular number or color. It becomes an all-consuming need to have only good colors in the house, or only lucky numbers on a math test. In fact, the child's teacher might be the first to notice this obsession because he refuses to answer certain questions because they contain unlucky numbers.

Compulsions

Compulsions are rituals that are performed in a certain way in order to relieve the anxiety caused by the obsessions. As you might imagine, they follow the obsessional fears fairly closely: contamination fears lead to hand-washing or excessive showering, fear of harm coming to your parents is relieved by checking to make sure that they're safe, preoccupation with the number five leads to repeating everything five times, and so forth. Although the compulsions are designed to relieve obsessional anxiety, they frequently make the child feel even more anxious as he struggles to "get it right." Getting it right or doing the ritual perfectly can be impossible. For example, one of our patients tried in vain to do ten "perfect" one-handed push-ups—the more he tried, the more tired he became, and the more impossible it was to complete the task. His parents struggled to understand what made one push-up count while another did not; his only explanation was that it "felt right" sometimes and didn't at others. This sense of completion or "getting it right" is very common to children with OCD. Stopping them before they have completed the ritual can cause them to become so anxious that they react violently. It is often difficult to know when to intervene and when to leave the child alone —his psychiatrist should help make the decision. The most common compulsions are:

Ritualized hand-washing, bathing, or cleaning. Hand-washing and cleaning rituals are designed to remove the dirt and germs the child perceives as contaminating him. He may wash his hands for brief periods many times each hour, or get "stuck" at the sink trying to get his hands "perfectly clean." Often, the excessive washing will cause his hands to become red and chapped, or even to crack open and bleed. Occasionally, children will develop severe skin problems because they use such harsh soaps or chemicals (rubbing alcohol, kitchen cleanser, etc.).

Checking compulsions. Children check in response to obsessions about harm coming to themselves or others and when they feel that they can't trust their senses (checking to make sure that what they saw was really there or that what they heard was really said). The checking rituals may appear to make sense, but really don't—such as a boy who fears that a fire will burn down his home and performs elaborate checking rituals to make sure that the stove is turned off, the coffee pot unplugged, and the front and back doors kept clear, but doesn't once check his home's smoke detector.

Repeating compulsions. As the name suggests, repeating compulsions require the child to repeat something over and over again—until he does it "perfectly" or until he has done it a certain number of times. It might be reading a paragraph, writing a particular letter, or performing a certain action. In other instances, the ritual is defined by doing things a certain number of times. For example, if Jack has to repeat things in twenties, getting dressed in the morning could take hours. He has to get up and down from the bed twenty times, repeat each step twenty times as he walks toward his closet, open and shut the closet door twenty times, and so forth. Often, the child becomes so discouraged by his rituals that he gives up and refuses to change his clothes or even to get out of bed in the morning. He avoids all activities that might set off the repeating rituals.

Ordering or arranging rituals. A child with ordering rituals might need to have her cup exactly two inches away from the top of her fork, her chair perfectly in line with the pattern of the tile, or the contents of her backpack arranged "just so." She may have only one arranging compulsion, or she may have dozens. Unlike the bedtime arranging rituals of healthy young children, in which all the stuffed animals must be lined up perfectly and then the covers tucked in, there is no particular pattern to the rituals in OCD. For example, a teen's clothes might be hung in the closet with military precision—each hanger one half inch away from its neighbors—but the rest of his room is a chaotic mess.

Counting compulsions. Many people count their steps as they walk along, or count telephone poles as they are driving down the highway. When their attention is diverted, they can stop counting without feeling upset. Children with counting compulsions become *very* upset if they are interrupted, because they feel that they must start over again and perform the counting ritual "perfectly." Often, they are counting because they have had a frightening obsessive thought and can get control over the obsession only by counting to fifty or one hundred. Other times, they have elaborate rituals around the counting, such as the little girl who had to hold her breath, tap her left index finger against her right palm, and focus her eyes on a particular color as she counted to fifty. If someone spoke to her while she was counting, she would have to start over again —perhaps this time doing fifty sets of fifties.

Need to tell, ask, or confess things. Children with doubting obsessions will frequently have compulsive questioning—they need to check if what they heard or saw was really true. However, unlike healthy young children who seem to be constantly asking questions about everything they see, the child with OCD asks the same question over and over again: "Did you shut the door, Mom?" "Yes, honey, I did." "How do you know?" "I know." "Are you sure you shut the door, Mom?" "Yes, I did." "But are you really sure you shut the front door? Maybe it was the back door that you shut." "Was it tightly shut?" And on and on they ask.

If It's Not OCD, What Else Could It Be?

Superstitions and Developmental Rituals

Nearly every child has at least one superstition—a magical rule that helps him control his universe. Sometimes, these superstitions continue into adulthood—you may still bend over to pick up a lucky penny, or avoid stepping on cracks to save your mother's back. These behaviors are silly and unnecessary, but they are not OCD. You are in control—you can decide to pick up the penny or to walk on by. Children's superstitious behavior is also clearly separable from OCD. The content is different, the children aren't upset by their superstitions, and they are in control of their behavior.

Developmental rituals may mimic OCD because the ritual is repeated in a compulsive, stereotyped way, but these rituals are normal and expected, particularly between the ages of two and six years. The rituals provide the child with comfort, rather than causing him to feel anxious about performing them correctly. Further, the rituals are usually time-limited—most children grow out of them by the time they are seven or eight years old. If a child's bedtime rituals abruptly increase in complexity, or they reappear after several years' absence, then they might be OCD—if there are other symptoms present.

Obsessive-Compulsive Personality Disorder

Typically, when people think they're talking about OCD, they're actually talking about obsessive-compulsive personality disorder. The personality disorder is closer to the cocktail party definition of OCD than obsessive-compulsive disorder itself is. People with obsessive-compulsive personality disorder are rigid, perfectionistic, excessively neat and clean, and overly concerned with rules and details (losing sight of the forest for the trees). If a child has obsessive-compulsive personality disorder, he is careful and compulsive about everything in his life. In contrast, OCD is characterized by the presence of discrete symptoms that have a very narrow focus, such as obsessive concerns about the AIDS virus. Obsessive-compulsive personality disorder can also be distinguished from OCD by its lack of distress. Rather than being tortured by their symptoms, children with obsessive-compulsive personality disorder are comfortable with their symptoms and often wish that others would be more like them.

Despite its lack of psychic distress, OCPD is a disorder. The symptoms often cause tremendous interference: children with OCPD are so preoccupied with the extraneous details of their school projects that they are unable to complete assignments on time; they are paralyzed by indecision —unable to decide what to wear in the morning, or what to eat for breakfast, or where to sit on the school bus; and they are perfectionistic to the point of impossibility—nothing gets done because it isn't ever quite good enough. Some children will overcome these disabilities by putting in tremendous amounts of extra effort, while others become overwhelmed and either give up (withdrawing into a constricted world that they can more easily control) or seeking treatment. Behavior therapy and anti-OCD medications are helpful for OCPD, although the response rate is less than that seen in children with OCD.

Pervasive Developmental Disorder (PDD) and Autism

Children with developmental disabilities, such as PDD or autism, can have stereotyped rituals that appear very similar to OCD. The child might wash his hands repeatedly, or repeat certain words or phrases over and over again, or be excessively concerned with the arrangement of his stuffed animals or his baseball card collection. In addition to the rituals, the child may have "obsessive" preoccupations with certain colors, numbers, or objects. The symptoms are very similar to the obsessions and compulsions in OCD and recent studies have shown that these symptoms respond to treatment with antiobsessional medications. In some cases, treating the stereotyped, repetitive behaviors has clarified the diagnosis —when they were gone, it was clear that the child still had problems interacting with others and communicating effectively. Pervasive developmental disorder and autism are both characterized by the inability to develop normal social interactions. The child expresses little or no emotion or affection and seems to be "off in a world of his own." Other symptoms of PDD and autism include abnormalities of speech, language, and communication, a "need for sameness," developmental delays, and abnormal responses to sensory stimulation—seeing the background as more important than the theme of the picture; or hypersensitivity to touch, textures, and tastes. PDD and autism have a broad spectrum of severity, ranging from mild social skills disabilities to severe social isolation and an inability to communicate. For further information, we suggest the following references: *Children with Autism: A Parent's Guide*, Michael D. Powers, ed. (Rockville, MD: Woodbine House, 1989) and *Thinking in Pictures and Other Reports from My Life with Autism*, Temple Grandin (New York: Vintage Books, 1995), and the following resources: The Autism Society of America, 7910 Woodmont Avenue, Suite 650, Bethesda, MD 20814; phone: 800-3-AUTISM, or Cure Autism Now, 5225 Wilshire Boulevard, Suite 503, Los Angeles, CA 90036; phone: 213-549-0500; http://www.canfoundation.org/ or E-mail: CAN@primenet.com.

Tics and Tourette Syndrome

There is a close link between OCD and tics—the two disorders occur frequently in the same children, and it is often difficult to distinguish between compulsions and tics (described in detail in chapter 15). If a child taps four times on his knee before getting up from a chair, he may have a repeating compulsion of OCD or a tapping tic from Tourette syndrome. Spitting, licking, touching, and tapping are all seen in tic disorders, but can also occur as compulsive rituals. In order to decide which disorder is causing the symptom, it is necessary for the child to be able to describe what led to the behavior. If it was a compulsion, an obsessive thought will have preceded it (for example, tapping in response to a fear of shouting out a swear word—the tapping decreases the anxiety associated with the fear of swearing); if it was a tic, he would have had only an urge or feeling preceding the tapping. If the child is young, or the tic/ritual has been going on for a long period of time, he may be unable to tell you why he did it. The correct diagnosis can then be made only by observing what other kinds of symptoms he is having and establishing a pattern, as discussed in chapter 15.

Treatment

Obsessive-compulsive disorder can be treated very effectively with medication, behavior therapy, or a combination of the two. The choice of treatment depends, in part, upon your child's age, his symptom patterns, and his developmental capabilities. For example, some children aren't able to participate in behavior therapy because they are too young to understand what is required of them or they have symptoms (such as counting) that are resistant to behavioral techniques; in those instances, medication may be the best choice. In others, behavior therapy is preferred—for example, when a child has experienced unwanted side effects from OCD medications. Deciding which treatment to try first depends upon your own preferences, as well as those of your child and his doctor. In some areas of the country, medications may be the only real treatment option, because qualified behavior therapists aren't available.

Psychological Therapies

The best psychological treatment of OCD is exposure with response prevention, a behavior therapy technique. Behavior therapy has been helpful to more than three-quarters of the children who completed the behavior therapy treatments. Qualified behavior therapists are now available in most U.S. cities, and, in addition, special behavior therapy manuals have been developed for use with children, including one devised by Dr. John March of Duke University. Behavior therapy isn't suitable for all children with OCD—very young children can't understand what is required of them, and children who have only obsessions or mental compulsions (like counting) find it difficult to gain control of their symptoms through behavior therapy. But for most children, behavior therapy offers a safe, effective solution.

Exposure with response prevention is based on the concept that compulsions are merely an attempt to control the anxiety caused by the obsessive thoughts. Studies have shown that obsessional anxiety mounts very quickly after exposure to a feared object, such as a dirty toilet seat, but it disappears equally quickly. Children with OCD don't wait for the anxiety to disappear—they can't stand feeling uncomfortable even for a few seconds and so they wash their hands in the hopes that the washing ritual will decrease their anxiety to a tolerable level. But the washing actually *increases* the anxiety. In exposure with response prevention, the child is taught that the anxiety will disappear by itself. In small but steadily increasing doses, the child is exposed to the thing(s) that he fears and prevented from performing his compulsive ritual. Initially, this causes some mild anxiety, but eventually the exposure doesn't cause any discomfort—the child has been desensitized to his fear.

Family education and family therapy are often recommended for OCD. Although neither can reduce the severity of the obsessions or compulsions, they can play a very important role in the child's recovery—helping his parents learn how and when to intervene in the compulsive behaviors, providing support to the child, his parents, and the other members of the family, and resolving various issues that can interfere with the child's recovery. The principles of family therapy are discussed in chapter 12.

Medications

Clomipramine (Anafranil) is a tricyclic antidepressant with special action on the serotonin system. In the late 1980s, studies done at the Child Psychiatry Branch of the National Institute of Mental Health demonstrated that clomipramine was very effective for the treatment of OCD in children. Since that time, a new class of serotonergic agents has been developed, the selective serotonin reuptake inhibitors or SSRIs: fluoxetine [Prozac], sertraline [Zoloft], paroxetine [Paxil], and fluvoxamine [Luvox]). These medications are discussed in detail in chapter 12. Because they have fewer side effects, the SSRIs are preferred over clomipramine, although both groups of drugs are very effective for OCD. Over 80 percent of children with OCD will respond to clomipramine or SSRI treatment with a reduction in symptom severity. The medications must be continued indefinitely, however, since the child's symptoms will return when the medication is stopped.

Helping Your Child Overcome His OCD Symptoms

Recognize your child's obsessive-compulsive behaviors as symptoms of OCD. If you have noticed that your child has any of the behaviors discussed earlier in the chapter, it's important to determine whether or not they might be symptoms of OCD. Ask your child if the symptoms bother him, and whether or not they are getting in his way. If you suspect OCD, it might be helpful to discuss the issue with your child's teacher. She may have seen one or more of the following behaviors:

Rereading and rewriting. Increased time required to complete an assignment, unexpected difficulty with comprehension, holes in paper or excessive erasures, or incomplete assignments or unfinished tests.

Contamination fears and washing compulsions. Sudden isolation or restricted play at recess—avoids certain people, objects, or places because they are "dirty," refuses to eat in cafeteria and won't participate in class food preparation project, refuses to touch doorknobs (always allows others to go through doorway first) or uses a paper towel to open door (some schools teach this in hygiene class, so this may no longer be a reliable sign), excessive number of trips to bathroom or excessively long bathroom visits *or* avoids public rest rooms completely. Chapped, or red, hands, even when weather is warm.

Counting and repeating rituals. Persists with an activity after everyone else has finished, repeatedly gets up and down from chair, drops pencil several times in a row, or has to return to classroom several times to "get something I forgot."

Provide support to your child, not to his OCD. The anxiety that your child feels is real, even if the obsession causing it isn't. Let your child know that you will keep him safe, but also tell him that there's nothing about the obsessive worries that can harm him. There's a very fine line between providing reassurance and responding to his obsession, so be careful not to become involved in the rituals. If you participate in his compulsive rituals, then it looks as if you believe the obsessions enough to help "protect" your child against them—that possibility is truly frightening to your child. If your child asks for reassurance, have him give it to himself by reflecting the question back to him.

Use distraction as a way to decrease your child's obsessive-compulsive symptoms. Activity is the best medicine a parent can give a child with OCD. Children are often symptom-free when they are concentrating hard on a game or activity, or they are playing outdoors—so, keep him busy!

Help your child avoid "avoiding"—the more he does, the more he can do. Parents tell us that the worst thing about their child's OCD is not being able to "make it better" by allowing him to stay in a "safe" or "clean" place. But if you protect him from the thing he fears, his OCD will become worse. OCD decreases with exposure (doing the hard things) and increases by avoidance—Howard Hughes became a miserable prisoner of his OCD because he had enough money to hire people to do everything "dirty" for him.

Get treatment for your child as soon as you recognize that he has OCD. The symptoms of OCD can be very distressing and can cause significant problems in your child's life. He deserves to feel better as soon as possible, and child psychiatrists are the specialists who can be most helpful. Whether the treatment is medication, behavior therapy, or a combination of the two, it is important for you to be an active partner in your child's treatment (see chapter 12 for additional information).

Further Reading

Baer, Lee, Ph.D. *Getting Control: Overcoming Your Obsessions and Compulsions*. Boston: Little, Brown, 1991.

Foa, Edna B., Ph.D. *Stop Obsessing! How to Overcome Your Obsessions and Compulsions*. New York: Bantam Books, 1991.

Greist, John H., M.D. *Obsessive-Compulsive Disorder: A Guide*. Madison, WI: Dean Foundation, 1995.

Rapoport, Judith, M.D. *The Boy Who Couldn't Stop Washing*. New York: Penguin Books, 1989.

Resources

The Obsessive Compulsive Foundation
P.O. Box 70
Milford, CT 06460
203-878-5669

The Obsessive Compulsive Information Center
Dean Foundation for Health, Research, and Education
8000 Excelsior Drive, Suite 302
Madison, WI 53717-1914
Phone: 608-836-8070
Fax: 608-836-8033

"My Son's Never Been a Problem Before, But Over the Past Week, He's Become Impossible"

PANDAS

"The creepies are coming back again, Dad," said Tommy, as he stood at the sink and washed his hands for the fourth time that morning.

"What do you mean, Tommy? What creepies?" Martin asked his son.

"Well, I get this funny jumpy feeling inside that makes me have to move all the time, and these stupid worries about germs and stuff. Haven't you ever noticed it?"

Martin had noticed it and he was worried. Not only was Tommy spending a lot of time in the bathroom washing his hands, but he had also developed an obsessive concern with the way his hair was combed and the way he brushed his teeth. He was suddenly hyper too, always fidgeting and moving about, like someone had revved his motor up too high. On top of that, his personality had changed overnight. Instead of being the easygoing boy whom everyone loved, Tommy was now a prickly, irritable stranger—everything had to be done his way, right away; if it wasn't, he exploded.

This wasn't the first time Tommy had gotten "the creepies." The first time, he had been away at camp and had become so homesick toward the end of the second week that he was sent home. Tommy hadn't really been homesick. He was doing many of the things that Martin was noticing now: washing his hands frequently, refusing to eat "dirty" foods, and worrying—worrying about everything, but especially about monsters, unseen germs, and harm coming to his father. Tommy wouldn't leave Martin's side when he was at home and would become inconsolably upset when Martin had to leave the house to go to work. The behavior was so worrisome that Tommy had paid a visit to Dr. Phillips, but the doctor hadn't been able to find anything wrong and had decided that it was probably an adjustment reaction to his first sleep-away camp. Dr. Phillips had encouraged Martin "to give Tommy a lot of extra love and attention and wait for it to blow over." The symptoms eventually subsided, but it had turned out to be a very rough summer.

Tommy started school that fall without any problems, only rarely talking about monsters or germs on his food. And then it started again—this time, on the Tuesday after Thanksgiving. Martin could remember the exact day the symptoms reappeared because once again they had exploded out of nowhere. Tommy had been sick with a slight cold over the long weekend, but had been well enough to go to school on Monday. He had had a good day, too, and went to bed excitedly planning which action figure he would take to school for sharing-time the next day. But when Tuesday morning came, Martin couldn't get Tommy to school because he refused to put on his shoes. "They're dirty! They're dirty!" Tommy kept screaming. "I can't put them on or they'll make me sick! Are you trying to kill me?"

Martin finally let Tommy leave the house in his slippers, but they didn't go to school, they went straight to Dr. Phillips's office.

"What's the matter, Tommy?" asked Dr. Phillips.

"I've got the creepies," answered Tommy. "You know, when kids get worries and have to do certain things."

"What kind of things?"

"Things that don't make sense—like washing my hands when they're not really dirty, or counting up to one hundred over and over again, or arranging my baseball cards in some goofy order," Tommy said. "That part's really weird. I don't even like the order I have to put them in. I just want the cards to be the way they're supposed to be, but something inside me makes me change them all around—and not just once, but like a zillion times."

"Anything else, Tommy?"

"Yeah. I get really scared at night now. I'm not a wimp or anything, but I have these terrible nightmares about monsters and things, and the monsters seem so real that I can't stand it. My dad has to leave the bathroom light on for me now and sometimes, if I've had a really bad dream, I'll sleep in the hallway outside his room. I figure the monsters won't be able to get me there."

"Hmm. I thought you said you knew that the monsters aren't real?" Dr. Phillips asked.

"Of course they're not real! But when I try telling my brain that in the middle of the night, it doesn't listen. It's just like the stupid worries in the daytime. I know my hands aren't really dirty, but I have to wash them anyway. Part of my brain is telling me to do it and the rest of my brain thinks it's stupid. I wish the stupid part would just shut up."

"Is there anything else I should know, Tommy?" Tommy shook his head no, so Dr. Phillips continued, "What have you noticed, Martin?"

Martin answered, "I've noticed all the things Tommy talked about and also that he's just not himself. He's really moody and irritable—not only is he prickly as a porcupine, but he acts like he's going to jump out of his skin. Look at him, he's squirming in his chair like he's got ants in his pants."

"I'm sorry, Dad."

"Son, it's okay. I know it's not your fault—that's why we're here to see the doctor."

Dr. Phillips asked a few more questions about Tommy's behavior, and then asked whether Tommy had been ill recently.

"Yes, now that you mention it," Martin replied. "He had a little cold this past weekend, with a slight fever, but everybody else was sick so I didn't really worry about it. You know, though, he also had a cold with a sore throat right before he had that episode last summer. Since he wasn't running a high fever, nobody at the camp checked it out."

"Let's check a throat culture today, then, and see if he has a strep infection," Dr. Phillips said. "I was just reading an article about a new kind of strep-triggered behavior problem and it sure sounds like Tommy might have it. I'll do a physical exam, check a throat culture, and get some blood to decide whether or not Tommy has had a recent strep throat infection."

Dr. Phillips performed his physical examination and found that Tommy's throat was slightly red and swollen. The rapid strep test came back positive, too, so Dr. Phillips wrote out a prescription for penicillin. "The penicillin will treat the strep throat, but it probably won't help Tommy's creepies," said Dr. Phillips, "so I'd like to suggest that you take Tommy to see a child psychiatrist."

"A child psychiatrist? That seems pretty extreme," Martin said. "Can't we just wait this out? It'll probably go away in a few weeks the way the other episode did, won't it?"

"Possibly, but Tommy won't feel very good in the meantime. I know it's a bit of a shock, so go home, talk it over, and we'll get together next week. I'll recheck Tommy's throat and we can decide about the child psychiatrist then."

When they returned, Dr. Phillips reported that Tommy's antistreptococcal titers were very high, indicating that either the present infection had been there for a while, or that he had had another infection a few weeks earlier. "The tests suggest that Tommy's problems might have been triggered by strep," he said, "but there's no way to know that for sure right now. If they were caused by the strep-triggered antibodies, it will take a while for them to disappear and his symptoms will continue until they do. Have you decided about the child psychiatrist?"

"Yeah, I don't need to see a psychiatrist anymore," Tommy answered. "I feel a lot better already because I know that this isn't my fault and that it will go away eventually. I've even noticed that I can stop myself from rearranging my baseball cards and washing my hands if I try really hard. I can pretty much ignore the worries, too. And at night, I just say, 'That's the creepies, they're not real,' and the monsters don't scare me."

"Sounds like you've discovered behavior therapy and thought-stopping, Tommy. I'm glad it's working so well." Dr. Phillips turned to Martin and continued, "The important thing now is for Tommy to stay healthy—if he has any signs of a strep throat, bring him in immediately."

"You can count on it, Doctor," Martin said, "We don't want any more creepies around here!"

What Do Strep Throat Infections Have to Do with Behavior Problems?

Researchers at the National Institute of Mental Health have recently discovered that some pediatric behavior problems are triggered by strep throat infections. The behavior problems include anxiety, obsessive-compulsive symptoms, hyperactivity, inattention, and motor and vocal tics. These symptoms occur together often enough to be considered a syndrome. In order to remind physicians of the key features of the syndrome, it was named PANDAS (pediatric autoimmune neuropsychiatric disorders associated with strep infections). The diagnostic features of PANDAS include:

Pediatric. Strep-triggered behavioral problems occur mainly in children who have not yet entered puberty. Most children are between the ages of five and nine when they have their first episode.

Autoimmune. Although the exact nature of the problem isn't yet known, PANDAS is thought to be similar to Sydenham's chorea (or Saint Vitus' dance), a type of rheumatic fever. Rheumatic fever occurs when a child has a prolonged strep throat infection (lasting at least five days before antibiotic treatment is started). The strep throat infections are caused by a type of streptococcal bacteria that survives, in part, by the use of molecular mimicry. Molecular mimicry means that the bacteria have "designed" themselves (through aeons of genetic evolution) to look like components of human tissues—this allows them to hide from the child's immune system. This is good news for the bacteria, but bad news for kids, since the molecular mimicry causes the production of antibodies that recognize not only the bacteria, but also the cells within the child's body that the strep was mimicking. The antibodies then mistake the child's own tissues for bacteria and set off an autoimmune (or self-directed) reaction. In the case of rheumatic heart disease, the antibodies mistakenly attack the heart; in rheumatic arthritis, it's the child's joints; and in Sydenham's chorea, parts of the child's brain. In PANDAS, it appears that the antibodies also target the brain, particularly an area known as the basal ganglia—a region at the base of the brain that helps to control our thoughts, movements, emotions, and behavior.

Neuropsychiatric disorders. Because the basal ganglia structures involved in PANDAS are responsible for so many functions, several different combinations of symptoms can occur. Obsessive-compulsive symptoms and motor or vocal tics (chapters 16 and 15, respectively) are most common, but separation anxiety (chapter 18) and symptoms of attention deficit hyperactivity disorder (chapter 13) can also occur. Neurologic problems include choreic movements (piano-playing movements of the fingers, or writhing dancelike movements of the arms, hands, and feet), hyperactivity, fidgetiness, and clumsiness. For some children, the first symptom of PANDAS is sloppy handwriting; for others, it is slight slurring of their speech (especially hard sounds like Ta, Pa, and Ka—Topeka, Kansas, is particularly "mushy" when children are having problems).

Associated with strep infections. In order for a child's symptoms to be considered as part of the PANDAS spectrum, a strep throat infection must start the process. In Sydenham's chorea, there can be quite a long lag between the strep throat infection and the beginning of the symptoms —sometimes as long as six to nine months. The first time a child is sick with symptoms of PANDAS, this may also be true, and it's often difficult to make the connection between a strep infection and the onset of the neuropsychiatric symptoms. But, in subsequent episodes, the infection will precede the symptoms by only a few days or weeks and may even still be present when the child's psychological symptoms are at their worst. Because strep throat infections happen relatively infrequently, the children will have an episodic course. They do very well for several months and then, suddenly, have a dramatic worsening of their symptoms. This intermittent course differs from the fluctuating symptom course seen in other childhood neuropsychiatric disorders because it has distinct relapses and remissions, rather than a waxing and waning pattern. Tommy's case is typical in that his symptoms were manageable until he got sick with a strep throat—then his symptoms "exploded" in severity and required treatment.

The other feature of note in Tommy's story was that his strep infection didn't cause a high fever, vomiting, or even a noticeable sore throat; instead, he appeared to have a mild cold. This presentation is increasingly common and parents are encouraged to be particularly vigilant about "colds" that are accompanied by behavior problems. A throat culture is the only way to determine whether or not a strep infection is present (just looking in the throat isn't enough—sometimes the infections don't cause pus, redness, or swelling of the tonsils). Because rapid strep tests are only about 85 to 90 percent as reliable as throat cultures, a regular throat culture should be done if the rapid strep test is negative (results of throat cultures are usually ready in two to three days). Finally, if your child does have a strep throat, it is important to give him his medication exactly as prescribed for the full treatment course. It takes ten days of penicillin treatment to eradicate the strep infection—less than that and you run the risk of the strep returning and causing antibodies to be produced.

———— Does Your Child Have PANDAS? ————

1. Does he have symptoms of:
     Obsessive-compulsive disorder (chapter 16);
     Motor or vocal tics (chapter 15);
     Late-onset attention deficit hyperactivity disorder (chapter 13);
     Separation anxiety disorder (chapter 18);
     Abrupt mood swings, personality change, or acting-out behaviors.
2. Did the symptoms begin suddenly or get dramatically worse abruptly ("overnight")?
3. Did the symptoms begin shortly after your child was sick with a strep throat infection (or had been exposed to strep by close contact with a child who had an infection)?

4. If he has had symptoms for a year or more, do the symptoms seem to relapse and remit (come on abruptly and then slowly disappear over a few months' time, rather than a fluctuating or waxing and waning course of severity) and have the relapses always been preceded by a strep throat infection (or exposure)?
5. Was your child between the ages of four and ten years when his symptoms first began?
6. Did one of your child's close relatives (your child's parents, aunts, uncles, grandparents) have rheumatic fever or Saint Vitus' dance and/or a history of obsessive-compulsive disorder or tics during childhood?

If you answered yes to questions 1, 2, 3, and 5 or 1, 4, and 5, your child may have PANDAS, particularly if the answer to question 6 is also yes.

How Do You Know If Your Child Has PANDAS?

The diagnosis of PANDAS depends upon establishing a clear relationship between strep throat infections and behavior problems—usually, this means that there have been at least two episodes of strep-triggered behavioral symptom exacerbations (onset of symptoms or relapses). To decide whether or not the symptoms were triggered by a strep infection, it helps to construct a time line comparing the child's medical records with her history of behavior problems. For example, in a child with PANDAS-related OCD, the time line might show that every time her antiobsessional medication dose was increased, she (or one of her brothers or sisters) had been sick with a strep throat. During times when her obsessive-compulsive symptoms were under control, she was also physically healthy.

Often, the past history won't provide enough information to be certain about the diagnosis of PANDAS. In those cases, it is important to begin to gather evidence of a relationship between strep infections and the child's behavior problems. The first step is to obtain antistrep titers when the child has been doing well for at least six weeks—these titers should be low (ASO and/or antistrepDNase B titers in the normal range). When her symptoms worsen, she should have a throat culture and another set of strep titers—the throat culture might be positive, but even if it isn't, the titers should have increased, if her symptoms are due to PANDAS.

(NOTE: Strep titers are often positive in perfectly healthy children because they are exposed so often to strep infections in the classroom. These titers can remain elevated for several months, and so a positive titer might be obtained during a symptom relapse but have nothing to do with that episode. Thus, it is just as important to establish that strep titers are low during periods of symptom remission as it is to show that titers are high when the symptoms are increased. Your pediatrician should know how to use sequential titers to determine whether or not an infection is related to symptom exacerbations.)

If It's Not PANDAS, What Else Could It Be?

PANDAS is an "etiologic subgroup" rather than a specific diagnosis. The children appear to share a common cause for their symptoms—a strep-triggered autoimmune disorder—but their behavioral symptoms differ, so they don't all have the same diagnosis. They might have strep-triggered obsessions and have a diagnosis of OCD or have motor and vocal tics and be diagnosed with Tourette disorder. The diagnosis of PANDAS would be in addition to the primary symptom diagnosis, rather than being a specific psychiatric diagnosis. To be included in the PANDAS subgroup, a child's symptoms must meet each of the five criteria described previously. If they do not, then it is likely that the symptoms are due to another cause and the proper diagnosis would be: obsessive-compulsive disorder (chapter 16), tic disorders (chapter 15), attention deficit hyperactivity disorder (chapter 13), or separation anxiety disorder (chapter 18).

Treatment of PANDAS

PANDAS-related tics and obsessive-compulsive symptoms respond to the same kinds of treatments as other forms of obsessive-compulsive disorder (OCD) or tic disorders. Therefore, any of the treatments recommended in chapters 15 (tics) and 16 (OCD) are suitable for children whose behavioral symptoms are due to PANDAS. In addition, there are specific treatments targeted at the immune system that offer promise in the treatment of PANDAS.

Immunologic Treatments

Two novel therapies, plasmapheresis and intravenous immunoglobulin (IVIG), are undergoing clinical trials at the National Institute of Mental Health (NIMH) for the treatment of PANDAS. Both treatments act directly on the immune system, and therefore aren't helpful if the child's behavioral symptoms weren't caused by an autoimmune disorder, such as PANDAS. Further, the treatments are not appropriate for many of the children who do have PANDAS, because they do not help chronic symptoms that are not directly related to an ongoing autoimmune process. Currently, the immunologic therapies are being used only to treat very ill, acute (recent) cases of PANDAS. If those patients have a good result, then the treatments may be tried in additional patients. At the present time, however, the use of immunomodulatory treatments for PANDAS is limited to a few research centers.

Plasmapheresis has been nicknamed "the blood cleaning procedure" by the children participating in the NIMH research studies. Essentially, that is what happens—during the course of five treatments (spread out over a two-week period), over 98 percent of the "bad" antibodies (actually, all types of antibodies, as well as other proteins in the blood) are removed from the child's circulation, the blood is "cleaned," and this stops the autoimmune reaction. In the plasmapheresis procedure, the child's blood is removed from his body through an outflow line (IV tube) and channeled into the apheresis machine. There, it is spun at high speeds to separate the formed elements of the blood (red blood cells, white blood cells, and platelets) from the liquid portion (the plasma, which contains the undesirable antibodies, among other things). The formed elements are mixed with a protein/saline (saltwater) mixture and returned to the child through an inflow line; the plasma is discarded or used for research studies. The treatment is dauntingly high-tech and carries the risk of serious side-effects, so it is not appropriate for most children, despite promising results from early studies.

Intravenous immunoglobulin (or IVIG) is the other treatment that is being tried in PANDAS. IVIG is a human blood–derived product that works through an unknown immunologic mechanism, but is thought to have effects similar to plasmapheresis (in essence, an internal blood-cleaning procedure). The children treated with IVIG are given an IV infusion of the medicine over a two-day period. Several of the children have had headaches, nausea, or vomiting during the treatment, but these side effects do not last very long. The IVIG infusion also appears promising as a treatment for PANDAS but the studies underway must be completed before we know whether or not IVIG and plasmapheresis will be useful as treatments for strep-triggered OCD and tic disorders. Until then, the symptoms should be managed with standard therapies, like SSRIs and behavior therapy.

Prevention of Strep Infections

Ongoing studies are examining whether twice-daily doses of penicillin can help prevent symptom worsenings in children with PANDAS. In rheumatic fever, penicillin is routinely prescribed as prophylaxis (prevention) against strep infections. This treatment is based on the theory that if a child is not infected with strep, then he won't produce new antibodies and further damage his heart, joints, or brain. It is far too early to recommend penicillin prophylaxis for PANDAS. Not only is there no definitive evidence that it works, but there also are serious risks associated with long-term antibiotic use, including yeast infections and antibiotic resistance (the strep bacteria don't become resistant, but other bacteria do, especially at the low doses used in strep prophylaxis).

Although we do not recommend penicillin prophylaxis, we do suggest that parents be extra vigilant about strep exposures in their children with PANDAS. If the child has been exposed to a strep throat infection or has a cold with slight fever, his doctor should take a throat culture. Early studies in rheumatic fever demonstrated that such surveillance strategies were very effective in decreasing rates of relapse and the same thing might be expected to be true for PANDAS.

Helping Your Child Overcome the Symptoms of PANDAS

Keep track of his symptoms. Since the diagnosis of PANDAS depends upon establishing a link between strep throat infections and symptom relapses, it is important for you to keep track of both your child's medical history and his behavioral symptoms. This does *not* mean that you need to keep exhaustive records. In fact, one of the best records we have seen was kept on the family's monthly wall calendar—having an entire year's data allowed us to establish rapidly the PANDAS pattern. This family chose to use initials to indicate who was sick that day with a cold or flu, with more specifics provided for the child with PANDAS (e.g., temp.

101°, sore throat, culture neg.). The same calendar was also used to note the child's symptom severity, both in terms of weekly ratings (0 to 4 severity) and days of unusually mild (smiling faces) or severe (frowning faces) symptoms. This is only one example; you and your child can design a system that best fits your own needs.

Keep your home free of strep. If your child has PANDAS, it is important to ensure that all family members are free of strep bacteria. Some people are "strep carriers," which means that they carry the strep bacteria around in their nose and throat without getting sick (or producing antibodies against the strep). Because they don't ever get sick themselves, they don't find out that they have the strep bacteria and can continue to pass them on to others, including children with PANDAS. A throat culture would still be positive for strep, however, so when your child is first diagnosed with PANDAS, it is important to check throat cultures on all family members. Any positive culture should be treated and a second culture obtained at the end of the course of antibiotics. If the culture is still positive, your doctor may prescribe a second course of penicillin, an alternative antibiotic, or an additional medication (such as Rifampin) to be taken for a few days in conjunction with the penicillin.

Sometimes it is very difficult to clear strep from a household, because as soon as one person is free of strep, another's culture is positive or they have symptoms of a strep throat. There is much speculation about where the strep "hides" in order to keep infecting the families. Some have blamed toothbrushes, while others have examined the family pets (including culturing dogs, birds, and hamsters!). At present, however, there is no clear evidence to suggest that strep is spread from animals to humans, but there is abundant evidence that strep is easily passed between humans by sharing toothbrushes, glasses, or kissing on the lips. Good hygiene practices (such as requiring children to wash their hands before eating) will help eliminate most cross-infections.

Further Reading

Because PANDAS is so new, there is nothing yet available in standard libraries. The following articles can be found in medical libraries.

Allen, A. J., Leonard, H. L., and Swedo, S. E. "Case Study: A New Infection-Triggered, Autoimmune Subtype of Pediatric OCD and Tourette's Syndrome." *Journal of the American Academy of Child and Adolescent Psychiatry* 31 (1992): 1050–56.

Swedo, S. E. "Sydenham's Chorea: A Model for Childhood Autoimmune Neuropsychiatric Disorders." *Journal of the American Medical Association* 212 (22) (1994): 1788–91.

Swedo, S. E., Leonard, H. L., Garvey, M., et al. "Pediatric Autoimmune Neuropsychiatric Disorders Associated with Streptococcal Infections (PANDAS): A Clinical Description of the First Fifty Cases." *American Journal of Psychiatry* 155 (1988): 264–71.

In addition, you are encouraged to consult the individual chapters in this book that are relevant to your child's symptoms. Each of these provides lists of specific resources.

18

"My Daughter Is Terrified to Let Me Go Out at Night, or Even to Go into Another Room Without Her"

Separation anxiety disorder

"Mommy, you can't go out. I need you here."

"Why do you need me, Teri?" Ann asked her daughter.

"Because I might have another bad dream and you're the only one who knows how to make them better," Teri said.

"I have to go, honey, I have a meeting at the church," her mother said. "But I'll be back long before you can have any bad dreams. Now, let's get you tucked into bed."

Ann took Teri into her bedroom and helped her climb up into the upper bunk of the bunk beds. She gave her daughter a kiss and hug, and tucked Teri's covers in tightly before turning off the overhead light.

"Mom," Teri cried. "You forgot to turn on my night-light."

"So I did," Ann replied. "I'm sorry, Teri. How about an extra kiss to make up for leaving you in the dark?"

"It's not the dark that scares me, Mom," Teri said. "What if you have an accident on your way home from your meeting? What if you die? Who will take care of me?"

"Darling, I'm not going to have an accident and I'm not going to die. I'm going to be just fine and so are you. Now, go to sleep."

As soon as her mother left the room, Teri climbed out of bed and went to the window to watch her mother drive away. She sat by the window for over two hours, until she saw her mother's car pull into the driveway, and then she scurried back into bed.

As she had promised, Ann went straight to her daughter's bedroom. As soon as she opened the door, Teri said, "Oh, Mommy, I'm so glad you're back home. First, I worried that you would get in an accident or that someone would sneak up on you and stab you. Then, I saw a big truck come by and that made me think that you had moved away and weren't ever coming back for me."

"Teri, that's one of the silliest things I've ever heard!" Ann replied. "If you saw the truck outside and all our things were still in here, how could that mean that I was moving away without you? Besides, you know that I would never move without taking you along—it would break my heart."

"I think that you shouldn't go away anymore," Teri said. "Then I wouldn't have to worry about you when you're gone. Please promise you won't leave me again—it's terrible when you're not here."

"I can't make that promise, Teri, but I can promise to tell you where I'm going before I leave," her mother said. "I don't want you to worry about me anymore, though. It's my job to worry about you—and right now I'm worried that you'll be too tired to get up for school in the morning. So, close your eyes and go right to sleep."

After tucking Teri in once again, Ann went to speak with her husband in the family room. "Sam, I'm really worried about Teri. She's always carried on more than the other kids when we go out in the evening, but now it's to the point where she worries about me even when I'm here. She's constantly checking in with me during the daytime and asking if I feel okay or if I'm being careful. These past few days, she hasn't left my side for more than a few minutes—if I go out to hang clothes on the line, she'll tag along after me and if I go to the bathroom, she'll be waiting outside the door when I come out. Have you noticed it too, or is it just me?"

Sam said, "Yes, I have noticed that she's acting strangely. She makes a huge fuss every morning as I am leaving for work—crying and begging me not to go. I practically have to peel her off my leg to get out the door. She calls me in the afternoon to find out what time I'm coming home and then she calls back ten minutes later to find out why I haven't left yet. She says that she wants me to leave 'before the traffic gets bad' so that she won't be so worried that I'm going to get hurt or killed on the way home. I don't get it—what's an eight-year-old doing worrying about whether or not her father drives carefully?"

"I don't know, but I know she shouldn't be," Ann replied. "I'm going to call and make an appointment with Dr. Foster, that new behavioral pediatrician in Dr. Jones's group. He's supposed to be an expert at problems like this."

When Dr. Foster asked Teri to tell him about her worries, she said, "I'm worried that my dad or my mom will get hurt or killed. I only feel safe when my mom's right next to me, so that I can touch her and make sure she's okay. But even touching her isn't working too well anymore. Sometimes I get scared even when she's right next to me."

Dr. Foster said, "That must be terrible. You know, Teri, lots of kids have scary nightmares and worries like you're having. They're part of an illness called separation anxiety disorder. There are several things that we can do to make you feel better. They'll take a little while to work, but in a few weeks, I bet you'll be able to go to sleep without feeling so scared and you won't have so many worries in the daytime either."

Separation Anxiety Disorder

Separation anxiety disorder affects about 2 to 3 percent of grade school children (about one in forty). The disorder is distinguished from other anxiety disorders by the fact that the worries are confined to fears that the child will be separated from her parents or her home. (Occasionally, children may develop symptoms of separation anxiety disorder that involve an ailing grandparent or a younger brother or sister, rather than her parents.) Separation anxiety disorder must be distinguished from normal separation difficulties, which are a developmental task of toddlers and children entering school for the first time, but are usually outgrown by the age of five or six (see chapter 4). Separation anxiety disorder starts some time later, frequently around ages seven to eleven, and usually has a discrete beginning—the child has previously been able to separate from her parents without difficulty and then develops a fear of separation. The separation fears are accompanied by psychological distress (anxiety) and physical discomfort, such as headache, stomachache, or symptoms of panic (rapid heartbeat, sweating, trembling, shortness of breath, choking, nausea or abdominal discomfort, dizziness, chills, or numbness and tingling sensations). In separation anxiety disorder, the symptoms also interfere with the child's ability to function normally—missed school days, social isolation, and disruptions in the child's or parents' daily routine are common.

The cause of separation anxiety disorder is unknown. Some mental health experts contend that separation anxiety disorder is just a variation of the normal developmental process and that treatment is not necessary. However, there is usually a delay of several years between the end of normal separation difficulties and the beginning of separation anxiety disorder. Further, the disorder causes both distress and interference, while the developmental difficulties cause neither. Recent medical studies suggest that separation anxiety disorder is not part of the normal developmental spectrum, but rather it is an anxiety disorder, which may be the childhood version of panic disorder and agoraphobia (fear of being in public places from which escape may be difficult and a fear of being alone). Separation anxiety disorder shares many features in common with agoraphobia, including reluctance to leave the "safety" of the home, fears about harm coming to loved ones, social isolation, avoidance of separations, and symptoms of panic. Further support for an association between the two disorders comes from studies demonstrating that adults with agoraphobia frequently had symptoms of separation anxiety disorder during childhood, and that similar treatments are helpful for both disorders.

Does Your Child Have Separation Anxiety Disorder?

1. Does she have recurrent episodes of distress when separating from home or her family members and/or in anticipation of such a separation?
2. Does she have persistent and excessive worries about losing a loved one or about something bad happening to one of her family members?
3. Does she have a persistent and excessive worry that something will happen to separate her from her family (such as getting lost or being kidnapped)?
4. Does she have a persistent reluctance to leave home (especially to go to school) because of worries about being separated from her family?
5. Does she have a persistent and excessive fear or reluctance to be alone?
6. Does she refuse to sleep away from home or have a persistent reluctance to go to sleep without one of her parents nearby?
7. Does she have repeated nightmares about being separated from her loved ones?
8. Does she have repeated complaints of physical symptoms such as headaches, stomachaches, nausea, or vomiting at times when she is separated from loved ones or is worrying about being separated from them?
9. Is she at least six years old?

If you answered yes to at least three of the first eight questions and yes to question 9, then your child may have separation anxiety disorder.

How Do You Know If Your Child Has Separation Anxiety Disorder?

A child with separation anxiety disorder worries that her parents will be taken from her and that something will make it impossible for them to return. She will cry or be excessively clingy when separating from her parents and may be reluctant to sleep alone or refuse to attend school. She also may have nightmares or frequent physical complaints, such as headache or stomachache. In mild cases of separation anxiety disorder, the child will be free of anxiety when she is in the company of her parents, but in more severe cases, she will have continued distress even in their presence—fearing that they might die, or become ill, or worrying in anticipation of the next separation. She may continually ask for reassurance, such as "Mommy, you're not going to die, are you? I couldn't stand it if you weren't here with me. Promise me that you'll let me die first, okay, Mommy?" or "Do you have to go to work on Monday, Daddy? Even if there's a blizzard? What would you do if there was a bad storm when I was here and you were at work?" or "Mom, if the house was on fire, would you let the firemen save me or would you get me out by yourself? I hope that you would come get me because then I'd know where you were."

Physical separations, such as having both parents go out for the evening, are obvious triggers of separation anxiety, but psychological separations can also trigger symptoms. Sleep is one such separation—the child is totally cut off from her parents when she falls asleep. Although most children are unaware of being alone as they sleep, the child with separation anxiety disorder is acutely aware of her vulnerability. To minimize the separation, she may insist on sleeping in or near her parents' bed or require one of her parents to sit with her as she falls asleep. If her parents choose the latter option, she may still end up in their bedroom, after she has been awakened by a nightmare or another anxiety-related sleep problem.

If It's Not Separation Anxiety Disorder, What Else Could It Be?

Normal Separation Difficulties

All toddlers have separation difficulties (see chapter 4), but these normal developmental anxieties usually disappear by the time the child reaches kindergarten. Separation anxiety disorder is distinguished from normal separation anxieties not only by its timing, but also by the amount of distress and interference associated with the symptoms. In the disorder, the anxiety, fears, and worries are severe enough to make the child uncomfortable and to be apparent to others, and the child's reluctance to be separated from her parents interferes with her ability to go to school, to play at another child's home, or to be left alone at home.

Other Anxiety Disorders

Generalized anxiety disorder (chapter 19) and social phobia (chapter 20) may be confused with separation anxiety disorder because the disorders share many features in common and frequently occur together. In generalized anxiety disorder, the child is not just worried about being separated from her parents, but about every aspect of her life. She would not only seek reassurance about her parents' health and well-being, but also about the weather, the safety of her food, her math grade, and a host of other subjects.

Social phobia is characterized by fears of public embarrassment and may lead to school refusal (chapter 4). However, the child with social phobia is not concerned about her parents' safety, nor is she excessively anxious about leaving home—as long as it is to go to a nonpublic setting, such as a friend's home. The child with social phobia would be comfortable going on a sleep-over, while the child with separation anxiety disorder would not, and the child with social phobia would fear (or avoid) performing a solo at a band concert, while the child with separation anxiety disorder would have no concerns about the performance—as long as her parents were close by in the audience.

PANDAS (Pediatric Autoimmune Neuropsychiatric Disorders Associated with Strep)

If the separation anxiety disorder begins abruptly and the symptoms worsen following strep throat infections, then it may be part of a newly characterized syndrome known as PANDAS (for pediatric autoimmune neuropsychiatric disorders associated with strep). Obsessive-compulsive symptoms or tics are usually present in PANDAS, so if your child has only separation anxieties, she is unlikely to have PANDAS (chapter 17).

Nightmares

Children with separation anxiety disorder have nightmares much more frequently than other children do. Often, they will blame their anxiety on a particularly vivid nightmare, and this makes some sense. We've all had nightmares that were so real or so frightening that we continued to feel uncomfortable the next day. On the other hand, nightmares could be viewed as a means of working through anxiety—the anxiety comes first and the nightmares follow. Although no one can tell which causes the other, it is clear that nightmares are a sign of increased anxiety. If your child suddenly begins having nightmares, it is important to look for sources of stress, such as a recent move, final exams, or increased family discord. Finding and eliminating the stress may be sufficient to eliminate the bad dreams. If the nightmares continue for more than two weeks, your child should see her doctor to make sure that the dreams aren't being caused by a physical problem, such as a sleep disorder (see chapter 22).

If your child's fears are primarily centered on being left alone and her distress over separations began abruptly and seemingly "out of the blue," then a psychological trauma, such as sexual abuse, should be considered as a possible cause for the symptoms. Chapter 7 describes the warning signs of sexual abuse, as well as prevention and treatment strategies.

Treatment of Separation Anxiety Disorder

Psychological therapies, particularly psychotherapy and behavior therapy, are the preferred treatments for separation anxiety disorder, with medications following closely behind. Most children will respond to treatment with psychotherapy (talk therapy or play therapy) or behavior therapy, and over three-quarters will respond to a treatment plan that combines behavior therapy with medication. Certain psychological treatments, such as cognitive-behavior therapy, are not suitable for young children (less than age eight or nine) because they require the child's active participation. Family therapy may increase the benefit of the individual treatments by providing a support system for the child's recovery, as well as reducing the impact of the child's symptoms on the family. (See chapter 12 for a complete description of each of these types of therapy.)

Psychological Treatments

Psychological treatments, such as behavior therapy, psychotherapy, and cognitive-behavior therapy, are the treatments of choice for many therapists who treat children with separation anxiety disorder. There are a variety of useful techniques available and the therapist can mix or match the elements to fit the child's individual needs. Behavior therapy, cognitive-behavior therapy, and psychotherapy appear to have the greatest benefit for separation anxiety disorder. Descriptions of the various psychological treatments are included in chapter 12.

Behavior therapy of separation anxiety disorder is based on the theory that all behaviors (including emotional responses, such as anxiety) are learned and can be unlearned by changing the pattern of reinforcements. The child with separation anxiety disorder has been practicing inappropriate leave-takings for so long that she has "unlearned" the right way to say good-bye and now needs to unlearn the wrong way of saying good-bye and then relearn the correct behavioral response. Relaxation therapy might be used in conjunction with the behavior therapy, particularly if the child has nausea, sweating, trembling, or a racing heartbeat in conjunction with her separation anxiety disorder.

Psychotherapy, such as art therapy, play therapy, or talk therapy, can be useful for the treatment of separation anxiety disorder, particularly when the separation difficulties arose from a particular worry or a traumatic event, or when the child is having trouble moving into the next developmental phase. Play therapy is used with younger children and traditional psychotherapy with older children to understand and eliminate some of the child's fears about separating from her parents, and to help the child achieve a sense of mastery over her worries. In treatment of a child with separation anxiety disorder, psychotherapy might be used to help the child understand and eliminate some of the fears about separating from her parents, as well as to relieve her pent-up anxieties by teaching her how to express the feelings in a positive way.

Medications

Medications are most effective for separation anxiety disorder when they are used as a "crutch" or short-term treatment, rather than as a long-term solution. The medications can be used to decrease anxiety during the early stages of behavior therapy and to help control anxiety in specific situations, such as the first few days back in school or when one of the child's parents must be away from home for a prolonged period of time.

Alprazolam (Xanax) and buspirone (BuSpar) are the anxiolytic, or antianxiety, drugs that are most often used for the treatment of separation anxiety disorder. These drugs are typically used only for brief periods of time in order to avoid physical dependence. Alprazolam (Xanax) is effective for the treatment of adults with panic disorder, but has not yet been shown to be better than placebo in the long-term treatment of separation anxiety disorder, despite the proposed connection between the two disorders. Alprazolam does help relieve anxiety related to specific stressful situations and can be used as a short-term aid to behavior therapy. (Chapter 19 provides additional information about the anxiolytic medications.)

Antidepressants, such as the tricyclics, imipramine (Tofranil) and clomipramine (Anafranil), or the serotonin-reuptake-blocking medications (SSRIs), fluoxetine (Prozac), fluvoxamine (Luvox), sertraline (Zoloft), and paroxetine (Paxil), can decrease the physical discomfort associated with anxiety and may also decrease the number of anxious episodes. About one-third to one-half of the children have depression at some point during their separation anxiety disorder, and the antidepressants may be particularly useful to these children because they work on both the anxiety and depression. The SSRIs are becoming increasingly popular for treatment of panic disorder in adults, so their use in children for this related disorder can also be expected to increase. (See chapter 12 for more information about the antidepressant medications.)

In some studies, imipramine and fluoxetine have been shown to be more helpful than placebos (sugar pills) for the treatment of symptoms of separation anxiety disorder, while other studies suggest that for the group as a whole, the antidepressants offer no advantage over the inactive compounds. In each of these studies, however, a few children have had dramatic improvements while taking the antidepressants, so it appears that a "Try it and see if it helps" approach may be in the child's best interest. The decision whether or not to use medication to treat your child's symptoms must be made by you and your child's doctor.

Helping Your Child Overcome Her Separation Anxiety Disorder Symptoms

Recognize the differences between separation difficulties and separation anxiety disorder. It is clear that your child's separation difficulties are in the expected range if she is four years old and is only tearful for a few minutes the first two mornings she attends a new preschool; it is equally clear that your child must have an anxiety disorder if she is ten years old, consumed with worry about being separated from you, and no longer leaves the house because of her fears. Between these two extremes, however, the distinctions are much less clear and it may be hard to decide if your child is closer to "expected" levels of separation difficulties or in excess of them. If you're not sure where your child's separation anxieties fall in the normal range, then seek consultation with her doctor, a school counselor, or her teacher—their extensive experience with children of a similar age will provide a context for your observations and should help clarify the right category for her separation difficulties.

Don't threaten your child with your absence. All children need (and deserve) a safe, comfortable environment in which to work through developmental issues such as establishing independence and developing their own identity. If your child isn't able to depend upon your love, support, and presence, she won't be able to handle these developmental challenges. A shockingly high proportion of parents—over 50 percent in one study—admit to having threatened to withdraw their love or even to abandon the child as a means of extorting good behavior. The parents might say, "If you don't sit down and finish your supper, I'm not coming back from my walk," or "If you can't behave, I'm going to send you to live with [your uncle Ralph, your grandparents, the gypsies]," or—if the parents are divorced—"[your mother/father]." (This is a double whammy —threat of abandonment and a reminder that the parents have already "abandoned" each other.) Although the parent who threatens to send the child "to the gypsies" is obviously making an idle threat, the child may not see it that way. The best solution is to avoid any comment that implies that you would leave your child or that she would be sent away from you.

Provide support for your child, but not for her separation anxieties. Your child's fears are very real to her and shouldn't be dismissed as "nothing to worry about," nor should they be given credibility: "I know you don't want me to go. I don't want to go either—it makes me sad and lonely to be away from my precious daughter." Both send an unintended negative message. In one case, the fears are dismissed as meaningless without considering their meaning for the child and, in the other, the parent increases the child's anxieties by concurring with her fears and extending them even farther. It is better to say, "I know that you're feeling scared and worried right now, but those feelings won't last very long and then you'll feel better." If your child is in therapy, remind her to use the tools that she's learned, whether it's practicing muscle relaxation or turning the anxiety-producing situation into an extra practice session. Finally, it's important that you remain in control of the situation. Don't let your child's anxieties force you to cancel your plans—avoidance increases anxiety, and the next time will be even more difficult.

Prevent separation anxiety disorder from becoming a cause of school refusal. See chapter 4 for an extended discussion of this issue. The bottom line is this: Your child should *never* miss school because of anxiety or separation difficulties. Going back the next day is always harder and it quickly becomes an impossible task to get the child back to her classroom.

Don't allow your child to be teased or humiliated about her fears and worries. Your child already feels bad about her separation fears. She thinks they're stupid, she fears they're "crazy" (they certainly don't make any sense to her—they just frighten her half to death), and she knows that only babies and young children are supposed to cry when their mother leaves. The teasing remarks are taken as confirmation of her inadequacies. Since it is impossible for her to ignore the teasing, it shouldn't take place. Stop teasing before it starts by requiring your family members to treat your child and her fears with respect. Ask your child's teacher to do the same thing in her classroom.

Seek help for your child now, rather than later. Children with separation anxiety disorder are suffering from constant worries, and may begin to fall behind in their emotional development because so much of their energy is being siphoned off to the anxiety disorder—the sooner they get help, the sooner they can get "back on track" with the task of growing up happily. If you're not sure whether your child needs treatment for her separation anxiety disorder, ask an expert. Schedule an appointment with your child's doctor or a consultation with a child psychiatrist of his recommendation.

Participate in behavior therapy and/or family therapy as requested. Behavior therapy is very helpful for separation anxiety disorder, but only if the child can successfully complete the course of treatment. If your child's therapist asks you to help your child with her behavior therapy homework, make sure that you know exactly what you are to do (and what your child must do for herself) and then complete your assignments on schedule. You may be asked to participate in some modeling exercises in the therapist's office or you may be given specific instructions about how to say good-bye to your child. These are not a criticism of your parenting, but rather an opportunity to improve specific aspects of your interactions with your child. Sometimes, your only job is to remind your child to do her behavior therapy homework, and then to leave the room. Just as she learned to play the piano, the child must do her own practicing if she is to master the new techniques.

If your teenager's anxieties stem from a sexual assault, provide her with love and support. If your teenager is sexually assaulted, she will need you to offer her unconditional love and support. The circumstances of the assault may make this difficult. She may have been raped at a party that she wasn't supposed to attend or after she had been drinking or using drugs; she may have been hitchhiking, or gone home with a guy she just met at a party; or she may have been attacked by that "nice boy from the club" whom you had encouraged her to date. Remember that sexual assault is a crime of violence, not passion, and your daughter is the victim —not you or her reputation. Her greatest fear is for her safety and you need to take steps to ensure that she is safe. Secondary fears include undetected internal injuries, an abnormal or "spoiled" appearance of her external genitalia, and an inability to have children. She will also feel ashamed of having been attacked and will blame herself—even if she couldn't have prevented the assault. Her shame may evoke feelings of doubt in you. Was she really assaulted, or was it consensual sex and she's "making up" this story because she got caught in the act? Did she lead him on? Could she have done more to prevent it? These doubts are normal, but must not be conveyed to your daughter. You must accept her story as the truth and deal with its consequences, starting with helping your child to feel safe again. Counseling is recommended for both of you. Your daughter will need professional help in dealing with her fears and self-doubts, and you will be better able to support her recovery if you have someone with whom you can share your concerns. Rape trauma centers offer both counseling sessions and support groups for adolescent victims.

Further Reading

Maloney, Michael, M.D., and Rachel Kranz. *Straight Talk About Anxiety and Depression*. New York: Facts on File, 1991.

Ross, Jerilyn, M.A. *Triumph Over Fear: A Book of Help and Hope for People with Anxiety, Panic Attacks and Phobias*. New York: Bantam Books, 1994.

Medical Texts That Might Be Helpful

Eisen, Andrew R., and Christopher A. Kearney. *Practitioner's Guide to Treating Fear and Anxiety in Children and Adolescents: A Cognitive-Behavioral Approach*. Northvale, NJ: Jason Aronson, 1995.

Leonard, Henrietta, M.D., ed. *Anxiety Disorders*. Child and Adolescent Psychiatric Clinics, Philadelphia, PA: W. B. Saunders. Vol. 2:4, October 1993.

March, John, M.D. *Anxiety Disorders in Children and Adolescents*. New York: Guilford Press, 1995.

Resources

Anxiety Disorders Association of America
11900 Parklawn Drive, Suite 100
Rockville, MD 20852
Phone: 301-231-9350
Fax: 301-231-7392
Internet: www.adaa.org
E-mail: anxdis@aol.com

"My Son Is So Nervous and Tense That He's Making Me Anxious"

Generalized anxiety disorder

Jordan, a small, dark-haired boy of ten, had been staring out the kitchen window for several minutes before he said, "It looks like it might storm today. I'd better take my poncho to school."

"Jordan, you won't need your poncho," his mother replied. "It's supposed to be a perfect day today—clear, warm, and sunny."

"I don't think so, Mom. There's a really nasty-looking cloud over there," he said as he pointed to the eastern sky.

His mother came to the window and looked at where Jordan was pointing. "Jordan," she said, laughing, "that puffy little cloud? That's a fair-weather cumulus—it can't make rain. All it can do is predict good weather. It's going to be a beautiful day."

Jordan persisted. "But what if a storm comes up and it starts raining just as I'm walking home from school? Or what if there's a tornado? It is tornado season, you know, and tornadoes can come up out of a clear blue sky."

His mother, Suzie, sighed and said, "Jordan, we've gone over this a thousand times before—there is <u>not</u> going to be a tornado today. There won't be a rainstorm, either. In fact, I can practically guarantee that not a single drop of rain will fall today."

"Practically guarantee?" Jordan interrupted. "So you're not sure either, hunh?"

"Yes, I'm sure, and since you insist, I will GUARANTEE that there won't be a drop of rain today," his mother replied with more than a trace of annoyance. "Now are you satisfied? I hope so, because I'm through with this conversation. Sit down and eat your breakfast."

"I don't want any breakfast," Jordan said. "My stomach hurts."

His mother's exasperated look turned to one of concern as she said, "Your stomach hurt yesterday, too. What's going on?"

"I don't know. It's been bothering me all week, maybe I have cancer or something."

"Jordan, you don't have cancer. But you shouldn't be having stomachaches so often. I'm going to make an appointment for you with Dr. Johnson. Now try to eat some breakfast—if you don't want the pancakes I made, you can have toast."

Jordan sat at the table and stared at his food for a few minutes before asking, "Mom, did you put my lunch in the refrigerator overnight or did you leave it out on the counter to spoil?"

"I put it in the refrigerator, Jordan. In fact, I was just about to get it out and put it in your backpack. It's nice and cold and it will be fine until lunchtime."

"You're sure?" Jordan persisted. "What about the yogurt—is it past the expiration date?"

"It's fine, Jordan," his mother answered. "Stop being such a worrywart!"

"I'm not a worrywart. I just don't want to get sick from the yogurt. My stomach already hurts."

"Fine," his mother said. "I'll make you a peanut butter and jelly sandwich."

"No!" Jordan said. "The peanut butter might get stuck to the roof of my mouth just as someone asks me a question and I won't be able to talk right and then everybody will laugh at me. That would be bad—really bad. Just give me the yogurt. I'd rather get sick."

"Okay, then, Jordan, yogurt it is. But hurry up and finish your breakfast or you'll miss your bus."

"Miss the bus?" Jordan gasped. "Oh no! I can't miss the bus. The driver would be so mad if he stopped and I wasn't there. I'll hurry." He took a bite of toast and then said, "But what about my stomachache? If I eat this, I might have to throw up on the bus. Throwing up on the bus is the worst—all the kids *would tease me and I'd die of embarrassment. Oh, why do these things always have to happen to me?"*

"Why indeed?" his mother whispered to herself.

This short exchange is only one of many that Jordan and his mother will have that day. Jordan never stops worrying—about everything from missing the bus or getting peanut butter stuck on the roof of his mouth, to having cancer or getting caught in a tornado. His worries aren't confined to just his own life either, he also worries about inner-city violence, the decline of the South American rain forests, and the spread of AIDS. There isn't anything that isn't a source of anxiety and worry to Jordan because he is suffering from generalized anxiety disorder.

Generalized anxiety disorder, or GAD, is classified as an anxiety disorder because the worries are persistent, pervasive, and severe enough to cause distress and impairment. Children with GAD worry constantly, often to the point of making themselves sick with headaches, stomachaches, or dizziness. The worries are so frequent and intrusive that the child can't relax fully and "just have fun"—in severe cases, he may not even be able to carry on a conversation or read a paragraph without interruption. The distress caused by the anxiety and the difficulties resulting from the chronic, intrusive nature of the worries are what separate GAD from normal childhood worries. (Also see chapter 12 for a discussion of severity criteria for disorders.)

Generalized anxiety disorder is quite common—affecting about one in twenty-five girls and one in fifty boys at some point during childhood or adolescence. The rate of GAD rises throughout the grade school years, and there is a marked increase in frequency among adolescent girls. Long-term studies have shown that GAD typically is present for only two to three years before resolving or changing into a different form (such as separation anxiety or social phobia). However, a few children will have symptoms that persist throughout adolescence and into adulthood—at present, it is impossible to tell which children will go on to have chronic anxiety.

Does Your Child Have Generalized Anxiety Disorder?

1. Does your child have excessive worries about a wide variety of subjects?

2. Do the worries cause your child to be anxious, nervous, or tense much of the time?
3. Have the worries been present for at least six months?
4. Does your child try to stop worrying and find that he can't control his anxiety?
5. Do the worries get in your child's way (cause interference with his friendships, schoolwork, or functioning at home)?
6. Does your child complain of at least one of the following symptoms?
   a. Restlessness or feeling keyed up or "on edge"
   b. Being easily fatigued
   c. Difficulty concentrating or mind going blank
   d. Irritability
   e. Muscle tension
   f. Sleep disturbances (difficulty falling asleep, waking in the middle of the night, or restless, unsatisfying sleep)

If you answered yes to questions 1 through 6, your child may have generalized anxiety disorder.

If you answered yes to questions 2, 4, and 5, but answered no to question 1 because your child doesn't worry about a wide variety of things, then your child may have:

Separation anxiety disorder (chapter 18), if his worries are mostly about the welfare of family members or his separation from home or family.

Hypochondriasis or somatization disorder, if his worries are about his health or the way his body is functioning.

Obsessive-compulsive disorder (chapter 16), if his worries are accompanied by compulsive rituals, or

Social phobia (chapter 20), if his worries are about being embarrassed in public.

How Do You Know If Your Child Has Generalized Anxiety Disorder?

"Worry early and worry often" is the motto of the child with GAD. He worries about his own safety, well-being, and happiness, and also about things far beyond his sphere of influence, such as tornadoes, terrorist bombings, or other catastrophes. He worries about things he's done and those he didn't do, things he's doing currently and those he'll do in the future. He ruminates about the B+ he got in math last year and the less-than-perfect score he received today, and also worries about his performance on the standardized tests next month and the likelihood of his being accepted by a college four years from now. Worries about the future are the most common symptom of GAD, perhaps because the future is associated with such uncertainty. For the child with GAD, any uncertainty or lack of predictability causes doubt, and the doubt leads to worries and anxiety. To avoid experiencing anxieties about the future, the child with GAD tries to gain control over all aspects of his life and he becomes rigid and careful about his daily schedule, schoolwork, and the way he eats, sleeps, and dresses. This rigidity, in combination with his chronic worries about adult issues like family finances and leaky roofs, makes him seem "old before his time."

The perfectionism associated with GAD is also a result of the child's anxieties about "doing well" and "being good." He tries hard to dress right, to say the right things, and to fit in with his classmates, but he still worries about having the wrong clothes, saying the wrong thing, or picking the wrong friends. He is overly sensitive to criticism and worries that others are noticing his imperfections. The child with GAD pushes himself to excel in sports and academics, but fears that he's a failure. In an effort to convince himself that his worries are unfounded, he seeks reassurance about the value of his achievements ("I helped the team when I scored that goal, didn't I?") or the quality of his work ("I got a ninety-eight on my test today, Dad. That's good enough to get an A, isn't it?"). He also requires reassurance that he's loved by his family, liked by his peers, and accepted as "normal." When his parents grow tired of answering his constant questions, they may ignore his need for constant support or become angry with his interruptions. When his peers become irritated with his need for reassurance, they may end the friendship or tease him about his worries, further contributing to his anxiety about fitting in with his peers.

The child with GAD is always nervous and tense, and often is irritable or "on edge." He is also ill much of the time. He has frequent headaches, stomachaches, nausea, dizziness, or "just not feeling well." The symptoms might vary from day to day, but they are almost always present, and typically worsen before a stressful event, such as taking a test or going away to camp. The child with GAD may have difficulty sleeping (see chapter 22) and might attribute this to his headache or stomachache, but usually his insomnia is caused by nighttime worrying.

Generalized anxiety disorder is often found in conjunction with other psychiatric disorders, such as depression or separation anxiety disorder. Between one-half to three-quarters of children with GAD are also suffering from depression or another anxiety disorder, such as separation anxiety disorder or panic disorder. Sometimes, the presence of depression or separation anxiety disorder can mask the child's GAD symptoms. Usually, however, GAD symptoms are increased in the presence of a second disorder—for example, depression decreases the child's ability to cope with his anxiety and causes greater impairment, while symptoms of separation anxiety disorder provide a catalyst for the child's worries, which quickly generalize to involve other concerns.

If It's Not Generalized Anxiety Disorder, What Could It Be?

Normal Childhood Worries

Every child has a number of different worries and concerns, and most children have at least one or two excessive fears (such as snakes, strange noises, or the dark). Normal worries may even increase to the point of full-blown anxiety on occasion, such as before a big test, an important ball game, or a solo performance. However, the worries are not persistent, and they do not cause distress or impairment. (See chapter 8 for further information about how to distinguish between normal worries and GAD.)

Stress-Induced Anxiety

When a child is experiencing excessive stress, such as his parents divorcing or the death of a grandparent, he may develop symptoms similar to GAD. Child abuse, including sexual abuse (chapter 7), also can cause excessive worries and symptoms of generalized anxiety. The stress-triggered anxiety can be distinguished from GAD by the nature and duration of the symptoms. Stress-triggered anxiety tends to focus on areas relevant to the stressor—for example, if the child's anxiety was triggered by the death of his grandmother, he might have worries about losing one or both of his parents and would seek reassurance about safety and health-related issues, but he would be unlikely to have excessive worries about school performance or being embarrassed in public.

Stress-triggered anxiety peaks in severity immediately following the stressful situation and fades away over the ensuing months. In GAD, the anxiety is a chronic problem and persists for at least six months before the diagnosis is considered. Children with GAD are usually described by their parents as "always" having been somewhat nervous and tense, while those with stress-triggered anxiety are more likely to have been anxiety-free before their symptoms were triggered.

Other Anxiety Disorders

Generalized anxiety disorder must be distinguished from other, more specific anxiety disorders and the content of the child's worries is key to making the correct diagnosis. If the fears mainly concern harm coming to the child's loved ones or the possibility that he won't be able to return home, the child is likely to have separation anxiety disorder (chapter 18). If the fears are centered on circumstances in which the child may come under scrutiny (such as eating in public or giving a speech), then social phobia (chapter 20) is the most likely diagnosis. Obsessive-compulsive disorder (chapter 16) would be considered if the child fears contamination or has repetitive rituals (compulsions) in conjunction with his worries.

Medical Illnesses

Children with chronic diseases, such as diabetes, asthma, or cystic fibrosis, often develop excessive concerns about their health and appearance. These can mimic the symptoms of generalized anxiety disorder, but shouldn't be confused with GAD because they are so closely related to the child's primary illness. Nonspecific illnesses, particularly those involving the gastrointestinal system, such as irritable bowel syndrome, ulcerative colitis, or Crohn's disease, can be more difficult to distinguish from GAD because these disorders cause chronic, intermittent physical symptoms (such as stomachaches and diarrhea), and they are frequently accompanied by increased anxiety and excessive health concerns. The anxiety may remain limited to the child's physical condition or it can become generalized and mimic GAD. The anxiety should be treated if it's a problem for the child, but the bowel disease should be brought under control first to ensure that the source of the child's worries has been eliminated.

Panic Disorder

Until recently, it was thought that children were not susceptible to panic disorder. But we now know that children do have panic attacks (albeit rarely) and the episodes are similar to those seen in adults. The panic attack comes on quickly and without warning, building to peak intensity within just a minute or two. The child feels sweaty and anxious, his heart pounds, and he has difficulty breathing or swallowing. He may feel as if he's choking or a heavy weight is crushing his chest, or he may experience an overwhelming fear that he's going to die or go crazy. In addition, he may have one or all of the following symptoms: chest pain or tightness, nausea, stomachache, dizziness, chills or hot flushes, and/or numbness or tingling in his fingers or toes. The episode lasts only a few minutes and is accompanied by extreme anxiety or, conversely, by feelings of being outside himself or detached from reality. When the panic attack is over, the child remains anxious and on edge, wondering what he did to cause the attack and worrying when the next one might occur.

The spells are so uncomfortable and disturbing that many children develop an intense fear of having a future panic attack. The child might avoid the place where the first attack occurred or places that are similar enough to trigger the memory. He might eventually refuse to leave the safety of his home, fearing that if he goes to school and has an attack, no one will be available to help him.

Panic attacks are serious medical conditions and a child with panic should always receive treatment. The goals of therapy are to decrease anxiety and prevent future attacks. Prompt treatment is crucial to the child's long-term prognosis, since one panic attack increases his chances of having a second and a second panic attack dramatically increases the chances of subsequent attacks. Panic disorder can be treated with behavior therapy, cognitive therapy, and/or medications. All have been found to be beneficial to adults with panic disorder, but at this point, there's no hard evidence that they are helpful to children. Anecdotal evidence suggests that antidepressant medications, such as desipramine or imipramine, or the antianxiety drugs clonazepam and alprazolam, hold the greatest promise.

Treatment of Generalized Anxiety Disorder

Generalized anxiety disorder can be treated with a variety of methods, including medications and psychological treatments, such as psychotherapy, behavior therapy, and cognitive therapy. Medications are the most effective treatment for GAD and therefore psychiatrists use them first in most cases. For some children, however, psychological treatments (particularly behavior therapy) may be the preferred choice since they have no side effects and offer the potential of long-term benefits (while medications appear to work only while the child is taking them).

Psychological Treatments

Psychotherapy includes talk therapy and play therapy. These are a good, safe choice for children with GAD because they allow the child to overcome his anxiety by talking through his worries and trying new things (thus decreasing avoidance, which reinforces fears and anxiety). Often, the therapist will encourage the child to imagine that his "worst" fears have come true and then to think about solutions to the situation. In the process, the therapist identifies the child's inner strengths and helps him to use those strengths to overcome his anxieties. Through continued practice, the child's fears are minimized and his coping skills are maximized so that he is able to gain control over his worries.

Behavior therapy and *cognitive-behavior therapy* are described in detail in chapter 12. When these techniques are used for GAD, the goal of therapy is to practice the worry until it no longer produces anxiety. During the treatment session, the therapist provides support to the child as he practices confronting his worries and ignoring (or tolerating) the accompanying anxiety. Between sessions, the child practices these exposures at home and learns that not only is the anxiety tolerable and transient, but also that he can decrease it by repeated exposure. Behavior therapy is often not suitable for use with children less than 8 or 9 years old as they haven't yet developed the skills needed to fulfill the requirements of the homework assignments.

Relaxation therapy teaches the child to control his breathing and to relax various muscle groups as a means of controlling the physical responses that accompany anxiety. By blocking the physical symptoms, it is easier for the child to ignore his anxiety and to participate in behavior therapy sessions. Relaxation therapy is useful not only as a help in therapy sessions, but any time the child begins to feel his heart racing or his hands trembling. He can also use relaxation therapy as a means of distracting his attention from the worries.

Medications

There are two families of medications that are used to treat childhood anxiety disorders: anxiolytic (antianxiety) drugs (such as alprazolam, clonazepam, and buspirone), and antidepressant drugs, such as imipramine, desipramine, and fluoxetine. Scientific studies have demonstrated that these medications are better than placebo (sugar pills) in reducing anxiety symptoms, and clinical experience has proven that they are safe and reasonably effective—about two-thirds to three-quarters of the children with GAD who take an anxiolytic or antidepressant medication will improve.

The antidepressant drugs appear to be the most effective medications for the treatment of GAD, with 75 percent of the children finding the medications helpful. Imipramine (Tofranil) and desipramine (Norpramin) are tricyclic antidepressant drugs that have a good record of success in childhood anxiety disorders, and the SSRIs (fluoxetine [Prozac], fluvoxamine [Luvox], sertraline [Zoloft], and paroxetine [Paxil]) are gaining popularity because they are both safe (few side effects) and effective. The antidepressant medications are discussed at length in chapter 12.

Anxiolytics or antianxiety drugs, such as alprazolam (Xanax), lorazepam (Ativan), and clonazepam (Klonopin), are also helpful for GAD. Each of these drugs is a benzodiazepine and has specific antianxiety effects. (Diazepam [Valium] is the best-known drug in this class, but it is not used for childhood anxiety disorders for a variety of reasons.) Lorazepam and alprazolam are short-acting medications that are particularly helpful for the anxious child who has both anxiety and insomnia—a bedtime dose allows him to fall asleep more easily, but the short-acting medication is gone by morning, so he is awake and alert in school the next day. Clonazepam (Klonopin) is a long-acting benzodiazepine and takes many hours to wear off. The child may feel groggy or sedated during daytime hours, even if the dose is taken early the evening before. The advantage of clonazepam is that it can prevent "withdrawal rebound"—a condition in which the child's anxiety increases dramatically as the drug wears off, and he feels more anxious and uncomfortable than he did before taking the medication. This rebound anxiety may be confused with worsening symptoms and so he is given more of the medication; the next time, the withdrawal is even worse, leading to a vicious cycle of increasing dosages and greater rebounding. Clonazepam minimizes withdrawal rebound because it wears off slowly enough to allow the child's body to compensate.

Side effects of benzodiazepine treatment include drowsiness, confusion, agitation, depression, and disinhibition (acting impulsively, or being wild or silly). An additional concern with benzodiazepines is the potential for physical dependency and the possibility that the drugs will be abused. Because the child's body adjusts to the presence of the medication, he becomes "dependent" on its presence—just as his anxiety can increase as the drug levels decline, physical changes may occur that can also be unpleasant. In essence, the child is "hooked" (physically, if not psychologically). For most children with GAD, the physical dependency is not a problem—the child's physician will decrease the medication dosage slowly over a few weeks' time and can then stop the drug without causing the child any discomfort. Because of the benzodiazepines' potential for abuse, however, the drugs should be avoided if one of the child's parents has a problem with alcoholism or drug abuse, or if the child (or teen) is at increased risk for drug abuse (see chapter 24).

Buspirone (BuSpar) is an antianxiety drug that is new to the United States and has not been used very often in children. Buspirone has a different mechanism of action than the benzodiazepines (it may actually be closer to the SSRIs in the way that it works). Buspirone is not associated with drug dependency or abuse and has few side effects, including dizziness, headaches, nausea, and fatigue. In the future, buspirone may prove helpful for the treatment of childhood anxiety disorders, since it was developed to treat anxiety in adults, but at present, there are not yet any studies demonstrating its utility for childhood anxiety disorders.

There are two classes of drugs that should *not* be used for childhood anxiety disorders: major tranquilizers and antihistamines. Despite their name, the major tranquilizers, such as haloperidol (Haldol), pimozide (Orap), or chlorpromazine (Thorazine), are not appropriate treatments for children with anxiety disorders. In fact, these drugs (also known as neuroleptics or antipsychotic medications) may actually increase anxiety among some groups of children. Further, the major tranquilizers have the potential to cause tardive dyskinesia (abnormal writhing movements of the face, hands, and feet). Tardive dyskinesia may continue even after the neuroleptic medication is stopped, and this long-term side effect is another reason why the major tranquilizers are not used to treat childhood anxiety disorders.

Antihistamines are also not appropriate for the long-term treatment of anxiety disorders. Because antihistamines are sedating, they can be used in the short-term management of an overly anxious child (to make him calmer and help him fall asleep), but they do not offer real help to the child with an anxiety disorder because they have no effect on anxiety. In an anxious child who is having trouble falling asleep, antihistamines might be used for two or three nights to produce sedation, but should not be used longer or they will cause secondary insomnia (also a rebound phenomenon).

Helping Your Child Overcome His Symptoms of Generalized Anxiety Disorder

Learn the differences between normal worries and anxiety disorders and seek treatment for GAD. The major differences between normal worries and the presence of an anxiety disorder are the degree of distress that the child experiences, the extent to which the anxieties interfere with daily functioning, and the length of time that the symptoms last. If your child's worries are causing anxiety, get in his way, or have been going on for over six weeks, he may need treatment. His pediatrician should be able to recommend a child psychiatrist who can do a formal evaluation and develop a treatment plan. Because psychological therapies are not usually the most effective treatments for GAD, it is important for your child to start with a child psychiatrist, rather than a psychologist or counselor, because the psychiatrist can prescribe medications if necessary.

Establish a stable, predictable base of support. A child with GAD has ever-present doubts and worries, particularly about his own safety and security. A stable family life can help decrease the child's anxiety by showing that his worries are unfounded, while a chaotic home environment can make the anxiety worse. For example, if your child is worried that "I'm not important to my family, so they'll forget to pick me up from soccer practice. I'll get kidnapped and never see them again," then he actually has three worries: (1) that he's not valued in the family, (2) he's going to be kidnapped as he waits on the soccer field, and (3) he'll be permanently separated from his parents. When you're twenty minutes late to pick him up, you reinforce the second part of the worry and, by generalization, the other two gain credibility. The next time your child has soccer practice, his fear will be much stronger and he may find it impossible to go to the soccer field alone.

Family routines should be established to provide an additional source of stability. The child with GAD requires structure and predictability as a means of fighting against his anxiety—the more he can use his previous experience to predict future events, the better prepared he is to "prove" to himself that the world isn't an incomprehensible mess. To increase your child's sense of security: establish daily and weekly routines for your family, avoid changing plans at the last minute, forewarn him about any changes in routine (such as having someone else pick him up from soccer practice), and help your child focus on those things that are under your control ("Yes, we are stuck in a bad traffic jam, Jordan, but we've got plenty of gas and I allowed extra time to get to the concert. It's going to be okay").

Don't wrap your child in a protective bubble. Although a stable, supportive environment is important for the child with GAD, this should not translate into a sterile, risk-free environment. If a child with GAD is protected from all risks and allowed to avoid all anxiety-provoking situations, his anxiety will increase—the more he avoids, the more there is to cause anxiety and to be avoided. Your child depends upon you to show him that his fears are groundless. If you are confident enough in his safety to allow/require him to follow through on his plans to stay overnight at a friend's house or to recite a poem in class, then he can draw upon that confidence when his anxieties begin to cast doubt on the situation; in contrast, if you "protect" him by not requiring him to participate, then you have confirmed the basis for his fears. Finally, every child needs to take chances in order to grow and develop properly, and the child with GAD is not an exception. He must be willing to fall off his bike in order to learn to ride, he needs to be able to admit his spelling mistakes in order to spell new words correctly, and he has to speak to at least one stranger in order to have a friend. Be prepared to offer your child some extra support and reassurance as he tests his limits, but keep those limits at the same distance as you would for a child who didn't have GAD.

Don't tease or ridicule your child about his worries and don't allow others to do so either. The child with GAD is a true "worrywart," but it's not helpful to remind him of his disorder, and it's harmful to label him as a worrier. Although the disorder is not caused by teasing or ridicule, it can be made worse by negative attention—children with GAD often worry that they're "crazy" or that they're an embarrassment to others. Teasing reinforces this worry and compounds their anxiety.

Further Reading

Additional references are listed in chapter 18.

Gittelman, Rachel, M.D. *Anxiety Disorders of Childhood*. New York: Guilford Press, 1986. This is a medical textbook.
Greist, John, M.D., Jeff Jefferson, M.D., and Isaac Marks, M.D. *Anxiety and Its Treatment: Help Is Available*. New York: Warner Books, 1988.
Sheehan, David V., M.D. *The Anxiety Disease*. New York: Bantam Books, 1983.

Resources

Anxiety Disorders Association of America
6000 Executive Boulevard, Suite 513
Rockville, MD 20851
Phone: 301-231-9350
Fax: 301-231-7392
Internet: www.adaa.org
E-mail: anxdis@aol.com

20

"My Daughter Is So Painfully Shy, She Won't Even Order Her Own Ice Cream"

Selective mutism and social phobia

"Naomi, what do you want to eat?" Rachel asked her seven-year-old daughter as they stood in line at the local fast food restaurant.

Naomi seemed to shrink to half her size as she shrugged her shoulders and gave her mother an "I don't know" look.

"I don't know either, Naomi," her mother replied in exasperation. "We can't hold up the line, so if you don't choose, I'm going to get you a hamburger and a soda. Is that all right?"

Naomi shook her head no and looked at the kid's meal display—desperately hoping that her mother would notice it and offer to buy her one. She really wanted the toy this week—all the kids in her class already had one, but as much as she wanted it, she couldn't bring herself to tell her mother, so she just stared at the signs and hoped that her mother would get the hint.

Rachel noticed the direction of her daughter's stares and asked, "Do you want a kid's meal?"

Naomi smiled and vigorously nodded her head yes! before hiding behind her mother and ducking her head so that her hair was once again covering her face.

"Oh, Naomi," Rachel said with a sigh. "What am I going to do with you?"

Naomi's teacher asked a similar question the next week at a special parent-teacher conference. "What are we going to do about your daughter?"

"Do about Naomi?" her father replied.

"What are we going to do about Naomi's refusal to talk?" Ms. Gold said. "Her shyness is definitely a problem, but I've taught dozens of shy children over the years and have had no real difficulties with getting them to warm up. Naomi is different. Not only is she reluctant to participate in group activities, but she won't read when it's her turn in the reading circle and she has never given me the answer to a single question that I've asked her. She seems to know the answer, but she's unable—or unwilling—to speak. For a while, I thought that Naomi's shyness was responsible for this and that she'd start to talk after she got comfortable in the classroom. But that isn't happening. She's made some friends and has started to participate in some of the classroom activities, but she's still not talking, not even to the other children in the class. I occasionally see her whisper something to her best friend, Juliana, when the two of them are standing off by themselves during recess. But as soon as someone comes within earshot, Naomi clams up again. The poor thing, it seems like she's really afraid of speaking in public," Ms. Gold concluded.

"You're precisely right, Ms. Gold," Rachel said softly. "Naomi isn't stubborn or naughty, she's got selective mutism. The doctors say that she's afraid to let people hear her voice, so she doesn't talk in public. I can't tell you how many vanilla cones she's eaten because she wouldn't tell me what flavor she wanted, or how many times I've had to rush to the bathroom with her because she wouldn't tell me that she had to go until everyone was out of hearing range. Then, when she got there, I had to go into the stall with her and sing so that no one would hear her tinkle."

"It sounds like this has been a problem for a long time," Ms. Gold said. "Why didn't you tell me about it? Maybe I could have helped."

Rachel replied, "I was going to schedule an appointment to see you, but I was waiting to see if maybe she'd be okay in your class. She did fine last year in kindergarten."

"Really?" Ms. Gold said incredulously. "Did she talk?"

"A little," Rachel continued. "I used to volunteer in her classroom and heard Naomi speak to the other children and even answer questions from the teacher. She never talked very loudly and didn't say much more than a syllable at a time, but she did talk. Maybe she was just more comfortable there—she'd been in the same small classroom with the same teacher and students since preschool, so it was almost like her second family."

"That certainly would be in keeping with selective mutism," Ms. Gold said. When Naomi's parents looked puzzled, she explained, "I spoke with the school's psychologist about Naomi and she also thought your daughter might have selective mutism. I'm glad to know that you've already seen a doctor and that she's getting help. It will be nice when Naomi is able to speak in class. I'm sure she has a lot to say," Ms. Gold concluded.

"Yes, she does," Naomi's father agreed. "She has a lovely voice, too. I hope that you get to hear it someday soon."

Selective Mutism and Social Phobia

Selective mutism and social phobia often occur together, perhaps because they both arise from similar apprehensions—fear of public critique or embarrassment. In selective mutism, the fear is related only to the child's speech, while in social phobia, the child fears being embarrassed by something that she does or says, or being seen by others and judged as weak, "crazy," stupid, or anxious.

Selective mutism is defined as the failure to speak in one or more situations, despite normal speech in other settings, such as the home. It ranges in severity from an inability to speak to strangers, such as store clerks or waiters, to complete mutism in all public settings, including the classroom and playground. Selective mutism was previously called "elective mutism" because therapists thought that the children were *refusing* to speak in public, rather than being *unable* to speak. The new name indicates not only a change in our understanding of the symptoms, but also a change in the professional attitude toward the disorder. Selective mutism is now best characterized as an anxiety disorder because the children report fearing the sound of their own voice or of having others hear their voice, and they develop a rapid heartbeat, shallow breathing, sweating, and trembling when they speak or hear their own voice (even on a tape recording). Since selective mutism is no longer considered to be a symptom of an oppositional disorder, psychiatrists can focus on helping the child overcome her fears and regaining her ability to speak in public, rather than breaking down her resistance against public speaking.

Social phobia is distinguished from excessive shyness (see chapter 9) because it causes difficulties in the child's life and also causes distress, in the form of anxiety, which is often associated with physical symptoms, such as sweating, blushing, trembling, light-headedness, diarrhea, and a racing heartbeat. The child with social phobia fears situations in which she must interact with new or unfamiliar persons, as well as settings in which she might be scrutinized by others. She is apprehensive about speaking or performing in front of others and avoids oral presentations or writing on the blackboard whenever possible (including feigning illness on the day that she's due to give her book report). Children can develop social phobia about any situation in which they might be observed. Fear of using public rest rooms may even be a symptom of social phobia, if the fear is related to having someone hear the child using the toilet, rather than concerns about cleanliness, as is seen in obsessive-compulsive disorder (chapter 16).

Does Your Child Have Selective Mutism?

1. Does she consistently fail to speak in certain situations, such as in class or in front of strangers?
2. Does her lack of speech interfere with her educational achievements or with her social relationships?
3. Has she been mute for at least one month (not counting the first month of school)?
4. Does she talk normally in at least one setting, such as at home with her family?
5. Is English her native language?

If you answered yes to all five questions, then your child may have selective mutism.

If you answered yes to questions 1, 2, and 3, but no to question 4, then your child may have mutism, but it is not selective mutism.

If you answered no to question 5, then your child's lack of speech may be related to difficulties adjusting to a new language, rather than selective mutism. The diagnosis might still apply if she is also unable to speak her native language in similar situations.

Does Your Child Have Social Phobia?

1. Does she show a marked and persistent fear of one or more social situations, including performances such as oral presentations, concerts, or plays?
2. Does she feel anxious, tense, or "frozen" in response to certain social situations?
3. Does she avoid social or performance situations? If not, does she seem extremely anxious or distressed as she endures them?

4. Do the fears interfere with her daily activities or peer relationships?
5. Has the fear of social situations lasted at least six months?
6. If she's older than twelve years of age, does she recognize that this fear is excessive or unreasonable?
7. Does she have physical symptoms of anxiety, such as sweating, blushing, racing heart, or trembling when confronted with certain social situations?

If you answered yes to questions 1 through 6, then your child may have social phobia.

If you also answered yes to question 7, then she probably has social phobia of sufficient severity to warrant treatment.

If you answered yes to questions 1 or 2 or 3, and also answered yes to questions 4 and 7, then your child may have panic disorder, rather than social phobia, and the distinction would be made by determining whether or not the anxiety was always related to a social situation or whether it could come on "out of the blue."

How Do You Know If Your Child Has Social Phobia or Selective Mutism?

Social phobia and selective mutism are both situation-dependent disorders and are not usually present when the child is home alone with her family. The children do have some characteristics that persist even in the safety of the child's home—these include being shy, timid, overly sensitive, anxious, fearful, and excessively clinging. Parents usually describe their child as "always having been this way," even though the selective mutism is not apparent until the child is at least three or four years old (nearly 70 percent of the children are first referred for treatment when they reach kindergarten). Social phobia usually begins later, during mid-adolescence, although it has been reported to occur in younger children who have another anxiety disorder or selective mutism.

Children with selective mutism talk freely in some situations, so it is clear that they are not suffering from deafness, a speech impediment, or another cause of mutism, but they do not talk out loud in public. The extent to which the children speak varies greatly. Some are able to speak only with immediate family members and won't talk at home if relatives or family friends are present, others can talk freely at home and to their friends at school and will even answer their teacher's questions with soft monosyllables, but wouldn't be able to order food in a restaurant or ask a store clerk for assistance. The children must depend upon gestures, shaking or nodding their head, or facial expressions to make their needs known in public. Frequently, their mothers seem to know exactly what they want, and if not, to be able to ask yes/no questions until they ascertain their child's needs. This close relationship was originally interpreted by child psychiatrists as evidence that the selective mutism arose from an unhealthy symbiosis between the mother and child, but it seems to be more of a reaction to the selective mutism—a means of coping with the child's inability to speak, similar to that developed by parents of toddlers who haven't yet learned to talk but have definite opinions about the kind of juice they want to drink or which pajamas they want to wear.

Social phobia is also situation-specific, with oral reports and class plays topping the list of situations that elicit anxiety. The child with social phobia worries almost incessantly about her performance for several days leading up to the event and may even lose sleep or have abdominal pain or diarrhea. She suffers through the presentation with sweating hands and racing heart, fearing that she'll do something embarrassing or that someone will notice her nervousness. When it's over, she feels a sense of tremendous relief for only a few moments before beginning to worry that she had not done well or that she said something inappropriate. The anxiety and physical discomfort make the book report just as horrible as the child had feared that it would be, which further increases her anxiety and her desire to avoid similar situations in the future.

Avoidance is the most common symptom of social phobia—children are reluctant to join an athletic team, choir, or orchestra because they don't want to be in the spotlight, they avoid formal speaking, and may avoid eating or writing in front of others, as well as avoiding the use of public bathrooms. Although formal speeches are the most-feared situation for children with social phobia, informal conversations give them the greatest overall distress, because they happen much more often. In one research study, children with social phobia reported that they had at least one anxiety-producing conversation every other day—whether it was confronting a classmate or turning down an invitation to a birthday party.

If It's Not Selective Mutism or Social Phobia, What Else Could It Be?

Selective mutism should be distinguished from an inability to speak secondary to deafness or other disabilities, and from other causes of mutism —such as expressive language delays, pervasive developmental disorder, and autism. Selective mutism should also be separated from reactive mutism, in which the silence is a response to a new situation or a traumatic event. Children frequently won't talk for their first few days of kindergarten or after starting a new school—this is often related to stranger anxiety and should disappear within the first month of school. Children may also become mute after a significant loss, such as a parent's death, or a severe trauma, such as sexual abuse or witnessing an assault of their parent. To ensure the child's safety, child abuse should always be considered when a child has mutism, but it will be found in only a small percentage of cases.

Excessive shyness may resemble social phobia and the distinction is made on the basis of the pattern of anxieties, as well as by the degree of distress and interference present (see chapter 9). For example, the shy child might have butterflies in her stomach as she gives her book report, but she wouldn't have spent days dreading it and suffer symptoms similar to a panic attack. Social phobia also may be confused with generalized anxiety disorder (see chapter 19), and the two conditions can be distinguished by the nature of the fears and worries. In general, a child with social phobia will have fears only about social situations, while the child with GAD will worry about many other things as well.

Treatment of Selective Mutism and Social Phobia

Selective mutism and social phobia are both helped by a variety of therapies, such as behavior therapy, individual psychotherapy (talk therapy), family therapy, and medication. At this time, there is little information available about the effectiveness of these treatments, although it appears that a combination of medication and behavior therapy may be optimal.

Psychological Treatments

Behavior therapists view selective mutism as the product of a long series of inappropriately reinforced negative behaviors, and the therapy is designed to teach the child a more positive manner of responding. Since the child's anxiety increases when she tries to speak and this inhibits further attempts at speech, the therapist first works on disconnecting the anxiety and the speaking. He helps the child learn to use relaxation techniques to control her anxiety and then supports and encourages her attempts to speak in a situation that is somewhat difficult for her. The child may not be able to speak in the therapist's presence, so her parents are taught to do the exercises. For example, the child might start out by whispering to the parent in the presence of someone seated across the room; at the next exercise, the stranger has moved a little closer and the parent has moved away; the exercises continue until the child is closer to the stranger than to her mother and she is able to speak in a loud voice.

Psychotherapy (talk therapy) for selective mutism is based on the theory that the child is using her silence as a means of punishing her parents or she is maintaining a family secret. Since the child can't speak, the therapist would use art therapy or play therapy in an effort to help the child work through these conflicts. Group therapy may also be effective, particularly for developing confidence with informal conversations. The therapist would initially focus on having the child participate fully in nonverbal group activities and then would involve her in those activities that emphasized verbal skills.

Contingency management is another version of behavior therapy and is used often to treat social phobia. It utilizes the irrational nature of the child's fears to convince her of their senselessness. In contingency management therapy, the child would be asked to imagine the worst possible outcome of the spelling bee ("I forget how to spell all the words" or "I wet my pants in front of the whole class") and then to examine these scenarios from an objective viewpoint ("I can't forget how to spell *all* the words. I've never gotten less than an A on any of our quizzes" or "I haven't wet my pants since I was two years old"). The success of contingency management therapy depends upon the child's ability to extrapolate her experiences to the point of absurdity, so it may not be useful for younger children.

Cognitive-behavior therapy is particularly useful for the treatment of social phobia because it not only desensitizes the child to her feared social situation, but also allows her to gain control over her fears. Cognitive-behavior therapy examines the role that negative thoughts play in increasing the child's anxiety and teaches the child how to replace the negative thoughts with positive ones. For example, if a child is worrying about being embarrassed in front of the class during a spelling bee, she is encouraged to replace that worry with a more realistic, positive thought, such as: "I've studied all my words and know them cold. I'll do fine!" The positive thoughts help to increase the child's self-confidence and self-esteem, as well as removing the negative influence of the worries and fears.

Medications

Medications that block serotonin reuptake are quite useful for the treatment of social phobia and recently have also been found to be helpful for selective mutism (these drugs are discussed in detail in chapter 12). Fluoxetine (Prozac) was shown to be of benefit to nearly three-quarters of adults with social phobia and appears to be similarly effective when used to treat children. When fluoxetine and fluvoxamine (Luvox) were tested as treatments for children with selective mutism, over 50 percent of the children improved, although it was rare to have the child regain full speaking capabilities. Sertraline (Zoloft) and paroxetine (Paxil) are two other serotonin-reuptake-blocking medications that may prove useful for the treatment of these disorders.

The traditional antianxiety drugs, such as diazepam (Valium), alprazolam (Xanax), and clonazepam (Klonopin), may play a role in the treatment of social phobia in adolescents, although one must be careful about rebound anxiety and physical dependence (see chapter 19). Phenelzine (Nardil), an MAO inhibitor, has been used effectively to treat social phobia in adults and has also been shown to be helpful in a few children with both social phobia and selective mutism, but its use with children is restricted by the necessity of following a special diet (see chapter 12). Beta-blockers, such as propranolol (Inderal) and atenolol (Tenormin), are used to block the physical symptoms of anxiety as part of treatment of social phobia in adults, but they are not used often with children because of the possibility that the child's blood pressure will fall below acceptable levels.

Helping Your Child Overcome Her Social Phobia and Selective Mutism

Recognize her "shyness" as social phobia and her "quietness" as selective mutism. Selective mutism and social phobia share characteristics with normal, expected behaviors (quietness and shyness, respectively) and may lie along a spectrum of behavioral responses. The difference between the disorders and the normal behaviors lies in the amount of distress associated with the symptoms and the degree of interference that results. If your child is exhibiting symptoms of anxiety related to her behavior, if she avoids situations in which she would experience anxiety, or if she is socially isolated or has problems at school as a result of her shyness/quietness, then it is outside the range of normal, expected behavior and is deserving of attention.

Encourage her to try new social situations and to speak in public. The effectiveness of behavior therapy suggests that when children with selective mutism are encouraged to speak in difficult situations, or those with social phobia are required to give a public performance, their anxiety disorder may actually improve. In contrast, children who are shy or quiet may develop social phobia or selective mutism if they are allowed to avoid all potentially stressful situations. Each time they "give in" to the fear, they reinforce it and it becomes more disabling. Rather than allowing your shy or quiet child to avoid situations that make her nervous, such as asking for directions or doing an oral report, encourage her to make the attempt. If she's giving a book report, provide her with plenty of opportunities to practice her speech, as well as suggestions for ways to stay calm during the exercise. However, if your child is truly frightened by an event, then she shouldn't be required to participate, because the risk of failure (and further negative reinforcement) is too great.

Prevent teasing and ridicule. For a child with fears about social interactions, there is nothing more devastating than to be teased about her symptoms. She is already afraid that people are laughing at her or finding fault with her behavior and the teasing just reinforces these fears. Stop teasing before it starts by establishing clear prohibitions against it and stiff consequences for infractions. Be careful that you don't inadvertently humiliate your child in your attempts to encourage her. Comments such as "Don't be such a wimp" or "You're such a baby" are not only hurtful, but they also reinforce the child's fears that she can't succeed.

Seek therapy early and complete any recommended treatment plans. As soon as you suspect that your child has selective mutism or social phobia, you should begin looking for a therapist to help her with her disorder. Both conditions respond well to treatment, particularly when it is begun early. Be prepared to take an active role in your child's therapy, particularly for selective mutism, because parents often provide much of the hands-on therapy required for complete recovery.

Further Reading

Berent, Jonathan, with Amy Lemley. *Beyond Shyness: How to Conquer Social Anxieties*. New York: Simon & Schuster, 1993.

Markway, Barbara, Ph.D., Cheryl Carmin, Ph.D., C. Alec Pollard, Ph.D., and Teresa Flynn, Ph.D. *Dying of Embarrassment: Help for Social Anxiety and Phobia*. Oakland, CA: New Harbinger Publications, 1992.

Marshall, John, M.D. *Social Phobia: From Shyness to Stage Fright*. New York: Basic Books, 1994.

Schneier, Franklin, M.D., and Lawrence Welkowitz, Ph.D. *The Hidden Face of Shyness: Understanding and Overcoming Social Anxiety*. New York: Avon Books, 1996.

Available through medical libraries:

Dow, Sara, Barbara Sonies, Donna Scheib, Sharon Moss, and Henrietta Leonard. "Practical Guidelines for the Assessment and Treatment of Selective Mutism." *Journal of the American Academy of Child and Adolescent Psychiatry* 34:7 (July 1995): 836–46.

Black, Bruce. "Social Anxiety and Selective Mutism." In *American Psychiatric Press Review of Psychiatry*, edited by L. J. Dickstein, J. M. Oldham, and M. B. Riba, vol. 15. Washington, D.C.: American Psychiatric Press, 1996.

Resources

Anxiety Disorders Association of America
11900 Parklawn Drive, Suite 100
Rockville, MD 20852
Phone: 301-231-9350
Fax: 301-231-7392
Internet: www.adaa.org
E-mail: AnxDis@AOL.COM

Developmental Speech and Language Disorders—Information Clearing House
National Institute on Deafness and Other Communicative Disorders
P.O. Box 37777
Washington, D.C. 20013
800-241-1044

Selective Mutism Foundation, Inc.
http://personal.mia.bellsouth.net/mia/g/a/garden/garden/index.htm
Write to:
Ms. Sue Newman
P.O. Box 450632
Sunrise, FL 33345-0632
        or
Ms. Carolyn Miller
P.O. Box 13133
Sissonville, WV 25360

Send self-addressed envelope with two stamps for information and
    quarterly newsletter.

"My Daughter Is So Sad and Blue— She Never Smiles or Laughs Anymore"

Depression and bipolar disorder

"Lisa, don't you have French club this afternoon?" Judy asked her sixteen-year-old daughter.

"I don't want to go," Lisa replied sullenly.

"Why not? You used to love it. Besides, you can use some more practice before your trip to Paris next month."

"I don't want to go to Paris, either. It's too far away and it's not going to be much fun."

Her mother replied, "Lisa, I'm so surprised to hear you say that! You've been saving up for this trip for three years—even before you started high school, you started talking about Paris."

"Yeah, well, people change," Lisa said as she walked out of the kitchen.

"Lisa, come back here! We haven't finished our conversation."

"I'm tired, Mom," Lisa replied without turning around. "I'm going to go take a nap."

"I wonder what's gotten into that girl?" Judy said to herself. "She doesn't want to go to Paris, she'd rather nap than be with her friends, and I haven't seen her smile in over a month. She seems so mopey, too. Well, maybe she'll feel better when she wakes up from her nap."

But Lisa didn't feel better. If anything, she felt worse as the afternoon went on. She had fallen asleep right away because she was totally exhausted from a recent bout of insomnia (Lisa was waking up every morning at 3:00 to 4:00 A.M. and then couldn't fall back asleep), but she woke up from her nap twenty minutes later feeling worse than when she had lain down. So, she stayed in bed for another forty minutes, trying to summon up the energy needed to tackle the mountain of homework she had to do, but it was just too overwhelming. "Besides," she thought, "I'm too stupid to figure out my algebra problems and it's going to be impossible for me to memorize the amendments to the Constitution, so why even try?" Instead, she picked up a well-worn copy of Glamour and flipped through the pages without really looking at them.

A few minutes later, her best friend, Meg, called to ask her to go to a party the next night. Lisa said, "I don't feel like it, Megs. I think I might be coming down with something."

"That's what you said last week, Lisa. Do you think you should go to a doctor or something?" Meg said.

"My mom's making me go tomorrow. I don't know why, though. I'm not sick. I just feel worn out and empty—like I'm a tube of toothpaste that somebody squeezed too hard."

"Maybe it's mono," Meg said. "My cousin had it and she felt awful for months."

"Great. Just what I need—several more months of feeling like this," Lisa said. "Well, I'll find out tomorrow. I'm going to go now, okay?"

"Okay, Lisa. Feel better!" Meg said and hung up.

The next afternoon, Lisa greeted her doctor by saying, "My best friend says I have mono and that's why I feel so worn out."

"Really?" Dr. Klein said. "Well, what else did your friend tell you?"

"That her cousin had it and was sick for months and months."

"That's true—mono can last a very long time," Dr. Klein said. "But let's make sure it's really mono before you decide that it'll be months before you feel better."

Dr. Klein asked Lisa a series of questions about her appetite, mood, and sleep habits.

"Hmm," Dr. Klein said. "Waking up early in the morning could explain your fatigue, but it isn't one of the signs of infectious mononucleosis. I suspect that you may be having a different problem, Lisa, but let's do an exam and find out."

When Dr. Klein felt Lisa's lymph glands and spleen, he found them to be completely free of any sign of mononucleosis. "Just as I thought," he said. "You don't have mono, Lisa. I think you're suffering from depression. That's actually good news, because it means that we can help you feel better by treating the depression. With mono, we'd just have to wait it out."

"How did she get depression?" Judy asked. "Things have been going well at home and at school—or at least they were until about a month ago."

"Nobody knows exactly why depression occurs," Dr. Klein said. "But it's clear that it doesn't take a specific stress for it to occur. It comes on suddenly and without good reason in some people. Even though we don't know the cause, we do know how to make the symptoms go away. Medications and psychological therapies are very effective. I'm going to refer you to a friend of mine—he's a psychiatrist who's had a lot of experience with adolescent depression. I'm sure that Lisa will like him and that he'll be helpful to her."

The psychiatrist was able to help Lisa a great deal. It took about three weeks for the combination of medication and cognitive-behavior therapy to start working and several more months for the depressive symptoms to disappear. But by early spring, Lisa was back to her previously happy and outgoing self— she even got a job doing telephone sales in order to make enough money to go to Paris!

Depression

For many years, people thought of depression as nothing more than a prolonged period of feeling sad or blue. Since the depression was "just" emotional, it wasn't taken seriously and people were told to "tough it out" or to "just get over it." We now know that depression isn't a voluntary condition, it's a brain disorder—an illness that affects both the mind and the body. Having a clinical depression is different from "being depressed," a term that we use to describe everything from a "bad hair day" to the grief we feel when losing a loved one. Depression is a psychiatric disorder that frequently occurs without explanation. Sometimes it follows a grief reaction, but it happens even more frequently without such a trigger.

Until the 1970s and 1980s, it was believed that depression didn't occur in childhood, perhaps because depressed children tend to be irritable, rather than appearing sad or "depressed." However, studies revealed that depression affects about one in one hundred children and about one in twenty-five teenagers. The rate in males is about one-half that of females (one in fifty adolescent boys has depression) and the number receiving treatment is even lower, suggesting that boys' depression is often missed, perhaps because they tend to have irritability, school failure, and behavior problems, rather than sadness or isolation.

Children with depression experience a variety of physical and psychological symptoms, varying from changes in appetite to impairments in concentration and memory. All children with depression feel sad or blue.

The feelings of sadness can be overwhelming and lead to hopelessness and helplessness, which puts the child at risk for suicide. In fact, depression accounts for over half of all suicides and may contribute to over 90 percent of attempts. Depression is also a risk factor for drug and alcohol use, as the teens search for something to "dull the pain."

Bipolar (Manic-Depressive) Disorder

Bipolar disorder, or manic-depressive disorder, is a form of depression. It is given special emphasis here because the diagnosis is being made with increasing frequency and it has several characteristics that distinguish it from typical depression. Until recently, physicians believed that manic-depressive disorder didn't occur in childhood and only rarely occurred during adolescence, but studies have shown that bipolar disorder affects about one out of one thousand children and increases in frequency during late adolescence and young adulthood to a rate of about one in one hundred adults. The disorder appears to be inherited in such a manner that it starts earlier in successive generations—if a child's mother or father has bipolar disorder, she is more likely to get bipolar disorder than other people, and to have it begin at a younger age than it did for her parent.

Bipolar disorder is distinguished from typical depressive disorders by the presence of mania. Mania is derived from the Greek word for madness, and the name refers to the psychotic symptoms, such as hallucinations and delusions, that are often seen in manic episodes. A child could have an abrupt onset of psychosis as the only symptom of mania, but, much more frequently, the manic episode is characterized by an exaggerated sense of well-being (euphoria) or excessive irritability—the children are either "higher than a kite" or they are short-tempered and fly into a rage with little provocation.

Mania causes disturbances of mood, perception, thoughts, and behavior, just as depression does. Some, but not all, of these symptoms are the opposite of those seen in depression. For example, in depression, the mood is too low for the circumstances, while in mania, the mood is artificially elevated, or "high." The child's thinking and her actions are speeded up, she needs little sleep, and she appears "hyper" or hyperactive (which is distinguishable from the hyperactivity of ADHD [chapter 13] by its onset at an older age). The child with mania speaks so rapidly that she can't be interrupted, but changes topics so abruptly that it's impossible to follow her train of thought. Her judgment is impaired and she might take unnecessary risks, such as driving fast or having unprotected sex.

She also might perceive herself as having special powers (like being able to fly or read minds) or special talents (such as having a great singing voice or being able to solve difficult mathematical formulas). Her inflated self-esteem and impaired judgment cause her to take on huge projects for which she has no talent, such as writing a novel or composing a symphony. She churns out volumes of gibberish, which even she can't interpret when she's no longer suffering from mania. In some cases, she completely loses touch with reality—having delusions that cause her to believe she's someone she's not, or that people are out to get her (paranoia), or hallucinations that cause her to see or hear things that aren't really there.

Does Your Child Have Depression?

1. Does she feel sad or "empty inside" much of the time?
2. Does she seem depressed or unusually irritable much of the time?
3. Has she lost interest in all, or almost all, activities?
4. Does she feel worthless, helpless, or excessively guilty over things outside her control?
5. Has she had a significant change in appetite (either increased or decreased) or weight (either weight gain or, more commonly, weight loss)?
6. Is she having trouble sleeping—either difficulty falling asleep or waking in the middle of the night and being unable to fall back asleep; or is she sleeping too much?
7. Do her actions and/or speech seem to be speeded up or slowed down?
8. Is she fatigued or lacking in energy?
9. Does she have trouble concentrating or making decisions?
10. Does she have recurrent thoughts of death or has she been thinking about hurting herself or killing herself?

Your child is likely to have depression if you answered yes to questions 1, 2, or 3 and at least four other questions *and* the symptoms have been present most of the time, every day or nearly every day, for over two weeks.

If the answer to question 10 is yes, your child is at risk for suicidal behavior and should receive professional help immediately.

Does Your Child Have Bipolar Disorder?

The diagnosis of bipolar disorder is based on the lifetime pattern of symptoms and can't be made from a checklist, but if your child has a history of depression, and she also has the following symptoms, the possibility of manic-depressive illness should be discussed with her physician.

Has your child had a distinct period of an abnormally and persistently elevated, expansive, or irritable mood that lasted at least one week?

During the period of mood disturbance have there been three or more of the following symptoms?

1. Inflated self-esteem or a sense that she is larger than herself?
2. Decreased need for sleep?
3. Much more talkative than usual or pressure to keep talking?
4. Feeling that her thoughts are racing or speech that is disconnected and jumps from one topic to another?
5. Marked increase in distractibility?
6. Markedly increased number of projects at home or at school, or a dramatic increase in social activities?
7. Increased involvement in pleasurable, but irresponsible, activities, such as shopping sprees, sexual indiscretions, or giving away her money or property?

How Do You Know If Your Child Has Depression?

Depression is a chronic disorder and symptoms must be present for at least two weeks before the diagnosis is considered. The time requirement separates a depressive episode from the normal mood changes of childhood and adolescence, as well as "adjustment reactions" to stressors at home, school, or in social relationships. As with other psychiatric disorders, distress and interference are also important components of the diagnosis. In depression, the child's persistent sadness and loss of interest in pleasurable activities are a source of distress, as are her feelings of guilt and worthlessness. When the depression is severe enough to cause physical symptoms, concentration difficulties, and school problems, it causes interference and the diagnosis is appropriately made.

Depression can cause disturbances in all aspects of a child's life—her thoughts, behavior, emotions, and physical health are all affected. The symptoms of depression vary greatly between children—one child might be restless, nervous, and "keyed up," while another is listless, sulking, and has decreased energy levels. This makes depression difficult to detect because young children typically have few symptoms and adolescents tend to "hide" their depression. The young child might appear emotionless or "flat" rather than sad, and complain only of not feeling good; when her pediatrician examines her, she might admit to feeling empty inside and not finding pleasure in her favorite TV show or video game (an inability to feel pleasure is one of the hallmark symptoms of depression).

The child with depression might seem to be "off in her own world" as she daydreams excessively. She can't concentrate well, so it's difficult for her to learn. She also may have memory problems, which make it difficult for her to remember physics equations, history facts, and, in some cases, people's names or faces—causing her social embarrassment or earning her a reputation of being "spacey" (if she covers by admitting she's forgotten) or rude (if she forgets that she's met someone before). It is also common for her to have trouble making decisions—the smallest decision, such as wearing the blue blouse or the red sweater, can require extraordinary weighing of the pros and cons. Large decisions can be impossible, so that a teen who is depressed may find she cannot fill out her college applications because she can't decide which schools she wants to attend.

The adolescent who is depressed is often more irritable, short-tempered, and aggressive than she is sad or withdrawn. For example, a teen with depression might be sent home from school for fighting or draw a technical foul in a wrestling match or basketball game for unnecessary roughness. The teenage boy might be able to tell you that he isn't happy anymore, but probably can't tell you that he's sad or apathetic—his behavior would tell you that.

The behavior problems most frequently seen in depression include "acting out" or disobedience, substance abuse (alcohol or drugs), and excessive risk-taking or self-destructive behavior, which leads to frequent accidents and possible suicide attempts. Social withdrawal is common and the child may isolate herself from her friends, her family, or both—spending more time alone in her room or sitting in front of the television or computer. School performance deteriorates when a child is depressed, not only because of the concentration difficulties, but also because of her lack of interest in the subjects. Declining school performance is one of the first signs of depression, and even before she feels sad or blue, the child with depression may begin getting poor grades, turning in messy, half-finished assignments, and com plaining of not being able to "keep up" with the lessons.

The physical symptoms of depression include decreased energy, fatigue, insomnia, appetite changes, and a variety of ailments, such as headaches, stomachaches, and chronic pain. Decreased energy and feeling "slowed down" are the most common complaints among depressed children, and may or may not be related to fatigue and sleep changes. Insomnia is also quite common—a child may have difficulty falling asleep, staying asleep, and/or waking too early. The most frequent pattern is for the child to have difficulty falling asleep and spend an hour or more worrying about various things before finally falling asleep. She may then wake between 2:00 and 4:00 A.M. and not be able to fall back asleep until it's time for her to get up in the morning. Depression can also cause the opposite problem—excessive sleepiness, in which the child goes to bed early, gets up late, and sleeps (naps) during the daytime. Appetite changes can also go in both directions—the child may have a sudden decrease in her appetite and lose weight without trying, or she may become ravenously hungry and gain three to five pounds in less than a month. These physical symptoms are fairly common and nonspecific, so they are not diagnostic of depression on their own, but should be considered in the overall picture, since they contribute to the child's impairment.

The child's age and developmental stage must be considered when determining whether or not she is depressed. A young child can't recognize her feelings as sadness and so won't be able to tell you that she feels sad, but she cries more easily than normal and has a sad expression on her face (unless she has a "flat" or expressionless facial appearance). By school age, the child with depression should be able to tell you that she feels unhappy, although she still might describe her mood as bored or angry rather than sad. She will be self-critical and might describe herself as ugly, unpopular, incompetent, or "a complete failure." In addition, she will be more sensitive to criticism or scrutiny from others and may withdraw from competitive sports or peer relationships rather than risk defeat or rejection. As her depression worsens, she may develop a sense of worthlessness, which is often accompanied by feelings of hopelessness and helplessness. Once the child feels that her situation is hopeless and that she is helpless to change it, she is at risk for suicidal behavior (which is defined as a preoccupation with death or harming oneself, or any action taken with the intent of hurting or killing oneself).

Suicide: "It Couldn't Happen to My Child"

There is no worse tragedy for a parent than to lose a son or daughter by suicide. None of us wants to believe that it could happen to our child, and yet there are over six thousand adolescent deaths by suicide each year in the United States. Suicide is currently the second leading cause of death for fifteen- to twenty-four-year-old adolescents (accidental deaths/ homicides are first). The number of suicide attempts is even higher: about ninety thousand teens attempt suicide each year; and approximately one out of every seventy-five teens will make an attempt sometime during their adolescence. Nearly all of these teens are suffering from depression, either as a primary problem, or in response to one of the triggers of depression: a loss (death, parents' divorce, or breakup of friendship or romantic relationship), physical or sexual abuse, pregnancy or abortion, school failure, embarrassment about appearance, financial problems, a humiliating experience, argument with a parent or peer, arrest or involvement in illegal activity, intoxication or chemical dependency (teens with alcohol or drug problems have a risk of suicide that is five to seven times greater than other teens), and concerns about sexuality (homosexual males are at the highest risk of any adolescent group for suicidal behavior).

Teens are particularly vulnerable to "accidental" suicides because they have an immature concept of death and view it as a temporary condition. They envision taking pills or slashing their wrists and then "waking up dead" so that they can take advantage of their parents' grief to get what they want. This sense of immortality is a particular problem for thirteen- to fifteen-year-old boys, who are more impulsive than girls and tend to use more lethal means for their attempt (such as a gunshot or hanging, rather than an overdose or slashing at their wrists).

Whenever a teenager talks about death or dying, it should be taken seriously. Healthy teenagers don't think about death or suicide, so if a teen threatens to kill herself, it is a cry for help, at the least. The adolescent should be encouraged to talk about her feelings of helplessness and hopelessness and also allowed to express her suicidal thoughts—neither of these will increase her chances of attempting suicide. The child shouldn't be left alone if she's contemplating suicide (particularly if she has a plan for how she would harm herself). She should be taken to a safe place where she can receive professional help, such as a mental health clinic or the emergency room of the closest hospital. If the teen is no longer suicidal when she gets there, that's wonderful news! Her cry for help has been heard without need for endangering her life.

If It's Not Depression, What Else Could It Be?

Normal Behavior or Adjustment Reactions

Depression can be distinguished from normal childhood behavior by the presence of distress and interference. Although adolescents may be excessively moody or irritable, become socially withdrawn, or feel sad more often than they did as children, they should not have prolonged periods of sadness or social isolation, nor should they have additional symptoms accompanying their blue moods (see chapter 11). Adjustment disorder with depressive symptoms is also common during adolescence. The depressive symptoms are identical to those in depression, but they do not last as long and are directly related to a stressful event, such as the child's parents divorcing.

Other Psychiatric Disorders

Many psychiatric disorders have depression as a secondary symptom. These include attention deficit disorder (chapters 13 and 14), obsessive-compulsive disorder (chapter 16), other anxiety disorders (chapters 18 through 20), and eating disorders, such as anorexia or bulimia (chapter 23). Substance abuse, including both excessive alcohol intake and drug use, can cause depression and can also be caused by depression. The relationship is often so entangled that it may be impossible to determine which came first (see chapter 24).

Medical Illnesses

There are dozens of physical causes of depressive symptoms, including medications, such as birth control pills or steroids; neurological disorders, such as seizures, migraine headaches, and tumors; endocrine conditions, including thyroid disease and diabetes; infectious diseases, like infectious mononucleosis and AIDS; or chronic diseases, such as lupus and chronic bowel disease. There are also several vitamin and mineral deficiencies that can cause depressive symptoms, such as fatigue, apathy, and concentration difficulties. Among adolescents, the most common of these would be iron-deficiency anemia, and deficiencies of zinc, copper, or the B vitamins.

Treatment of Depression

In general, medications are the preferred treatment for childhood depression because the disorder is usually at least moderately severe before it's recognized. Mild depression is the only form of depression that is amenable to treatment with psychological treatments, such as psychotherapy or cognitive-behavior therapy. However, for both mild and moderately severe depression, a treatment plan that incorporates a combination of medication and psychological techniques is even better than either alone because the two treatments work through different mechanisms and the combination offers the greatest potential for benefit. In the current health care payment environment, however, such combination therapy may not be offered. Further, parents should be aware that almost all treatment for depression is done on an outpatient basis. This is appropriate only if the child is not at risk for suicide; otherwise, she must be hospitalized in order to ensure her safety.

Psychological Therapies

Psychotherapy: Play therapy for young children or psychotherapy (talk therapy) for older children and teens can be helpful in resolving some of the issues that contribute to the depression. In psychotherapy, the focus is on understanding the thoughts and behaviors that contribute to the depressive feelings, and the therapist utilizes games, puzzles, and stories to facilitate the therapy, particularly in the younger child. In adolescents, group therapy can be very effective, as the teens are more likely to express their feelings to each other than they are to an adult. The therapist ensures that the group targets specific issues and keeps the discussion moving in a positive direction.

Family therapy and family education can be used to decrease stress related to family issues, as well as to provide family members with models for more effectively dealing with problem situations.

Cognitive therapy and cognitive-behavior therapy are described in detail in chapter 12. The goal of cognitive therapy is to help the adolescent become aware of her depressive thoughts and their destructive impact, and then to replace the negative thoughts with more accurate, positive, or constructive ways of thinking. Cognitive-behavior therapy works particularly well for the depression that occurs in children with ADHD and learning disabilities (see chapters 13 and 14). The child's behavior disorder makes her vulnerable to receiving more negative reinforcement than positive reinforcement and she doesn't learn to cope in a positive fashion. In cognitive-behavior therapy, a new pattern of thinking is taught as a new pattern of behaving is modeled through direct reinforcements for positive behaviors and ignoring or negative reinforcement for inappropriate, negative behaviors.

Medications

There are three general classes of medications that can be used as antidepressants: the selective serotonin reuptake inhibitors (SSRIs), the tricyclic antidepressants, and the monoamine oxidase inhibitors (MAOIs). Information about each of these groups of drugs is provided in chapter 12. The SSRIs have become the drug treatment of choice for depression in children and adolescents, as the medications are both safe and effective. The tricyclic antidepressants are also used frequently, although they have a higher rate of side effects. There are three monoamine oxidase inhibitors (MAOIs): phenelzine (Nardil), tranylcypromine (Parnate), and isocarboxazid (Marplan). The MAOIs are reserved for use in severely ill patients who have not responded to other medications. They should not be used as routine treatments because of the potential for serious side effects if the MAOIs are taken in conjunction with certain foods or medications. If MAOI therapy is required, the psychiatrist should ensure that the patient and her parents know precisely what is involved with the treatment and particularly which foods and medications must be avoided. With proper precautions, the MAOIs can be a lifesaving treatment, as they frequently work when other medications have failed.

Other antidepressants are used infrequently in children because of limited experience in adults. These antidepressants include trazodone (Desyrel), buproprion (Wellbutrin), nefazodone (Serzone), and venlafaxine (Effexor). Each of these medications has a unique formulation and a particular effect on the balance of brain messenger chemicals, which may prove to be beneficial. However, at this time, there is almost no information about their safety or effectiveness in children. Until there is greater experience with their use, these antidepressants should not be used to treat children or adolescents unless they have failed other medications, or the child seems to need a particular effect.

Medications for Bipolar Disorder

Medications are lifesaving in bipolar disorder and are used both to stop the manic or depressive episodes, and to stabilize the excessive mood swings. Mania should be considered as a medical emergency, since the teen is at risk for reckless behaviors and psychosis while she is in the manic phase, and suicide or self-injurious behavior when the mania turns into depression, as inevitably occurs. Acute episodes of mania usually are treated in the hospital and the staff must take special precautions to protect the child during the period of mood stabilization.

Depression in bipolar disorder is treated with an antidepressant (as described above), while mania can be treated with lithium (Eskalith or Lithobid) or another of the mood stabilizers. If a child is having delusions, hallucinations, or serious perceptual difficulties, she should also be treated with antipsychotic drugs, such as the neuroleptics (haloperidol [Haldol], chlorpromazine [Thorazine], trifluoperazine [Stelazine], or thioridazine [Mellaril]) or atypical antipsychotics (clozapine [Clozaril], risperidone [Risperdal], or olanzapine [Zyprexa]).

Lithium (Eskalith or Lithobid) has been used for over forty years to decrease the "highs" of mania, to help decrease irritability and rage attacks, and to prevent excessive mood swings. It is helpful to nearly three-fourths of the adults who receive it, but less is known about how many children will respond. Two other medications, valproic acid (Depakote or Depakene) and carbamazepine (Tegretol), are also being used as mood stabilizers in bipolar disorder. These medications are anticonvulsants (or antiseizure drugs) that were found to help stabilize moods in adults with bipolar disorder. Carbamazepine and valproic acid work well in adults, but have their own risk of side effects, so lithium is still the first choice for mood stabilization in children.

Lithium has several side effects, including nausea (worse if given on an empty stomach), weight gain, hand tremors, increased thirst and urination, drowsiness or fatigue, and acne. Bed-wetting can also occur, particularly in children who were older when they stopped wetting the bed. The enuresis is thought to be due to the changes in fluid balance caused by the lithium salt. Laboratory studies and an ECG are needed before starting lithium therapy because it is a salt that can displace other salts in the body (like sodium and potassium). This also means that lithium toxicity (poisoning) can occur if the child becomes dehydrated, such as might occur when she has been running around outside on a hot day. Adequate fluid intake is essential whenever a child is taking lithium.

Helping Your Child Overcome Her Depression

Recognize the signs of depression. Depression can begin slowly and insidiously, so you and your child may have become accustomed to her isolation, tearfulness, or extreme irritability. Use the checklist to determine whether or not your child might be suffering from depression. In addition, you can ask her how she's feeling—she will probably be able to tell you that she doesn't feel happy anymore or that she's feeling empty inside. If so, she should see a doctor to determine whether she has depression.

Take action when you notice that your child is depressed. If your child is depressed, she needs professional treatment. Get it by contacting her physician, a school counselor, or the mental health center for referral to a therapist.

Prevent excessive stress and other risk factors for depression. Stress doesn't cause depression, but it can worsen the condition, so it should be avoided. If there are stressors that are under your control (such as unnecessary bickering over grades or her choice of clothes), then eliminate them. It will improve your mental health, as well as hers.

Recognize the signs of suicidal behavior and intervene immediately. If your child says, "I wish I were dead," "I can't take it anymore, I want out," or "You'd be better off without me," or she shows signs of suicidal behavior, you need to react. Don't ignore it and hope that it will go away by itself—it won't! Talking about suicide doesn't "put ideas into her head" or push her into hurting herself; quite the opposite, it can sometimes prevent a suicidal act. Talk to your child, find out what's troubling her, let her know that you're willing to listen, and that you're going to keep her safe. Her greatest fear is that no one will help her and she really will have no choice but to harm herself.

Don't leave your child alone if she's suicidal. Take her to her doctor's office or to the emergency room at the hospital. If your child has a suicide plan and doesn't feel as if she can depend on herself not to act on it, call an ambulance to take both of you to the emergency room. This situation is a medical emergency and your child needs help immediately!

In order to determine that your child is no longer suicidal, she must have a comprehensive assessment by a psychiatrist, in addition to the emergency room physician. If it's determined that your child poses no immediate risk to herself, she may be released to your care. When you take her home, you should still provide her with close supervision—letting her know that you're there for her safety and security. You should also suicide-proof your home. Dispose of *all* extra pills (including aspirin and Tylenol—both can cause a lethal overdose). Keep any remaining medications in a locked cabinet to which your child doesn't have access. Get guns and other weapons out of the house and off your property, as the risk of suicide increases tenfold if there is a gun in the house. And, finally, follow through on the doctor's recommendations for therapy. Often, there is a "honeymoon" period after the initial crisis passes in which the child feels better and insists that she "was so stupid to even think about it. I'll never do it again." Unfortunately, the honeymoon always passes and then she is at even greater risk for suicidal behavior, so make sure that she's hooked up with a therapist before the depression returns.

Further Reading

Cytryn, Leon, M.D., and Donald McKnew, M.D. *Growing Up Sad: Childhood Depression and Its Treatment*. New York: W. W. Norton, 1996.

Greist, John H., M.D., and James W. Jefferson, M.D. *Depression and Its Treatment*. New York: Warner Books, 1992.

Herskowitz, Joel, M.D. *Is Your Child Depressed?* New York: Pharos Books, 1988.

Kerns, Lawrence L., M.D., with Adrienne Lieberman. *Helping Your Depressed Child: A Reassuring Guide to the Causes and Treatments of Childhood and Adolescent Depression*. Rocklin, CA: Prima Publishing, 1993.

Lee, Essie E., and Richard Wortman, M.D. *Down Is Not Out: Teenagers and Depression*. New York: Julian Messner, 1986.

McCoy, Kathleen, Ph.D. *Understanding Your Teenager's Depression: Issues, Insights and Practical Guidelines for Parents*. New York: Berkley, 1994.

Nelson, Richard E., Ph.D., and Judith C. Galas. *The Power to Prevent Suicide: A Guide for Teens Helping Teens*. Minneapolis, MN: Free Spirit Publications, 1994.

Oster, Gerald D., Ph.D., and Sarah S. Montgomery, M.S.W. *Helping Your Depressed Teenager: A Guide for Parents and Caregivers*. New York: John Wiley & Sons, 1995.

Seligman, Martin E., Ph.D., with Karen Reivich, Lisa Jaycox, Ph.D., and Jane Gillham, Ph.D. *The Optimistic Child: A Revolutionary Program That Safeguards Children Against Depression and Builds Lifelong Resistance*. Boston, MA: Houghton Mifflin, 1995.

Shamoo, Tonia K., and Philip G. Patros. *"I Want to Kill Myself": Helping Your Child Cope with Depression and Suicidal Thoughts*. San Francisco: Jossey-Bass, 1990.

Shapiro, Patricia Gottlieb. *A Parent's Guide to Childhood and Adolescent Depression*. New York: Dell Publishing, 1994.

Resources

American Association of Suicidology
2459 South Ash
Denver, CO 80222

American Foundation for Suicide Prevention
120 Wall Street, 22nd Floor
New York, NY 10005
Phone: 212-363-3500
Fax: 212-363-6237
Internet: http://www.afsp.org

Depression Awareness, Recognition and Treatment Campaign
Office of Scientific Information
National Institute of Mental Health
5600 Fishers Lane, Room 7C-02
Rockville, MD 20857
301-443-4513

National Alliance for the Mentally Ill
200 North Glebe Road, Suite 1015
Arlington, VA 22203
800-950-6264

National Depressive and Manic-Depressive Association
730 North Franklin, #501
Chicago, IL 60610
800-82N-DMDA

National Foundation for Depressive Illness
P.O. Box 2257
New York, NY 10116
800-248-4344

"My Son Sleeps All Weekend and Still Can't Wake Up on Time on Monday Morning"

Sleep disorders and seasonal affective disorder

"Rick, you're going to be late!" Margaret called up the steps for the third time that morning.

"Rick? Do you hear me?" she called again. Not hearing an answer, she ran up to his bedroom and knocked on the closed door. "Rick? Can I come in?" Again, no answer, so Margaret pushed the door open and found her son still in bed, snoring loudly.

"Richard!" she shouted loudly enough to wake the dead—and her twelve-year-old son. She continued in a slightly softer but clearly irritated voice. "Richard! I can't believe you're not up yet. Your ride comes in exactly seven minutes and if you miss it, I'm not taking you to school. You're going to have to walk and you'll be tardy. Considering that you've been tardy so many times already that the next time you're late you've got a two-week detention coming, I'd think you'd be working a little harder to prevent it."

"I know, but I don't feel good, Mom," Rick whined, with his eyes still half closed. "My head hurts and I'm so tired I can't move. Can't I just stay home and sleep until I feel better?"

Margaret reached over to touch his forehead. "Hmm, you don't have a fever, but you certainly look terrible. I guess you can stay in bed this morning. In fact, you can stay in bed until I can get you an appointment with Dr. Scott—this morning sickness of yours has been going on for too long now."

Dr. Scott's receptionist gave Rick an appointment for early in the afternoon. Even though Rick slept for another three hours, he was still tired when he had to get up.

"Hi, Rick," Dr. Scott said when he entered the room. "What brings you in today?"

"My mother made me come," Rick said irritably. "She thinks I sleep too much."

"Do you?" Dr. Scott asked.

"No. I don't think I get enough sleep. I'm always tired."

"I'll say," his mother said. "Rick is so irritable these days, it's really hard to live with him. He and his older sister fight constantly."

"Anything else?" Dr. Scott asked Rick and his mother.

"Yes," Rick said. "I'm hungry all the time! Even though I've been trying to cut back, I've gained at least ten pounds this past month. Another good reason to quit the wrestling team—I'd never make weight."

"What was the other good reason that you quit?" Dr. Scott asked.

"I didn't like it anymore. The coach was always yelling at me to try harder and I just didn't want to."

"He's not trying in school either, Doctor," Margaret added. "His grades for the past quarter were down in every subject from what they were during fall quarter. He sleeps instead of studying at night—he even naps on weekends for several hours. It's like he's gone into hibernation mode or something."

"Is there anyone else in the family who has a pattern of winter weight gain, excessive sleeping, and irritability?" Dr. Scott asked.

"Yes," Margaret said. "My husband and I are both irritable and grouchy all winter. We both get the blues, too. I don't think my husband's ever gone into a full-blown depression, but I have—several times. It's better now that we plan for a winter vacation in the Caribbean."

"I think Rick may need to go with you this winter," Dr. Scott said. "He seems to be suffering from winter blues, or seasonal affective disorder. I suspect that he, too, would benefit from a week in the Caribbean, but in the meantime, let's get him started on some light therapy. A light box is the most reliable means of giving light treatments, although he could get much the same benefit by sitting outdoors on a sunny day for at least an hour."

"We'll try the light box, Doctor," Margaret said. "I'd like Rick to get back to his normal self as quickly as possible."

Rick used the light box every day for an hour in the morning, and at the end of the first week, he was feeling much better. He was sleeping and eating normally and he had returned to his usual good humor—even his schoolwork had improved enough for him to be able to miss a week to travel to the Caribbean with his family.

Seasonal Affective Disorder or Winter Blues

Seasonal affective disorder (or SAD) is a form of depression that recurs regularly during the winter months. Unlike the other forms of depression described in chapter 21, SAD is identified more by its physical symptoms, such as excessive sleepiness, increased appetite, and weight gain, than by any particular psychological symptoms, such as a sad mood or apathy. In fact, the children are frequently unaware of their irritability and are surprised when their parents complain about their snappishness and short temper.

A study done by researchers at the National Institute of Mental Health revealed that about one in one hundred grade school children suffer from SAD each winter, with increasing rates throughout middle school and high school years. High school seniors appear to have SAD at a rate comparable to adults—about one in twenty girls and one in forty boys. The disorder is easily treated, once recognized, but unfortunately many people don't yet know that it can occur during childhood and adolescence, and therefore children aren't yet receiving the appropriate diagnosis and treatment.

——— **Does Your Child Have Winter Blues?** ———

Does your child have:

1. Extended periods of irritability or depression (see chapter 21) during the winter of several different years *and* no similar symptoms during the summer?
2. Physical symptoms in association with irritability or depression?
   a. Increased sleep requirements—difficulty getting out of bed in the morning
   b. Lack of energy and fatigue
   c. Increased appetite, particularly for carbohydrates and sweets ("cravings"), often leading to weight gain
   d. Difficulty thinking clearly—memory lapses, poor concentration, and increased distractibility

3. Evidence of impairment in functioning—e.g., deterioration in grades or school performance, social isolation, or failure to complete tasks at home or at school

If you answered yes to questions 1, 2, and 3, your child may have seasonal affective disorder. His physician will be able to determine if his symptoms are consistent with winter blues or another seasonal disorder.

How Do You Know If Your Child Has Winter Blues?

Children with SAD can have such dramatic changes in mood and energy that they appear to be two different people in the winter and the summer. In the summer, they are happy, energetic, and view life as filled with many exciting possibilities. In the winter, they are grouchy, tired, and pessimistic. When the winter days are short, the child can't see any opportunities for fun or enjoyment, and if he did, he wouldn't have the energy to try them. He's miserable and makes those around him miserable as well.

Irritability and poor school performance are the most frequently reported symptoms of SAD in children and adolescents. The overlap between SAD and the school calendar can make it difficult to diagnose the disorder in school-age children and adolescents because the winter blues usually begin just as the child's academic requirements are increasing. Thus, his deteriorating school performance is blamed on "the material being a little harder this year than he's been used to" or the child "just is not applying himself well," rather than on the cognitive changes that accompany SAD. However, the child is trying his best—often putting in longer hours than he did in the early fall or previous spring—but he can't comprehend the materials because of the memory lapses and concentration difficulties that are associated with SAD. In actuality, the association between SAD and the school calendar is not that close. The child's SAD will begin in mid-November or early December and peak in January and February, before disappearing some time in March or early April. This corresponds with the second and third quarters of the academic year, but the child's school performance should be unblemished for the first reporting period. If SAD is to blame for a child's school failures, his report cards should show a consistent pattern of good first quarter marks and then deteriorations in the second and third marking periods. His fourth quarter marks may also be poor because he has been struggling with cognitive deficits throughout the winter and can't bring his grades back up in the last part of the school year. However, he might recall that "it's easier to pay attention and to remember things in the spring," or he may actually have a rebound in his grades.

In addition to the changes in mood and energy level, a child with SAD may experience a variety of physical symptoms, including increased appetite, carbohydrate cravings, and increased sleep requirements. The child feels ravenously hungry, particularly during the early winter months, and often satisfies his appetite and carbohydrate cravings by bingeing on sweets and breads. The presence of holiday treats contributes to the problem and it's not unusual for a child with SAD to gain five to ten pounds in a month's time. He also sleeps excessively, up to ten or twelve hours each night, and yet will still complain of constant fatigue.

Sleep Disorders

Childhood sleep disorders are the other cause of constant fatigue. Sleep disorders affect an unknown number of American children. Although physicians agree that the problem is a common one, it is difficult to ascertain the exact number of children affected because sleep disorders span such a wide spectrum and have such a wide variety of symptoms, from excessive sleepiness and fatigue to difficulties with falling asleep or staying asleep. The child's age and developmental stage also influence the types of sleep problems that he may experience—nightmares and night terrors are common in young children, but insomnia is rare, while in older adolescents, insomnia is increasingly common and night terrors affect less than one in five hundred teens.

——— Does Your Child Have a Sleep Disorder? ———

Does your child frequently experience difficulties with:

1. Falling asleep (more than twenty minutes) or staying asleep?
2. Waking up in the morning?
3. Being too sleepy during the daytime?
4. Feeling fatigued—yawning, lack of energy, or complaints of feeling tired?
5. Nightmares (more than one per week) or night terrors?

6. Sleep-walking, sleep-talking, or other sleep-related behavior?
7. Restless sleep?

If you answered yes to questions 1, and 3 or 4, then your child may have insomnia. If you answered yes to questions 1 and 2, and also 3 or 4, your child may have a circadian rhythm disturbance (such as the "night owl" syndrome of adolescence).

If you answered yes to questions 5, 6, or 7, then your child may have a sleep disruption (parasomnia). Parasomnias are not always a problem—your child's doctor can decide whether or not they are disturbing your child's sleep.

How Do You Know If Your Child Has a Sleep Disorder?

Sleep disorders are divided between those that disrupt the sleep process and lead to insufficient, excessive, or inefficient sleep (dyssomnias—pronounced *dis-some-knee-yas*) and those in which behaviors intrude upon ongoing sleep (parasomnias). There are several common childhood disorders in each category. Each of the dyssomnias and parasomnias has its own unique set of symptoms and each is managed slightly differently, so they will be described individually, rather than trying to generalize the description to include all the disorders.

Dyssomnias

Circadian rhythm disturbances are nearly universal during adolescence, as the teen's body clock is disturbed by changing hormone levels (see also chapter 11). It is common during adolescence for a child to develop a delayed sleep phase or to become "a night owl" who is unable to fall asleep before midnight, and is not ready to awaken before 9:00 to 10:00 A.M. Unfortunately, the requirements of school and work prohibit him from following his natural sleep patterns, and so he builds up a sleep debt. His attempts at "catching up" on his sleep over the weekend cause additional disruptions in his biological clock and further antagonize the situation. The teen ends up chronically sleep-deprived and totally out-of-sync with his daily schedule.

The only natural "cure" for delayed sleep phase is to allow the teen to follow his body's clock. This can be accomplished during summer vacations if he can work the evening shift, go to bed around 2:00 A.M., and then sleep until midday or later. However, during the school year, his body's clock must be reset through either phase delay or phase advance treatment. In phase delay treatment, the child goes to bed one to two hours later each night and gets up one to two hours later during the day —for example, he might go to bed at 2:00 A.M. tonight and get up at noon tomorrow; then, tomorrow night, he goes to bed at 3:30 A.M. and gets up at 1:30 P.M. This continues until he's moved completely around the clock to an acceptable bedtime—at that point, his internal clock is reset and he can resume a normal sleep schedule. This is obviously impossible to accomplish if the child has to attend school, but might be possible during school vacations. Phase advance therapy is usually preferable because it's done in much smaller increments and can be accomplished during the school year. The teen's wake-up time is advanced by ten to fifteen minutes a day and he goes to bed ten to fifteen minutes earlier each night until he reaches an acceptable bedtime. Phase advance therapy only works if the early morning awakening is applied consistently—the child cannot "sleep in" on weekends, because that disrupts his body's clock again. Phase advance therapy is more effective when it is combined with morning light therapy. This shuts off secretion of melatonin, the hormone responsible for sleep, and helps the child to wake up fully.

Insomnia is another common sleep disorder during childhood. Insomnia is defined as difficulties falling asleep or staying asleep and it is actually not a disorder, but a symptom of several different disorders, such as sleep pattern disruptions, asthma and other medical conditions, and chronic hyperarousal (the child's nervous system is overly sensitive to external stimuli and so he awakens too easily). Psychiatric disorders, such as depression or anxiety disorders, can also cause insomnia, as can a poorly established bedtime ritual. For example, the colicky infant who always falls asleep while being held may not learn to fall asleep in his bed; when he is older and spontaneously awakens in the night (which is common when a disturbance occurs during a transition from one sleep state to another), he lies awake for prolonged periods because he doesn't know how to fall back to sleep on his own.

Insomnia is usually diagnosed through a sleep log, in which the parent and/or child records the time that the child went to bed, fell asleep, and any periods in which he was awake during the night. The child is asked to record any difficulties he had falling asleep, and his parent notes any circumstances that could contribute to the insomnia (such as his watching a scary movie before bedtime). As you might imagine, keeping an accurate sleep log for a young child can be difficult because he can't help record his middle-of-the-night awakenings. In those instances, an overnight sleep study may be required to clarify the sleep pattern and help determine the appropriate treatment. The treatment of insomnia is directed at the cause of the sleep difficulties, rather than the insomnia itself. It should be noted that medications aren't very effective in treating children's insomnia and also carry a risk of side effects, so they should be avoided.

Obstructive sleep apnea syndrome (OSAS) occurs when the child's airway is blocked during sleep. In addition to obstruction from enlarging tonsils, children can develop OSAS from inborn defects of the palate, nose, or throat. For example, children with Down's syndrome are at risk for OSAS because their tongues are too large for their mouth and throat, and obstruct the upper airway.

Narcolepsy is rare in childhood, but can happen during adolescence. Narcolepsy is a chronic disorder that is characterized by four distinctive symptoms: (1) excessive daytime sleepiness with irresistible sleep attacks; (2) "drop attacks," or sudden loss of muscle tone in the arms and legs; (3) hallucinations associated with onset of sleep; and (4) sleep paralysis—an inability to move for a few minutes after the child awakens or as he falls asleep. The child is particularly disturbed by the hallucinations and sleep paralysis because he is conscious when they occur.

Narcolepsy is treated by a combination of medications and increased amounts of sleep (sufficient sleep at night, plus twenty- to thirty-minute naps two or three times daily). Stimulant medications (such as methylphenidate, pemoline, or dextroamphetamine) are used to counteract the excessive daytime sleepiness, while antidepressant medications can help treat the muscle weakness and drop attacks.

Parasomnias

Night terrors (also known as sleep terror disorder): Night terrors are a problem of the young child aged eighteen months to five years. They usually occur about one to three hours after the child falls asleep, at the point that he's moving from deep non-REM sleep to REM sleep. When a child has a night terror, he will sit bolt upright in bed, scream as if he's being murdered, and stare out with glassy, unseeing eyes. He appears terrified—his heart is beating quickly, his breathing is shallow and irregular, and he's sweating profusely. He is inconsolable and difficult to awaken. The night terror lasts for thirty seconds to five minutes and then the child calms down and continues sleeping. He doesn't remember the event at all the next day (although his parents are often quite traumatized by the experience).

Night terrors are not harmful and don't require treatment. However, they may be less frequent if the child takes a brief thirty- to sixty-minute nap in the afternoon (in order to smooth the transition from non-REM to REM sleep). If the night terrors begin later in childhood or during adolescence, an electroencephalogram (EEG) should be obtained to rule out a sleep-related seizure disorder.

Sleepwalking and other sleep-related behaviors: The school-age child may develop sleepwalking or other behaviors associated with partial arousal from sleep. Sleepwalking is uncoordinated and purposeless, so the child can injure himself by crashing into objects or falling down the stairs during a sleepwalking episode. It is therefore important to make the child's environment "sleepwalking-proof." Gates can be installed at the top of the stairs to prevent him from falling down a flight of stairs, his window can be sealed, or the doors locked at night to prevent him from roaming into dangerous areas, and an alarm system could be utilized to notify his parents when he's up and out of bed. If the sleepwalker can be kept safe, there is no need for specific treatment. He will probably outgrow it during adolescence.

Nightmares are frightening dreams that occur at the end of REM sleep and are recalled if the child is abruptly awakened—either by an external disruption or by the fear he feels in response to the dream. No one knows why nightmares occur, but they usually start between the ages of three to six years and affect nearly one-half of all children. Nightmares are easily distinguished from night terrors because they occur later in the night, they are remembered, and the child will awaken if the nightmare is severe enough to make him cry out in fear. Treatment of nightmares is directed at reducing any stress that may be contributing to the child's anxiety and providing him with comfort and reassurance after the frightening dream.

Bed-wetting and other sleep-related conditions: Bed-wetting (or enuresis) is discussed in detail in chapter 6. A variety of other medical and neurological illnesses can also cause sleep problems, which might include sleep-related asthma, gastroesophageal reflux, and sleep-related headaches. These all cause middle-of-the-night awakening, in addition to symptoms of shortness of breath, heartburn, or headache, respectively. Sleep-related epilepsy can also occur, although it is rare. Psychiatric disorders that disrupt sleep include depression, schizophrenia, manic-depressive illness, anxiety disorders, panic disorder, and substance abuse.

These conditions should be considered any time a grade school child begins to develop sleep difficulties.

Helping Your Child Overcome His Excessive Sleepiness

Maintain a consistent sleep-wake schedule. If your child has SAD or a sleep disorder, his biological clock can be disrupted by fluctuations in bedtime and wake-up time. It is important to establish an appropriate bedtime and to put your child to bed at the same time each evening—even on weekends. Setting the bedtime appropriately depends both on your child's sleep requirements and on his natural rhythms. For example, if he consistently falls asleep after 9:30 P.M. even when put to bed at 8:30 P.M. and he awakens spontaneously in the morning, then he's getting enough sleep with a 9:30 P.M. bedtime. On weekends, he must also go to bed at 9:30 P.M. and arise at about the same time as on school days to ensure that his clock remains "in sync," otherwise he won't be able to get up on time on Monday morning.

The child with SAD needs to maintain a regular schedule year-round. He will sleep less in the summer, but should still go to bed at about the same time as he does in the fall and spring, while in winter, he will want to sleep more, but must get up at the appointed hour, as "sleeping in" will worsen his depression.

Use light as an aid to keeping your child's clock "in sync." Sunlight is the timekeeper for your child's internal clock. In the winter, keep your child's drapes open and allow the sun to pour in as soon as it rises; in summer, his drapes should be drawn to prevent early-morning awakening. If your child's bedroom is on the west side of the house, or he doesn't have windows that permit sunlight to enter, he may need supplemental light in the morning to shut off melatonin secretion and help him wake up. A bedside lamp on a timer set to turn on about thirty to sixty minutes before his alarm goes off will help him awaken more easily.

Use light as a natural antidepressant. Light can also be used as an antidepressant, particularly during the wintertime. Our research team demonstrated that light is a very effective treatment for children's winter blues when it is administered according to a carefully regimented treatment schedule. If light is being used to treat a full-blown winter depression, it should be done by a trained mental health professional. However, if your child is suffering only from the "winter blahs" or the doldrums which overwhelm most of us in January and February, you can initiate therapy on your own. Once again, it merely requires a bedside lamp set to go off thirty to sixty minutes before the child's alarm clock does. In addition, your child should be exposed to unfiltered (outdoor) sunshine for at least twenty to thirty minutes in the morning. If that isn't possible, it's important for him to get outside for recess at noon daily. Don't forget to continue the "light therapy" on weekends and during dark, cloudy days (the amount of light present on the grayest day is still enough to have some antidepressant effects).

Recognize that your child is suffering from a sleep disorder and get help for him. Most sleep disorders aren't treated because they're never recognized as a problem. If your child is groggy and difficult to arouse in the morning, tired and irritable throughout the day, or he has difficulty falling asleep in a timely fashion at night, he may have a sleep disorder. If you're concerned about the possibility, arrange for him to have a full diagnostic evaluation by his physician.

Further Reading

Rosenthal, Norman, M.D. *Winter Blues: Seasonal Affective Disorder—What It Is and How to Overcome It.* New York: Guilford Press, 1993. For mail orders, call 800-FIX-BLUES.

Schaefer, Charles E., ed. *Clinical Handbook of Sleep Disorders in Children.* Northvale, NJ: Jason Aronson, 1995.

Smyth, Angela. *SAD: Who Gets It? What Causes It? How to Cure It.* London: Thorsons, 1990.

Resources

National Organization for Seasonal Affective Disorder (NOSAD)
P.O. Box 451
Vienna, VA 22180

Society for Light Treatment and Biological Rhythms (SLTBR)
P.O. Box 478
Wilsonville, OR 97070

Also, see the resources section of chapter 21 for further information on depression.

"My Daughter Is Obsessed with Her Weight"

Eating disorders: obesity, anorexia, and bulimia

"Have you noticed how skinny Kristen has gotten?" Richard asked his wife, Peggy, as they ate breakfast together late one Sunday morning.

Peggy replied, "Yes, I know, she's been dieting for the past few months. She's done really well, too. I can't believe how fast she lost all that baby fat. She looks great, doesn't she?"

"Well, not really," Richard said. "Actually, she looks sick. I think this diet of hers has gone too far—she's too pale, and all that's left of her is skin and bones. At least, I think that's all there is. It's hard to tell what she looks like under all those layers of clothes. I don't think that I've seen her wear anything except baggy sweatshirts and oversized sweatpants in weeks."

"Well, now that you mention it, she does seem a little too thin. But at least she's doing something about her weight. You know how concerned I've been that Kristen would end up as fat as your sister Sharon or the other heifers in your family."

Richard replied, "Peg, I don't like to hear you putting Sharon down. She's not fat. She's just a little overweight."

"A little overweight?! She must weigh at least two hundred fifty pounds. If Kristen's diet can keep that from happening, I'm all for it!" Peg said emphatically.

"Still," Richard said, "Kristen is only fourteen and she's taken this diet and exercise thing much too seriously. I'm really worried about her. Why don't you schedule an appointment for her with the pediatrician?"

Peggy replied angrily, "If you want Kristen to be seen by the pediatrician, then you take her in. It would be a nice father-daughter outing—probably the first one in over six months."

"I'm not the one who chooses not to spend time together," Richard replied. "Kristen won't have anything to do with me."

"She's not too fond of me either," Peggy said less angrily. "She barely speaks to me anymore. She doesn't talk to her sister or her friends either. She just exercises—doing calisthenics in her room or running in the park. The only way I could get her to the doctor would be to jog there with her and I won't do that."

"I guess neither of us can do it alone, so we should both go," Richard decided. "Please call and make an appointment for next week sometime and I'll rearrange my schedule to be there."

Kristen's appointment was the following Tuesday. While the nurse weighed her and took her vital signs, Richard and Peggy spoke privately with Dr. Adams. "I'm not sure what's wrong, Doctor," Richard said. "All I know is that Kristen is far too thin. She exercises constantly and I bet she hasn't eaten more than fifteen lettuce leaves and a couple of bites of vegetables at any one meal for the past three months."

"That's not true," Peggy interrupted. "Remember when we had that big dinner last weekend? You told her she had to eat everything that we put on her plate and she did. It took her a long time, but she ate every bite."

"Yes, but you only gave her a small potato, three bites of meat, and a few green beans. And even at that, she went into the bathroom afterward and threw it all up," Richard said.

"You can't prove that," Peggy countered. She was about to continue, when Dr. Adams interrupted the argument by asking, "Would you both agree that her weight is a concern to you?"

"Yes," Richard replied immediately.

"Yes," Peggy agreed. "I wasn't worried about her weight until Rick and I talked about it last week, but since then I've been watching her—she really doesn't eat very much and she's lost a lot of weight. I bet she's down to about a hundred pounds."

"It's a good thing you brought her in to see me, then," Dr. Adams said. "I'll go see Kristen now. After I've examined her, we'll all meet together and discuss this further. If you're right, and she's dieting when she's already too thin, then she may not listen to much of what gets said, but it's still important for her to hear it."

Dr. Adams walked to the exam room and took Kristen's chart from the door. She was shocked to discover that her patient's weight was recorded as only 78 pounds—the nurse must have made a mistake. Kristen had weighed 130 pounds at her last checkup and couldn't have lost 52 pounds, or 40 percent of her body weight, in a year. She hadn't grown either. She should have been at least five feet five inches and her height was recorded again as five feet three inches. Dr. Adams decided to say hello to Kristen before having the nurse reweigh her. As soon as she entered the exam room, she knew there wasn't any need to recheck the measurements—Kristen wasn't just thin, she was emaciated.

Kristen mumbled hello to her doctor and then complained about being cold, so Dr. Adams got her a blanket and helped her wrap it around her shoulders. She then asked, "Kristen, do you know why your parents brought you here today?"

"Yeah, they think I'm too thin."

"Do you think you're too thin?" Dr. Adams asked.

"No, I don't, and I don't know why they're always nagging me to eat. I still have thunder thighs and my hips are huge. See?" she said, and pointed to her emaciated thighs and pelvis.

Dr. Adams asked Kristen a few more questions and performed a complete examination, but Kristen's initial answer had confirmed the diagnosis of anorexia nervosa. Despite the fact that Kristen weighed only seventy-eight pounds, she considered herself "fat" and was dieting to lose more weight. Etch marks on the back of her teeth showed that she had been vomiting frequently—a sign that she also had bulimia. Dr. Adams knew that the combination of severe anorexia and bulimia was very serious and arranged for Kristen to be hospitalized immediately. When Dr. Adams spoke with Kristen and her parents, Richard and Peggy agreed with the diagnosis and the plan for therapy, but Kristen balked at the suggestion that she was suffering from anorexia, just as Dr. Adams had predicted.

Eating Disorders

There are three major eating disorders that affect children and adolescents: anorexia, bulimia, and binge-eating disorder. Anorexia is characterized by excessive thinness, decreased food intake, and distortions in body self-image (the anorexic girl thinks she's fat even when she's dangerously thin). Bulimia or binge-purge disorder is diagnosed when a teenager has recurrent episodes of excessive, out-of-control food intake (binges) and inappropriate compensatory behaviors (purging), such as self-induced vomiting, misuse of laxatives, enemas, or diuretic agents, fasting, or excessive exercise. Binge-eating disorder has recurrent episodes of excessive food intake, but is not associated with purging behavior. Compulsive overeating is also classified as an eating disorder, but it is rarely a problem in childhood or adolescence and is not discussed here.

The eating disorders vary in severity and symptom presentation, but all share in common an unhealthy approach to calorie intake, alterations in body size or function, and an excessive preoccupation with food, eating, and appearance. The disorders are relatively uncommon in childhood (although anorexia can begin as young as seven or eight years of age), but increase in frequency during adolescence, particularly among teenage girls. The rate of anorexia in the general population is about 0.5 percent (one in two hundred people have a history of anorexia) and varies by gender and socioeconomic status—the rate is highest among white middle-class girls and lowest in boys (only 10 percent of patients with anorexia are male). Bulimia is more common than anorexia and affects up to 4 percent (one in twenty-five) of college-age women.

It isn't clear how eating disorders develop, but there are several plausible theories. One recent theory raises serious concerns for parents because it suggests that anorexia may be the direct result of rapid weight loss. The researchers theorize that when a teenager undertakes a starvation diet, her body responds to the starvation by changing levels of certain chemicals in the brain. These alterations not only decrease the teen's metabolic rate to conserve energy, but also decrease her appetite and core body temperature (which explains Kristen's constant chills) and possibly cause distortions in her body image, leading her to think that she's fat when she's obviously not. This theory is in keeping with the observations that males who run long-distance races and girls who are training as gymnasts and ballet dancers are at the highest risk for developing anorexia—perhaps because their athletic training puts such emphasis on maintaining an excessively thin physique and extremely low body fat content.

Some psychiatrists and psychologists theorize that anorexia arises from a teenage girl's unconscious concerns about her development as a woman and her wish to avoid further maturation. By decreasing her body weight to the point where her breasts and hips disappear and her menstrual periods cease, she is able to forestall puberty. Other theories suggest that anorexia is a result of disturbed family relationships, the consequence of societal or cultural pressures (such as the emphasis on low-fat diets or the trend toward models and movie stars being ultrathin), or a symptom of severe depression (see chapter 21). Each of these theories has merit and it is possible that all are correct—anorexia could be caused by multiple factors. At present, however, the cause of anorexia and the other eating disorders is unknown.

Does Your Child Have an Eating Disorder?

1. Is she excessively thin (less than 85 percent of expected weight) and yet continues to diet and/or exercise to lose weight?
2. Does she think she's fat or that she needs to lose weight even though she's too thin?
3. Does she fear gaining weight or becoming fat even though she's underweight?
4. Has she stopped growing in height, and/or have her menstrual periods ceased?
5. Does she have recurrent episodes of eating unusually large quantities of food in a short period of time (a "binge")?
6. Have the binge episodes occurred at least twice a week for three months or longer?
7. Does she feel that the episodes of binge eating are outside her control?
8. Does she overvalue her body size and shape (for example, attributing her lack of a date on Friday night to having gained five pounds over the last few weeks)?
9. Does she engage in inappropriate methods to prevent weight gain ("purging"), such as self-induced vomiting, fasting, excessive exercise, or misuse of laxatives, diuretics, enemas, or other medications?

If the answer to questions 1 through 4 is yes, then she may have anorexia.

If the answer to questions 5 through 7 is yes, then she may have binge-eating disorder.

If the answer to questions 5 through 8 is yes, then she may have bulimia:

If the answer to question 9 is no, it is the nonpurging type.
If the answer to question 9 is yes, it is the purging type.

How Do You Know If Your Child Has an Eating Disorder?

Despite the obvious physical symptoms that characterize the eating disorders, they frequently go unrecognized for prolonged periods of time. This may be due to the fact that the physical changes are initially subtle (or even desirable) and increase slowly and gradually. For example, Kristen's mother didn't recognize her excessive thinness until her husband pointed it out to her. The eating disorders also go unnoticed because the adolescents hide their symptoms for as long as possible. They may recognize the senselessness of their behaviors and keep them secret in an effort to avoid embarrassment (such as hiding cookie wrappers following a binge), or they may fear that their parents will intervene in the diet and exercise regime before they've reached their goal—this is particularly true for girls with anorexia, since they are driven to achieve an impossible goal. Eating disorders are also missed because parents assume that the disorders are always associated with excessive thinness, but, in actuality, anorexia is the only disorder that has abnormal weight as a diagnostic criterion. The other eating disorders occur not only in girls who are underweight, but also in girls who are normal weight and above.

The eating disorders share many features in common and there is considerable overlap between the various disorders, as demonstrated in the diagnostic checklist. The symptoms common to all three eating disorders include: abnormal food intake, preoccupation with food or eating, and distortions of body self-image.

Abnormal Food Intake

Abnormal food intake includes both the amount of food eaten and the manner in which it is consumed. Inadequate calorie intake characterizes anorexia, while episodes of excessive calorie consumption (bingeing) are the hallmark of bulimia and binge-eating disorder. In anorexia, calorie consumption is often decreased to less than six hundred calories a day in an effort to maintain weight loss despite the decreases in basal metabolic rate and exercise tolerance. It is difficult to conceive of such extreme food restrictions going unnoticed for any period of time, but it happens quite often. The teenager skips breakfast without question because she's "never eaten breakfast" or she's "in a hurry"; she easily dodges lunch because she's at school; and she avoids dinner by scheduling a conflicting event or telling her parents, "I'll eat something later. I had a big lunch at school [ate right after school, have too much homework to do, don't feel well right now, etc.]." In homes where the family eats dinner together every night, these excuses aren't sufficient, so she hides her uneaten food in a napkin and disposes of it after the meal or she volunteers to clear the table so that she can dump her meal down the garbage disposal. She might also take very small helpings, avoid meat, cheese, and other high-calorie foods, and spend the mealtime drinking water, cutting her meat into tiny pieces, and pushing her food around the plate.

Binge eating, as its name implies, is the consumption of excessive amounts of food in a limited period of time. The binge-eating episodes are associated with eating much more rapidly than normal and stuffing oneself to the point of physical discomfort; afterward, the adolescent feels guilty, disgusted, and depressed about the overeating. The binge eating usually occurs when the teenager can eat alone, even though she's not particularly hungry (for example, she might wait until 2:00 A.M., when everyone else is asleep, to sneak into the kitchen for a binge). Usually, the foods chosen are "forbidden foods" that are high in fat and calories, such as chips, doughnuts, cake with rich frosting, ice cream, and others. The binge eating may last for only a few minutes or extend as long as several hours, and throughout the binge, the adolescent will feel that she is unable to stop gorging herself because she is not in control of her eating. She recognizes that her behavior is irrational and hides it as long as possible. To avoid detection because of missing foodstuffs, she may buy special foods for the binges and hide them in her room, disposing of the wrappers in secret. However, since the binge-eating episodes aren't under her control, any binge eating that is frequent enough to qualify as an eating disorder should be apparent to the vigilant parent.

To maintain a stable body weight, it is necessary to have calorie balance (calories in = calories out). In bulimia, this is achieved by balancing bingeing with purging. Active purging is the expulsion of unwanted calories through self-induced vomiting, the use of laxatives or enemas to hasten stool evacuation, and/or use of diuretics to increase fluid loss (decreasing both weight and "bloating"). Purging can also take the form of excessive exercise to burn off the calories consumed or drastic decreases in calorie consumption—fasting or extremely low-calorie diets.

Preoccupations with Food or Eating

Very often, an adolescent with an eating disorder has had a long-standing interest in food, which first became apparent early in childhood when she took over cooking for the family or spent her weekend afternoons preparing complicated recipes. As the eating disorder developed, her interest took on an obsessive quality and increased in direct proportion to the degree to which she had restricted her calorie intake. This is a natural consequence of self-imposed starvation since her body responds to any prolonged caloric deprivation by increasing food-seeking behavior. In anorexia, food becomes a true obsession and the young woman with anorexia may spend almost all of her time thinking about food—planning what she will eat, when she will eat it, and how many calories she will spend on each serving (accurate to within one or two calories). With binge-purge disorders, the preoccupation is not only with what she will eat, but also with resisting the urge to binge eat and calculating compensatory deprivations following a binge-eating episode.

Distortions of Body Self-Image

In the chapter's opening vignette, Kristen weighed only seventy-eight pounds and yet she viewed herself as fat. This is typical of young women with anorexia and, in fact, is the key feature that distinguishes anorexia from other forms of excessive dieting. Bulimia is also characterized by a distorted self-image and is diagnosed only when the girl's self-evaluation is unduly influenced by her food intake, weight fluctuations, or changes in appearance. These self-evaluations often have an irrational quality: a patient with bulimia might insist that she didn't get elected to class office because "I was too bloated when I gave my election speech" or a girl with anorexia might draw a picture of herself with grossly enlarged hips and thighs. In some cases, the body-image distortion is completely irrational and is similar to a psychotic delusion. For example, an anorexic patient might not recognize her own picture because "The girl in the picture is so much thinner than I am." For therapy to be effective in eating disorders, these irrational beliefs must be erased and the girl must achieve an accurate view not only of her body size and appearance, but also of its role in determining her happiness and success.

If It's Not an Eating Disorder, What Else Could It Be?

The eating disorders are so unique that there are no medical mimics, nor are there any other psychological disorders that have similar symptoms. Even in the few diseases, like end-stage cancer or AIDS, that cause significant anorexia (usually due to decreased metabolic needs), there are no accompanying body-image distortions, so these medical conditions should never be confused with anorexia nervosa.

Treatment of Eating Disorders

Treatment of eating disorders is aimed at eliminating body/self-image distortions, as well as restoring normal body weight and normal eating patterns. Eating disorders are notoriously difficult to treat and successful outcomes have usually been the result of multiple simultaneous therapies, such as a combination of individual psychotherapy, family therapy, cognitive-behavior therapy, and medication. Depending upon the severity of the eating disorder, treatment may be started in a clinic setting or in the hospital, but it should always be done by a team of health professionals experienced in the treatment of eating disorders. Many communities have an eating disorders treatment unit; if yours doesn't have one, then your child's doctor may refer your child to the closest teaching hospital. Before enrolling your daughter in a treatment program, make sure that you understand the goals of the therapy, the role that you will play in her recovery, the benchmarks for success (for example, the tasks your child must accomplish and the weight she must reach before the feeding tube is removed), and the expected length of treatment (usually at least six months of intensive therapy followed by several years of maintenance treatment).

Psychotherapy remains the mainstay of treatment for anorexia and bulimia. Individual and group sessions have proven to be beneficial in helping the patient to overcome fears about her appearance or the future, and to see her body in a way that more closely resembles its true shape and size. The long-term goals of psychotherapy are to increase the teen's coping skills so that she no longer has to depend upon dieting as a symbol of control, and to improve her self-image so that thinness and weight loss aren't necessary as external markers of self-worth. Psychoanalytic approaches may also be useful in the treatment of anorexia, particularly if the adolescent needs to master key developmental tasks, such as accepting her sexuality and establishing her independence.

Family therapy is also helpful for adolescents with anorexia. Studies have shown that adolescents receiving traditional psychotherapy plus family therapy were much more likely to recover than those who received only psychotherapy. Usually, the goal of family therapy is to reinforce the patient's recovery and to strengthen the family's support network, but occasionally it may be used to work through problems in the family that contribute to the eating disorder, such as poor family communications or conflicts over the teen's emerging independence.

Cognitive-behavior therapy utilizes elements of both cognitive therapy and behavior therapy to help the adolescent learn appropriate responses to various environmental cues, and then to practice them, incorporate them, and eventually accept them. Cognitive therapy starts with education about the anorexic and bulimic symptoms, and then attempts to normalize the adolescent's eating patterns, before progressing to issues of self-esteem, stress management, and control. In behavior therapy, undesirable responses are unlearned (for example, the patient might binge each time she watches a romantic movie and would have to extinguish both the binge-eating urge and the behavior of bingeing), and then the extinguished behavior is replaced by a positive, healthy response (eating a normal-sized portion of popcorn during the movie, or if moderation is too difficult, abstaining from food during and after the movie).

Cognitive-behavior therapy appears to be particularly useful for bulimia and for the binge-purge type of anorexia, perhaps because the target behaviors (that is, binge eating, vomiting, and laxative use) are easy to identify and prevent. For example, cognitive-behavior therapy of a girl who had both anorexia and bulimia might include the requirement that the patient eat everything served to her at her regularly scheduled meals and then sit at the table for a specified period of time following the meal to prevent purging. During the after-meal period, a staff member might review the nutritional contents of the meal or help the teenager appreciate her feelings of fullness and satiety.

Previously, medications were not used much in the treatment of eating disorders because they offered little advantage over psychological treatments alone. In various controlled studies, major tranquilizers (such as chlorpromazine, pimozide, and haloperidol), minor tranquilizers (such as Valium and others), amitriptyline (an antidepressant drug), and appetite-enhancing medications (such as cyproheptadine) were shown to have no benefits over placebo (sugar pills). However, recent research has demonstrated that desipramine (a tricyclic antidepressant) and the serotonin-reuptake-blocking antidepressants are useful for the treatment of eating disorders. (See chapter 12 for a full description of the antidepressant medications.) The SSRIs [fluoxetine (Prozac), fluvoxamine (Luvox), sertraline (Zoloft), and paroxetine (Paxil)] work by blocking various serotonin reuptake and have been shown to be superior to placebo in the treatment of eating disorders, perhaps because they induce changes in serotonin regulation that alter the brain's response to food intake (thus allowing the adolescent to recognize her hunger and fullness) and also decrease the obsessive preoccupation with food and the compulsive urges to binge eat and purge.

Helping Your Child Overcome an Eating Disorder

Decrease your child's risk of developing an eating disorder. Children who overvalue food's importance, or who are self-conscious about their appearance, are at increased risk of developing eating disorders. To decrease these risks, your child should enter adolescence with a solid knowledge about nutrition and healthy eating habits, and with a positive self-image that allows her to value her body for its strengths rather than denigrating its weaknesses. She should also view food as a source of energy and not as a substitute for love or affection. One of the best ways to teach your child these things is by setting a good example—eat a healthy diet, snack when you're hungry and not when you're bored or lonely, avoid cyclic dieting, and don't be critical of your own figure flaws.

Help teens who need to lose weight do it safely and sensibly. All weight-reduction diets should be supervised by a physician or registered dietitian, particularly during childhood and adolescence, when there is a risk of inducing an eating disorder through starvation dieting. Your child's doctor may prescribe a specific weight-loss diet or he may refer your child to a dietitian or nutritionist for instructions. The weight loss should be limited to one or two pounds per week and the weight should be shed as a result of both modest reductions in calorie intake and increased caloric expenditure (exercise!).

Learn to recognize the eating disorders. Eating disorders are distinguished from other eating problems by the presence of unhealthy patterns of food consumption and preoccupation with food and/or appearance. Both the behavioral and psychological symptoms must be present, but if you are concerned about either aspect, it is a good idea to have your child examined, since she may be hiding some of the more serious symptoms from your view.

Remain vigilant to the development of eating disorders. The peak ages for anorexia are between thirteen and fourteen and seventeen and eighteen, while bulimia can develop at any time between the ages of thirteen and twenty-one, so it is important to remain vigilant to symptoms of eating disorders throughout your child's adolescence.

Respond to your concerns by seeking treatment. Your child may be embarrassed or threatened by your discovery of her eating disorder and try to prevent you from seeking treatment for her. Don't be dissuaded! The eating disorders can be life-threatening and it is imperative that your child starts treatment as soon as possible and that she stays in treatment until she is fully recovered. Getting her to go to the first therapy session may be very difficult and you should be prepared for all kinds of excuses and stalling tactics. It may also be difficult to get her to follow through on the requirements of her therapy. For example, during treatment for anorexia, if a teen's weight dips below a critical level, a feeding tube has to be placed; she will often refuse to cooperate and her parents must give consent for the tube's placement. Some parents try to "help" their child by refusing to give permission for the feeding tube to be put in place. Not only does this not help, but it seriously undermines the therapy and threatens the teen's safety. An experienced treatment team will anticipate these difficult moments and will provide you with information and encouragement to help you support your child appropriately.

Participate in therapy and posttherapy care when requested. Family therapy is a very helpful part of the treatment of adolescents with eating disorders. If you are asked to participate in family therapy, educational courses, or other treatments, you should do so. It is an ideal opportunity to solve problems that could hamper your child's recovery.

Further Reading

Abraham, Suzanne, and Derek Llewellyn-Jones. *Eating Disorders: The Facts*. New York: Oxford University Press, 1992.

Berg, Frances M. *Afraid to Eat: Children and Teens in Weight Crisis*. Hettinger, ND: Healthy Weight Journal, 1997.

Bruch, Hilde. *The Golden Cage: The Enigma of Anorexia Nervosa*. New York: Vintage Books, 1978.

Costin, Carolyn. *Your Dieting Daughter: Is She Dying for Attention?* New York: Brunner/Mazel Publishers, 1997.

Jablow, Martha M. *A Parent's Guide to Eating Disorders and Obesity*. New York: Dell, 1992.

Kolodny, Nancy J. *When Food's a Foe: How to Confront and Conquer Eating Disorders*. Boston: Little, Brown & Company, 1992.

Moe, Barbara. *Coping with Eating Disorders*. New York: Rosen Publishing Group, 1991.

Siegel, Michele, Judith Brisman, Margor Weinshel, and Margot Weinshel. *Surviving an Eating Disorder: New Perspectives and Strategies for Family and Friends*. New York: HarperCollins, 1992.

Sherman, Roberta Trattner, and Ron A. Thompson. *Bulimia: A Guide for Family and Friends*. Lexington, MA: Lexington Books, 1990.

Resources

ANAD—National Association of Anorexia Nervosa and Associated Disorders
Box 7
Highland Park, IL 60035
Phone: 847-831-3438
Fax: 847-433-4632
Internet: http://www.healthtouch.com

ANRED—Anorexia Nervosa and Related Eating Disorders, Inc.
P.O. Box 5102
Eugene, OR 97405
Phone: 541-344-1144
Internet: http://www.anred.com

"My Son Is Drinking and Using Drugs"

Alcoholism and drug abuse

"Hello? Smith residence, Jack Smith speaking."

"Hello, Mr. Goodson. This is Police Officer Clark from the Fourth Precinct. I'm calling about your son, John."

"Is he all right?" Jack asked.

"Yes, sir. He's fine. But he's been arrested for drug possession. We were called in to investigate a noise complaint on Third Street and found your son at an unsupervised party with a small quantity of marijuana. He was obviously drunk and he failed a Breathalyzer test, so he may also be charged with underage drinking—that will be up to the judge at his arraignment hearing tomorrow. Right now, though, I need you to come down to the station."

"Of course, I'll be right over," Jack said.

When Jack arrived at the police station, he arranged bail for John and then was led to a small windowless room where his son was sitting with two other boys. All three wore the same expression on their face—a combination of pain, nausea, fear, and guilt.

"How are you, John?" Jack asked.

"I don't feel so good," John answered. "I'm sick to my stomach and my head hurts. Plus, it's really scary in here. If you don't take me home, they're going to put me in a cell with some gang members they just arrested."

"How do you know that?"

"Officer Clark told me."

"He may have just been trying to scare you, John," Jack said. "Police sometimes do that in the hopes that you'll think twice before getting into trouble again. What happened, anyway?" Jack asked.

John looked at the other two boys before answering with false bravado: "Messed up and got caught."

"I know that, I just posted your bond," Jack said. "I was wondering why you did something so stupid. You're only fourteen—you're not supposed to be going to parties unless we know about it, much less drinking alcohol or smoking pot. What on earth were you thinking?"

Before John could respond, Jack looked at the two other boys and said, "Don't try to answer that—this isn't the time or place to have that discussion."

As soon as they left the police station, John said, "I'm sorry, Dad. It won't happen again."

"You bet it won't!" Jack said. "You'll be grounded for the rest of this year and won't have an opportunity. I only hope that it's not already too late. The police are really cracking down on drug use and underage drinking, and the judge may be tempted to throw the book at you. If you're convicted of underage drinking, you could lose your driver's license before you even get it—you might not be able to drive until you're eighteen or twenty-one! Besides that, the judge might charge you with a felony for possession of marijuana. It is an illegal drug, you know."

"They busted me for half a joint, Dad!" John whined. "It wasn't even mine, I was just holding it for somebody else."

"Whether you were holding it or smoking it doesn't matter, John, the law says possession. You were in possession of the marijuana when the police arrived and you're in very deep trouble. With them, and with me."

Jack was right. The law is clear that possession, rather than intent or use, is what counts. The law was written to prohibit possession of drugs and alcohol (by underage minors) because possession is a fact that can't be disputed. Drug use, excessive or underage alcohol intake, substance abuse, and addiction are all associated with frequent cover-ups and denial. Parents must remember this as they deal with their children and adolescents. The child will deny that he has a problem, even when caught red-handed or when the alcohol or drugs are causing substantial difficulties in his life.

Cigarettes, Alcohol, Marijuana, and Other Drugs

Cigarettes and alcohol are the most common drugs abused by school-age children and adolescents, and yet, until recently, they were rarely targeted by drug abuse prevention programs. Politics and money clearly played a role in this, as the cigarette and alcohol industries have powerful lobbies and the potential for large campaign donations. However, the trend began to change as the rate of alcohol-related deaths among adolescents climbed to unacceptable levels and tobacco advertisements began to target children and young adolescents (examples include the Joe Camel cigarette advertisements and numerous smokeless tobacco ad campaigns).

Prevention programs obviously aren't yet working, since experimentation with drugs and alcohol has reached epidemic proportions. Recent studies show that 70 percent of teenagers will try cigarettes (many during seventh and eighth grade) and 90 percent will try alcohol before graduating from high school (two-thirds of eighth graders admit to having tried alcohol). Many teens (and adults!) consider experimentation with cigarettes, drugs, and/or alcohol to be a "rite of passage," but it's not. There is no developmental task that requires a teen to try drugs and alcohol. There are, however, many developmental factors that predispose the adolescent to experimentation: among others, the fact that he's seeking a new identity, the importance of peer approval, and the decreasing influence of his parents' opinions. Parents should therefore expect their child to experiment with cigarettes, alcohol, and other drugs (starting as early as fifth or sixth grade in some communities), but they should not accept it as inevitable. The preteen's parents should establish rules against smoking cigarettes, drinking alcohol, and using other drugs, and should have clearly established consequences for infractions, and then follow through on the rules as they would for any other problem behavior. This is the best safeguard against substance abuse that can be provided to the child.

Substance abuse occurs in about 10 percent of adolescents that experiment with drugs or alcohol. Substance abuse is defined as the recurrent use of drugs or alcohol in a way that causes clinically significant impairment or distress. Psychological dependence is usually present in substance abuse, which makes it difficult to quit the drug (the child is "hooked"). If the child has both psychological and physical dependence upon the drug, he is addicted and it can be impossible to quit unless he has medical treatment. Physical dependence occurs when a child develops both drug tolerance and withdrawal—he requires increasing amounts of the substance to achieve intoxication or a "high" (tolerance) and he suffers physical symptoms when prevented from accessing the substance (withdrawal). Cigarettes and most street drugs can cause addiction (nicotine is one of the most addictive substances known), but marijuana does not—although it can produce psychological dependence, there is no physical dependence with marijuana use. Alcoholism is also an addictive disorder because the individuals develop both tolerance and withdrawal symptoms (which can be life-threatening in some cases).

The risk of becoming addicted to drugs or alcohol is increased by genetics (inheritance), depression and other psychiatric disorders, and patterns of alcohol/drug use by the child's parents. The vast majority of the 10 percent of children who develop substance abuse problems will have a genetic predisposition, as a family history of drug or alcohol addiction increases a child's risk tenfold. The children may also have witnessed inappropriate patterns of cigarette, alcohol, or drug use by their parents. This is one instance in which "Do as I say and not as I do" will not work. Parents must get control of their own substance use problems before their children reach the age of risk, including stopping cigarette smoking, inappropriate alcohol intake, or use of illicit drugs.

Psychiatric disorders are the third risk factor for substance abuse. A child with depression or an anxiety disorder may use alcohol or other drugs to "self-medicate" in the hopes that he'll feel better when he's intoxicated or high. In other instances, the child's vulnerability to substance abuse is increased because the underlying disorder has eroded his self-esteem. For example, a teen who has untreated ADHD or unrecognized learning disabilities and is overwhelmed by his schoolwork—he's trying his best, but he's labeled as "lazy" or "stupid" because of his poor performance—may turn to alcohol or drugs to feel better or more important. But when he starts using drugs, his performance deteriorates further and he's caught in a vicious cycle of poor self-esteem leading to drug use which erodes his self-esteem and performance further and leads to more drug use.

Does Your Child Have a Problem with Drugs or Alcohol?

1. Has his school performance changed? Is he having problems with:
   a. Downward turn in grades?
   b. Not doing his homework?

c. Increased absenteeism, lateness, skipped classes, or sleeping in class?

d. Increase in disciplinary actions, such as detentions?

2. Has his attitude toward his family changed significantly? Has he become:

a. Withdrawn or isolated?

b. Disobedient?

c. Hostile, angry, or irritable?

d. Secretive?

3. Have his peer relationships changed? Has he:

a. Rejected his old friends?

b. Become vague about his current friends? Never introduced you to them?

c. Become secretive about phone calls or meetings with his friends?

d. Started staying out past curfew with them without explanation?

e. Started attending parties with people not known to you?

4. Has he changed? Do you worry that he has:

a. An unhealthy appearance or sudden indifference to hygiene or grooming?

b. Frequent complaints of physical problems— stomachaches, headaches, insomnia?

c. Periods of poor physical coordination, slurred speech, or disorientation?

d. Memory lapses, short attention span, or difficulty concentrating?

e. Weight changes or dramatic change in appetite?

f. Unpredictable mood swings?

g. Signs of depression, hopelessness, or suicidal behavior?

h. Physical signs of drug or alcohol use: reddened eyes, nagging cough, brown-stained fingertips, alcohol hangover, headache, vomiting after parties, blackouts, or smell of alcohol, tobacco, or marijuana?

Although there is no particular combination of signs and symptoms that confirms a "diagnosis" of substance abuse, if a child has a deterioration in his school performance (yes to question 1), which is accompanied by a change in relationships (yes to questions 2 or 3), the first consideration should be drug and/or alcohol use.

If the answer to question 4 is yes, the child needs help, even if it's not related to drug or alcohol use.

How Do You Know If It's a Problem with Substance Abuse?

The warning signs of alcohol or drug use are subtle and the symptoms of substance abuse are easily confused with other conditions, including normal adolescent rebellion. School failure is the most reliable sign of substance use, but it obviously can be due to a large number of causes. The problem is that if the child denies using drugs or alcohol, it can be impossible for his parents to determine whether or not he's telling the truth, since even health professionals must depend upon chemical tests (such as urine toxicology screens) to prove that a child has used drugs. Confrontations or furtive investigations can create additional problems for the parent-child relationship, and also may fail to determine whether or not the child has a problem with substance abuse. Therefore, we don't recommend that parents try to determine the cause of their child's problem behaviors, but rather get help from outside the family as soon as they become concerned that their child *might* be using drugs. If the source of the problems is something other than drugs or alcohol, the child will be able to get help for that condition; if the problems are related to substance abuse, treatment can begin.

If It's Not Substance Abuse, What Else Could It Be?

Any of the psychiatric disorders can cause symptoms similar to those described in this chapter's checklist, but depression is the most frequent mimic. Depression is characterized by many of the same symptoms as drug use—social isolation (withdrawing from friends and family), physical discomforts, insomnia, memory changes, and difficulties paying attention, among others (see chapter 21 for a full description). Further, depression can contribute to the development of a child's drug use. Therefore, if a child is exhibiting social isolation, withdrawal from his family, deterioration in his school performance, or physical symptoms, both depression and substance use should be considered in the diagnosis.

Attention deficit hyperactivity disorder (ADHD), learning disabilities, and conduct disorder can contribute to substance abuse, but should not be mistaken for drug or alcohol use because they start earlier in childhood (see chapters 13 and 14).

Treatment for Drug and Alcohol Abuse

The treatment of drug addiction or alcoholism requires that the physical dependence be treated before the issue of psychological dependence can be addressed. Detoxification, or the abrupt withdrawal of alcohol and drugs, can be life-threatening if the teen is severely addicted, so it is usually done in a hospital or drug rehabilitation center. There are a variety of successful approaches that can be used for detoxification, depending upon the substances to which the child is addicted and the philosophy of the treatment team. In general, the child and his parents should be told what will be done to help clear the alcohol or drugs from the child's body, and it should be clear that the primary goal of the early stages of therapy is protection of the child's physical safety.

Treatment of psychological dependence may also be started as an inpatient or in a residential treatment facility. The units are locked because the urge to obtain drugs is so strong that the child may take unsafe risks to obtain them, such as running away from the treatment center rather than abstaining from the drugs. He may also bargain, plead, cajole, or beg his parents to have him released prematurely—knowing how to say no is one of the first things his parents will be taught in their sessions with the therapist. Family education and family therapy are an integral part of the drug treatment program, and his parents must participate in their own therapy sessions if the child's treatment is to be fully successful.

Children and teenagers do best when they receive treatment in a program specifically designed to meet their needs. These programs are available through drug and alcohol rehabilitation centers, local mental health clinics, and at colleges, universities, and some high schools. Peer group counseling is one of the most successful forms of therapy, as recovering teen alcoholics are powerful role models for the teens who are just entering therapy. The adolescent may also participate in a twelve-step support group, such as Alcoholics Anonymous (AA) or Narcotics Anonymous (NA). His participation in AA or NA will continue after discharge from the treatment program, and, indeed, throughout his life he will be encouraged to use the support groups as an aid to overcoming his vulnerability to substance abuse.

If a child is entering treatment for drug or alcohol abuse, or if a substance abuse problem is being considered, it is imperative that he also receive a complete diagnostic workup for a psychiatric disorder. If a psychiatric disorder is diagnosed, it should be treated with medications and/or psychological therapies, because that will increase the chances of the child's recovery from the substance abuse. The workup and treatment of psychiatric disorders are done in addition to the treatment for the substance abuse, *not* as a substitute for dealing with the drug or alcohol problems.

Helping Your Child Avoid Problems with Drugs and/or Alcohol

Anticipate that your child is going to be exposed to drugs and alcohol. Your child will encounter situations in which he is asked to try cigarettes, alcohol, marijuana, and possibly cocaine or other drugs. He needs to know why he should say no, and how to do so effectively. This education should start in elementary school and continue throughout your child's adolescence. In addition to the health risks (which become meaningless to the invulnerable teenager), it may be helpful to discuss the fact that these substances are illegal. Your child could be arrested if caught with marijuana or other drugs, or risk losing his driver's license if he drives while intoxicated.

Your child should practice saying no until he can do it easily and without embarrassment. Role-playing can be very helpful in this regard. In addition to practicing saying no, he should also take the part of his friend—this helps him to understand that he would be willing to hear no if it were said. Your child will find it easier to say no if he has support for this position from his friends and family members. Get to know his friends well and make sure that they don't drink or use drugs, meet his friends' parents to confirm that they are also against drug use, and encourage your child to participate in groups such as Students Against Drunk Driving.

Become aware of the warning signs of drug and alcohol use. Although the signs of substance abuse can be subtle, they are almost always detectable. If your child has a sudden deterioration in his schoolwork, withdraws from family or friends, or begins to exhibit secretive or hostile behaviors, drug or alcohol use should be suspected.

Don't deny that your child has a problem with substance use. Some signs of drug or alcohol use, such as burning incense or obvious intoxication, aren't subtle but fail to get appropriate attention for the child's substance abuse problem, because they are ignored by his parents. This is not helpful to the child. Nor is it helpful to make excuses for his behavior, to cover up for his intoxication with the school or his other parent, or to bail him out of drug-related problems by giving him money or allowing him to steal from the family's piggy bank. Enabling behaviors such as these worsen the child's substance abuse problem and must be avoided.

Provide safeguards, especially for life-threatening situations. Limits can help protect your child, but they aren't all that is necessary to keep him safe. You must also provide specific safeguards against dangerous situations, even if they seem to contradict your family's rules. For example, your child should not be allowed to drink alcohol when he is underage because it is illegal and potentially dangerous, but the life-threatening danger comes from drinking and driving a car, or riding with someone who has been drinking. Thus, although you must establish negative consequences for drinking alcohol, they shouldn't be so severe as to make it impossible for your child to admit to you that he's been drinking and needs a ride home. Further, you should discuss the situation ahead of time with your child, so that he knows that your ultimate goal is his safety.

Seek professional help for problems related to drug and alcohol use. Drug and alcohol use can quickly escalate to substance abuse. No one, particularly your child, can promise that he's "just experimenting" and won't become addicted. Early intervention, by an experienced team of professionals, is the best protection against a lifetime problem with alcoholism or drug dependency.

Become active in teacher-parent-child coalitions to prevent drug and alcohol use. Parents of teenagers and teachers can be a powerful influence in the community. If they are involved in local coalitions for drug/alcohol abuse prevention, they can provide an important perspective on the behavior of children and adolescents that can make the efforts of the other community members even more effective.

Further Reading

Drews, Toby Rice. *Getting Your Child Sober: A No-Fault Guide for Parents and Professionals.* South Plainfield, NJ: Bridge Publishing, 1987.

Levant, Glenn. *Keeping Kids Drug Free: D.A.R.E. Official Parent's Guide*. San Diego, CA: Laurel Glen Publishing, 1998.

Neff, Pauline. *Tough Love: How Parents Can Deal with Drug Abuse*, rev. ed. Nashville, TN: Abingdon Press, 1996.

Van Ost, William C., M.D., and Elaine Van Ost. *Warning Signs: A Parent's Guide to In-Time Intervention in Drug and Alcohol Abuse*. New York: Warner Books, 1988.

Vogler, Roger E., Ph.D., and Wayne R. Bartz, Ph.D. *Teenagers and Alcohol: When Saying No Isn't Enough*. Philadelphia, PA: Charles Press Publisher, 1992.

Resources

Al-Anon/Alateen Family Group Headquarters, Inc.
P.O. Box 862
Midtown Station
New York, NY 10018-0862
800-344-2666

American Council for Drug Education (ACDE)
164 West 74th Street
New York, NY 10023
800-488-DRUG or 212-595-5810, ext. 7860
Nationwide referral service puts you in touch with local drug/alcohol support groups.

D.A.R.E. (Drug Abuse Resistance Education)
Box 512090
Los Angeles, CA 90051-0090
800-223-DARE

MADD (Mothers Against Drunk Driving)
511 East John Carpenter Freeway
Irvington, TX 75062
800-GET-MADD or 214-744-6233

Narcotics Anonymous
World Service Office
P.O. Box 9999
Van Nuys, CA 91049
800-662-4357 or 818-780-3951

National Clearinghouse for Alcohol and Drug Information
P.O. Box 2345
Rockville, MD 20847-2345
800-SAY-NOTO

National Federation of Parents for Drug-Free Youth
P.O. Box 3878
St. Louis, MO 63122
800-554-KIDS or 314-968-1322

National Institute on Drug Abuse
5600 Fishers Lane, Room 10A03
Rockville, MD 20857
800-638-2045 or 301-443-4577

National PTA Drug and Alcohol Prevention Project
700 North Rush Street
Chicago, IL 60611
312-577-4500

Partnership for a Drug Free America
800-624-0100 (for information about how to talk to your children about
    drugs)

Hotlines
Cocaine helpline: 800-COCAINE
Crisis hotline: 800-421-6353 (in California, 800-352-0386)
National Council on Alcoholism Information: 800-NCA-CALL
National Drug Abuse Hotline: 800-622-HELP

Acknowledgments

Is It "Just a Phase"? would not have been possible without the knowledge we've gained from our teachers and colleagues, the experiences we've shared with our patients and their parents, and the faithful support of our families and friends. We are particularly indebted to:

Our mentors—Judy Rapoport, Sidney Berman, Joseph Noshpitz, Marilyn Benoit, William Ayres, John Dunne, Jack McDermott, David Ingall, Herb Philipsborn, John Reichert, Glen Aylward, and Darrell Kirch, among countless others.

Our friends and collaborators at the National Institute of Mental Health, Brown University, and elsewhere—Ellen Leibenluft, Marjorie Garvey, Xavier Castellanos, Collette Parker, Susan Leitman, Jay Giedd, Susan Perlmutter, Marge Lenane, Lorraine Lougee, Billinda Dubbert, Jean Silvestri, Mira and David Irons, Ann Doll, Doug Beer, Jane Eisen, Mark Riddle, John March, Peter Strick, and Pat Levitt.

Our children—Elizabeth, Emily, Katie, Alexander, and Nathaniel; their physicians—Sharon Kiernan, Frank Palumbo, Sherahe Fitzpatrick, Wilson Utter, Judith Shaw, Jean Massie, and Frank Galioto; and their wonderful teachers—Mary Fisher, Sasha Wall, Susan Bauer, Melissa Carleton, Lisa Ruskowski, Ruth Donahue, Jane Houser, Barbara Burnett, Linda Chin, Marie Pelosi, M. Fish, Sheila Clawson, Martina Dalton-

Quinn, Emily Goff, Melinda Foley-Marsello, Melinda Van Lare, Connie Raymond, Barbara Scattergood, Sarah Adams, and all the others at Moses Brown School, Lone Oak Montessori, Spring Hill Elementary, and Longfellow Middle School. They've taught us so much about parent-teacher and parent-physician partnerships, as they've nurtured our children's minds, bodies, and spirits.

Our unparalleled support systems at work and home—Mai Karitani, Marsha Spirito, Diane Gnepp, Maxine Steyer, Bob Dennis, Pam Pearson-Green, Joan Harvey, Brenda Sandler, Greg Swedo, and Ken Rickler.

And, most important, the many talented people who share credit for the creation of Is It "Just a Phase"?:

Arielle Eckstut, our treasured agent, and Robert Asahina, president of Golden Books Adult Publishing Group, who turned a dream into reality with their support and encouragement;

Elizabeth Spencer, our editorial assistant, who spent countless hours in the library and on the Web finding references and ensuring the accuracy of the referrals;

Helen Goliash and Elizabeth Swedo, who faithfully and accurately prepared the drafts of the manuscript;

Suzanne Noli, who created the beautiful book jacket, and Karen Mc-Dermott, who made sure that people would have an opportunity to see it;

Lara Asher, who always had a smile in her voice and the answers to our many questions—just when we needed them most; and

Laura Yorke, our editor, who provided clarity and focus to the manuscript, and allowed the message of help and hope to radiate throughout the pages of Is It "Just a Phase"?

Index

anxiety:
  definition of, 123
  PANDAS as trigger of, 248
  relaxation therapy for, 174–175
  school refusal and, 63, 73, 75
  selective mutism and, 291
  sympathetic nervous system and, 132
  see also fear
anxiety disorders, 170
  agitation and, 16–17
  bed-wetting caused by, 320
  diagnostic measures for, 170–171
  fear vs., 105, 109, 116
  hyperactivity and, 157
  insomnia and, 318
  moodiness and, 160, 164
  nightmares and, 108
  picky eaters and, 33
  school refusal and, 66
  selective mutism and, 286
  substance abuse and, 339
  symptoms of, 85, 89–90, 108, 170–171
  therapies for, 173, 175
  worry and, 121, 124, 128, 160
  see also GAD; separation anxiety disorder
appetite, 303, 316
appetite-enhancing medications, 332
Asendin (amoxapine), 178
asthma, 276, 318, 320
atenolol, 292
Ativan (lorazepam), 279
attention deficit disorder, *see* ADD
attention deficit hyperactivity disorder, *see* ADHD
autism, 145, 148, 239–240, 290
Azrin, N. H., 88

bad habits, 80–91
  habit reversal and, 88–89
  learned behaviors and, 81
  OCD vs., 85, 89, 90
  parental guidelines for, 86–89
  pediatric help for, 90–91
  teachers and, 89–90
  tic disorders vs., 85–86, 90
  treatments for, 84
  see also hair-pulling
basal ganglia, 249
Baum, L. Frank, 104
bedtime rituals, 81, 318
bed-wetting, 32, 92–101, 320–321
  causes of, 93–98, 320
  lithium and, 308
  medications for, 178
  parental guidelines for, 98–100
  pediatric help for, 100–101
behavioral inhibition, 105–106
behavior therapy, 174
  for ADD, 208–211
  for ADHD, 23, 189
  age restrictions for, 241, 278
  for bad habits, 84
  contingency management as, 291
  for fear, 113, 116
  for GAD, 277, 278
  for misbehavior, 57
  for obsessive-compulsive personality disorder (OCPD), 239
  for OCD, 174, 241–242
  for panic disorder, 277
  for school refusal, 63, 74–75
  for selective mutism, 290–291
  for separation anxiety disorder, 174, 263, 264, 267–268

for social phobia, 290–291
  star charts as, 87–88
Benzedrine, 190
benzodiazepines, 279–280
bereavement, 156–157
beta-blockers, 292
binge-eating disorder, 326
binge-purge disorder, 38, 325, 330
bipolar (manic-depressive) disorder, 160, 296–311
  bed-wetting and, 320
  definition of, 299–300
  diagnostic checklist for, 301
  medications for, 307–308
  moodiness vs., 160
  symptoms of, 160, 299–300, 301
  treatments for, 305–308
birth control pills, 305
birth defects, 97
bladder infections, 96
body self-image, 27, 31–32, 39, 325, 330, 331
boredom, 12–13, 14, 70, 206
boys:
  development of, 11–12
  sexual obsessions and, 234–235
  testosterone and, 157
Boy Who Couldn't Stop Washing, The (Rapoport), 235
Bradley, Charles, 190
brain, 3–4, 183
Brown, Jeffrey, 74–75, 113–114
bulimia, 27, 28, 325–326, 332
  see also eating disorders
buproprion, 193, 307
BuSpar (buspirone), 265, 279, 280

cancer, 33
carbamazepine, 308
Catapres (clonidine), 193, 225
child abuse, 50, 57, 61, 70
child psychiatrists, 23, 116, 267, 281
Children with Autism: A Parent's Guide (Powers), 240
chlorpromazine, 280, 308, 332
choreic movements, 249
choreoathetosis, 222
chronic bowel disease, 305
chronic hyperarousal, 318
cigarettes, 338–339
clomipramine, 91, 178, 242, 265
clonazepam, 277, 279
clonidine, 193, 225
Clozaril (clozapine), 308
clue diary, 30
cocaine, 17
cognitive-behavior therapy (CBT), 161, 263, 264
  for anxiety disorders, 175
  for depression, 175, 298, 306
  for eating disorders, 331
  for GAD, 278
  for panic disorder, 277
  for social phobia, 291–292
colds, 250
complex tics, 218
compulsions, 233, 236–238, 240
conduct disorder, 16, 50–52, 342
consequences, 42–45, 50, 71, 161
consistency, 18, 22, 42–43, 45, 50, 194, 195, 212
contamination fear:
  GAD vs., 276
  moodiness and, 160
  OCD and, 229–231, 232, 233–234, 236, 243, 276
  picky eaters and, 33
  treatments for, 174
contingency management, 291
Crohn's disease, 33, 69, 276

Dr. Susan Anderson Swedo is a board-certified pediatrician and a fellow of the American Academy of Pediatrics. She is the head of behavioral pediatrics at the National Institute of Mental Health (NIMH) and former scientific director of the NIMH Intramural Research Program. She is the coauthor of *It's Not All in Your Head* and has written nearly one hundred professional papers. Dr. Swedo lectures frequently at universities, medical colleges, and national and international professional meetings. She received *Good Housekeeping* magazine's nomination as one of the "Best Mental Health Experts in the U. S." She lives near Washington, D.C., with her husband and three daughters.

Dr. Henrietta L. Leonard is a board-certified child psychiatrist in practice at Rhode Island Hospital and is the training director of the child psychiatry program at Brown University School of Medicine. She is a member of the American Academy of Child and Adolescent Psychiatry and the American Psychiatric Association. Dr. Leonard is the coauthor of *It's Not All in Your Head* and has written more than ninety professional articles. She has edited a text on childhood anxiety disorders that has been acclaimed as one of the best sources of treatment information available. She received the NIMH's WISE Award for Scientific Achievement. Dr. Leonard has been listed twice in *Good Housekeeping* magazine as one of America's leading child psychiatrists. She lives in Providence, Rhode Island, with her husband and two sons.